AI, Corporate Social Responsibility, and Marketing in Modern Organizations

Muhammad Nawaz Tunio
University of Sufism and Modern Sciences, Pakistan

IGI Global
Publishing Tomorrow's Research Today

Vice President of Editorial Melissa Wagner
Managing Editor of Acquisitions Mikaela Felty
Managing Editor of Book Development Jocelynn Hessler
Production Manager Mike Brehm
Cover Design Phillip Shickler

Published in the United States of America by
IGI Global Scientific Publishing
701 East Chocolate Avenue
Hershey, PA, 17033, USA
Tel: 717-533-8845
Fax: 717-533-8661
Website: https://www.igi-global.com E-mail: cust@igi-global.com

Library of Congress Cataloging-in-Publication Data

Names: Tunio, Muhammad Nawaz, 1984- editor.
Title: AI, corporate social responsibility, and marketing in modern organizations / edited by Muhammad Nawaz Tunio.
Description: Hershey, PA : IGI Global Scientific Publishing, [2025] | Includes bibliographical references and index. | Summary: "This book explores this convergence, offering a comprehensive examination of how AI is reshaping the landscape of CSR and marketing in today's business environment"-- Provided by publisher.
Identifiers: LCCN 2024053030 (print) | LCCN 2024053031 (ebook) | ISBN 9798337302195 (hardcover) | ISBN 9798337302201 (paperback) | ISBN 9798337302218 (ebook)
Subjects: LCSH: Social responsibility of business. | Marketing. | Artificial intelligence.
Classification: LCC HD60 .A353 2025 (print) | LCC HD60 (ebook) | DDC 658.4/08--dc23/eng/20250204
LC record available at https://lccn.loc.gov/2024053030
LC ebook record available at https://lccn.loc.gov/2024053031

British Cataloguing in Publication Data
A Cataloguing in Publication record for this book is available from the British Library.

This book is dedicated to those who strive to create a more sustainable, ethical, and innovative future for businesses and society.

Table of Contents

Detailed Table of Contents

This investigation looks at the association among domestic trade entrepreneurial mindset, innovations openness, and enhancing entrepreneurial practices in the context of domestic trade in the Eastern Horn of Africa. Using a quantitative research approach, the investigation examined information from 370 domestic ventures, using approaches like Exploratory Factor Analysis (EFA) and Structural Equation Modeling (SEM) with AMOS software. The outcomes manifest a substantial affirmative association among entrepreneurial mindset of family owned trade and innovations openness, implying that domestic firms with a robust entrepreneurial mindset are more likely to contribute in innovative practices. The investigation adds to the current literature by stressing the worth's of cultivating an entrepreneurial orientation and using peripheral joint ventures in domestic firms. Real world consequences underscore the need for domestic trade to foster an innovative ethos, engage in training, and form strategic alliances.

CSR is crucial for family businesses, including hotels, which are a significant employer globally. The COVID-19 pandemic has impacted the hospitality sector, leading to digital transformation and contactless technology adoption in European hotels. To maintain competitiveness, European family-owned hotels should implement sustainable practices, enhance digital connectivity, provide health and well-being amenities, invest in employee training, and adopt contactless technologies. A thorough review of secondary research is conducted to find out the CSR practices implied by European Family businesses hotels. It is concluded that incorporating artificial intelligence and machine learning into CSR efforts can strengthen commitment to sustainability and social responsibility. Further the hotel industry, which holds a market share of over 50% in Europe, is expected to grow at a CAGR of 7.0% between 2022 and 2023.

AI-driven market intelligence is revolutionizing how businesses analyze and respond to market dynamics. This chapter explores the integration of artificial intelligence (AI) tools in competitive analysis and market positioning. It discusses the foundations of market intelligence, the role of AI in enhancing competitive strategies, and the practical tools and technologies available for implementation. The chapter also addresses the challenges and ethical considerations associated with AI, including data quality, integration with legacy systems, and privacy concerns. Future trends such as autonomous systems, enhanced personalization, and the convergence of AI with augmented and virtual reality are examined. The implications of these advancements for businesses, managers, and society are analyzed, emphasizing the need for responsible AI use and strategic innovation. This comprehensive

weakness, opportunity, threat) analysis of Artificial Intelligence with some quality contents and portraits. The resultant of the research paper smoothens the augmentation knowledge body of the nurturing the contents of the smart or modish universities, smart pedagogy, smart teachers & learners, role of the Artificial Intelligence in the field of education and the applications supporting the Artificial Intelligence.

The present research investigation is an effort to explain the importance of the mother tongue in human life, including academic achievement, intellectual development and enculturation. This research has also focused on the challenges and opportunities of artificial intelligence in language learning. The method of narrative review of the literature was used to review recent research on artificial intelligence in language learning. The findings of this review are consistent with various research done in the field of Language and artificial intelligence, which highlight the critical role of technologies of artificial intelligence in Language learning along with some challenges associated with the context and meaning of Language.

Foreword

The convergence of Artificial Intelligence (AI), Corporate Social Responsibility (CSR), and Marketing is shaping a new era for modern organizations. In a world where technology is transforming every aspect of business, the integration of AI into core strategies has become essential for companies seeking to remain competitive, socially responsible, and customer-focused. This book, *AI, Corporate Social Responsibility, and Marketing in Modern Organizations*, delves into these dynamic intersections and offers a comprehensive exploration of how AI can enhance CSR efforts and revolutionize marketing in today's business landscape.

Over the past few decades, CSR has evolved from a voluntary practice to a strategic imperative for businesses worldwide. Consumers, investors, and stakeholders now expect companies to address pressing social and environmental issues while delivering value to their customers. However, balancing profit with purpose has always been a challenge, requiring organizations to rethink their operations, supply chains, and community engagement. Enter AI—an advanced tool that is not only transforming how businesses operate but also redefining how they can better fulfill their social responsibilities.

AI's ability to process vast amounts of data, generate insights, and optimize decision-making processes presents unparalleled opportunities for enhancing CSR initiatives. For instance, AI-driven tools can track and reduce a company's carbon footprint, improve workplace safety, and create more ethical supply chains. In addition, AI can help companies engage with consumers who are increasingly concerned about sustainability and corporate ethics, offering transparency and responsiveness that foster deeper trust and loyalty.

In marketing, AI is changing the game by providing businesses with the ability to analyze consumer behavior in real time, personalize interactions, and predict future trends with remarkable accuracy. By combining AI with CSR, organizations can craft marketing strategies that not only resonate with their target audiences but also demonstrate their commitment to making a positive impact on society. This alignment between ethical marketing and responsible business practices is critical for companies aiming to build lasting relationships with their customers.

What makes *AI, Corporate Social Responsibility, and Marketing in Modern Organizations* particularly valuable is its timely focus on the integration of these three powerful forces. This book brings together cutting-edge research and practical applications, offering insights into how AI can amplify CSR efforts while simultaneously transforming marketing strategies. It challenges readers to consider the potential of AI not just as a tool for efficiency but as a catalyst for ethical and responsible business transformation.

The authors present a forward-thinking approach to CSR and marketing, illustrating how AI can be leveraged to meet the increasing demands for corporate transparency and accountability. In addition to its theoretical contributions, the book offers real-world examples and case studies that demonstrate how modern organizations are successfully integrating AI into their CSR and marketing initiatives. These examples highlight the tangible benefits of AI, from improving customer satisfaction and brand loyalty to enhancing environmental sustainability and social equity.

This book also addresses some of the challenges and ethical considerations that come with AI adoption. As AI becomes more embedded in business operations, questions around data privacy, algorithmic bias, and the social implications of automation must be addressed. The authors do an excellent job of balancing the excitement surrounding AI's potential with a thoughtful discussion of its limitations and risks, providing readers with a nuanced understanding of the topic.

As we stand at the intersection of technological innovation, corporate responsibility, and evolving consumer expectations, this book serves as an essential guide for business leaders, marketers, academics, and students alike. It equips readers with the knowledge and tools needed to harness AI's power responsibly while maintaining a strong focus on social impact and ethical marketing practices.

In conclusion, *AI, Corporate Social Responsibility, and Marketing in Modern Organizations* is a pioneering work that offers both vision and practical insights. It not only explores the future of business but also lays the foundation for a new paradigm where technology, responsibility, and innovation converge to create a better world. I congratulate the editor, Dr. Muhammad Nawaz Tunio, and the contributing authors for producing such an insightful and timely book. I am confident that this work will inspire leaders in all sectors to embrace AI as a force for good, driving positive change in both business and society.

Erum Shaikh

HoD, Department of Business Administration, Shaheed Benazir Bhutto University, Sanghar Campus, Pakistan

Preface

The business landscape of the 21st century is being reshaped by rapid technological advancements, shifting consumer expectations, and the increasing importance of corporate responsibility. In this context, Artificial Intelligence (AI) has emerged as a transformative force that is revolutionizing how modern organizations operate, engage with their stakeholders, and fulfill their social responsibilities. At the same time, Corporate Social Responsibility (CSR) has become a strategic imperative, and marketing has evolved to emphasize authenticity, transparency, and purpose. The book *AI, Corporate Social Responsibility, and Marketing in Modern Organizations* seeks to explore the powerful synergies between these three domains, offering insights into how AI can drive more responsible, ethical, and effective business practices.

As AI continues to permeate various sectors, it is no longer just a tool for enhancing operational efficiency or streamlining workflows. AI's potential to influence organizational strategies is far-reaching, especially in the realms of CSR and marketing. Businesses today are expected not only to provide exceptional products and services but also to contribute positively to society and the environment. This book examines how AI can be integrated into CSR initiatives to meet these demands, helping organizations to better address societal challenges, such as climate change, ethical supply chains, and social equity, while still achieving their business goals.

In the realm of marketing, AI offers unprecedented opportunities for personalization, customer engagement, and data-driven decision-making. As consumers become more conscious of the ethical implications of their purchasing decisions, companies are leveraging AI to create marketing strategies that align with their CSR commitments. By doing so, they are able to build deeper connections with their customers, foster brand loyalty, and position themselves as leaders in both innovation and corporate responsibility.

This book is divided into sections that address key themes within AI, CSR, and marketing. It provides an overview of AI's capabilities, followed by discussions on how these technologies can enhance CSR efforts and improve marketing practices. Each chapter is supported by real-world case studies and examples that highlight how forward-thinking organizations are already using AI to advance their CSR and marketing goals.

Some of the critical topics covered in this book include:

- **AI for Sustainable Business Practices**: How AI can be used to reduce carbon footprints, manage resources more efficiently, and promote environmental sustainability.
- **Ethical AI and Corporate Governance**: The role of AI in promoting transparency, accountability, and ethical decision-making within organizations.
- **AI-Driven Marketing**: How businesses are using AI to better understand consumer behavior, personalize marketing efforts, and foster stronger customer relationships.
- **Challenges and Opportunities in AI-Enhanced CSR**: The ethical considerations, risks, and potential of AI in shaping responsible business practices and public perception.

This book is intended for a wide audience, including business leaders, marketers, entrepreneurs, CSR professionals, and students who are keen to understand the intersection of AI, corporate responsibility, and marketing. By providing both theoretical frameworks and practical insights, this book serves as a resource for those looking to implement AI technologies in a way that is not only beneficial for business growth but also aligned with the broader goals of sustainability and social responsibility.

As the editor of *AI, Corporate Social Responsibility, and Marketing in Modern Organizations*, I would like to extend my gratitude to the contributing authors who have shared their expertise in AI, CSR, and marketing. Their insights provide a comprehensive look at how these fields can work together to create a more sustainable and ethical future for businesses and society

I hope that this book will inspire readers to think critically about the role of AI in shaping the future of business and encourage them to explore innovative solutions that balance profitability with purpose.

ORGANIZATION OF THE BOOK

Chapter 1: Family Business Entrepreneurial Orientation Effect on Improving Entrepreneurial Processes by Mediation of Open Innovation in Horn of Africa

The first chapter looks at the association among domestic trade entrepreneurial mindset, innovations openness, and enhancing entrepreneurial practices in the context of domestic trade in the Eastern Horn of Africa. Using a quantitative research approach, the investigation examined information from 370 domestic ventures, using approaches like Exploratory Factor Analysis (EFA) and Structural Equation Modeling (SEM) with AMOS software. The outcomes manifest a substantial affirmative association among entrepreneurial mindset of family owned trade and innovations openness, implying that domestic firms with a robust entrepreneurial mindset are more likely to contribute in innovative practices. The investigation adds to the current literature by stressing the worth's of cultivating an entrepreneurial orientation and using peripheral joint ventures in domestic firms. Real world consequences underscore the need for domestic trade to foster an innovative ethos, engage in training, and form strategic alliances.

Chapter 2: Use of Artificial Intelligence (AI) for Improving Human Resource Management (HRM) Functions

Artificial intelligence is affecting every area of business. It technology is used by all forms of organizations for improved productivity and performance. Hence, there is no exception for the HRM function in which applications AI found to be extremely beneficial. Therefore, this chapter is written specifically to understand the uses and significance of AI to HR functions. Therefore, contents are not only limited to literature and evidence but also the theoretical perspective as well as empirical gaps and implications to provide rigorous understanding to the readers. Thus, the implications, scope, and significance of this chapter have many folds as it is beneficial for academicians, researchers, scholars and policymakers to understand the use of AI for HRM functions for a better development of community and society,

Chapter 3: Role of Green Corporate Social Responsibility and Corporate Social Responsibility in Enterprises: Evidence from Europe

CSR is essential for companies to meet financial, social, and environmental goals. European companies can improve society and the environment by incorporating CSR into environmental policies. Businesses globally have invested approximately $16.6 trillion in CSR, which promotes environmental sustainability. Record-high carbon emissions, waste energy, pollution, wastewater, and water scarcity have boosted natural resource demand. GCSR actions increase organizational, environmental, economic, and ethical performance. This qualitative study analyses European SME statistics from publicly available online publications, journals, books, reports, government and public industries, and agency statistics using secondary data collecting.

Chapter 4: How the Family Business Hotels of Europe are Rebuilt After COVD-19: Leveraging CSR Practices for Post Pandemic Resilience

CSR is crucial for family businesses, including hotels, which are a significant employer globally. The COVID-19 pandemic has impacted the hospitality sector, leading to digital transformation and contactless technology adoption in European hotels. To maintain competitiveness, European family-owned hotels should implement sustainable practices, enhance digital connectivity, provide health and well-being amenities, invest in employee training, and adopt contactless technologies. A thorough review of secondary research is conducted to find out the CSR practices implied by European Family businesses hotels. It is concluded that incorporating artificial intelligence and machine learning into CSR efforts can strengthen commitment to sustainability and social responsibility. Further the hotel industry, which holds a market share of over 50% in Europe, is expected to grow at a CAGR of 7.0% between 2022 and 2023.

Chapter 5: AI-Driven Market Intelligence: Enhancing Competitive Analysis and Market Positioning

This chapter explores the integration of artificial intelligence (AI) tools in competitive analysis and market positioning. It discusses the foundations of market intelligence, the role of AI in enhancing competitive strategies, and the practical tools and technologies available for implementation. The chapter also addresses the challenges and ethical considerations associated with AI, including data quality, integration with legacy systems, and privacy concerns. Future trends such as autonomous systems, enhanced personalization, and the convergence of AI with augmented and virtual reality are examined. The implications of these advancements for businesses, managers, and society are analyzed, emphasizing the need for responsible AI use and strategic innovation. This comprehensive overview provides insights into leveraging AI to optimize market intelligence and drive business success.

Chapter 6: Accelerating the Development of New Products and Services with AI-Enabled Innovation Management

This chapter explores the role of Artificial Intelligence (AI) in innovation management, focusing on its potential to accelerate the development of new products and services. It examines how AI technologies, including machine learning, natural language processing, and generative design, transform each stage of the innovation lifecycle—from idea generation to market introduction. The chapter also addresses key challenges such as ethical considerations, data quality, and integration issues, offering strategic recommendations for effective AI implementation. Future trends, including advanced AI capabilities, integration with emerging technologies, and ethical AI practices, are discussed to provide a forward-looking perspective. By leveraging AI, organizations can enhance decision-making, improve efficiency, and drive successful innovation. This chapter aims to equip readers with insights and strategies to harness AI effectively in their innovation processes.

Chapter 7: Artificial Intelligence as the New Face of Marketing Activites and Functions: Theory, Concepts, Illustrations, and Implications

Artificial Intelligence is the tool utilized by every organization and all of its functions to generate, synthesize, and analyze data. Marketing also has no exception in which AI can be used for the betterment of various activities and functions. However, the perceived level of risk may affect the use drastically. Therefore, this chapter has been written purposively to highlight the use of AI for marketing to make researchers, academicians, managers, and policy makers understand AI's role in improving marketing efforts.

Chapter 8: Enhancing Marketing and Brand Communication with AI-Driven Content Creation

This chapter explores the evolution of AI in content creation, from generative models to immersive technologies like augmented reality (AR) and virtual reality (VR). It examines the impact of AI on personalization, SEO optimization, and the ethical challenges associated with AI-generated content, including issues of authenticity, creativity, and misinformation. The chapter concludes by discussing future trends in AI-driven content creation, emphasizing the importance of human-AI collaboration to achieve innovative and responsible content strategies.

Chapter 9: AI in Customer Service Automation: Balancing Efficiency with Human Touch

This chapter investigates the evolving role of AI in customer service automation, focusing on balancing efficiency with human interaction. AI technologies, including advancements in Natural Language Processing (NLP), predictive analytics, and integration with Augmented Reality (AR) and Virtual Reality (VR), are transforming customer service by enhancing personalization and streamlining operations. However, challenges such as maintaining emotional intelligence, ensuring ethical use of AI, and addressing privacy concerns remain critical. The chapter discusses strategies for leveraging AI while preserving the essential human touch and highlights future trends and innovations shaping the customer service landscape. By navigating these developments, businesses can optimize customer interactions and create more effective, empathetic, and responsive service environments.

Chapter 10: Leveraging AI to Tailor Customer Engagement with Personalized Marketing Strategies

This chapter delves into the role of AI in shaping personalized marketing strategies, emphasizing the advancements in machine learning, natural language processing, and predictive analytics. It discusses how AI enhances customer engagement through hyper-personalization, integrating technologies like augmented reality (AR) and virtual reality (VR), and addresses the ethical considerations and challenges involved. Practical tips and best practices for implementing AI-driven personalization, including data quality management, tool selection, and ethical practices, are provided. Future trends such as predictive analytics and AI-generated creative content are highlighted as key areas for continued development. Businesses that effectively harness these AI capabilities can achieve significant improvements in customer satisfaction and loyalty.

Chapter 11: AI for Personalizing Customer Interactions: Improving Engagement and Satisfaction

This chapter investigates the transformative impact of AI on personalizing customer interactions, examining key technologies such as machine learning, natural language processing, and predictive analytics. It highlights the benefits of AI-driven personalization, including enhanced engagement, improved customer satisfaction, and increased conversion rates. Challenges such as data privacy, ethical considerations, and integration complexities are also discussed, alongside best practices for effective implementation. Future trends, including hyper-personalization and AI integration with augmented reality, are explored to provide insights into emerging opportunities and innovations. By addressing both the potential and challenges of AI in personalization, this study offers a comprehensive overview of how businesses can leverage AI to optimize customer interactions and drive long-term success.

Chapter 12: AI-Driven Customer Engagement Strategies for Small Businesses

This chapter explores how AI technologies, such as chatbots, personalized marketing, and customer analytics, transform customer interactions. By leveraging AI, small businesses can deliver tailored experiences, predict customer behavior, and optimize engagement across multiple channels. The study examines the implementation of AI tools to automate customer service, segment audiences, and create dynamic marketing campaigns. It also addresses potential challenges, including data privacy concerns and the need for technological adoption. Through case studies and empirical analysis, this research highlights the benefits and limitations of AI-driven engagement, providing insights into best practices for integrating AI into small business operations. Ultimately, the study aims to offer a comprehensive understanding of how AI can be effectively utilized to build stronger customer relationships, growth in the competitive market landscape.

Chapter 13: The Modish Universities and the Impact of Artificial Intelligence on IT

The impact of COVID-19 was severe and adverse on the entire human community and from there emerged out the combination of the smart classrooms adopted by the Universities with the assistance of Artificial Intelligence. The smart classes used to exist earlier also however, the extensive usage started only after the insurgence of pandemic fear where every education body initiated the search of digital platforms to continue the education and the academic operations. Traversing the procedures, shape, structure, planning, strategy and skills, this research paper has explored the various concepts, the implemented tools and has also done a SWOT (strength, weakness, opportunity, threat) analysis of Artificial Intelligence with some quality contents and portraits. The resultant of the research paper smoothens the augmentation knowledge body of the nurturing the contents of the smart or modish universities, smart pedagogy, smart teachers & learners, role of the Artificial Intelligence in the field of education and the applications supporting the Artificial Intelligence.

Chapter 14: Challenges of Artificial Intelligence (AI) in Language Learning

The last chapter is an effort to explain the importance of the mother tongue in human life, including academic achievement, intellectual development and enculturation. This research has also focused on the challenges and opportunities of artificial intelligence in language learning. The method of narrative review of the literature was used to review recent research on artificial intelligence in language learning. The findings of this review are consistent with various research done in the field of Language and artificial intelligence, which highlight the critical role of technologies of artificial intelligence in Language learning along with some challenges associated with the context and meaning of Language.

Muhammad Nawaz Tunio
University of Sufism and Modern Sciences, Pakistan

Acknowledgment

The journey of bringing *AI, Corporate Social Responsibility, and Marketing in Modern Organizations* to life has been both challenging and rewarding. This book is the result of the collective efforts of many individuals whose insights, guidance, and support have been invaluable throughout the process. I would like to express my deepest gratitude to all those who contributed to making this work possible.

First and foremost, I would like to extend my sincere thanks to the contributing authors. Their expertise in the fields of Artificial Intelligence, Corporate Social Responsibility, and Marketing has greatly enriched the content of this book. Their commitment to exploring the powerful synergies between these domains and their dedication to advancing knowledge in this rapidly evolving area are reflected throughout the chapters. Without their contributions, this book would not have been possible.

I would also like to express my profound appreciation to Dr. Ahmed Nawaz Tunio, Professor at Sindh Agriculture University, Tandojam, Pakistan for his continued support and guidance. His leadership and vision were instrumental in shaping the direction of this book, and his encouragement kept the project moving forward at every stage.

A special thanks to the editorial team and publishing staff, whose hard work behind the scenes ensured the smooth progress of this book from concept to completion. Their professionalism, attention to detail, and dedication have made this book possible, and I am grateful for their unwavering support.

Finally, I am deeply grateful to my family, friends, and colleagues for their encouragement and patience throughout this journey. Their support has been a source of strength, allowing me to stay focused and committed to the completion of this work.

Introduction

The rise of Artificial Intelligence (AI) is one of the most significant technological developments of the 21st century, transforming industries across the globe. At the same time, Corporate Social Responsibility (CSR) has evolved from a voluntary business practice into a core strategic priority for organizations seeking to align profitability with social and environmental impact. In parallel, marketing, too, has undergone a radical shift—moving from product-centric strategies to purpose-driven, customer-focused approaches. The convergence of AI, CSR, and modern marketing presents an unprecedented opportunity for businesses to create value in ways that were previously unimaginable.

AI, Corporate Social Responsibility, and Marketing in Modern Organizations explores this convergence, offering a comprehensive examination of how AI is reshaping the landscape of CSR and marketing in today's business environment. As AI technologies become more advanced and widely adopted, they are enabling organizations to achieve their CSR goals more efficiently and innovatively. Simultaneously, AI-powered marketing tools are giving companies deeper insights into customer behavior, enabling them to tailor their products and messages in ways that resonate with socially conscious consumers.

The Intersection of AI, CSR, and Marketing

At the core of this book is the understanding that AI is not merely a tool for operational efficiency but a transformative force that can drive positive social impact. AI's capabilities extend far beyond data analysis and automation; it has the potential to help companies achieve their CSR objectives by optimizing resource use, improving transparency, and enabling more responsible supply chain management. When applied to marketing, AI allows businesses to engage with consumers in more meaningful ways, addressing their growing demands for transparency, sustainability, and corporate ethics.

Today's consumers expect brands to be more than just providers of goods and services—they expect them to be active participants in solving global challenges such as climate change, inequality, and social injustice. This shift in consumer expectations is pushing businesses to rethink how they approach CSR and how they communicate their values to the market. AI is playing a critical role in this transformation by helping organizations make smarter, data-driven decisions that align with their CSR goals while also enhancing their marketing efforts.

Why This Book?

This book is born out of the recognition that modern organizations must navigate a complex and rapidly changing business environment. To remain competitive, companies must adopt AI technologies that not only improve their operational efficiency but also help them fulfill their ethical and social responsibilities. Moreover, they must develop marketing strategies that reflect their commitment to CSR, thereby building trust and loyalty among consumers who are increasingly concerned about the impact of their purchases on society and the environment.

The purpose of *AI, Corporate Social Responsibility, and Marketing in Modern Organizations* is to provide a roadmap for businesses seeking to leverage AI to enhance both their CSR initiatives and marketing strategies. Through a combination of theoretical insights, case studies, and practical applications, this book aims to show how AI can be a powerful enabler of responsible business practices and sustainable marketing.

Key Themes of the Book

This book is structured around several key themes, each of which highlights a different aspect of the relationship between AI, CSR, and marketing:

1. **AI for Responsible Business**: This section explores how AI can be used to enhance corporate social responsibility efforts. Topics include AI's role in promoting sustainable supply chains, reducing environmental impact, and improving workplace diversity and inclusion. It also addresses the ethical considerations of AI, such as ensuring that AI systems are designed and used in ways that avoid bias and promote fairness.
2. **AI in Marketing**: Here, the focus shifts to how AI is transforming marketing by enabling companies to better understand and engage with their customers. This section delves into AI-powered tools such as predictive analytics, personalized

marketing, and sentiment analysis, all of which allow businesses to create more targeted and relevant campaigns that align with their CSR objectives.

3. **Integrating AI with CSR and Marketing Strategies**: The book emphasizes the importance of integrating AI with both CSR and marketing strategies. It discusses how companies can align their AI-driven marketing efforts with their broader CSR goals, ensuring that they are not only meeting customer expectations but also contributing to a larger societal mission.
4. **Challenges and Opportunities**: No exploration of AI would be complete without addressing the challenges that come with its adoption. This section highlights the risks associated with AI, including privacy concerns, the potential for algorithmic bias, and the ethical dilemmas that arise when deploying AI in CSR and marketing initiatives. It also explores the opportunities that AI presents, particularly in terms of innovation and the potential for creating more inclusive and sustainable business models.
5. **Case Studies and Real-World Applications**: Throughout the book, readers will find case studies that illustrate how leading companies are successfully using AI to enhance their CSR and marketing efforts. These examples provide valuable insights into the practical applications of AI, demonstrating how it can be leveraged to drive both social impact and business success.

Who Should Read This Book?

AI, Corporate Social Responsibility, and Marketing in Modern Organizations is designed for a wide range of readers, including business leaders, marketing professionals, CSR practitioners, entrepreneurs, and students. Whether you are looking to understand the strategic implications of AI for your organization, or you are a marketing professional aiming to align your campaigns with your company's CSR values, this book offers actionable insights and guidance.

As AI continues to revolutionize the way businesses operate, those who understand how to harness its potential in responsible and ethical ways will be the ones who thrive. This book aims to equip readers with the knowledge and tools they need to succeed in this new era of business, where technology, ethics, and marketing are more interconnected than ever before.

In conclusion, the goal of this book is not just to explore the technical possibilities of AI, but to inspire a more thoughtful and responsible approach to its adoption in modern organizations. By integrating AI with CSR and marketing, businesses can create value not only for themselves but also for society as a whole, leading to a more sustainable and equitable future.

Muhammad Nawaz Tunio

University of Sufism and Modern Sciences, Bhitshah, Pakistan

Chapter 1

Family Business Entrepreneurial Orientation Effect on Improving Entrepreneurial Processes by Mediation of Open Innovation in the Horn of Africa

Shashi Kant
https://orcid.org/0000-0003-4722-5736
Bule Hora University, Ethiopia

Tafese Niguse
https://orcid.org/0009-0008-6536-6392
Bule Hora University, Ethiopia

Metasebia Adula
https://orcid.org/0000-0001-5732-2850
Bule Hora University, Ethiopia

ABSTRACT

This investigation looks at the association among domestic trade entrepreneurial mindset, innovations openness, and enhancing entrepreneurial practices in the con-

DOI: 10.4018/979-8-3373-0219-5.ch001

text of domestic trade in the Eastern Horn of Africa. Using a quantitative research approach, the investigation examined information from 370 domestic ventures, using approaches like Exploratory Factor Analysis (EFA) and Structural Equation Modeling (SEM) with AMOS software. The outcomes manifest a substantial affirmative association among entrepreneurial mindset of family owned trade and innovations openness, implying that domestic firms with a robust entrepreneurial mindset are more likely to contribute in innovative practices. The investigation adds to the current literature by stressing the worth's of cultivating an entrepreneurial orientation and using peripheral joint ventures in domestic firms. Real world consequences underscore the need for domestic trade to foster an innovative ethos, engage in training, and form strategic alliances.

INTRODUCTION

The mindset for entrepreneurial orientation of domestic ventures is vital in strengthening entrepreneurial practices, especially in locations like the Eastern Africa where fiscal dynamics are fast shifting (Adula et al., 2023). Globally, domestic firms make up a sizable component of the private sector, contributing to employment and fiscal growth. Their distinct features, like long-term vision and civic devotion, place them in the forefront of promoting innovation and entrepreneurship. This investigation investigates the link among domestic trade entrepreneurial mindset and the adoption of innovations openness, with the goal of learning how this association might improve entrepreneurial practices in the Eastern Africa (Fikadu et al., 2023). The term "entrepreneurial orientation" comes from strategic administration literature and refers to the practices, approaches, and decision-making styles of organizations that prioritize innovation, reactiveness, and option taking (Jabo et al., 2024). This concept has gained momentum in empirical research, proposing that a robust entrepreneurial mindset might improve outcome and strategic advantage. According to research, domestic firms frequently demonstrate a specific entrepreneurial approach, defined by a combination of traditional worth's and creative approaches. However, the integration of innovations openness—a approach that facilitates cooperation and idea distribution across organizational boundaries—is still underexplored in this context (Nsom, 2021).

Despite the potential benefits, domestic ventures in the Eastern Africa confront a number of real world problems, like restricted access to intellectual capitals, poor infrastructure, and socio-fiscal instability. These limitations might limit their capacity to engage in innovations openness and fully utilize their entrepreneurial orientation (Birhane et al., 2024). Also, there is a substantial lack in empirical research on how innovations openness mediates the link among domestic firm entrepreneurial mindset and entrepreneurial practices in this region. Most prior research has concentrated on developed economies, leaving a considerable gap in our understanding of the particular practices at work in the Eastern Africa (Al Alawi et al., 2023).

This chapter seeks to fill these research gaps by offering a thorough examination of the factors driving entrepreneurial practices in domestic firms, with a focus on the mediating function of innovations openness. By combining current literature and offering fresh empirical information, the investigation will provide substantial insights to future scholars and policymakers. The research identified real world approaches that domestic firms might use to improve their entrepreneurial practices through innovations openness, eventually informing governmental actions that promote regional entrepreneurial growth. This chapter seeks to fill these research gaps by offering a thorough examination of the factors driving entrepreneurial practices in domestic firms, with a focus on the mediating function of innovations openness. By combining current literature and offering fresh empirical information, the investigation will provide substantial insights to future scholars and policymakers. The research will identify real world approaches that domestic firms might use to improve their entrepreneurial practices through innovations openness, eventually informing governmental actions that promote regional entrepreneurial growth.

BACKGROUND OF INVESTIGATION

The entrepreneurial mindset of domestic ventures has arisen as an substantial field of research, particularly in emerging locations like the Eastern Africa (Guyo et al., 2024). Domestic ventures are particularly positioned to foster fiscal growth because of their natural flexibility, long-term vision, and robust civic alliance. Despite these benefits, trade confronts substantial hurdles in executing effective entrepreneurial approaches, notably in incorporating innovations openness into organizational operations (Fikadu et al., 2023). In the Eastern Africa, domestic ventures frequently face challenges like restricted access to financing, poor infrastructure, and legal barriers that hamper their capacity to innovate. These problems are manifested in a case investigation involving a domestic-owned firm in Ethiopia. Despite its robust entrepreneurial drive and dedication to sustainable practices, the firm struggled to implement innovations openness models due to a lack of engagement with peripheral partners including colleges and research organizations. This led to missed chances for information distribution and technical breakthroughs, which might have increased productivity and customer strategic advantage (Uba et al., 2022).

Similarly, a textile-focused domestic firm in Kenya struggled to capitalize on innovations openness owing to conventional administration approaches that stressed internal procedures over peripheral alliance (Dereso et al., 2023). The corporation understood that implementing novel approaches might nurture competency and product quality, but was stymied by a fear of agility and a reluctance to collaborate with peripheral partners. This story demonstrates a frequent barrier: ethnic resistance with in domestic firms. Established conventions can hinder innovation and adaptability to changing customer needs. (Nsom, 2021) Also, empirical research reveals that domestic firms in the region frequently lack the human capital required to successfully execute novel approaches. A research done in Somalia learned that many domestic trade are run by people who have little exposure to current trade approaches, resulting in a mismatch among their entrepreneurial goals and real skills. This situation highlights the vital need for training and growth programs focused at enhancing the abilities of domestic firm executives and staff, allowing them to embrace an entrepreneurial mindset that contains innovations openness (Akbar et al., 2021). The challenges faced by domestic ventures in the Eastern Africa are exacerbated by peripheral issues like political instability and fiscal uncertainty, which can create an unstable trade sphere. For illustration, a domestic-owned manufacturing firm in Sudan failed to recruit investors owing to persistent wars and regulatory uncertainty. This volatility not only limited their capacity to develop, but also reduced their customer strategic advantage (Al Alawi et al., 2023).

STATEMENT OF PROBLEM

The entrepreneurial mindset of domestic firms has the potential to dramatically improve entrepreneurial practices, particularly by including innovations openness (Panigraghi et al., 2023). Ideally, domestic firms must use their distinct strengths—like long-term vision, civic associations, and flexibility—to stimulate innovation and generate fiscal progress in the Eastern Africa. However, the contemporary reality is in sharp contrast to this ideal situation. There are many inconsistent information gaps, indicating that although some domestic firms effectively incorporate innovative approaches, many others struggle, yielding equivocal conclusions about the general influence of entrepreneurial mindset on outcome outcomes (Fikadu et al., 2023). Empirical research manifests a link among entrepreneurial mindset and increased firm success, although the conclusions are sometimes contradictory across circumstances. For illustration, although some domestic trade improve their flexibility and customer responsiveness through innovations openness, others fail to profit on similar tactics due to entrenched old traditions and a reluctance to welcome peripheral cooperation. This mismatch underscores theoretical gaps in our idea incubation of how ethnic and institutional proxies affect the link among entrepreneurial mindset and innovation in domestic firms (Tjano et al. 2020).

Also, there are substantial gaps in research about the exact mechanisms by which innovations openness mediates the effects of entrepreneurial mindset on entrepreneurial practices. Existing research has mostly focused on developed economies, ignoring the particular challenges and options found in the Eastern Africa. This lack of contextual awareness restricts the outcomes' significance to domestic firms operating in poor countries, where socio-fiscal and political issues heavily effect entrepreneurial activity (Uba et al., 2022). Real world issues exacerbate the situation even further. Domestic firms in the Eastern Africa frequently confront intellectual capital limits, insufficient infrastructure, and legislative hurdles that limit their capacity to contribute in innovations openness (Durga et al., 2024). Also, ethnic issues might cause resistance to agility, making it harder for these organizations to implement novel procedures. For illustration, many domestic trades favor short-term stability over long-term innovation, resulting in missed chances in a highly competitive firm (Poli, 2024).

This investigation seeks to fill these gaps by conducting a thorough investigation of the link among domestic trade entrepreneurial mindset, innovations openness, and entrepreneurial practices in the Eastern Africa. By combining empirical research with regional case studies, the venture will investigate the unique constraints that domestic ventures confront and propose best practices for utilizing innovations openness. Also, it will contribute to theoretical frameworks by investigating innovations openness's mediating function, providing insights that might be used to drive future research and policy. Lastly, the goal of this research is to give real world advice for domestic ventures and politicians in the Eastern Africa, so nurturing a more hospitable sphere for innovation and entrepreneurship.

THEORETICAL FOUNDATION

The Intellectual capital-Based View (RBV): It holds that a firm's competitive advantage is derived from its unique intellectual capitals and skills. In the context of domestic firms, this theory highlights the worth's of intangible assets like domestic reputation, trust, and social capital, which might improve entrepreneurial mindset and promote creative practices. Domestic ventures frequently have deep-rooted idea incubation and contacts in their communities, which allow them to learn and capitalize on options for innovation. However, the RBV also emphasizes the possible limits that these firms confront, particularly when their intellectual capitals are not well matched with the demands of a fast changing customer economic approach (Uba et al., 2022).

The Dynamic Capabilities Framework: It builds on the RBV by emphasizing a firm's capacity to integrate, grow, and reconfigure internal and peripheral competences to handle dynamically changing situations. This approach is especially substantial for domestic firms attempting to implement innovations openness since it emphasizes the need of agility and adaptation in their entrepreneurial operations. Domestic firms with robust dynamic capacities might successfully harness peripheral expertise and intellectual capitals, nurturing an innovative ethos that improves their competitive position. However, nurturing these competencies remains a problem, particularly in light of limited intellectual capitals and traditional administration approaches (Tjano et al., 2020).

Domestic Trade Theory: It focuses on the distinct traits and behaviors of domestic-owned trade. This theory investigates how domestic dynamics, governance frameworks, and the interaction of domestic and firm interests effect entrepreneurial behavior and innovative outcomes. Domestic firms frequently worth's long-term stability and heritage, which might together stimulate and stifle innovation. Understanding these interactions are vital for determining how families affect decision-making practices and how much innovations openness they accept (Arshad et al., 2020).

Among these theories, the Dynamic Capabilities Framework is the primary theoretical lens for this investigation. It provides a complete grasp of how domestic firms might shift their entrepreneurial perspective to effectively leverage innovations openness. By emphasizing the capacity to build and reorganize intellectual capitals in response to economic agility, this framework offers a solid platform for investigating how domestic firms in the Eastern Africa might traverse their particular problems while enhancing their entrepreneurial practices. This perspective not only allows for a more in-depth idea incubation of the elements that influence innovation in domestic firms, but it also informs real world advice for cultivating an adaptable and collaborative ethos in a fast changing fiscal world (Poli, 2024).

DEFINITION AND ORIGIN OF CONCEPTS

Entrepreneurial Orientation (EO): It refers to firms' procedures, approaches, and decision-making styles that worth are innovation, pro-activeness, and propensity for option. EO evolved from the strategic administration literature, notably Miller's (1983) books. These academics identified EO as a substantial predictor of trade outcome, arguing that firms with a robust entrepreneurial mindset are more likely to recognize and capitalize on novel customer options. EO is often predefined using proxies like as innovativeness, propensity for option, and pro-activeness, which collectively define a firm's entrepreneurial posture. The notion has now developed, with academics investigating its influences in a diversity of settings, including domestic ventures, where the mindset might be affected by domestic worth's and long-term goals (Idonije et al., 2022).

Open Innovation: It refers to the practice of organizations using peripheral ideas, information, and expertise in conjunction with their internal skills to expedite innovation practices. This approach differs from typical closed innovation models, in which ventures depend entirely on internal intellectual capitals to produce novel products. The word originated from the awareness that in today's enhancing interconnected global economy, organizations might profit considerably from peripheral alliances, joint ventures, and information agility. Innovations openness highlights the worth's of networks and Eco approaches, allowing firms to access into a diversity of sources of invention, which is especially substantial for domestic trade looking to improve their entrepreneurial practices in a competitive Eco approach (Arshad et al., 2020).

Family Owned Business: It refers to trade that are owned and operated by members of the same domestic, with domestic dynamics having a substantial effect on trade operations and decisions. The definition of a domestic firm varies, but it typically involves domestic ownership, domestic engagement in administration, and a desire to pass the firm down to future generations. The investigation of domestic ventures dates back to early fiscal theories, but it gained popularity in the late twentieth century as scholars began to realize the distinct traits and obstacles that domestic-owned firms confront. Gersick et al. (1997) made substantial contributions to this topic by investigating the connection among domestic and trade approaches, stressing how domestic worth's, governance frameworks, and succession planning affect corporate outcome & innovations openness (Idonije et al., 2022).

EMPIRICAL LITERATURE REVIEW

Family owned Business and Entrepreneurial Orientation

The empirical research on the effect of entrepreneurial mindset in domestic firms on entrepreneurial success finds a robust association that highlights domestic firms' particular characteristics. Research repeatedly manifests that domestic firms with a robust EO—defined by aspects like as innovativeness, propensity for option, and pro-activeness outperform their non-domestic counterparts in terms of entrepreneurial success. For illustration, Miller and Le Breton-Miller (2006) learned that domestic firms with a robust EO are healthier at outcome and grabbing customer opportunities, resulting in improved outcome outcomes and long-term sustainability (Idonije et al., 2022). Also, the association among EO and entrepreneurial success is especially clear in the context of innovation. This assumption is assisted by research (Chelliah et al., 2022), which manifests that domestic trade that contribute in innovative approaches benefit substantially in customer outcome and customer satisfaction. This is due in part to their capacity to harness familial associations and networks, which allows them access to principle intellectual capitals and idea incubation that can promote innovation (Arshad et al., 2020). In addition to innovation, propensity for option is an substantial aspect of EO that drives entrepreneurial success. Domestic firms that are ready to take calculated options frequently gain a competitive advantage, especially in volatile customer circumstances. According to Zahra (2005), domestic firms that take on a lot of option are healthier positioned to adapt to agility and seek novel endeavors, which improve their long-term profitability? This ability to overcome uncertainty is vital for entrepreneurial success, particularly in places experiencing fiscal and political crises (Alameeri, 2023).

Also, the dedication to long-term success, which is common in domestic firms, has a substantial effect on entrepreneurial achievements. Domestic trade often worth's sustainability and heritage over short-term profits, which can lead to more strategic decisions. According to Astrachan and Shanker (2003), this long-term orientation promotes domestic firms to engage in innovation and growth, nurturing an atmosphere conducive to entrepreneurial success (Idonije et al., 2022). However, the literature also emphasizes the challenges that domestic firms might confront in reaching their entrepreneurial potential. Ethnic influences, like a propensity for stability over agility, might limit the entrepreneurial mindset of domestic trade. According to research, domestic firms might be option averse due to worries about protecting domestic reputation and wealth, thereby restricting their participation in creative practices (Momanyi, 2023).

H1: Domestic Trade Entrepreneurial Mindset has substantial association.

Family Business EO and innovations openness

Empirical research into the association among entrepreneurial mindset (EO) in domestic firms and innovations openness adoption reveals a multifaceted interplay with substantial effect on innovation outcomes. Domestic ventures, which have traditionally been distinguished by their distinctive worth's and long-standing dedication to stability, sometimes find themselves at a crossroads when it comes to adopting novel approaches. According to research, a robust EO, which contains quality's like as propensity for option, reactiveness, and innovativeness, can have a positive influence on domestic firms' desire to pursue innovations openness. Domestic firms with high EO are more likely to seek peripheral alliances and joint ventures, enhancing their potential for innovation through shared idea incubation and intellectual capitals (Alameeri, 2023). The ethnic factors inherent in domestic firms influence their approach to innovations openness. According to Cennamo et al. (2019), domestic firms with a robust commitment to innovation generate ethos in which staffs feel empowered to seek peripheral ideas and collaborate with partners, resulting in increased inventive output. This collaborative orientation improves the firm's flexibility to customer agility while also strengthening its competitive position (Momanyi, 2023).

However, domestic firms face hurdles in fully leveraging their entrepreneurial orientation to generate innovations openness. According to research, ethnic resistance to peripheral influence might stifle alliance because many domestic trades prefer to depend on internal intellectual capitals and established approaches. According to Zahra et al. (2004), while domestic firms might be proactive, their option-averse orientation might prevent them from engaging in innovations openness approaches that demand vulnerability and confidence in peripheral partners. The friction among the urge for innovation and the unwillingness to venture outside customary bounds is a substantial hurdle (Nsom, 2021). Also, the research highlights the role of leadership in assisting the integration of EO and innovations openness. Domestic firm leaders that exhibit an entrepreneurial orientation and actively assist innovation are vital to overcoming internal opposition and cultivating an Eco approach that worth's peripheral cooperation. Block and Wagner (2010) found that domestic trades driven by visionary managers are more likely to follow innovations openness approaches, which improves their general innovation skills and customer responsiveness (Jocic et al., 2023).

The empirical research demonstrates a beneficial association among domestic firms' entrepreneurial mindset and their participation in innovations openness. Domestic trade that adopt a robust EO are healthier positioned to utilize peripheral alliances and collaborative efforts, hence achieving innovative outcomes. However, ethnic barriers and leadership dynamics must be overcome in order to fully realize the promise of innovations openness. Understanding these factors is vital for nurturing strategies that will assist domestic ventures succeed in an enhancing linked and competitive trade world (Momanyi, 2023).

H2: Domestic Trade Entrepreneurial Mindset has substantial effect on innovations openness

Innovations openness and improving entrepreneurial practices

The empirical research on the effect of innovations openness on entrepreneurial practices emphasizes the agility power of collaborative innovation approaches in boosting trade outcome and agility. Henry Chesbrough popularized the notion of innovations openness, which stresses the utilization of peripheral ideas and customizing avenues in addition to internal intellectual capitals to speed the innovation practice. According to research, organizations that implement innovations openness strategies might dramatically improve their entrepreneurial practices, resulting in healthier product creation, shorter time-to-customer, and more responsiveness to consumer requirements (Hakeem et al., 2024).

A substantial research by Laursen and Salter (2006) provides robust evidence that organizations that use innovations openness approaches report healthier levels of inventive production. Their outcomes manifest that integrating peripheral idea incubation—via associations with education institutes, research institutes, and other firms—allows firms to tap into multiple ideas and skills, so boosting their innovation potential. This peripheral interaction enables not just the production of novel ideas, but also the improvement of current procedures, resulting in more successful entrepreneurial outputs (Nsom, 2021). Also, innovations openness promotes an iterative approach to entrepreneurship, defined by quick prototyping and feedback loops. Empirical research, like that done by Enkel et al. (2009), manifests that firms who use innovations openness might iterate their goods and services more quickly by integrating consumer input and ideas from peripheral partners. This iterative approach improves the entrepreneurial cycle by allowing organizations to swiftly adjust to customer needs and technical improvements, enhancing general responsiveness and strategic advantage (Savitri & Syahza, 2021).

Innovations openness has a predominantly substantial part in enhancing entrepreneurial practices in high-tech areas. Mathafena et al., (2023) found that innovations openness benefits organizations in fast-paced sectors by allowing them to stay nimble and inventive. Working jointly with peripheral organizations allows these firms to have access to cutting-edge expertise and customer information, together of which are vital for long-term growth and innovation (Hakeem et al., 2024). However, the literature also underscores the obstacles of using innovations openness. Firms might face challenges in managing peripheral joint ventures, like intellectual property issues and the blending of different corporate ethoss. According to West and Bogers (2014), these obstacles can undermine the efficacy of innovations openness ventures, emphasizing the importance of corporations developing strategic frameworks that promote cooperation while protecting their interests (Al Alawi et al., 2023). Also, the importance of firm ethos on the success of innovations openness ventures must not be underestimated. According to research, organizations with a assistive ethos that fosters propensity for option and experimentation are more likely to effectively incorporate innovations openness into their entrepreneurial practices. For illustration, Chesbrough and Rosenbloom (2002) found that organizations with a robust innovation ethos are healthier positioned to capitalize on peripheral ideas and turn them into commercial goods and services (Igudia et al., 2020).

H3: Innovations openness has substantial effect on enhancing entrepreneurial practices

Mediation effect of innovations openness among EO and entrepreneurial practice

The entrepreneurial mindset (EO) of domestic firms in the Eastern Africa is vital for enhancing entrepreneurial practices, notably through the mediation of innovations openness. Domestic ventures, which are common in this region, can have distinguishing features like a long-term vision, extensive civic alliance, and a robust dedication to tradition, which might affect their approach to innovation. According to research, a robust EO—characterized by propensity for option, innovation, and pro-activeness—allows domestic trade to find and capitalize on novel options, enhancing their general entrepreneurial practices. In the Eastern Africa, where fiscal issues and customer instability are prevalent, a robust EO can assist domestic ventures handle uncertainty more successfully (Hakeem et al., 2024).

Innovations openness plays a substantial role in mediating this association, allowing peripheral ideas and intellectual capitals to be integrated into domestic firm entrepreneurial practices. By embracing innovations openness, these ventures might increase their ability to collaborate, share information, and co-create with peripheral partners like other trade, academic institutions, and local communities. This collaborative approach not only broadens the innovation pipeline, but also speeds up the creation and execution of novel ideas, resulting in healthier goods and services. Empirical research demonstrates that domestic firms that actively contribute in innovations openness might greatly increase operational competency and customer responsiveness, establishing a ethos of continuous improvement (Nsom, 2021).

However, the obstacles that domestic ventures confront in the Eastern Africa must not be disregarded. Factors like restricted intellectual capital availability, infrastructure shortcomings, and sociopolitical instability might impede their capacity to fully exploit their entrepreneurial mindset and embrace innovations openness. Also, ethnic orientations with in domestic trade might generate reluctance to peripheral alliance, since traditional norms frequently prioritize internal decision-making and option avoidance. Overcoming these hurdles needs a strategic shift in thinking, encouraging domestic firms to see innovations openness as a approach to improve their entrepreneurial practices rather than a threat to their existing traditions (Nsom, 2021).

H4: Innovations openness substantially mediates the association among domestic trade entrepreneurial mindset and enhancing entrepreneurial practice

CONCEPTUAL FRAMEWORK

Based on theoretical and empirical outcomes, the following conceptual framework was formulated.

Figure 1.Conceptual framework (Authors)

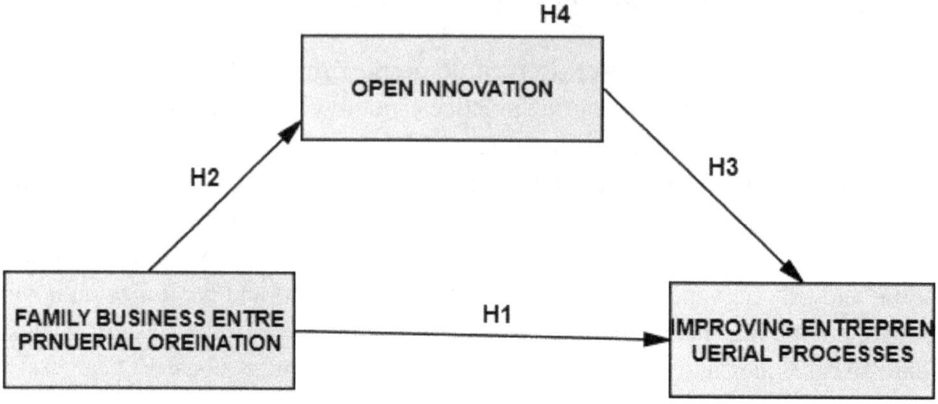

RESEARCH METHODOLOGY

This investigation used a quantitative investigation approach to look at the effect of entrepreneurial mindset and innovations openness on the entrepreneurial practices of domestic firms in the Eastern Africa. A sample size of 370 domestic ventures was selected to ensure adequate statistical power for the investigation. A stratified random sampling approach was used to choose participants, resulting in a representative distribution across diverse sectors and areas in the Eastern Africa. To guarantee that the information was suitable for factor analysis, the Kaiser-Meyer-Olkin (KMO) measure was produced. A KMO score greater than 0.70 proposed that the sample size was appropriate for further investigation. Following that, Exploratory Factor Analysis (EFA) was used to determine the underlying structure of the components associated with entrepreneurial mindset, innovations openness, and entrepreneurial practices. The EFA intended to minimize information dimensionality while also confirming the number of factors that could be retrieved from survey questions. The information was analyzed using Structural Equation Modeling (SEM) with AMOS software to examine the hypothesized correlations among the components. SEM enabled an evaluation of the direct and indirect effects of entrepreneurial mindset on entrepreneurial practices, as mediated by innovations openness. The model fit was assessed using a diversity of indices, including the Chi-square statistic, Comparative Fit Index (CFI), and Root Mean Square Deviation of mean of Approximation (RMSEA), to ensure that the model accurately reflected the information.

Scale Development

The scale for evaluating entrepreneurial mindset, innovations openness, and entrepreneurial practices was created after conducting a thorough analysis of related literature. The constructions were operationalized using a succession of carefully built pieces based on known scales from earlier research. For illustration, Lumpkin and Dess' (1996) aspects of innovativeness, propensity for option, and reactiveness served as the foundation for the entrepreneurial mindset construct. Questionnaires were contained to capture characteristics like the readiness to offer novel questionnaires and the proclivity to take cautious options. Innovations openness was assessed using scales developed from Chesbrough (2003), which emphasized alliance with peripheral partners and the utilization of peripheral ideas to improve innovation practices. Questionnaires contained remarks on the frequency of alliances with research institutes and the use of client feedback into product growth. The entrepreneurial practices construct was created by combining components from the literature on entrepreneurial success and operational competency, including studies that emphasize the need of adaptability and response to customer situations. Each item was created to represent distinct behaviors and outcomes associated with the entrepreneurial practices of domestic firms. Before completing the scale, a pilot research was undertaken with a smaller sample of domestic ventures to ensure that the questionnaires were clear and relevant. Minor improvements were made based on participant feedback, ensuring that the scale was valid and trustworthy for the wider research. The final instrument consisted of well-defined questions that effectively predefined the constructs, laying the groundwork for the quantitative analysis done in this investigation.

DATA Analysis

Table 1. KMO and Bartlett's test

Kaiser-Meyer-Olkin Measure of Sampling Adequacy.		**.860**
Bartlett's Test of Sphericity	Approx. Chi-Square	1428.838
	Df	88
	Sig.	.000

Source: Authors

Table 1 manifests the outcomes of the Kaiser-Meyer-Olkin (KMO) Measure of Sampling Adequacy and Bartlett's Test of Sphericity, which are together vital for determining the information's eligibility for factor analysis. The KMO score of 0.860 depicts robust sampling adequacy, above the widely recognized criterion of 0.70. This manifests that the correlations among the proxies are high enough to assist the use of component analysis, demonstrating that the information set has a substantial level of redundancy. A KMO number closer to 1.0 often implies that factor analysis might produce relevant outcomes, but worth's less than 0.50 signals that the information is unsuitable for such a investigation. Bartlett's Test of Sphericity provides additional evidence that the information is suited for factor analysis. With estimated Chi-Square worth's of 1428.838 and a significance level (Sig.) of 0.000, the outcomes manifest that the correlation matrix is not an identity matrix, implying that there are substantial correlations among proxies. The null assumption of Bartlett's Test is that the proxies are unrelated in the population. A substantial result ($p < 0.05$) permits us to reject this assumption. This outcome assists the conclusion that the proxies are eligible for factor analysis; since they manifest substantial inter correlation to warrant factor extraction. These tests, taken collectively, give a compelling reason for moving forward with exploratory factor analysis (EFA) and demonstrate that the information set is robust enough to learn underlying patterns among the constructs being researched. The affirmative KMO and Bartlett's Test outcomes depict that the following analyses will most likely provide valid insights into the alliance among entrepreneurial mindset, innovations openness, and entrepreneurial practices in domestic firms.

Table 2. Total variance explained

N	Initial Eigen-worth's			Squared Loadings Extraction Sums			Squared Loadings Rotation Sums		
	Total	% of Variance	Cumulative %	Total	% of Variance	Cumulative %	Total	% of Variance	Cumulative %
1	4.41	31.285	31.285	4.41	31.285	31.285	3.00	21.451	21.451
2	1.37	9.787	42.022	1.37	9.787	41.019	2.16	15.491	35.842
3	1.29	9.087	52.109	1.29	9.087	52.109	1.99	14.178	52.109
4	.951	6.782	57.889						
5	.871	6.219	63.117						
6	.775	5.519	68.634						

Abstraction Method: PCA
Source: Authors

Table 2 précises the overall variance explained by the retrieved components in the exploratory factor analysis (EFA) performed with Principal Component Analysis (PCA). The table displays three crucial metrics: beginning eigen worth's, extraction sums of squared loadings, and rotation sums of squared loadings, which collectively reveal the dimensionality of the constructs being studied. The chief eigen worth's manifest that the chief component has an eigen worth's of 4.41, which accounts for 31.285% of the total variance. This considerable amount proposes that this single component accounts for a vital percentage of the information's variability, implying that it is the dominating underlying element. The following components, notably the second and third, also contribute to the general variance, with eigen worth's of 1.37 and 1.29, accounting for 9.787% and 9.087% of the variance, respectively. These three components account for more than 52% of the variation, demonstrating a valid representation of the underlying structures.

The worth's for the chief three components in the Extraction Sums of Squared Loadings are consistent with the original eigen worth's, demonstrating the extracted factors' dependability. The chief component continues to explain 31.285% of the variation, while the second and third components maintain contributions of 9.787% and 9.087%, respectively. The combined proportion of 52.109% across all three components emphasizes their significance in capturing the principle characteristics of the information. The Rotation Sums of Squared Loadings manifest how the distribution of variance agility after the rotation operation, which is intended to improve interpretability. After rotation, the chief component's total variance falls to 21.451%, proposing that, while the volatility remains large, it is more equally spread throughout the components. The second and third components similarly had higher totals of 15.491% and 14.178%, indicating a healthier demarcation of the constructions. This redistribution depicts that the rotation successfully clarified the connections among the proxies, resulting in a more interpretable factor structure.

Confirmatory Factor Analysis

The principle component arrangement of a group of guided proxies is validated using a kind of statistics known as confirmatory principle component examination. Investigators can use CFA to assess hypotheses based on the underlying frame job and correlations among observable proxies. To test the premise that there is a association among the proxies being directed and the latent notions that underlay them, the investigation used CFA (see Table 3).

Table 3. Covariance

Covariance			Estimate	S.E.	C.R.	P	Hy.
open innovations	**<-->**	**Family Business entrepreneurial orientation**	**.239**	**.019**	**8.229**	**.00**	**H2**
open innovations	<-->	Enhancing entrepreneurial practice	.313	.029	7.689	.00	**H3**
Family Business entrepreneurial orientation	<-->	Enhancing entrepreneurial practice	.253	.23	7.829	.00	**H1**

Source: Authors

Table 3 manifests the covariances among the investigation's core constructs: innovations openness, domestic trade entrepreneurial mindset, and enhancing entrepreneurial practices. The table contains principle statistical indicators like covariance worth's, deviation of means (S.E.), vital ratios (C.R.), and related p-worth's, all of which contribute to understanding the connections among these constructs. The correlation among innovations openness and domestic firm entrepreneurial approach is stated to be 0.239, with a deviation of mean of 0.019. The crucial ratio of 8.229 is extremely high, resulting in a p-worth's of ".00," which depicts a statistically substantial association. This manifests that when domestic firms develop a more entrepreneurial mindset, they are more likely to engage in innovations openness approaches. The affirmative correlation depicts that these dimensions are affirmatively connected, which assists the premise that entrepreneurial mindset improves the potential for innovation within domestic trade.

Also, the correlation among innovations openness and improved entrepreneurial practices is calculated as 0.313 with a deviation of mean of 0.029. The crucial ratio of 7.689, collectively with a substantial p-worth's, manifests a robust association. This research proposes that innovations openness not only promotes novel ideas and practices, but it also directly assists to the advancement of entrepreneurial practices with in domestic firms. The affirmative covariance manifests that organizations that effectively use innovations openness tend to be more efficient and adaptable in their entrepreneurial operations. Also, the correlation among domestic firm entrepreneurial orientation and enhancing entrepreneurial practices is 0.253, with a deviation of mean of 0.23. The crucial ratio of 7.829, collectively with a enormous p-worth's, assists the assumption that a robust entrepreneurial mindset has a direct effect on the improvement of entrepreneurial practices. This affirmative link proposes that domestic firms with a proactive and inventive mindset are healthier equipped to improve operational outcome and customer responsiveness.

Table 4. Validity concern

	CR	AVE	MSV	MaxR(H)	FBEM	IO	EME
FBEM	0.728	0.640	0.222	0.848	**0.650**		
IO	0.761	0.660	0.129	0.760	0.168	**0.659**	
EME	0.788	0.607	0.271	0.794	0.378	0.188	**0.681**

Note: FBEM= family business *entrepreneurial mindset; IO= Innovations openness; EME= Improving entrepreneurial Practice*

Source: Authors

Table 4 offers essential validity measures for the investigation's components, with an emphasis on Composite Reliability (CR), Average Variance Extracted (AVE), Maximum Shared Variance (MSV), and Maximum Reliability (MaxR(H). These proxies are vital for determining the consistency and validity of measuring scales for domestic trade entrepreneurial mindset, innovations openness (OI), and enhancing entrepreneurial practices. The constructions' Composite Reliability (CR) ratings manifest a high level of internal consistency. The CRs for entrepreneurial mindset of family owned trade, OI, and entrepreneurship approach nutriments are 0.728, 0.761, and 0.788, respectively. In general, CR worth's more than 0.70 are regarded acceptable, indicating that all three constructions provide accurate measurements. This conclusion assists the reliability of the scales created for this investigation.

The Average Variance Extracted (AVE) worth's corroborate the constructs' validity. The AVEs for entrepreneurial mindset of family owned trade, OI, and entrepreneurship approach instruments are 0.640, 0.660, and 0.607, respectively. An AVE score greater than 0.50 manifests that the concept captures a substantial percentage of the variation in the questionnaires, validating the scales' validity. All three structures fulfill this standard, implying that they accurately measure the specified dimensions. The maximum shared variance (MSV) worth's give information about the constructs' discriminant validity. The MSVs for entrepreneurial mindset of family owned trade, OI, and entrepreneurship approach instruments are 0.222, 0.129, and 0.271, respectively. These low numbers imply that the conceptions share little variation, assisting the idea that they are separate from one another. This is assisted by an examination of the correlations across constructs, which must be smaller than the square root of their respective AVE worth's to prove discriminant validity. Lastly, the Maximum dependability (MaxR(H)) worth's manifest the constructions' overall reliability, with entrepreneurial mindset of family owned trade at 0.848, OI at 0.760, and entrepreneurship approach instruments at 0.794. These outcomes surpass the allowed level, assisting the conclusion that the measurement scales are dependable and effective.

Mediating role Examination

Figure 2.Structural equation model (Authors)

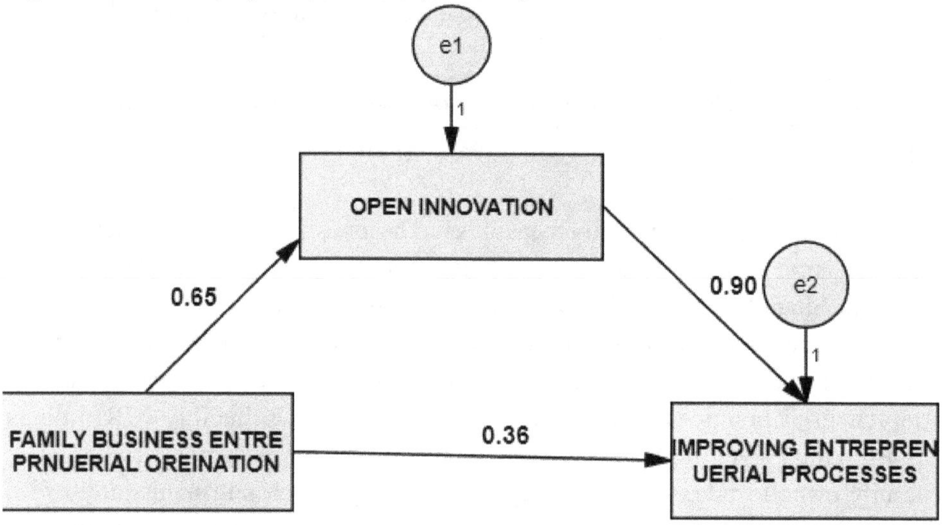

Model fit indices

Table 5. Model fitness

Sig.	Chi-Sq	RMR	Fitness Goodness	Fitness Confirmatory	TLI	RMSEA
0.004	1.950	.038	0.938	0.909	0.908	.032

Source: Authors

Table 5 manifests the model fit indices, which are substantial metrics for assessing the appropriateness of the structural equation model (SEM) utilized in the investigation. These indexes contain the Chi-square statistic's significance, Root Mean Square Residual (RMR), Goodness of Fit Index (GFI), Confirmatory Fit Index (CFI), Tucker-Lewis Index (TLI), and Root Mean Square Deviation of mean of Approximation (RMSEA). Collectively, these indicators assist determine how well the proposed model matches the observed information. The Chi-square worth is given as 1.950, with a significance level (Sig.) of 0.004. A large Chi-square depicts that there is a mismatch among the observed and anticipated covariance matrices, implying that the model does not fit completely. However, given the low worth's of the Chi-square compared to the degrees of freedom, this can also depict that the model is relatively well-specified, particularly in bigger samples where the Chi-square can be affected by sample size.

The Root Mean Square Residual (RMR) worth's of 0.038 depicts a low residual among the observed and expected correlations, proposing a good match. Lower RMR worth's often imply greater model fit, and worth's less than 0.05 are frequently regarded acceptable. The Goodness of Fit Index (GFI) and Confirmatory Fit Index (CFI) scores are 0.938 and 0.909, respectively. The GFI represents the proportion of variance accounted for by the model, whereas the CFI accounts for sample size, hence proving the model's adequacy.

The Tucker-Lewis Index (TLI) worth of 0.908 further assists the model fit, since worth's greater than 0.90 propose a robust match. This index considers the model's multifaceted, indicating that it is adequately parsimonious while yet fitting the information well. Lastly, the Root Mean Square Deviation of mean of Approximation (RMSEA) is given as 0.032, which is much lower than the criterion of 0.05, proposing a good match among model and information. RMSEA worth less than 0.05 are usually regarded propulsive of a robust model fit, while worth's among 0.05 and 0.08 depict an adequate fit.

Table 6. Regression examination

Relative			**Approx.**	**S.E.**	**C.R.**	**P**	**Ass.**
Open Innovations	**<---**	**Family Business Entrepreneurial Orientation**	**.764**	**.145**	**6.583**	**.00**	**H2**
Enhancing Entrepreneurial Practice	<---	Open Innovations	.332	.135	2.849	.00	H3
Enhancing Entrepreneurial Practice	<---	Family Business Entrepreneurial Orientation	.954	.188	7.962	.00	H1

Source: Authors

Table 6 manifests the regression outcomes. The table displays essential statistical measures like regression constants (Relative), deviation of means (S.E.), vital ratios (C.R.), p-worth's, and associated assumptions. The regression constant for innovations openness predicted by domestic trade entrepreneurial approach is 0.764, with a deviation of mean of 0.145 percent. The crucial ratio of 6.583, collectively with the substantial p-worth manifested by.00, reveals a robust affirmative association among entrepreneurial mindset of family owned trade and OI. This depicts that domestic firms with a robust entrepreneurial mindset are far more likely to engage in innovations openness approaches. This information lends assist to Assumption 2 (H2), demonstrating that domestic firms with an entrepreneurial orientation have a higher potential for innovation. The regression constant for enhancing entrepreneurial practices and innovations openness is 0.332, with a deviation of mean of 0.135. The crucial ratio of 2.849 and the substantial p-worth's manifested that innovations openness has a positive effect on the growth of entrepreneurial practices. This research assists Assumption 3 (H3), which states that domestic firms that implement innovations openness approaches improve their operational procedures and general entrepreneurial effectiveness. The robust association is found among strengthening entrepreneurial practices and domestic firm entrepreneurial mindset, with a regression constant of 0.954 and a deviation of mean of 0.188. The crucial ratio of 7.962, collectively with the large p-worth, proposes a very robust affirmative correlation. This outcome confirms Assumption 1 (H1), demonstrating that a robust entrepreneurial perspective not only promotes innovations openness but also directly assists to the strengthening of entrepreneurial practices with in domestic firms.

Table 7. Mediating effect

	Influence	**Worth**	**Path Influence**
Family business Entrepreneurial orientation → Entrepreneurial Improvement Practice	Direct Influence	.36	Direct influence stated
Family business Entrepreneurial orientation → open innovations → Entrepreneurial Improvement Practice	Indirect Influence	.65*.90=.585	Indirect Influence Ensued
	Whole influence	.945	Partial mediation

Source: Authors

Table 7 manifests the mediating role effects, together directly and indirectly via innovations openness. The metrics contained in the table give useful information on the nature of these associations and the level of mediation required. The direct effect of domestic firm entrepreneurial mindset on the entrepreneurial improvement practice is calculated as 0.36. This direct effect reveals a substantial association, implying that a robust entrepreneurial mindset with in domestic trade contributes directly to the improvement of entrepreneurial practices. This conclusion emphasizes the need of cultivating an entrepreneurial orientation as a basic component for enhancing operational outcome and responsiveness in domestic firms. When the indirect connection is examined, the outcomes propose that entrepreneurial mindset of family owned trade has an effect on OI, which then influences entrepreneurship approach instruments. The path influence is computed as 0.65 (entrepreneurial mindset of family owned trade's influence on OI) multiplied by 0.90 (OI's influence on entrepreneurship approach instruments), obtaining a result of 0.585. This substantial indirect effect proposes that innovations openness acts as a principle arbitrator in the link among entrepreneurial mindset of family owned trade and entrepreneurship approach instruments. It implies that domestic firms who actively contribute in innovative practices are well able to agility their entrepreneurial drive into tangible agility to their operations. This underlines the need of peripheral alliance and idea incubation distribution in enhancing the efficacy of entrepreneurial exertions.

The general influence, depicted by the total effect of entrepreneurial mindset of family owned trade on entrepreneurship approach instruments, is computed as 0.945. This high cumulative worth's emphasizes the association's general strength when together direct and indirect paths are taken into consideration. The symbol of "partial mediation" manifests that, while innovations openness makes a vital contribution to the interaction among entrepreneurial mindset of family owned trade and entrepreneurship approach instruments, direct influence remains robust. This manifests that domestic firms' direct efforts, as well as their collaborative participation in innovations openness, benefit entrepreneurial improvement practices.

DISCUSSION

The outcomes manifest that entrepreneurial mindset of family owned trade has a robust beneficial influence on together innovations openness and entrepreneurial practices, emphasizing the necessity of instilling an entrepreneurial orientation in domestic firms. The outcomes depict that domestic trade with a robust entrepreneurial mindset is more likely to contribute in innovative practices, which improves operational competency and flexibility to customer agility. This outcome was similar with the outcome of Nyoach et al. (2024) & Arshad et al., (2020). The mediating function of innovations openness was identified as a substantial aspect in the link among entrepreneurial mindset of family owned trade and entrepreneurship approach instruments. According to the outcomes, domestic firms that aggressively seek innovations openness generate fresh ideas while also streamlining their entrepreneurial practices. This research emphasizes the importance of peripheral cooperation and information agility in building innovative skills. In locations like the Eastern Africa, where intellectual capitals are scarce and customer dynamics are constantly shifting, innovations openness might give domestic trade with the competitive advantage they require to succeed. This investigation adds to the current literature by focusing on the dynamics of domestic firms in a developing country, providing insights into how entrepreneurial mindset and innovations openness might be effectively used to improve entrepreneurial practices. The outcomes have real world applications for domestic firm owners and policymakers. Fostering an entrepreneurial ethos and assisting innovations openness approaches might assisted domestic ventures improve their resilience and outcome, eventually contributing to the region's general fiscal growth.

CONCLUSION

The outcomes manifested that having a robust entrepreneurial orientation not only promotes participation in innovations openness practices, but it also directly leads to the improvement of entrepreneurial practices. This underlines the crucial significance of instilling an entrepreneurial orientation in domestic ventures, as it acts as a catalyst for innovation and operational competency. The mediating function of innovations openness emphasizes the importance for domestic trade to comfortable peripheral joint ventures and idea incubation distribution. These firms might have access to a diversity of ideas and intellectual capitals through innovations openness, which is vital for adjusting to customer agility and nurturing long-term success. This is especially substantial in the Eastern Africa, where fiscal burdens and intellectual capital scarcity necessitate novel answers for existence and strategic advantage.

MANAGERIAL INFLUENCES

The outcomes of this investigation have numerous principle administration influences for domestic ventures operating in the Eastern Africa. Chief and foremost, it is vital for domestic firm executives to foster a robust entrepreneurial ethos with in their firms. This entails nurturing an approach that fosters propensity for option, inventiveness, and responsiveness among stakeholders. Chiefs might strengthen the firm's capacity to learn and exploit on novel options, resulting in healthier trade outcome. Also, the substantial function of innovations openness as a arbitrator emphasizes the worth's of peripheral associations and cooperation. Chiefs must actively seek out networks with other firms, research institutions, and civic organizations to allow information distribution and intellectual capital agility. Encouraging cooperation not only improves the firm's innovative skills, but it also allows for the integration of varied ideas, which might lead to more effective problem answer and flexibility in a fast changing customer.

Also, training and growth programs that focus on creative thinking and collaborative approaches might be advantageous. Chiefs might develop a more flexible and responsive workforce by providing employees with the skills and mindset required to engage in innovations openness. This proactive approach to talent growth might considerably improve the entrepreneurial operations of domestic trade. Lastly, establishments and assist groups must incubate the region's particular obstacles for domestic ventures and give tailored assist to promote an entrepreneurial approach. This might contain intellectual capitals and fiscal benefits to promote inventiveness and assistance. By fostering a approach, stakeholders might assist domestic trade and subsidize to the Eastern Africa's general fiscal growth.

PRACTICAL INFLUENCES

The investigation's outcomes have many real world influences for domestic firms in the Eastern Africa, particularly in terms of enhancing their entrepreneurial capacities through strategic measures. Chief, domestic firms must prioritize fostering an entrepreneurial mindset by incorporating innovative approaches into their everyday operations. This might be accomplished by cultivating a mindset that worth's innovation and promote to take predefined options. Conducting novelty meetings, free-associating meetings, and rewarding staffs who incubate novel ideas or nurture existing procedures are all illustrations of real world actions. The function of innovations openness as an arbitrator depicts that domestic trade must aggressively pursue peripheral alliances. This might comprise developing joint ventures with education institutes, exploration organizations, and other trade of agility information and intellectual capitals. Participating in firm forums, incubation centers, and networking events might assist establish ties and lead to joint ventures. Such associations can assist the firm's innovation capacity by providing access to novel expertise and customer information. Also, domestic ventures must have procedural approaches for gathering and incorporating feedback from consumers and peripheral partners. Steady surveys, emphasis clusters, and civic engagement programs might assist firms healthier understand customer demands and tailor their services accordingly. This real world approach not only nurtures client connections, but also guarantees that the firm stays current with firm trends and requests.

THEORETICAL INFLUENCES

The outcomes of this investigation have substantial theoretical influences for the spheres of entrepreneurship and domestic trade studies. This investigation adds to the increasing frame of works highlighting the implication of an entrepreneurial mindset in domestic trade by outcome a vigorous association. It confirms the idea that an entrepreneurial mindset is not just a required quality, but also a vital driver of innovation and operational competency, matching with previous theories that advocate for domestic ventures' proactive participation in their communities. Also, the investigation emphasizes the mediating role of innovations openness, arguing that it acts as a conduit for entrepreneurial mindset to transfer into nurtured entrepreneurial practices. This outcome expands the theoretical idea incubation of how domestic trade might use peripheral intellectual capitals and alliances to improve their innovative capabilities. It is consistent with and builds on the innovations openness concept, arguing that the dynamic interaction among internal entrepreneurial tendencies and peripheral collaborative practices is vital for effective innovation in domestic firms.

RECOMMENDATION

Based on the investigation's outcomes, numerous recommendations are made for domestic ventures in the Eastern Africa looking to improve their entrepreneurial capabilities through innovations openness and a robust entrepreneurial mindset. Chief, domestic trade must foster a ethos of innovation by encouraging propensity for option and innovative thinking. Chiefs must develop rules that promote creative ideas and promote people to explore without fear of failure. Regular brainstorming sessions and innovation workshops can assist to build an approach conducive to the growth of novel ideas. Additional, domestic firms must actively seek out associations with other entities like colleges, research institutes, and other firms. Alliance on joint initiatives allows domestic firms to get access to novel expertise, customer insights, and best practices that might assist them innovate more effectively. It is advised that firms join firm networks and innovation clusters, which allow for information agility and collaborative issue solving. Also, domestic firms must engage in training programs that foster together entrepreneurial and collaborative capabilities among staff. Workshops on design thinking, agile approaches, and successful association administration might provide teams with the tools they need to effectively contribute in innovations openness. These educational practices will not only improve individual capabilities, but will also result in a more unified and adaptive workforce.

FUTURE DIRECTIONS

Future investigation on the link among domestic trade entrepreneurial mindset, innovations openness, and enhancing entrepreneurial practices must look at various interesting areas. Chief, longitudinal studies might be done to see how these associations agility over time, especially in response to changing customer situations and fiscal settings. Understanding the dynamics of these components at various phases of a domestic trade's lifespan would give useful insights into how entrepreneurial mindset and innovations openness adapt to and effect outcome in diverse situations. Also, future research must look at the precise contextual elements that might modify the connections revealed in this investigation. Ethnic factors, firm peculiarities, and the socio-fiscal sphere in the Eastern Africa might all have a substantial effect on how domestic firms engage in entrepreneurial practices and innovations openness.

REFERENCES

Adula, M., Birbirsa, Z. A., & Kant, S. (2023). The effect of interpersonal, problem solving and technical training skills on performance of Ethiopia textile industry: Continuance, normative and affective commitment as mediators. *Cogent Business & Management*, 10(3), 2286672. Advance online publication. DOI: 10.1080/23311975.2023.2286672

Akbar, F., Bon, A. T. B., Alshaikh, M. E., & Wadood, F. (2021). Mediating effects of inbound innovations openness on entrepreneurial mindset and firm outcome. *Review of International Geographical Education Online*, 11(5), 519–541.

Al Alawi, A. M., Al Kindi, K., Al Shukaili, A., & Ahmed, E. R. (2023). Entrepreneurial practices, innovation, and job creation: The role of demographics and inventiveness as moderators. *International Journal of Innovation Science*. Advance online publication. DOI: 10.1108/IJIS-12-2022-0232

Alameeri, M. S. (2023). Contextual effects of expertise adoption, subjective wellbeing, entrepreneurial behavioral microfoundations and social relations on entrepreneurial innovation: a investigation of SMEs in Kuwait.

Arshad, M. Z., Meirun, T., Javaid, M., Ali, M., Arshad, M. H., & Maneerat, C. (2020). The importance of learning mindset and entrepreneurial mindset on SMEs outcome. *International Journal of Disaster Recovery and Trade Continuity*, 11(1), 1220–1228.

Asefa, K., & Debela, K. L. "Effect of Transformational Leadership on Organizational Performance: The Mediating Role of Employee Commitment and Expert Systems (AI) Inclusion in Ethiopia," *2023 International Conference on Communication, Security and Artificial Intelligence (ICCSAI)*, Greater Noida, India, 2023, pp. 305-310, DOI: 10.1109/ICCSAI59793.2023.10421269

Ato Sarsah, S., Tian, H., Dogbe, C. S. K., Bamfo, B. A., & Pomegbe, W. W. K. (2020). Effect of entrepreneurial mindset on radical innovation outcome among manufacturing SMEs: The mediating role of absorptive capacity. *Journal of Strategy and Administration*, 13(4), 551–570.

Birhane, M., Amentie, C., Borji, B., & Kant, S. Are Ethiopian Coffee Farmers Proficient to Predict Capital Structure with Mediation of AI Based Knowledge Systems and Asset Liquidity? In AI in Agriculture for Sustainable and Economic Management (pp. 199-215). CRC Press.

Chelliah, M. K., Aravindan, K. L., & Muthaiyah, S. (2022). Entrepreneurial mindset and innovations openness promote the outcome of services SMEs: The mediating role of cost leadership. *Administrative Sciences*, 13(1), 1. DOI: 10.3390/admsci13010001

Dereso, C. W., Kant, S., Muthuraman, M., & Tufa, G. (2023). Effect of Point of Service on Health Department Student's Creativity in Comprehensive Universities of Ethiopia: Moderating Role of Public-Private Partnership and Mediating Role of Work Place Learning. In: Jain, S., Groppe, S., Mihindukulasooriya, N. (eds) Proceedings of the International Health Informatics Conference. Lecture Notes in Electrical Engineering, vol 990. Springer, Singapore. https://doi.org/DOI: 10.1007/978-981-19-9090-8_13

Durga, P., Godavarthi, D., Kant, S., & Basa, S. S. (2024). Aspect-based drug review classification through a hybrid model with ant colony optimization using deep learning. *Discov Computing*, 27(1), 19. DOI: 10.1007/s10791-024-09441-w

Fikadu, G., Kebede, K., & Kant, S. (2023). Entrepreneurship Mindset to Nurture the Halal Food Firm Future in Ethiopia. *Journal of Islamic Fiscal and Trade Research*, 3(1), 43–56.

Guyo, D. M., Kero, C. A., & Kant, S. (2025). Is Marketing Intermediaries' Mediation Required for Livestock and Products Marketing to Improve the Economic Status of Pastoralist Communities in Ethiopia? In AI in Agriculture for Sustainable and Economic Management (pp. 216-234). CRC Press.

Guyo, K., & Kero, C. A. "Mediation of Marketing Intermediaries and AI Adoption Between Livestock Products Marketing and Economic Status of Pastoralist in Ethiopia," *2023 International Conference on Communication, Security and Artificial Intelligence (ICCSAI)*, Greater Noida, India, 2023, pp. 311-316, https://doi.org/DOI: 10.1109/ICCSAI59793.2023.10421261

Hakeem, A., Raissi, N., & Matoussi, H. (2024). Rationality and dynamism on entrepreneurial mindset to the pace of internationalization: The moderating role of ecoapproachal munificence. *Journal of International Entrepreneurship*, •••, 1–35.

Idonije, P. I., Dangana, E. A., Ameh, A. A., & Okafor, G. O. (2022). Entrepreneurial Mindset and Sustainable Job Creation: A Investigation of Small and Medium Firms in South-South, Nigeria. Journal of Trade Administration. *Innovation and Inventiveness*, 1(1), 254–277.

Igudia, E., Uba, C. D., & Wale-Oshinowo, B. (2020). Understanding Small Trade Entrepreneurial Activity in the Nigerian Bottom of The Pyramid (BoP) and Informal Economy.

Jabo, B., & Kant, S. "Impact of Technical CRM on Ethiopia Bank Human-Computer Interface and Competitive Advantage as Mediators of Performance," 2024 IEEE International Conference on Computing, Power and Communication Technologies (IC2PCT), Greater Noida, India, 2024, pp. 679-682, https://doi.org/DOI: 10.1109/IC2PCT60090.2024.10486237

Jocic, M. R., Morris, M. H., & Kuratko, D. F. (2023). Familiness and innovation outcomes in domestic firms: The mediating role of entrepreneurial mindset. *Journal of Small Trade Administration*, 61(4), 1345–1377.

Kant, S., & Adula, M. (2024). AI Learning and Work Attitude Mediation Between Reward and Organizational Support in Ethiopia. In Gomathi Sankar, J., & David, A. (Eds.), *Generative AI for Transformational Management* (pp. 109–136). IGI Global., DOI: 10.4018/979-8-3693-5578-7.ch005

Kant, S., & Adula, M. (2024). Mediated by AI-Based Generative Re-Enforcement Learning and Work Attitude: Are Intrinsic Rewards Transforming Employee Perceived Organizational Support? In Gomathi Sankar, J., & David, A. (Eds.), *Generative AI for Transformational Management* (pp. 83–108). IGI Global., DOI: 10.4018/979-8-3693-5578-7.ch004

Kant, S., & Adula, M. (2024). Human-Machine Interaction in the Metaverse in the Context of Ethiopia. In Impact and Potential of Machine Learning in the Metaverse (pp. 196-212). IGI Global. DOI: DOI: 10.4018/979-8-3693-5762-0.ch008

Makhloufi, L., Laghouag, A. A., Ali Sahli, A., & Belaid, F. (2021). Effect of entrepreneurial mindset on innovation capability: The mediating role of absorptive capability and organizational learning capabilities. *Sustainability (Basel)*, 13(10), 5399. DOI: 10.3390/su13105399

Mathafena, R. B., & Msimango-Galawe, J. (2023). Entrepreneurial mindset, customer mindset and opportunity exploitation in driving trade outcome: Moderating effect of interfunctional coordination. *Journal of Entrepreneurship in Emerging Economies*, 15(3), 538–565. DOI: 10.1108/JEEE-03-2021-0114

Momanyi, J. S. (2023). Entrepreneurial Mindset, Trade Incubation, Trade Strategies and Outcome of Start-ups in Nairobi City County, Kenya (Doctoral dissertation, University of Nairobi).

Nsom, N. K. (2021). Evaluating the Measures of Enhancing Trade Growth in Sub-Saharan Africa: The Case of Cameroon.

Nsom, N. K. (2021). Evaluating the Measures of Enhancing Trade Growth in Sub-Saharan Africa: The Case of Cameroon.

Nyoach, T. D., Lemi, K., Debela, T., & Kant, S. (2024). Does Organizational Commitment Mediate the Relationship between Employee Relationship Management and Bank Performance? The Case of Banks in Ethiopia. *International Journal of Organizational Leadership*, 13(2), 355–376. DOI: 10.33844/ijol.2024.60419

Panigrahi, A., Pati, A., Sahu, B., Das, M. N., Nayak, D. S. K., Sahoo, G., & Kant, S. (2023). En-MinWhale: An ensemble approach based on MRMR and Whale optimization for Cancer diagnosis. *IEEE Access : Practical Innovations, Open Solutions*, 11, 113526–113542. DOI: 10.1109/ACCESS.2023.3318261

Poli, T. A. (2024). Mediating Role of Entrepreneurship Capability in Sustainable Outcome and Women Entrepreneurship: An Evidence from a Developing Country. *Journal of Ecohumanism*, 3(3), 2006–2019. DOI: 10.62754/joe.v3i3.3553

Savitri, E., Dp, E., & Syahza, A. (2021). Can innovation mediate the effect of adaptability, entrepreneurial mindset on trade outcome? *Advanced Science Letters*, 11(8), 2301–2312.

Tjano, R. N., & Janse van Rensburg, L. J. (2020). The association of self-efficacy and entrepreneurial intentions on the commitment of the next generation in domestic-owned agritrade. *Acta Commercii*, 20(1), 1–12.

Uba, C. D., Igudia, E., & Wale-Oshinowo, B. (2022). Understanding small trade entrepreneurial activity in the Nigerian bottom of the pyramid and informal economy. *International Journal of Entrepreneurship and Small Business*, 46(3), 353–375. DOI: 10.1504/IJESB.2022.124461

KEY TERMS AND DEFINITIONS

Family Business: A family business is a commercial organization owned and operated by one or more family members. It can range from small enterprises to large corporations. Key characteristics often include family influence in management and decision-making, as well as a focus on long-term goals and values that reflect the family's legacy.

Entrepreneurial Orientation: Entrepreneurial orientation refers to the strategic posture of a firm that embodies a willingness to take risks, innovate, and proactively seek out new opportunities. It typically includes dimensions such as innovativeness, proactiveness, and risk-taking. Companies with a strong entrepreneurial orientation are often more adaptable and competitive in dynamic markets.

Entrepreneurial Process: The entrepreneurial process is the series of steps that entrepreneurs take to create and grow a new venture. This process generally includes identifying opportunities, developing a business idea, gathering resources, launching the business, and managing its growth. It often involves continuous learning and adaptation as the entrepreneur navigates challenges and opportunities.

Open Innovation: Open innovation is a concept that encourages organizations to use external ideas and paths to market in conjunction with their internal capabilities. This approach involves collaborating with external partners, such as other businesses, research institutions, or customers, to drive innovation and accelerate the development of new products or services. It contrasts with traditional closed innovation models where all research and development occur internally.

Chapter 2
Use of Artificial Intelligence (AI) for Improving Human Resource Management (HRM) Functions

Muhammad Faisal Sultan
Khadim Ali Shah Bukhari Institute of Technology, Pakistan

Shahid Khan
Khadim Ali Shah Bukhari Institute of Technology, Pakistan

Nazia Abdul Rehman
Federal Urdu University, Karachi, Pakistan

Harris Masood
Federal Urdu University, Karachi, Pakistan

ABSTRACT

Artificial intelligence is affecting every area of business. It technology is used by all forms of organizations for improved productivity and performance. Hence, there is no exception for the HRM function in which applications AI found to be extremely beneficial. Therefore, this chapter is written specifically to understand the uses and significance of AI to HR functions. Therefore, contents are not only limited to literature and evidence but also the theoretical perspective as well as empirical gaps and implications to provide rigorous understanding to the readers. Thus, the implications, scope, and significance of this chapter have many folds as it is bene-

DOI: 10.4018/979-8-3373-0219-5.ch002

ficial for academicians, researchers, scholars and policymakers to understand the use of AI for HRM functions for a better development of community and society,

BACKGROUND

In recent times use of technology for attaining business goals and objectives is very common. However, with the introduction of artificial intelligence (AI), there is a strong probability that businesses will touch new Horizon through the achievement of their objectives in an efficient manner. This postulate is valid as AI can perform all the tasks that humans are supposed to perform (Pandey, 2020). According to studies, the use of big data along with the Internet of Things (IoT) is primarily responsible for the emergence of AI-based technologies. Recently, AI-based technologies have the main support and power in organizations that are used to create business model innovation, process transformation & competitive advantage, etc (Chowdhury et al., 2023).

Studies also claim that the use of AI is effective for day-to-day & long-term pieces of work. Moreover, the use of AI can not only enable firms to perform work related to different areas and fields but also reduce work pressure on employees (Vinithkumar & Sanjeev, 2019). This happens as AI associates technology and processes with individuals to generate innovative outcomes & also pushes margins in terms of time and cost efficiency (Pandey, 2020). However, some people might perceive the use of AI as the job executioner but on the other side, AI is the tool that will revamp HR practices. However, the overall benefits of AI will surpass the cost of acquisitions and drawbacks of AI associated with HR functions (Pandey, 2020).

INTRODUCTION

The future of Human Resource Management revolves around humans and digitization. HRM is the function that pioneers automation in the work process (Pandey, 2020). Therefore, studies are shreds of evidence significant use of AI in HR functions to support the working of the team uniquely. Studies define AI as a tool that is developed and trained by humans to perform delicate and intelligent operations related to the intellectual skills of humans (Vats et al., 2024). Hence with the growth of AI, it is required by HR departments to make people, teams and leaders understand the role of AI in the workplace without compromising on personal, group, and organizational values (Pandey, 2020). Recent surveys of literature e.g., Pandey, (2020); Vats et al. (2024) and Vinithkumar and Sanjeev (2019) etc., also evidence a significant surge in the literature related to the use of AI in HR functions to improve performance, reduce cost and overcome extra burden from employees. Recent studies also claim that the adoption of AI by HR departments is not only based upon the value that has been created by AI for HR processes but the implementation of AI in HR departments may also create value for customers, employees, and organizations.

STATEMENT OF PROBLEM & PURPOSE OF STUDY

Human Resource Management (HRM) plays a significantly important role in the success of the organization. Therefore, it is necessary to use HRM and related functions effectively and efficiently to ensure hassle-free organizational working. However, HR functions are perceived to be critical for organizational success. Hence, if any of these functions are not been managed in the desired and effective manner then these may not only result in an increase in cost but will also cause bottleneck decisions and will ultimately decrease the organizational performance & productivity (Kaushik et al., 2023).

However, the use of AI cannot replace the element of Human input. Therefore, in developing countries like Pakistan, there is a need for thorough policy-making to increase the use of AI in developing countries (Bibi, 2019). Hence, this paper is purposively written to indicate the uses and benefits of AI for HR and related functions in developing countries like Pakistan. Hence, this study is one of the pervasive studies that is beneficial for multiple stakeholders as it is beneficial for academicians, researchers, and policymakers to understand the significance of AI to conduct more studies to flourish the use of AI in HR and related functions.

LITERATURE REVIEW

In recent times companies have started to adopt AI in various HR functions to improve the Efficiency and effectiveness of HR functions (Vinithkumar & Sanjeev, 2019). Hence it is optimal to believe that there is a massive scope for the use of AI for HR functions especially for talent acquisition, learning and development compensation payroll, etc (Pandey, 2020). Studies also term the use of AI in HRM functions is a time of need as the use of AI is also beneficial for HR professionals and through coping effectively with the AI at the workplace HR personnel may become able to understand problems, issues, and related trends in advance (Vinithkumar & Sanjeev, 2019). Hence, it is optimal to indicate that the implementation of AI may improve employee's overall experience but this ease and customization is not without the threats of unethical use of the technology (Chukwuka & Dibie, 2024).

Improving the process of recruitment:

Vinithkumar and Sanjeev (2019) highlighted the use of AI in the process of recruitment and reflected that the use of AI is massively important for screening CVs, sending auto-generated messages to candidates scheduling interviews, etc. The study mentioned the role of Chabot or automated answering machines is very important and significant for resolving problems and issues related to the process of recruitment. Studies also indicated the use of AI in the process of recruitment through effective screening of candidates, scheduling of interviews & sending messages to applicants, etc (Yawalkar, 2019). Vats et al (2024) also evidence the use of AI in the process of recruitment as in recent times the use of AI can flourish resume scanning, scanning of networks to find the most suitable candidates, assessing the probability of candidate success, and communicating with candidates through chatbots and devising unique resume, etc. Hence, the major benefits of using AI in the process of recruitment are the speed and volume of candidate search and scanning. Other than this use of AI is also efficient in assessing the structure of salary that is prevailing in the market for different situations. Moreover, through using AI HR personnel can also post jobs automatically to different forms of social media sites to churn ratio through the most recent and attractive keywords.

Other than these activities using AI will also remove vagueness from the process of recruitment by adding the most appropriate interviewers to the panel to increase the reliability of the recruitment process. Lastly, the use of AI in the process of recruitment will also reduce cost per hire and increase the churn ratio of applicants throughout the process of recruitment and selection (Bibi, 2019).

Improving the Process of Selection:

The use of AI may also create a pleasant effect on the overall selection process. According to the studies use of AI will improve the selection of employees through selecting the right person for the right job. Hence, the use of AI may also optimize the overall procedure of identifying the best applicant as per the requirement and job specification (Yawalkar, 2019). Studies also revealed that using AI only requires HR personnel to plot jobs in the employee tracking system and the system will automatically highlight the best candidate for the job (Bibi, 2019).

Enhancement of Workplace Learning:

There is a definite impact of advanced technology and AI on workplace learning. In modern times companies are using advanced and sophisticated tools e.g., Eagazify, Obie, and Niles for providing feedback and sharing knowledge. Similarly, Microsoft 365 is a modern tool that is used to increase employee productivity & also to reduce time constraints, etc. Hence, it is optimal to declare that the use of advanced technologies and AI is also enhancing the company's overall performance through effective management of behind-the-scenes roles (Vinithkumar & Sanjeev, 2019).

Improving Efficiency of Employees:

The use of AI is also beneficial for the increase of employee productivity. According to the studies use of AI will be proficient for supplementary activities like data collection, copying data, processing data filling reports, etc. Hence, employees may remain focused on their prime tasks and responsibilities which ultimately increases employee efficiency (Sanyaolu & Atsaboghena, 2022).

Optimizing the Process of Performance Management:

Studies indicated that the use of AI is also beneficial for the improvement of performance management. The use of AI will not only reduce the time spent on unnecessary and traditional methods of employee evaluation but will also improve the level of accuracy of the process (Chukwuka & Dibie, 2024).

The use of AI is also beneficial for real-time observation of the achievement of objectives and rendering feedback at the time of non-compliance. Therefore, AI is also termed as an effective tool to assess the performance of every employee. The use of AI is also beneficial for the removal of biases from the process of performance management and will also be used to provide a detailed set of instructions and benchmarks that are required to be achieved to ensure performance (Sanyaolu & Atsaboghena, 2022). According to studies from Pakistan use of AI is not limited to traditional methods of performance appraisals from spread sheets and the use of sophisticated tools will automatically figure out the performance and non-performers. Thus, support decisions related to promotions, demotions, and transfers effectively and efficiently (Bibi, 2019).

Proficient On-Boarding: On-Boarding is the stage in which HR introduces new hires to the other members of the organization. The use of AI is also important for onboarding as the use of AI will automate the entire process of onboarding. Through using AI new hires may easily communicate with the other team members as well as high-ups of the organization. On the other end use of AI-based chatbots may also improve the overall performance of onboarding by collecting required information from the new hires, organizing information, and making new hires sequentially fill out the required form, etc. AI-based onboarding mechanism may also be hassle-free for the new hires as AI will arrange the process with flexible time and location schedules. Lastly, the AI-supported process of onboarding will result in and will also assist new hires to get indulged into the system with convenience and ease (Sanyaolu & Atsaboghena, 2022).

Efficient for Training and Development Initiatives: HR managers are required to ensure the skill set of employees resembles the requirement of the employer. The use of AI is also found to be important in this regard. Fundamental uses of AI in training and development initiates are to make learners engaged, track skills application, develop soft skills, develop leadership skills, and embark on conflict management skills. Moreover, the use of AI will also be beneficial for creating customized and personalized training programs for new hires. Lastly, the use of AI is also important for assessing the training matrices to figure out the needs of every person related to learning and development (Sanyaolu & Atsaboghena, 2022).

Efficient in Reward Management:

Compensation Management is perceived to be one of the most important tools for the removal of employee dissatisfaction and fostering motivation. In recent times studies have indicated that the role of AI is to assess the gaps between the wages or compensation of employees working at the same level to achieve fair compensation practices at the organizational level.

Moreover, relying on recent technology HR can also predict future trends in employee compensation practices. Hence, HR may become able to set fair compensation packages for employees that are based on their education, skills knowledge, etc (Sanyaolu & Atsaboghena, 2022).

Increases Employee Engagement:

The use of AI is also effective in checking the rate of employee engagement and their level of happiness. This assessment is beneficial to gauge the level of motivation in different departments, teams, and employees. Various tools may extract the required information from emails, memos media comments, etc., to predict the level of employee engagement (Sanyaolu & Atsaboghena, 2022). Studies from Pakistan also supported these points as the use of AI will decrease overall return on investment (ROI) by increasing the level of employee engagement. Moreover, by using AI it is easy to predict the performance patterns of employees to understand the psycho-emotional traits that are the major cause of employee performance (Bibi, 2019)

Predicting Effective Career Paths:

For a long time, HR personnel have been actively involved in providing effective career paths to employees to aid their career journey. However, with the advent of technology HR departments are taking the assistance of AI to provide the right career paths and help employees achieve excellence in their fields and work life. Hence, in contemporary times recent technologies are used by HR departments to train, develop, and employ personnel. Recently employers have been considering incorporating tools that are progressive in assessing employee emotions. These forms of tools and applications have a long way in assessing the employee attitude, engagement, and role. According to studies these technologies will be used to forecast the training and development required by different groups of employees for better performance (Sanyaolu & Atsaboghena, 2022).

Optimizes the rate of Employee Retention:

The use of AI is also imperative for optimizing retention strategies. According to the studies use of AI can easily predict those employees who may leave the organization shortly. Thus, the use of AI also tends to plan effective motivational practices to increase the rate of retention (Sanyaolu & Atsaboghena, 2022).

Overcome Burden from HR Personnel:

The use of AI will also reduce the administrative burden on HR personnel. Hence, using AI may also result in better problem-solving and proactive initiatives that ultimately reduce the extra administrative burden on HR personnel (Yawalkar, 2019). One of the other studies e.g., Vats et al (2024) indicated that the use of AI may also be helpful at the helpdesk where the use of Chat-bot may be practiced to answer queries made by employees and customers. Similarly, the use of AI may also reduce administrative activities e.g., monitoring of training and verification of employee competencies, etc. Hence, there are multiple uses of AI in HR that may aid in the substantial reduction of administrative tasks from HR personnel.

RESEARCH METHODOLOGY

Research Methodology is the part of the research that describes various points, elements, and parameters that are used in the research to make it cost-effective, focused, and rigorous. However, research methodology is not only used to describe the parameters, points, and elements that are used in the research but also to highlight the reason for preferring any particular point or parameter rather than others (Kothari, 2004). Hence, to make this section adequate and effective to make other researchers, academicians, and policymakers understand the scientific method applied to develop this study we followed Sekaran and Bougie (2016) to divide the research methodology into parts. However, sampling design is not been used in this study as this study is a book chapter that is written in a different way as compared to a general research paper (Roediger III, 2006).

Research Design:

The purpose of this study is descriptive as it aims to indicate and highlight various benefits, uses, and edges that may be achieved through using AI in HRM functions. Hence, no qualitative or quantitative assessment has been made and the study follows the indications of Sekaran and Bougie (2016) as a descriptive study that is based on a cross-sectional time horizon and minimal interference from researchers. However, it is not imperative to devise the research design without including the concept of research onion devised by Saunders et al (2007) which reflects that this study is to make readers grasp detailed benefits that may be achieved through implementing AI in HR functions to improve performance of HR department and organization. Moreover, this study is also developed on traces of research gaps from relevant literature. Hence, it is based on epistemology while the philosophical stance used to relate philosophy with research approaches and research strategy is post-positivism which applies to qualitative as well as quantitative studies.

The research approach used in devising this study is deductive, the research strategy is archival and the methodological choice is mono-method as indicated by Saunders et al. (2015)

Figure 1. Sphere of HR benefits indicating benefits of using AI for HR core and related functions (Researcher's own creativity)

IMPLICATIONS AND DISCUSSIONS

The use of AI is much beneficial for HR and related functions as indicated by the previous studies e.g., Chukwuka and Dibie (2024); Sanyaolu & Atsaboghena (2022); Vats et al (2024) and Vinithkumar & Sanjeev (2019), etc. A literature survey reveals that most of the recent studies reflect the operational and strategic benefits of using AI in HRM and related functions. Hence, on the base of the points extracted from the literature researchers have developed a diagrammatic view of the universe of benefits that the use of AI may provide to HRM and related functions.

Therefore, Figure 1 has been developed to highlight the benefits that are evident from the literature and can benefit HRM and related functions. The oval shape is the sphere of benefits of AI that can be achieved and integrated into HR functions. Rectangle indicated the benefits that are reflected through literature and remaining are the benefits that are for the improvement of related functions. Understanding these points and models might be found effective and beneficial for academicians, researchers, and policymakers. To highlight these related benefits study incorporated the implications from Bibi (2019) that the use of AI may also improve the payroll management system and may also decrease the time required to process and approve bills etc. Other than that use of AI may also assist in project completion and assessment i.e., the use of AI is an efficient tool to assess the estimated date of project management, and assessing these points will assist the HR department in incorporating required input with the perspective of the human resources.

REFERENCES

Bibi, M. (2019). Execution of artificial intelligence approach in human resource management functions: Benefits and challenges in Pakistan. *Sarhad Journal of Management Sciences*, 5(1), 113–124. DOI: 10.31529/sjms.2018.5.1.8

Chowdhury, S., Dey, P., Joel-Edgar, S., Bhattacharya, S., Rodriguez-Espindola, O., Abadie, A., & Truong, L. (2023). Unlocking the value of artificial intelligence in human resource management through AI capability framework. *Human Resource Management Review*, 33(1), 100899. DOI: 10.1016/j.hrmr.2022.100899

Chukwuka, E. J., & Dibie, K. E. (2024). Strategic Role of Artificial Intelligence (AI) on Human Resource Management (HR) Employee Performance Evaluation Function. *International Journal of Entrepreneurship and Business Innovation*, 7(2), 269–282. DOI: 10.52589/IJEBI-HET5STYK

Kaushik, P., Miglani, S., Shandilya, I., Singh, A., Saini, D., & Singh, A. (2023). HR Functions Productivity Boost by using AI. *International Journal on Recent and Innovation Trends in Computing and Communication*, 11(8), 701–713. DOI: 10.17762/ijritcc.v11i8s.7672

Kothari, C. R. (2004). Research methodology: Methods and techniques. New Age International

Pandey, S. (2020). Exploring the role of Artificial Intelligence (AI) in transforming HR functions: An Empirical Study in the Indian Context. *International Journal of Scientific Research and Engineering Development*, 3(5), 719–732.

Roediger, H. L.III. (2006). Reviewing Book Chapters. In Sternberg, R. J. (Ed.), *Reviewing scientific works in psychology* (pp. 89–100). American Psychological Association., DOI: 10.1037/11288-006

Sanyaolu, E., & Atsaboghena, R. (2022). Role of Artificial Intelligence in Human Resource Management: Overview of its benefits and challenges. *ResearchGate*, (December), 1–8.

Saunders, M., Lewis, P., & Thornhill, A. (2007). Research methods. *Business Students 4th edition Pearson Education Limited, England, 6*(3), 1-268

Saunders, M. N. K., Lewis, P., Thornhill, A., & Bristow, A. (2015). *Understanding research philosophies and approaches: Research methods for business students.* Pearson.

Sekaran, U., & Bougie, R. (2016). *Research methods for business: A skill building approach*. John Wiley & Sons.

Vats, I., Kirilenko, O., & Novak, V. (2024). Benefits of using artificial intelligence in core HR processes. *Monthly Informational and Analytical Journal*, 3(-), 8–12. Advance online publication. DOI: 10.37634/efp.2024.3.1

Vinithkumar, S., & Sanjeev, S. (2019). Artificial Intelligence in Human Resource Management. *International Journal of Research and Analytical Reviews*, 6(1), 20–24.

Yawalkar, M. V. V. (2019). A study of artificial intelligence and its role in human resource management. [IJRAR]. *International Journal of Research and Analytical Reviews*, 6(1), 20–24.

Chapter 3 Role of Green Corporate Social Responsibility and Corporate Social Responsibility in Enterprises: Evidence From Europe

Samrah Jamshaid
https://orcid.org/0000-0002-6060-2463
Northeast Normal University, China

Kiran Shahbaz Khan
COMSATS University Islamabad, Pakistan

Saadia Ali
Bahria University, Islamabad, Pakistan

Rabia Kishwer
Islamic International University, Islamabad, Pakistan

ABSTRACT

CSR is essential for companies to meet financial, social, and environmental goals. European companies can improve society and the environment by incorporating CSR into environmental policies. Businesses globally have invested approximately $16.6 trillion in CSR, which promotes environmental sustainability. Record-high carbon emissions, waste energy, pollution, wastewater, and water scarcity have boosted natural resource demand. GCSR actions increase organizational, environmental,

DOI: 10.4018/979-8-3373-0219-5.ch003

economic, and ethical performance. This qualitative study analyses European SME statistics from publicly available online publications, journals, books, reports, government and public industries, and agency statistics using secondary data collecting.

INTRODUCTION:

Understanding the value of CSR in regard to society and stakeholders such as employees, customers, and suppliers, amongst other groups, is not difficult to do. Because it represents a potential point of divergence, this issue is significant not just in the context of social welfare but also in its own right. Consumers are more likely to support organizations and practices that have a positive influence on the world as a whole, and they offer businesses that are ethically responsible a competitive advantage in the market. Organizations rely on this information to identify opportunities and threats, as well as to plan, carry out, oversee, and develop long-term goals that will allow them to continue expanding in terms of financial stability (for the company as well as society as a whole) and economic production (Shaikh, et al., 2019). The research indicates that a company's motivation to give back to society, which is the driving factor for the adoption of CSR by SMEs, is increased when there are substantial economic incentives and a high level of internationalization inside the firm (Grimstad, et al., 2020). The connection between corporate social responsibility and the prosperity of SMEs can be partially explained by the moderating effect of reputation management (Bahta, et al., 2020). CSR programs with the goal of assisting small and medium-sized enterprises (SMEs) in problem-solving should be designed with those organizations' unique requirements and conditions in mind (Hadi, et al., 2020). According to the findings of our study, the biggest reason that small and medium-sized businesses (SMEs) do not participate in CSR initiatives is because they do not have the financial backing to do so (Zou, et al., 2021). Because CSR has a significant positive impact on corporate financial performance, businesses should enthusiastically adopt CSR in response to the call of the nation, as stated in the principles of corporate social responsibility (CSR). This is especially true for more stable businesses and state-owned enterprises (Wu, et al., 2020). The interest in corporate social responsibility (CSR) as a means of seeking to obtain that competitive edge has developed as a result of greater competition among firms as well as pressure from governments. When a firm is able to successfully incorporate social responsibility into its corporate culture, it can realize a number of benefits, including an advantage in the marketplace, benefits for the community, and possibly even savings for the government. The concept that is known as “corporate social responsibility” stipulates that businesses have a need to behave in a responsible manner in the communities in which they operate their operations (commonly shortened as "CSR"). Because of the wide range of cultural backgrounds that exist, the phrase "socially responsible" can be interpreted in a variety of very specific ways by various enterprises. The idea of a "triple bottom line," which contends that businesses should track not only their financial success but also the influence they have on society and the environment, is widely utilized by corporations. This concept argues that businesses should track not only their financial success but also the influence they have on society and the environment. Those who believe that this idea is correct believe that corporations have a responsibility to monitor more than just their financial status. It is of critical importance in developing the corporate identity of financial institutions and securing the commitment of employees and other internal stakeholders (Shaikh, et al., 2022). CSR is influenced indirectly by firms' environmental policies since these policies, in turn, have an impact on the firms' internal procedures and environmental practices (Shah, et al., 2016). Corporate social responsibility (CSR) activities provide environmental, social, and economic benefits, and these benefits are especially relevant for the rising manufacturing and service industries of emerging countries (Ahmed, et al., 2021). CSR is consisted of and focuses on the following main areas of activity: the preservation of the environment, the quality and safety of construction, the engagement of the community, the engagement of employees and clients, and the administration of CSR (Jiang, et al., 2016). Studies have identified a correlation between environmental corporate social responsibility and technical innovation, which is in line with both CSR and environmentally sustainable development (Lui, et al., 2021). According to the findings of the research, strategic considerations were the key driver for the establishment of a CSR project that places an emphasis on environmental conservation (Babiak, et a., 2021). This chapter presents an overview of corporate social responsibility (CSR), green CSR, the disagreement around their definitions, and how European businesses can benefit from understanding these concepts.

Background

Organizational leaders may endure poor organizational performance and lose profitability if they don't undertake CSR activities (Yim et al., 2019). Corporate executives need to act responsibly if they want to be respected by their stakeholders. Corporate social responsibility (CSR) leaders can achieve their financial aspirations as well as societal and environmental objectives by strategically assisting firms in successfully meeting stakeholder expectations (Franklin, 2023). Without a doubt, the incorporation of Corporate Social Responsibility (CSR) and Green CSR emerges as a pressing imperative for firms functioning in the European setting. By collaborating with stakeholders, fostering transparency, and incorporating moral and environmentally responsible business practices into daily operations, European enterprises can effectively contribute to social well-being and ecological preservation. They get one step closer to a more responsible and sustainable future by doing this. Literature highlights the crucial necessity of incorporating CSR practices into organizational environmental plans since every facet of CSR exhibits a favorable link with environmentally sustainable development (Shahzad, et al., 2020). The mechanism study also demonstrates how CSR has an impact on promoting green innovation, assisting environmental investments, and enhancing corporate governance—aspects essential for promoting high-quality corporate progress (Xue, et al., 2022). Environmental issues include record-high carbon emissions, waste energy, pollution, wastewater, and water scarcity have dramatically increased the consumption of natural resources over the past 50 years, making 2020 the hottest year on record (Kannan et al., 2022; W. Simmou et al., 2023). Due to its rising ethical focus on the environment and social good (Fernandez-Gago et al., 2020), CSR has become and remains more urgent (Govindan, 2022). Businesses around the world have invested more than $16.6 trillion in CSR initiatives, according to the 2020 report from The Forum for Sustainable and Responsible Investment. Due of this, CSR is frequently viewed as an important element of long-term viability (Fandos-Roig et al., 2021; W. Simmou et al., 2023). Concern for the environment has become so widespread and important in recent years that the UN General Assembly gave the climate summit top priority at its 74th session on September 24, 2019. The implementation of environmental management practices is currently a top priority for all parties involved (Yu et al. 2017), and it is now expected of industrial organizations to participate in the creation of green products and procedures (Bresciani et al. 2022; Yu et al. 2017). (Niazi et al., 2023). According to the KPMG poll on sustainability reporting, in 2020, 81% of the top 5200 firms worldwide would report on sustainability, up from 18% in 2002. (KPMG, 2020). Additionally, it is acknowledged in the action plan for funding sustainable growth of the European Commission, which calls for "better-integrating sustainability in ratings and market research." According to S&P (2017), they discovered 717 instances in which environmental and climatic conditions were pertinent to the assessment and 106 instances in which they caused a change in the rating. Meles and others (2023) Between 60 and 70 percent of the world's pollution is caused by small and medium-sized enterprises (SMEs), which are also major forces behind job creation and economic growth globally (Mendes et al., 2022). But SMEs' approaches to addressing environmental issues are not generally recognized (Kortetm aki et al., 2022). All parties involved must move quickly to decrease the environmental effects of their industrial activity (Baah et al., 2021; W. Simmou et al., 2023). The European Commission launched the European Green Deal (EGD) in 2019, a roadmap of green measures to make the EU economy resilient and carbon neutral until 2050.According to the EGD, the major axes of green transformations are clean energy, sustainable industry, building and renovation, the "from farm to fork" approach, eradicating pollution, sustainable mobility, biodiversity, and sustainable finance. Companies are interested in green transformations and establishing their green brands in order to be appealing in national and particularly international markets and correspond to customers' desires. As a result, "The 2030 Agenda for Sustainable development," which includes 17 objectives and 169 targets to be met by 2030, was adopted by United Nations Member States. One of them is fostering green corporate social responsibility (Us, Pimonenko & Lyulyov, 2023). According to Niazi et al. (2023), GCSR might be accomplished by putting GHRM customs, green goods, and green activities into practice. According to Suganthi (2020), the inclusion of GCSR-related activities boosts organizational effectiveness. Higher environmental, economic, and ethical performance of organizations was a result of GCSR initiatives (Niazi et al., 2023). According to W. Simmou et al. (2023), environmental performance of SMEs is greatly improved by external (Environment and Community) and internal (Employees) GCSR-related techniques.

What is CSR

The phrase "Corporate Social Responsibility" (CSR) is used to refer to an approach to doing business in which stakeholders other than shareholders are taken into account in all decisions. According to Eric Orts of the University of Pennsylvania, corporate social responsibility (CSR) has been established at least since the 1930s, despite its recent surge in popularity (NCBI, 2007). CSR is often distinguished from philanthropy in definitions since it is more directly related to the core business and can increase profits. Corporate social responsibility (CSR) is a set of practices that balances the bottom line with other stakeholders (HEC, 2019). CSR is the idea that businesses should contribute to the communities in which they operate (HBS,2021). The goal of a company's CSR efforts is to persuade all of the company's stakeholders that those efforts will have a positive effect on those stakeholders (Afridi, et al., 2023). It can also refer to a company's activities that go above and beyond what is required by law or are otherwise beneficial to society (Gatti et al., 2019; Mansour et al. 2022). Employees are inspired to do good work when their employers make environmental and social responsibility (CSR) a priority. It also implies that companies should think about the effects of their actions on society and the environment, not only on the bottom line. The United Nations Industrial Development Organization UNIDO (2022) defines corporate social responsibility (CSR) as "the process by which an enterprise reconciles the conflicting demands of its economic, environmental, and social environments with the interests of its shareholders and other stakeholders" (Wirba, A. V. 2023). According to the European Commission (2006), government involvement in CSR is essential despite the fact that CSR agendas and activities are founded on voluntary action by firms and serve as a tool for accountability and responsibility (Wirba, 2023). Companies should fulfil their CSR responsibilities by voluntarily working to improve the social well-being of the communities in which they operate. At its core, it is a process for dividing up a company's profits and losses among its various internal and external parties, such as employees, shareholders, investors, customers, vendors, and community groups. The OECD has designated an alternative to CSR called Responsible Business Conduct (RBC), which is defined as "making a positive contribution to economic, environmental, and social progress in order to achieve sustainable development and minimize negative effects from an enterprise's direct and indirect activities, products, or services" (OECD, 2023). Corporate social responsibility (CSR) is not a new concept, but over the past decade its focus has shifted from labor issues and local philanthropy toward environmental actions. More and more companies desire to go "green" and are building to LEED (Leadership in Energy and Environmental Design) certification standards, joining the Chicago Climate Exchange, and producing corporate social reports to make public their environmental performance in accordance with the Global Reporting Initiative (Lyon, et al., 2010). Many businesses view CSR as a crucial tool for enhancing their brand's reputation and corporate image (Shafique et al., 2021). Green CSR refers to an organization's ecologically friendly practises that safeguard society, the environment, and the firm's bottom line. The development of the positive association between green perceptions and green purchasing behaviour depends on understanding good consumer perceptions of hotel green CSR programs. This trend is being driven by a number of factors, including managerial altruism, cost-cutting efficiency improvements, the emergence of a new generation of environmentally conscious consumers, and more astute business leaders who prevent political conflict before it arises rather than responding to public pressure after the fact. Despite creeping concerns that some of the resulting corporate actions may be mere "greenwash," for the most part they are welcomed by employees, consumers, investors, regulators, and the public. But is it really socially desirable for managers to take on costly environmental initiatives that are not required by law. The concept of "corporate social responsibility" is one that is becoming increasingly familiar to people all around the world. On the other hand, the author had never previously been exposed to such a detailed explanation of sustainable development. The terms "social responsibility," "environmental responsibility," and "economic responsibility" are referred to collectively as "corporate social responsibility," or CSR for short. It is necessary for a firm to be able to apply all three of these criteria consistently if it intends to remain in that location over the long term. If a business is primarily concerned with making money, it may give off an impression of being greedy. It is a concern that if they only pay attention to the environment, they will pay less attention to the well-being of the employees. If they are just concerned with meeting their social responsibilities, they run the risk of not giving the marketing of their products the attention it deserves. In other words, these three aspects ought to coordinate their efforts in order to produce a financially viable, environmentally conscientious, and welcoming place of employment. According to the opinions of several experts, the term "sustainable" is chosen over "CSR" because of its higher familiarity.

What is GCSR?

Environmental CSR is a crucial component of corporate social responsibility (CSR), and it is included in this idea. Organizations have a duty to protect the environment, and environmental CSR can serve as a strategic direction for achieving long-term development objectives. The vast majority of the research that is currently available defines environmental CSR using a three-pronged framework. One perspective on environmental corporate social responsibility (CSR) that is more narrowly focused says that it entails a number of environmental measures that businesses voluntarily put into place, with the emphasis of these initiatives being on resources or energy. Second, a process-based viewpoint claims that environmental CSR entails streamlining organizational procedures to lessen the environmental impact those operations have. The third and final point of view is a product-based one, according to which businesses can offer environmentally friendly goods and services thanks to environmental CSR. In a broad sense, it refers to the consideration of social and environmental issues in conjunction with commercial operations, and it encourages participation of the key stakeholders in the firm's environmental initiatives. Green is a way of thinking and a social movement that advocates for environmental preservation and improvement. It can be said that the environmental component of CSR entails the responsibility to address the environmental effects of the company's operations and the minimization of behaviours that might negatively affect how future generations enjoy the nation's resources. Companies that practice "corporate social responsibility" are those that are dedicated to having a positive social or environmental impact on society. Additionally, it can foster good will toward an organization's reputation and positively impact the performance and health of a brand. Because of a brand's "go green" or "go social" credentials, consumers are keen to support it, but the real question is if they are willing to pay more for it. Businesses share the same level of responsibility that individuals do when it comes to global environmental issues like ozone depletion, global warming, or the loss of biodiversity, especially when large industries are involved. Three actions in green management could lessen the harmful effects of business operations on the environment. Which are: Industrial ecology, life-cycle analysis, and design for disassembly. The environmental impact of a product throughout the course of its life cycle is the subject of life cycle analysis. Industrial ecology is the design of industries as self-contained ecosystems with a focus on product reuse and recycling. Companies that are committed to having a good social or environmental influence on society engage in corporate social responsibility. Additionally, it can improve the reputation of an organization and the health and performance of a brand. Because of a company's "go green" or "go social" credentials, consumers are prepared to support it, but are they willing to pay more. Environmental, social and governance and corporate social responsibility are related but different concepts that can be combined to boost corporate sustainability. These two terms have some overlapping meaning and are sometimes used interchangeably. But with new tightening expectations on corporate practices and increasing concerns surrounding environmental sustainability, businesses should know what these terms mean, how they differ and where they overlap.

CSR AND ENTERPRISES OF EUROPE

It's important to recognize how complementary regulation helps to foster an atmosphere where businesses can voluntarily fulfil their social duty. In order to further advance the EU's interests and values in ties with other regions and nations, it aims to reassert the EU's worldwide influence in this area. Additionally, it will aid in directing and coordinating the policies of EU Member States, hence lowering the possibility of varying strategies leading to increased costs for businesses with operations in several Member States. The goals of the Europe 2020 strategy for smart, sustainable, and inclusive growth, including the target of 75% employment, are supported by CSR. When private sector companies offer public services, ethical business practices are extremely crucial. Enterprises have a social obligation to assist in reducing the social repercussions of the current economic crisis, including job losses. CSR provides a set of ideals that can be used to create a society that is more cohesive and to support the shift to a sustainable economic system. CSR When it comes to concerns about corporate responsibility and sustainability, Europe has the most powerful business network in the continent. We bring together over 10,000 firms on a local, European, and global scale and act as a source of inspiration and support for these businesses with the help of our corporate members, National Partner Organizations (NPOs), and Associated Partners. They provide assistance to businesses and entire industries as they undergo transformation, collaborate to develop actual solutions, and advance the cause of sustainable growth. They are in favor of structural change in accordance with the Sustainable Development Goals, and their goal is to collaborate with the leaders of Europe and the other stakeholders to develop a comprehensive strategy for a sustainable Europe by the year 2030. CSR Europe is the leading European business network for corporate social responsibility, with around 75 multinational corporate members and is currently comprised of 38 multinational firms originating from a wide variety of sectors and locales (Idowu, et al., 2013). CSR Europe is a network that is comprised of 35 national partner organizations, and it currently provides its services to over 10,000 firms across Europe.

Figure 1. CSR Europe's corporate members (lhttps://www.csreurope.org/our-network#:~:text=CSR%20Europe's%20network%20of%2035,than%2010%2C000 %20companies%20in%20Europe)

CSR enables businesses to better anticipate and profit from rapidly changing societal expectations and operating situations since it necessitates contact with internal and external stakeholders. Thus, it can encourage the establishment of new markets and open doors for expansion. Businesses can create long-term consumer, employee, and citizen trust as a foundation for sustainable business models by addressing their social responsibilities. Increased levels of trust in turn serve to foster a climate where businesses can innovate and expand. The lives of people in the EU and around the world are significantly impacted by the actions of corporations. Not only in terms of the goods and services they provide, the employment opportunities they produce, or the jobs they create, but also in terms of the workplace atmosphere, human rights, health, the environment, innovation, education, and training. Enterprise competitiveness is becoming increasingly dependent on a strategic approach to CSR. Risk management, cost reductions, financial access, client connections, human resource management, and the ability to innovate can all be advantages of it. Despite the fact that many companies choose to voluntarily embrace CSR policies, governments may decide to control both corporate behaviour and CSR activities using two distinct incentive structures. Regulation requires not only the establishment of disclosure norms but also the imposition of positive legal requirements on businesses. The government can also encourage firms to engage in ethical practices by granting tax advantages and credits to those businesses who do so. In March of 2006, with the assistance of members of the business community and organizations such as BusinessEurope, SMEunited (formerly known as UEAPME), and CSR Europe, the European Commission launched the CSR Alliance. The Alliance has the goal of contributing to the expansion of CSR across Europe. It demonstrates the significance as well as the impact of voluntary business engagement. It emphasizes innovative approaches to CSR, fosters the development of new approaches, and makes it simpler for private efforts to be undertaken in this area. It is a haphazard association that does not have official procedures, a charter, or any norms or criteria that have been specified. The European Commission does not have direct management responsibility for the Alliance. Both the support of business organizations and the support of the business community itself are necessary for its success. More than 150 different companies have shown their support for the Alliance up to this point.

Figure 2. Higher visibility of CSR activities (https://www.businesseurope.eu/european-alliance-csr)

The idea of CSR has lately gained popularity in Europe, where firms are increasingly participating in CSR initiatives. CSR is "a concept whereby corporations integrate social and environmental considerations in their business operations and in their relationship with their stakeholders in a voluntary bias," according to the European Commission's definition from 2002. Prior to the 1990s, CSR initiatives tended to be put into place as a result of efforts to "do good to appear good." Now that a strategic strategy is being adopted, which is defined as "performing well and doing better," we can see this transition (Perrini, F., 2006). CSR Europe membership organization consisting of large European companies has defined the following main elements of CSR activities:

Figure 3. CSR

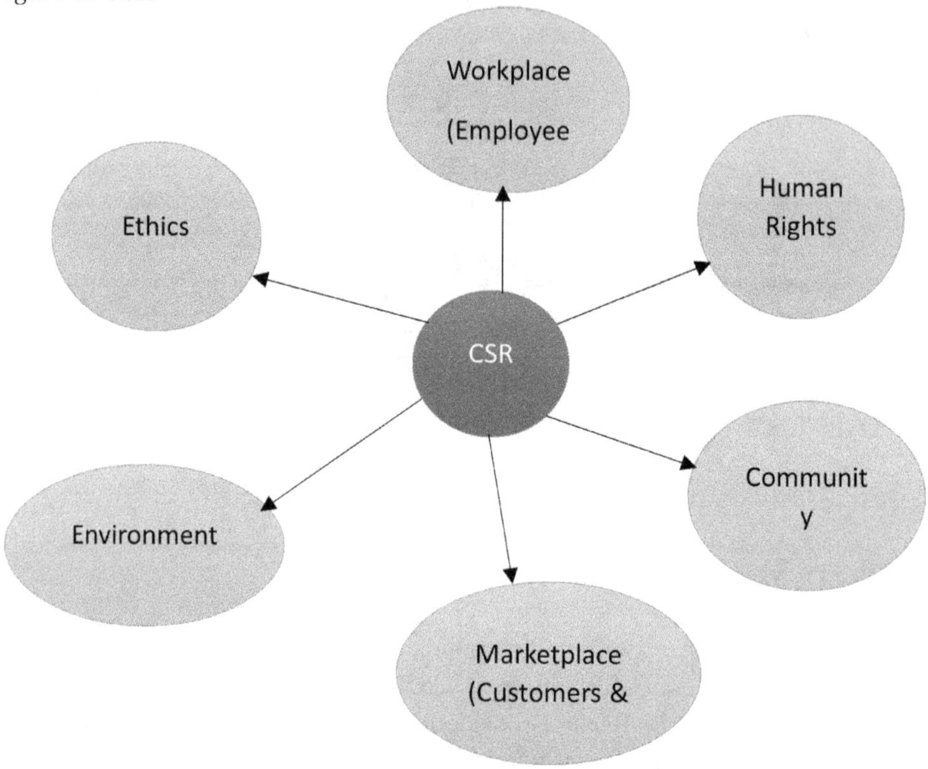

CSR Programs by EU:

Corporate social responsibility (CSR) refers to efforts taken by businesses that go above and beyond what is required by law to protect society and the environment. Businesses are more likely to fulfil their social duty willingly when certain regulatory mechanisms are in place. The European Union's treaty goals of sustainable development and a fiercely competitive social market economy can be considerably advanced by businesses through CSR. CSR efforts demand a significant investment of time and money from the firms and their shareholders. However, there is increasing interest in CSR projects in the modern business sector. Business executives value CSR programs, and customers also want businesses to contribute more to their communities and societies. On the other hand, if CSR efforts are not a proven method or strategy to improve financial or organizational performance, shareholders may not support the idea of spending wealth and resources in CSR projects. CSR supports the objectives of the Europe 2020 strategy for intelligent, sustainable, and equitable growth, including the target of 75% employment. Ethical business ethics are highly important when private sector organizations provide public services. Businesses have a social responsibility to help lessen the negative social effects of the present economic crisis, such as job losses. CSR provides a set of ideals that can be used to create a society that is more cohesive and to support the shift to a sustainable economic system. Corporate social responsibility helps gain customer trust by caring about issues such as Earth Day, raises awareness, and encourages social change. Although there are thousands of companies doing their part, the efforts of large global corporations have far-reaching results that can impact global issues, from hunger and health to global warming and climate change. Corporate social responsibility comes in many forms. Even the smallest company can impact social change by making a simple donation to a local food bank. Companies are said to exhibit CSR if they acknowledge that they have a duty to protect the environment and implement policies to guarantee that they are doing more for society than just generating a profit. The premise behind CSR is that instead of just evaluating and reporting on their earnings, organizations need to have a broader picture of what success looks like.

How to improve CSR:

Figure 4. How to improve CSR (https://blog.submittable.com/improve-csr/)

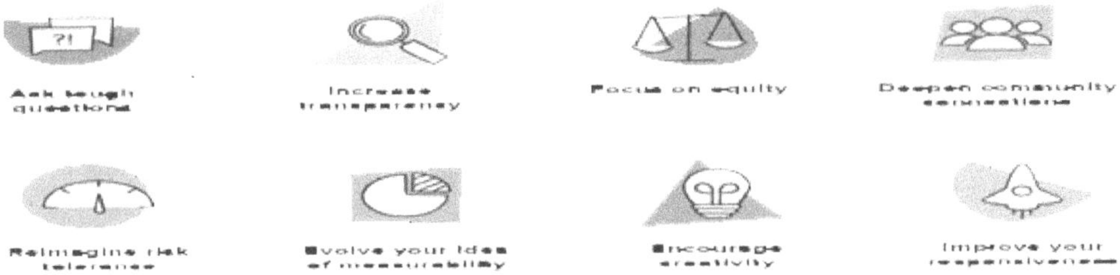

A little over 42% of today's millennials have "begun or deepened" their relationships with businesses they believe have favorable social or environmental effects. 70% of Gen Z buyers want to make ethical purchases from businesses by 2023, according to Deloitte (McKinsey, 2018). Businesses in Europe do better than businesses in Continental Europe's more coordinated market economies (CMEs) on the majority of CSR metrics. This is because Anglo-Saxon businesses have more liberal market economies (Jackson, et al., 2010). Companies with stronger CSR performance have better financial results and pay less for bank debt since there is a correlation between CSR and firm financial success (Du et al., 2023) (Zhang, et al., 2023). The SDGs have caused multinational firms to redefine CSR in the context of sustainability more broadly, and they are prepared to offer advice to SMEs as part of a larger supply chain collaboration process (Williams, et al., 2023). However, the ability of enterprises to sustainably build their businesses is favorably connected with their attention to CSR among their workers, clients, vendors, and governments (Ma, et al., 2023). Leading companies that participate in CSR and green CSR include the following:

Table 1. Leading companies that participate in CSR and green CSR

Renewable Innovation	**Johnson & Johnson**
Social issues	Google
Sustainability	Coca-Cola, New Belgium Brewing Company
Carbon neutral & pay equity	Ford Motor Company
Employee rights	Netflix & Spotify
Access to healthcare	Pfizer
Philanthropic Donations	Wells Fargo
Social media & journalism	The Washington Post
Packaging	LEGO
Climate neutral	Bosch
Local communities	The Walt Disney Company
Clean technology	General Electronics

(source; 16 Brands Doing Corporate Social Responsibility Successfully I Digital Marketing Institute. (2022, November 10). Digital Marketing Institute. https://digitalmarketinginstitute.com/blog/corporate-16-brands-doing-corporate-social-responsibility-successfully)

Here the top 10 most sustainable enterprises headquartered in Europe.

Table 2. Top 10 most sustainable enterprises headquartered in Europe

Schneider Electric	**Ørsted A/S**	**Nestlé**	**Novozymes A/S**	**Moncler**
Neste Oyj	Unilever	Adidas	SAP	Siemens AG

In today's rapidly shifting business climate, companies are evaluated not just on their financial performance, but also on how devoted they are to confronting social, economic, and environmental concerns. In the past, companies were evaluated solely on their financial performance. As a component of a company's total reputation, corporate social responsibility (CSR), which influences both the value of a brand and the faith that customers have in that brand, has grown in importance. Companies have a responsibility to stay current on CSR statistics and trends in order to modify their strategies and procedures in response to the growing popularity of this concept. The striking fact that 76 percent of businesses use CSR reporting as a defense against threats to their brand reputation paints a clear picture of the significant role that CSR plays in contemporary business strategy. Without a doubt, this fact gives a clear picture of the important role that CSR plays in contemporary business strategy. This astonishing number indicates how consumers are becoming more conscious of an organization's social and environmental duties in a world where they are prioritizing those responsibilities. The inclusion of this intriguing information into a blog article on data regarding corporate social responsibility indicates the efficacy of CSR in strengthening company image while negotiating the treacherous terrain of public perception. More than one thousand different international companies are participating in the United Nations' Corporate Social Responsibility (CSR) program known as the Global Compact. The staggering number of over one thousand multinational firms who are actively participating in the UN's CSR effort, the Global Compact, indicates the widespread commitment to ethical business practices that exists within the corporate sector. This unquestionable rise in engagement underlines the growing significance of CSR in today's society, which occurs when businesses actively recognize their obligation to make contributions that are helpful to the local community, the global community, and their stakeholders. When researching Corporate Social Responsibility (CSR) statistics, it is impossible to ignore the insightful results of a Harvard Business Review study. The study discovered a significant positive relationship between CSR and an organization's financial performance. This convincing data ultimately ignites an exciting narrative that supports the idea that deliberate CSR activities may help firms achieve financial success. The overwhelming proof of the crucial role that corporate social responsibility plays in the business sector is the fascinating Boston College study revealing that 66 percent of CEOs name improved employee morale as the top benefit of CSR programs. This fascinating statistic emphasizes the significant significance that decision-makers have on fostering a supportive environment for their employees given the correlation between great employee morale and increased production. Internationally recognized principles and guidelines, especially the most recent updates to the OECD Guidelines for Multinational Enterprises, offer authoritative direction for businesses looking to adopt a formal approach to CSR, particularly large businesses. This fundamental collection of globally accepted principles and directives serves as the foundation of a freshly enhanced worldwide framework for CSR. It is important to completely align European CSR policy with this framework. These principles and recommendations state that CSR must at the very least address issues relating to human rights, labor and employment practices (such as training, diversity, gender equality, and employee health and well-being), environmental issues (such as biodiversity, climate change, resource efficiency, life-cycle assessment, and pollution prevention), and the fight against bribery and corruption. The CSR agenda also includes community involvement and development, the integration of people with disabilities, and consumer issues, including privacy. Both the disclosure of non-financial information and the promotion of social and environmental responsibility throughout the supply chain are acknowledged as significant cross-cutting problems. Employee volunteering is recognized by the Commission as a form of CSR in a statement on EU policies and volunteering that was recently adopted.

CONCLUSION

Although neither "CSR" nor "Environmental CSR," which we will refer to collectively as the "green CSR idea," are particularly original concepts, the significance of CSR's focus on the environmental effects of firms is. This is a new development. It only looks that a company is giving back to the customers or clients it serves when it offers assistance with issues relating to the environment, society, the economy, stakeholders, and voluntarism in any form. There is a wealth of empirical evidence in the published research that demonstrates that corporate social responsibility (CSR), when carried out correctly, results in enormously beneficial outcomes for both the society and the individual businesses involved. CSR activities are beneficial to a company's long-term performance because they increase customer consciousness regarding environmental protection, moral consumption, and corporate social responsibility. CSR programs might have a variety of audiences in mind, including employees, customers, vendors, and policymakers. The fact that the study was carried out only on companies based in Europe is one of the limitations. Another limitation is the likelihood that the findings would be different if a more complete analysis of the industrial sector is carried out. As people become more aware of the effects of climate change, there is an increase in the amount of pressure that is being put on government agencies to promptly enact new legislation that is aimed to defend the environment. It is anticipated that environmental rules will grow far more stringent in the years to come and that these laws will be strictly implemented all across the world. This will have an impact on the economy as a whole, not just on certain companies such as those dealing with energofage or those that release hazardous or lethal substances into the air, water, or land. The fundamental concept of corporate social responsibility (also known as CSR), according to which firms should strive for the highest possible levels of input efficiency and output effectiveness, is one of the most essential elements in the achievement of successful corporate innovation. Corporations that prioritize financial expansion over lowering their environmental imprint and the wasting of resources are putting themselves in the path of a significant risk from the perspective of environmental activists. Citizenship in the community and environmental responsibility go hand in hand and are two aspects of the same concept. However, sustainability has become one of the most widely discussed themes in recent years, particularly in the media, on college campuses, and in government organizations. It took some time for the many different groups that claimed ownership of the term "sustainability" to come to an agreement on a single definition of the concept. However, given the phrase's political value, it is imperative that we have a solid understanding of this intricate notion as soon as possible. Businesses that have a strong sense of corporate social responsibility (CSR) are more likely to achieve a healthy balance when it comes to their financial, environmental, and community goals. CSR stands for "corporate social responsibility." The conservation of the environment should be a top priority for businesses of all sizes, from SMEs to Less, and this should be accomplished through CSR and GCSR. This is particularly true in European countries.

REFERENCES

Afridi, S. A., Afsar, B., Shahjehan, A., Khan, W., Rehman, Z. U., & Khan, M. A. (2023). Impact of corporate social responsibility attributions on employee's extra-role behaviors: Moderating role of ethical corporate identity and interpersonal trust. *Corporate Social Responsibility and Environmental Management*, 30(2), 991–1004. DOI: 10.1002/csr.2017

Ahmed, R., & Štreimikienė, D. (2021). Environmental Issues and Strategic Corporate Social Responsibility for Organizational Competitiveness. Journal of Competitiveness. .DOI: 10.7441/joc.2021.02.01

Baah, C., Amponsah, K. T., Issau, K., Ofori, D., Acquah, I. S. K., & Agyeman, D. O. (2021). Examining the interconnections between sustainable logistics practices, environmental reputation and financial performance: A mediation approach. *Vision (Basel)*, 25(1), 47–64. DOI: 10.1177/0972262920988805

Babiak, K., & Trendafilova, S. (2011). CSR and environmental responsibility: Motives and pressures to adopt green management practices. *Corporate Social Responsibility and Environmental Management*, 18(1), 11–24. DOI: 10.1002/csr.229

Bahta, D., Yun, J., Islam, R., & Bikanyi, K. (2020). How does CSR enhance the financial performance of SMEs? The mediating role of firm reputation. *Ekonomska Istrazivanja*, 34(1), 1428–1451. DOI: 10.1080/1331677X.2020.1828130

Bresciani S, Rehman SU, Alam GM, Ashfaq K, Usman M (2022). Environmental MCS package, perceived environmental uncertainty and green performance: in green dynamic capabilities and investment in environmental management perspectives. Rev Int Bus Strat(ahead-of-print).

Du, M., & Li, Y. (2023). *Tax avoidance, CSR performance and financial impacts: evidence from BRICS economies*. International Journal of Emerging Markets., DOI: 10.1108/IJOEM-05-2022-0747

Essential Corporate Social Responsibility Statistics in. 2023 • ZipDo. (2023, June 13). ZipDo. https://zipdo.co/statistics/corporate-social-responsibility/

EUR-Lex - 52011DC0568 - EN - EUR-Lex. (n.d.). EUR-Lex - 52011DC0568 - EN - EUR-Lex. https://eur-lex.europa.eu/legal-content/EN/ALL/?uri=CELEX %3A52011DC0568

Fandos-Roig, J. C., S'anchez-García, J., Tena-Monferrer, S., & Callarisa-Fiol, L. J. (2021). Does CSR help to retain customers in a service company? *Sustainability (Basel)*, 13(1), 1–21. DOI: 10.3390/su13010300

Fern'andez-Gago, R., Cabeza-García, L., & Godos-Díez, J. L. (2020). How significant is corporate social responsibility to business research? *Corporate Social Responsibility and Environmental Management*, 27(4), 1809–1817. DOI: 10.1002/csr.1927

Franklin, A. (2023). Implementing Corporate Social Responsibility Strategies to Enhance the Profitability of Firms (Doctoral dissertation, Walden University).

Gatti, L., Vishwanath, B., Seele, P., & Cottier, B. (2019). Are we moving beyond voluntary CSR? Exploring theoretical and managerial implications of mandatory CSR resulting from the new Indian companies act. *Journal of Business Ethics*, 160(4), 961–972. DOI: 10.1007/s10551-018-3783-8

Govindan, K. (2022). Theory Building Through Corporate Social Responsibility 4.0 for Achieving SDGs: A Practical Step Toward Integration of Digitalization With Practice- Based View and Social Good Theory. *IEEE Transactions on Engineering Management.*

Grimstad, S., Glavee-Geo, R., & Fjørtoft, B. (2020). SMEs motivations for CSR: An exploratory study. *European Business Review*, 32(4), 553–572. DOI: 10.1108/EBR-01-2019-0014

Hadi, N., & Udin, U. (2020). Testing the Effectiveness of CSR Dimensions for Small Business Entrepreneurs. *Journal of Open Innovation*. Advance online publication. DOI: 10.3390/joitmc7010006

Idowu, S. O., Capaldi, N., Zu, L., & Gupta, A. D. (Eds.). (2013). *Encyclopedia of corporate social responsibility* (Vol. 21). Springer. DOI: 10.1007/978-3-642-28036-8

Jackson, G., & Apostolakou, A. (2010). Corporate Social Responsibility in Western Europe: An Institutional Mirror or Substitute? *Journal of Business Ethics*, 94(3), 371–394. DOI: 10.1007/s10551-009-0269-8

Jiang, W., & Wong, J. (2016). Key activity areas of corporate social responsibility (CSR) in the construction industry: A study of China. *Journal of Cleaner Production*, 113, 850–860. DOI: 10.1016/j.jclepro.2015.10.093

Kannan, D., Shankar, K. M., & Gholipour, P. (2022a). Paving the way for a green transition through mitigation of green manufacturing challenges: A systematic literature review. *Journal of Cleaner Production*, 368, 132578. DOI: 10.1016/j.jclepro.2022.132578

Kortetm¨aki, T., Heikkinen, A., & Jokinen, A. (2022). Particularizing nonhuman nature in stakeholder theory: The recognition approach. *Journal of Business Ethics*, •••, 1–15. DOI: 10.1007/S10551-022-05174-2/TABLES/2

Liu, Y., Chen, Y., Ren, Y., & Jin, B. (2021). Impact mechanism of corporate social responsibility on sustainable technological innovation performance from the perspective of corporate social capital. *Journal of Cleaner Production*, 308, 127345. Advance online publication. DOI: 10.1016/j.jclepro.2021.127345

Lyon, T. P., & Maxwell, J. W. (2010). Does Green Corporate Social Responsibility Benefit Society? In Issues of the Day (pp. 90-91). Routledge.

Ma, C., Yu, C., & Latif, Y. (2023). CSR and Sustainable Growth in China's Technology Firms between 2010 and 2021. *Sustainability (Basel)*, 15(3), 2101. Advance online publication. DOI: 10.3390/su15032101

Mansour, M., Aman, N., Al-Ghazali, B. M., & Shah, S. H. A. (2022). Perceived corporate social responsibility, ethical leadership, and moral reflectiveness impact on pro-environmental behavior among employees of small and medium enterprises: A double-mediation model. *Frontiers in Psychology*, 13, 967859. DOI: 10.3389/fpsyg.2022.967859 PMID: 36507031

Meles, A., Salerno, D., Sampagnaro, G., Verdoliva, V., & Zhang, J. (2023). The influence of green innovation on default risk: Evidence from Europe. *International Review of Economics & Finance*, 84, 692–710. DOI: 10.1016/j.iref.2022.11.036

Mendes, A. C., Ferreira, F. A., Kannan, D., Ferreira, N. C., & Correia, R. J. (2022). A BWM approach to determinants of sustainable entrepreneurship in small and medium- sized enterprises. *Journal of Cleaner Production*, 371, 133300. DOI: 10.1016/j.jclepro.2022.133300

MNE Guidelines - OECD. (2023). MNE Guidelines - Organisation for Economic Co-operation and Development. https://mneguidelines.oecd.org/mneguidelines/

Perrini, F. (2006). Corporate social responsibility: doing the most good for your company and your cause.

Responsibility, W. I. C. S. 4 Types | HBS Online. (2021, April 8). Business Insights Blog. https://online.hbs.edu/blog/post/types-of-corporate-social-responsibility

Shafique, I., Kalyar, M. N., & Mehwish, N. (2021). Organizational ambidexterity, green entrepreneurial orientation, and environmental performance in SMEs context: Examining the moderating role of perceived CSR. *Corporate Social Responsibility and Environmental Management*, 28(1), 446–456. DOI: 10.1002/csr.2060

Shah, K., Arjoon, S., & Rambocas, M. (2016). Aligning Corporate Social Responsibility with Green Economy Development Pathways in Developing Countries. *Sustainable Development (Bradford)*, 24(4), 237–253. DOI: 10.1002/sd.1625

Shahzad, M., Qu, Y., Javed, S., Zafar, A., & Rehman, S. (2020). Relation of environment sustainability to CSR and green innovation: A case of Pakistani manufacturing industry. *Journal of Cleaner Production*, 253, 119938. DOI: 10.1016/j.jclepro.2019.119938

Shaikh, E., Brahmi, M., Thang, P. C., Watto, W. A., Trang, T. T. N., & Loan, N. T. (2022). Should i stay or should i go? explaining the turnover intentions with corporate social responsibility (CSR), organizational identification and organizational commitment. *Sustainability (Basel)*, 14(10), 6030. DOI: 10.3390/su14106030

Shaikh, E., Khoso, I., & Chandio, F. (2019). Effects of Corporate Social Responsibility on Organizational Performance: A Conceptual and Literature Review. Grassroots (17260396), 53(1).

Simmou, W., Govindan, K., Sameer, I., Hussainey, K., & Simmou, S. (2023). Doing good to be green and live clean!-Linking corporate social responsibility strategy, green innovation, and environmental performance: Evidence from Maldivian and Moroccan small and medium-sized enterprises. *Journal of Cleaner Production*, 384, 135265. DOI: 10.1016/j.jclepro.2022.135265

Suganthi, L. (2020). Investigating the relationship between corporate social responsibility and market, cost and environmental performance for sustainable business. *South African Journal of Business Management*, 51(1), 1–13. DOI: 10.4102/sajbm.v51i1.1630

True Gen'. Generation Z and its implications for companies. (2018, November 12). McKinsey & Company. https://www.mckinsey.com/industries/consumer-packaged-goods/our-insights/true-gen-generation-z-and-its-implications-for-companies

Us, Y., Pimonenko, T., & Lyulyov, O. (2023). Corporate Social Responsibility and Renewable Energy Development for the Green Brand within SDGs: A Meta-Analytic Review. *Energies*, 16(5), 2335. DOI: 10.3390/en16052335

What is Corporate Social Responsability (CSR)? HEC Paris. (2019). https://www.hec.edu/en/faculty-research/centers/society-organizations-institute/think/so-institute-executive-factsheets/what-corporate-social-responsability-csr

Who we are. (2023). Deloitte. https://www.deloitte.com/global/en/about.html

Williams, S., & Murphy, D. (2023). Learning from Each Other: UK Global Businesses, SMEs, CSR and the Sustainable Development Goals (SDGs). *Sustainability (Basel)*, 15(5), 4151. Advance online publication. DOI: 10.3390/su15054151

Wirba, A. V. (2023). Corporate Social Responsibility (CSR): The Role of Government in promoting CSR. *Journal of the Knowledge Economy*, 15(2), 1–27. DOI: 10.1007/s13132-023-01185-0

Wu, L., Shao, Z., Yang, C., Ding, T., & Zhang, W. (2020). The Impact of CSR and Financial Distress on Financial Performance—Evidence from Chinese Listed Companies of the Manufacturing Industry. *Sustainability (Basel)*, 12(17), 6799. Advance online publication. DOI: 10.3390/su12176799

Xue, Y., Jiang, C., Guo, Y., Liu, J., Wu, H., & Hao, Y. (2022). Corporate Social Responsibility and High-quality Development: Do Green Innovation, Environmental Investment and Corporate Governance Matter? *Emerging Markets Finance & Trade*, 58(11), 3191–3214. DOI: 10.1080/1540496X.2022.2034616

Yim, S., Bae, Y. H., Lim, H., & Kwon, J. (2019). The role of marketing capability in linking CSR to corporate financial performance. *European Journal of Marketing*, 53(7), 1333–1354. DOI: 10.1108/EJM-08-2017-0526

Zhang, L., & Su, W. (2023). Corporate social responsibility, internal control, and firm financial performance. *Frontiers in Psychology*, 13, 977996. Advance online publication. DOI: 10.3389/fpsyg.2022.977996 PMID: 36660285

Zou, Z., Liu, Y., Ahmad, N., Sial, M., Badulescu, A., Zia-ud-Din, M., & Badulescu, D. (2021). What Prompts Small and Medium Enterprises to Implement CSR? A Qualitative Insight from an Emerging Economy. *Sustainability (Basel)*, 13(2), 952. Advance online publication. DOI: 10.3390/su13020952

Chapter 4
How the Family Business Hotels of Europe Are Rebuilt After COVD-19:
Leveraging CSR Practices for Post-Pandemic Resilience

Maryum Bibi
Northeast Normal University, China

Maria Ahmed Ajaz
Iqra University, Pakistan

Ali Said Akaak
https://orcid.org/0000-0003-4281-5315
College of Economics and Business Administration, Oman

Sadia Noureen
Bahria University, Pakistan

Syed Bilawal Ali Shah
https://orcid.org/0000-0001-9100-3802
University of Malaya, Malaysia

ABSTRACT

CSR is crucial for family businesses, including hotels, which are a significant employer globally. The COVID-19 pandemic has impacted the hospitality sector, leading to digital transformation and contactless technology adoption in European hotels. To maintain competitiveness, European family-owned hotels should implement sustainable practices, enhance digital connectivity, provide health and well-

DOI: 10.4018/979-8-3373-0219-5.ch004

being amenities, invest in employee training, and adopt contactless technologies. A thorough review of secondary research is conducted to find out the CSR practices implied by European Family businesses hotels. It is concluded that incorporating artificial intelligence and machine learning into CSR efforts can strengthen commitment to sustainability and social responsibility. Further the hotel industry, which holds a market share of over 50% in Europe, is expected to grow at a CAGR of 7.0% between 2022 and 2023.

INTRODUCTION

On a global scale, family businesses are the most significant type of corporate ownership and the most significant type of employers (Smyrnios, et al., 1998). It is described as "an operational firm where the majority of the authority is held by members of the same family." A network of families, a multigenerational family (grandparents included), or a nuclear family (parents and children) could be this (Solutions, F. B., 2013). The intersection of organizational behaviour and family businesses hasn't been much studied, but there are many intriguing research issues there that could be helpful to both disciplines of study. The timing is ideal for making such investments, making family companies an intriguing backdrop for behavioral scientists to study. These firms are conceptually distinct from those that aren't family businesses because of the significant participation of kinship links in the business (Sharma, et al., 2014). In comparison to non-family firms whose governance is restricted to the company alone, family businesses place a larger emphasis on both the family and the business as a whole and have better results for the family and equivalent outcomes for the business (Basco, et al., 2009).

The largest 500 family businesses, according to the International Monetary Fund, employ 24.52 million people, generated US$8.02 trillion in sales in 2022, an increase of 10% from 2021, and boosted the world economy by 6%. Additionally, it is anticipated that the growth rate of these businesses would be 2.7 percent in 2023. (Robertsson, H., 2023). These days, social media has an impact on the travel sector for women who own family businesses, and Facebook, Instagram, and Twitter are crucial tools for female entrepreneurs in the sector (Eman, et al., 2023). Over the past 20 years, research on corporate social responsibility (CSR) in the tourism industry has gradually changed due to an increase in literature, an emphasis on theoretical contributions, and a change in vocabulary (Zanfardini, et al., 2016). The demand for natural resources has increased due to record-high carbon emissions, waste energy, pollution, wastewater, and water scarcity, and corporations worldwide have invested around $16.6 trillion in CSR, which supports environmental sustainability. One of the worst global epidemics in recent memory, COVID-19 has had a major yet diffuse impact on health systems, economies, and civilizations. The COVID-19 pandemic started slowly, but by December 31, 2019, the Wuhan Municipal Health Commission in China had reported a cluster of pneumonia cases.

In less than a month, there had been more than 200 fatalities worldwide, prompting the World Health Organization (WHO) to declare a global health emergency (Jamshaid, et al., 2023). On March 11, 2020, the WHO classified COVID-19 outbreaks a pandemic due to an increase in cases in April in the USA and Europe (Jamshaid, et al., 2020). According to data from UNTWO, the pandemic had a significant influence on international visitor numbers, which after years of consistent yearly growth witnessed a shocking -73 percent decline in arrivals in 2020 and -71 percent in 2021 due to travel restrictions in response to Covid-19 (UNWTO,2021). With 1 billion fewer foreign arrivals and US $ 1.1 trillion in international tourism receipts, 2020 is acknowledged as the worst year in tourism history. According to the World Tourism Organization's (UNWTO) most recent statistics, the level of tourism has decreased by almost 74% from 30 years ago. Everyone had a rough time during the COVID-19 pandemic, and it also made the environment more vulnerable to problems like the increase in global temperatures and the depletion of natural resources. However, this pandemic has given people the chance to find hope, see COVID-19's destruction of the tourism industry as an error, and work on the present and future of the hospitality and tourism industry with more socially and environmentally sustainable communities.

In the same way, it brought about a transition and difficulties in the digital world. In the early stages of the epidemic, practically all business operations in the area ceased, with India experiencing an uncontrollable death rate while China implemented stringent travel restrictions and locked down its entire cities, outlawing all intercity trading. COVID-19 had an impact on several nations at different periods, in different ways, and to varying degrees, but efforts to control the outbreak led to national lockdowns, significant travel restrictions, and border closures, which made the tourist industry one of the worst-affected industries. This study aims to produce a reliable and precise measurement of family companies for use in additional studies. The COVID-19 epidemic has had a major influence on the hotel business, causing mental health problems and a rise in employee attrition. Controlling the epidemic and implementing public institutions' policies are essential for the industry to recover. As human contact decreases and the risk of getting the virus rises, family-run hotels in Europe have started integrating contactless technology to offer a safer and contamination-free tourist experience. For hotel businesses to exceed guest expectations, streamline operations, maintain competitiveness, and quickly adjust to a rapidly changing market, digital transformation is essential.

European family-owned hotels should implement sustainable practices, enhance digital connectivity and automation, provide amenities for health and well-being, make an investment in employee training, and adopt contactless technologies in order to enhance visitor experiences, promote sustainability, and accommodate shifting traveler preferences. The pandemic has brought attention to the demand for contactless services, including mobile payments and check-ins. Strategic partnerships between hotels and diverse businesses have resulted from the quick adoption of next-generation technology, such as contactless hospitality. A key step towards sustainability is the incorporation of artificial intelligence (AI) and machine learning (ML) into European hotel CSR efforts. These companies will be able to strengthen their commitment to sustainability and social responsibility by utilizing AI and ML capabilities as technology develops.

BACKGROUND

One of the most well-liked tourist locations in the Mediterranean, the Balearic Islands get more than 1% of all international travelers. New locations in the eastern Mediterranean are opening up as the European Union expands to the east, forcing hotel management to adapt their practices. Innovation is a crucial instrument for achieving this, and the hotel industry has a special opportunity to benefit from these transformations by offering a pleasant environment and limitless employment opportunities. The attraction and retention of professional and unskilled hospitality talent, however, continues to be a problem on a global scale. The success of such a strategy depends on real-world encounters that serve as inspiration, which prompts a review of the realities of managerial positions in the hotel industry. Family enterprises are the oldest type of business in human history and make up the vast majority of businesses in Greece, Europe, and the rest of the world (Koumentakis, S., 2021).

Millions of hotels are owned by families worldwide, and some of them date back many years and even many generations. Running a hotel is quite similar to managing a large family where there is always something new. Perhaps the internet goes down today, you win a prestigious award tomorrow, a family member shows in unexpectedly the following week when the hotel is already full, or one day the police knock on your door to question a member of your family. Therefore, having a family business like a hotel and operating it to preserve the history are regular occurrences, and owners continue to operate their hotels even in the worst-case scenario of the economy. Nishiyama Onsen Keiunkan, for instance, which is a Japanese resort close to Mount Fuji and the oldest family-run hotel in the world, survived COVID-19. It has been in operation since 705 A.D. and has been passed down within the same family for 52 generations. The Olde Bell in Hurley, England, which opened about

900 years ago in 1135 (Fes, N. 2021), is the oldest family-run hotel in Europe. They also survived in COVID-19. These hotels can quickly spread epidemics like COVID-19 because they are frequented by a varied range of people in terms of race, nationality, age, and culture (Yu, et al., 2021). Despite the importance, history, and contribution that family businesses make to the GDP of any country, it is alarming that more studies on family businesses are now open to the same kind of criticism. This is caused, in part, by the fact that academic prestige is valued more highly than new and practical knowledge (Miller, et al., 2021).

The sustained success and growth of family-owned enterprises are essential to the health of both the global economy and the economies of any individual country. The tourism and hospitality industries were severely impacted, and since they are crucial to any nation's economy and employment, they require substantial national and international aid from reputable groups. The worldwide hospitality industry increased at a compound annual growth rate (CAGR) of 7.0 percent from $4,390.59 billion in 2022 to $4,699.57 billion in 2023, according to the Hospitality Global Market Report 2023. This rapid growth rate is partially a result of the lifting of international travel restrictions. Due to the current state of the world economy, it is anticipated that the market would continue to expand but more slowly, with a Compound Annual Growth Rate (GAGR) of +5,8 percent predicted between 2022 and 2032.

Figure 1. Travel & tourism forecast (2022-2032) (https://hospitalityinsights.ehl .edu/hospitality-industry)

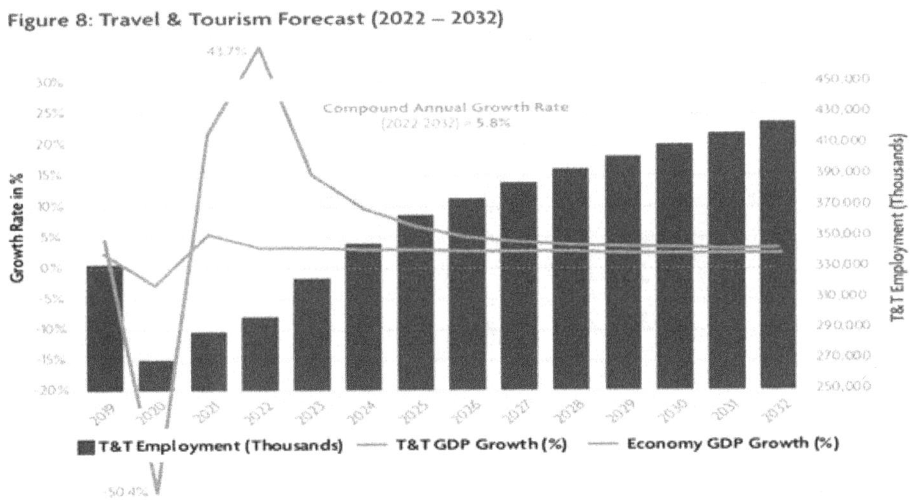

The COVID-19 pandemic has had a tremendous impact on the hospitality sector, especially in Europe, where firms have suffered greatly as a result of lockdown measures. For instance, the Italian hospitality sector had a sharp decline in foreign hotel guests and a 99.1% market collapse in April 2020. Social management challenges like risk assessment, crisis management, innovation implementation, and sustainability initiatives are faced by the hotel industry. The governments have been collaborating with their tourism and travel industries on recovery plans in the post-COVID era. Travel bubbles may present an opportunity for a fully open system and for regaining travellers' confidence (Anna Fink, 2020). After COVID-19, the focus has shifted to domestic tourism in the majority of the countries, and this move is aiding in recovery, in contrast to how the tourist sites have been classified by the international travel restriction. While some nations focus on domestic tourism, others provide trip packages for their neighbours. The COVID-19 pandemic has had an impact on the hospitality sector globally, and family-run hotels in Europe that have rebuilt and used CSR strategies for post-pandemic resilience draw in foreign visitors. Family-owned hotels engaged in 40 various CSR initiatives to lessen the COVID-19 pandemic's harmful consequences, including the following:

Figure 2. Self-created presentation of what CSR acts performed by family business hotels for community

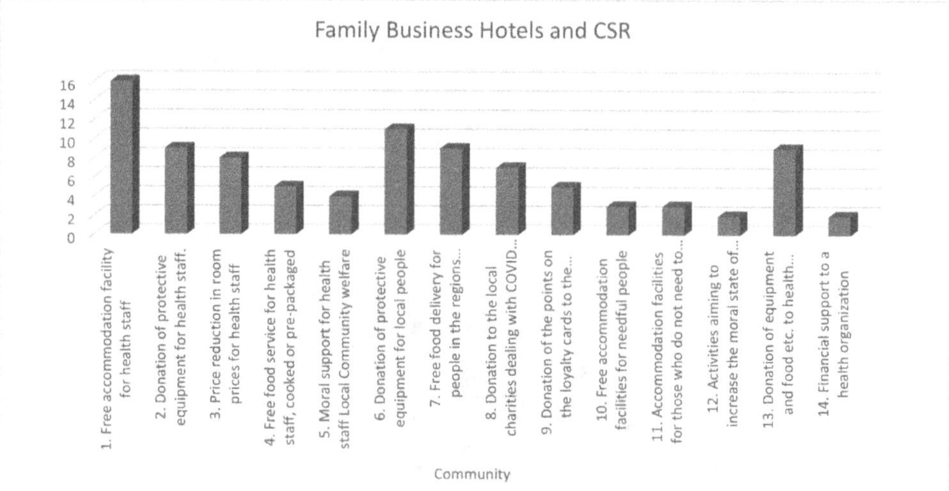

The above graph is showing how the family business hotels in Europe helped the community by 14 different CSR activities, 12 CSR activities for their Employees are shown in below pie-chart and 14 CSR acts for their customers shown in next bar graph (Figure 4).

Figure 3. Self-created presentation of what CSR acts performed by family business hotels for employees

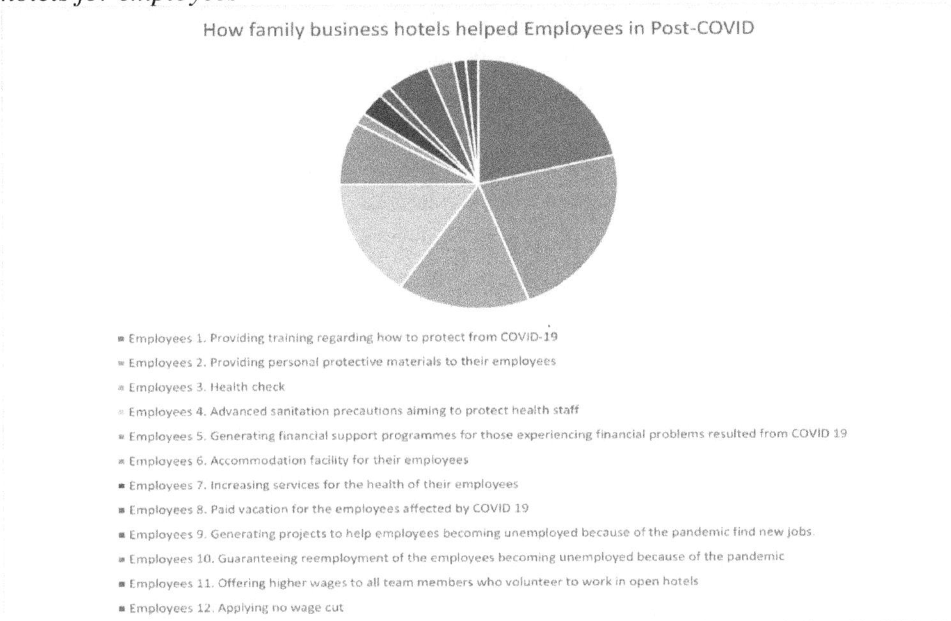

Figure 4. Self-created presentation of what CSR acts performed by family business hotels for customers

CSR AND FAMILY BUSINESS HOTELS

A company that is owned and operated by members of the same direct or extended family is referred to as a "family business" (Jamshed, et al., 2023a). In the hospitality industry, hotels are frequently owned by numerous distinct families. The bulk of these hotels are still maintaining their legacy and maintaining control over a sizable section of the hospitality industries in which they operate, according to a deeper investigation into the history of these hotels. The St. Moritz Hotel and Spa in Switzerland, founded in 1856, the Corus Hotels, founded in the United Kingdom in 1876, and the St. Moritz Hotel and Spa, founded in Switzerland, both in 1856, are the oldest known family-owned hotels (Jamshed, et al., 2023b). The hotel sector, which has a market share of more than 50%, is one of Europe's most significant economic foundations (Jamshed, et.al, 2023c). The European Commission defines corporate social responsibility (CSR) as "the obligation of firms for their influence on society" (COM,2011). There are three ways it can affect employees: directly through environmental awareness, indirectly through environmental commitment (Shah, et al., 2023).

CSR has positive effects on customer behavior and organizational performance, and currently, many organizations are launching CSR initiatives, which increase customer satisfaction and attract new clients, both of which have an impact on business earnings and the strength of a company's competitive advantage. CSR for the benefit of the company's workforce, clients, suppliers, and governments is associated with sustainable business growth (Ma, et al., 2023). Innovation is essential for the survival of family-run hotels in Europe because it promotes sustainable growth and makes it possible to use cutting-edge tourism strategies. However, non-economic variables including aversion to risk, family disputes, and closure to external sources make the innovation drivers in family enterprises weaker. Hotels in Europe have implemented a number of novel concepts, including market selection, strategic human resource management, employee empowerment, market responsiveness, behavior-based evaluation, and marketing synergy. An organic real-time food service scenario has been used to research the development of culinary food products. While the creation of a particular culinary product by itself may not result in a sustainable advantage, an organizational competency in innovation development may give businesses a sustainable advantage through a process of ongoing product innovation.

Consumers are prepared to pay a premium (often more than 15%) for eco-friendly hotels and restaurants that serve food made from organic, locally sourced, or non-genetically modified foods, according to multiple studies. It's interesting to note that customers who are aware of a company's CSR efforts are much more willing to "forgive" the business for a minor service error, allowing for a quicker service recovery (Boston, 2017). In order to address their remarkable relationships with their companies, many businesses are choosing CSR activities for branding. They also make their customers through social activities by the business. After branding through CSR activities, these businesses have developed a positive reputation in the market and can improve their financial performance, which can draw in customers and stakeholders. Corporate social responsibility (CSR) and corporate financial performance (CFP) are two facets of the same coin that complement one another. The better a firm performs financially, the more potential there is for it to engage in CSR activities, and the more actively a company participates in CSR activities, the better it performs financially.

Participating in CSR activities can be a tactic used by businesses to draw investors and enhance financial performance; as such, the decision to spend money on CSR should be assessed and studied similarly to other investment decisions made by businesses. Family-run hotels should create a CSR program that prioritizes improving service standards, brand recognition, and guest satisfaction because strong customer loyalty will help the industry compete (Veloso, et al., 2021). CSR helps the business sector develop sustainably, and without it, sustainable development cannot be achieved (Behringer, et al., 2016). The tourism business can advance sustainable development because it can contribute to local autonomy and sustainability, which call on people to work together globally and consider how their activities will influence the environment and future generations (Jamshed, et al.,2023b) No matter which way CSR is viewed, there is ample evidence in the literature to show that when it is done properly, the community and the relevant businesses benefit greatly (Koi-Akrofi, J. 2023).

Since the 1990s, hotels have been growing daily as a result of embracing CSR principles, and CSR has also grown in numbers while research has increased in volume (Farrington et al., 2017). Ismail et al. (2019) claim that family business owners have a significant impact on the spread of vital concepts like innovation as well as the fostering of an entrepreneurial mindset in their staff members. Additionally, this model emphasizes crucial qualities like imagination, independence, initiative, assertiveness, and risk-taking, all of which are closely related to family culture and the stage of a company's life cycle (Massa, L.; Tucci, 2013). Since 85 percent of firms receive financial support from family members, FFI Global Data Points states that family engagement is crucial for new businesses to succeed. In every economy, families hold the great majority of privately held businesses (FamilyFirm, 2023). Only through consumer company identity and trust can CSR have an impact on customer satisfaction, and CSR practices considerably increase customer loyalty thanks to the mediating effects of these two factors (Jiddi, F. E., 2023).

FAMILY BUSINESS HOTELS AND GDP

Yogi Berra once said, “It's like deja vu all over again.” The same topics, including performance, innovation, internationalization, succession, CSR, entrepreneurial orientation, and the connections between these characteristics and various aspects of family governance in various industry and geographic contexts, seem to be the focus of an increasing amount of quantitative family firm research. The hospitality sector is the largest sector of the economy, and the European sector accounts for about half of the sector globally (Jamshed, K. et al., 2023d). Collaborative innovation can help family enterprises innovate more effectively by allowing them to overcome resource constraints and draw on the knowledge, cash, technology, and information of other organizations. However, research on this topic is still in its infancy (Feranita, et al., 2017). More so than non-family organizations, family businesses leverage mature knowledge in their innovation processes (Gusenbauer, et al., 2023). Family businesses are long-term by nature and usually adopt a long-term view in their strategy and decision-making, which helps to maintain market stability (Lumpkin, et al., 2011). More so than non-family organizations, family businesses leverage mature knowledge in their innovation processes. Additionally, family businesses appear to respect mature expertise more than non-family businesses (Gusenbauer, et al., 2023). The global market for hotels and resorts reached its peak in 2019 at 1.52 trillion dollars. The coronavirus (COVID-19) pandemic caused the market size to fall under one trillion dollars in 2020 and 2021. The market size was anticipated to reach $1.21 trillion in 2023 as shown in below graph.

Figure 5. Anticipated market size (https://www.statista.com/statistics/1186201/hotel-and-resort-industry-market-size-global/)

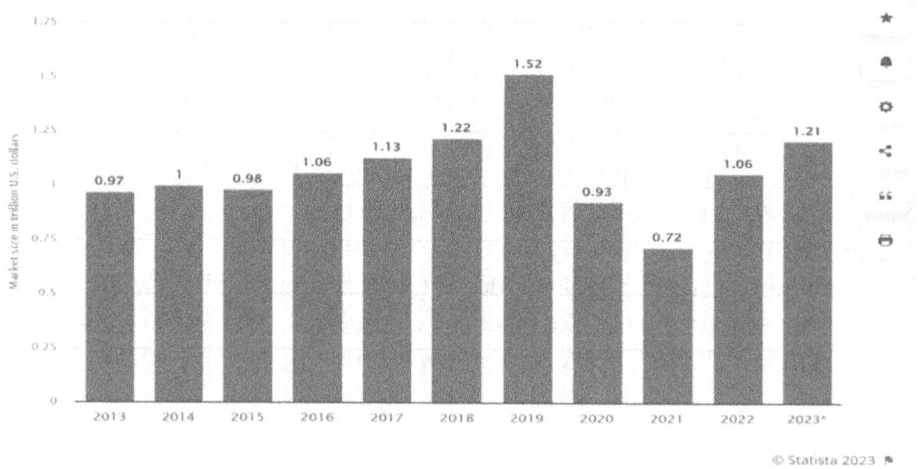

It is impossible to overestimate the contribution of family-owned hotels to the global GDP in the business sector. These hotels significantly impact the whole economic environment through their operations and services. 2022 saw a 23 percent decline in travel and tourism's overall contribution to the world gross domestic product (GDP) compared to 2019, the year before the coronavirus (COVID-19) pandemic started. In total, travel and tourism contributed 7.7 trillion dollars to the world economy in 2022. This amount was predicted to stay 5% below pre-pandemic levels in 2023, rising to an estimated 9.5 trillion US dollars.

Figure 6. Predicted impact of travel & tourism on world economy (https://www.statista.com/statistics/233223/travel-and-tourism--total-economic-contribution-worldwide/)

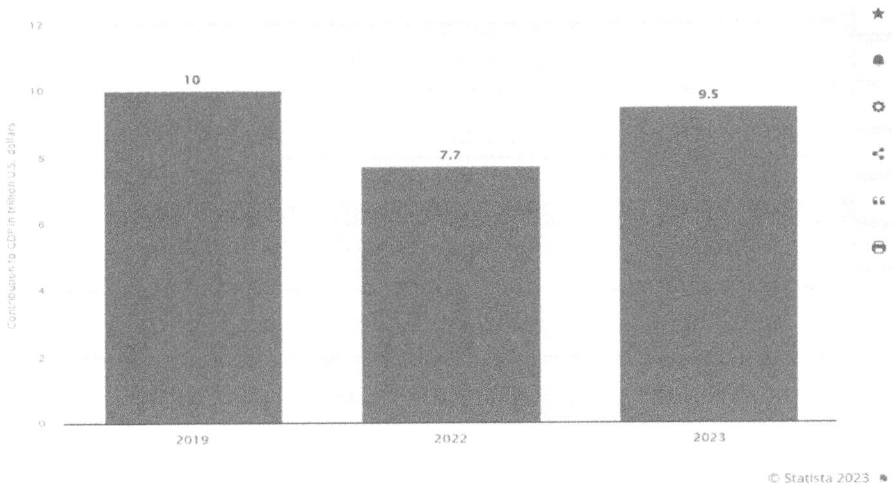

POST PANDEMIC AND EUROPEAN FAMILY BUSINESS HOTELS

According to studies by Sönmez et al. in 2020 and Teng et al. in 2021, depression, anxiety, and stress had an impact on hotel employees' intentions to leave their jobs, making the hospitality sector one among the most adversely affected economic sectors by the COVID-19. Its recovery depends on the ability to contain the epidemic and on how well public institutions have implemented macroeconomic policies to boost overall economic recovery (Anguera-Torrell, et al., 2020). Instead, through the perception of overall organizational justice, the impact of government support for hotels on hotel employees during the COVID-19 pandemic positively impacted employee job satisfaction and organizational commitment, while the ethical climate of hotels had a negative impact on the relationship between job satisfaction and organizational commitment (Salem, et al., 2021). In order to create a more sterile and untainted tourist experience while lowering human touch and raising the risk of getting the virus during the COVID-19 pandemic, family-owned hotels in Europe have started introducing contactless technologies.

In practically every industry, value creation, delivery, and capture have been impacted by digital transformation (Vaska et al., 2021), and hotel customers value digital engagement in their hotel experience (Brochado, et al., 2016). Particularly in large businesses, digital transformation is a challenging process that calls for a certain set of abilities and resources. In order to achieve or maintain a competitive advantage and please stakeholders, it includes using digital technology. Therefore, when planning and managing digital transformation initiatives in family-owned hotels, tried-and-true methods for developing IT strategies are still useful (Wynn, et al., 2022). In order to meet guest expectations, manage operations, maintain competitiveness, and quickly adapt to a rapidly changing market, European hotels largely rely on digital transformation. The nature of these hotels' digital transformation programs and their competitive environment have an impact on their direction and pace. European family-owned hotels use a variety of tactics to keep a competitive edge and offer distinctive tourist experiences. These tactics include multigenerational appeal, multigenerational service, local authenticity, direct family engagement, long-term goals, engaging storytelling, and specialty marketing. These tactics have been shown to have a favorable effect on customers' experiences and company success.

European family-run hotels should implement sustainable practices, enhance digital connectivity and automation, offer amenities for health and well-being, promote local experiences, spend on employee training, and use contactless technologies in order to enhance visitor experiences, promote sustainability, and adjust to shifting traveller preferences. The epidemic has brought attention to the demand for contactless services, including smartphone check-ins and digital payments, where the usage of technology and individual mental characteristics affects the adoption of digital payments (Musyaffi, et al., 2021). Since the older generations accepted the usage of mobile devices for shopping and payments in a reduced proportion, digital commerce appears to be the norm for millennials in the epidemic period (Akram, et al., 2021). While limiting physical touch, hoteliers nonetheless want to give visitors a personalized experience. When done correctly, visitors receive a distinctive, high-touch user experience without having to worry about contracting the virus. Listed below are a few quick examples of how this could be done: Digital menus, ordering through apps, websites, or phones, and payment methods like contactless terminals or the same can all be used in restaurants. Digital check-in and check-out, guest communication via chat applications, email, or website chat bots for Q&A,

and greater food and beverage integration into the overall hotel experience are all possible in hotels (Bassford, C. 2021). This has sped up the adoption of cutting-edge innovations like contactless hospitality, which can handle operations like reservations, check-ins, and room service.

The importance of strategic collaborations between hotels and various businesses has increased in the hospitality industry. Vertical alliances involve partnerships between hotels and various businesses like airlines, travel agencies, car rental services, restaurants, shopping malls, and card service providers. Horizontal alliances involve collaborations between hotels, such as chains, management contracts, and franchises. Another important step towards sustainability is the use of artificial intelligence (AI) and machine learning (ML) into European hotel CSR programs. Energy efficiency, waste management, visitor satisfaction, sustainable supply chains, informed decision-making, carbon footprint reduction, community involvement, eco-friendly mobility, and reporting transparency are all included in this integration. The use of ML and AI capabilities demonstrates the progressive nature of European hotels and strengthens their CSR impact. These companies will be able to strengthen their commitment to sustainability and social responsibility by utilizing AI and ML capabilities as technology develops. Considering that 70% of millennials seek a contactless hotel experience, it can be concluded that contactless technologies are quickly becoming an indispensable part of contemporary hotel amenities. Although pandemics are not new to the hospitality sector, the COVID-19 pandemic has altered the industry's fundamental beliefs. As a result, many hotels have revived their products and policies and revamped them to be ready for any future pandemics (Shah, et al., 2023b).

CONCLUSION

Family businesses are the most significant kind of corporate ownership and employers around the globe where the largest 500 family firms in the world employ 24.52 million people and generate $8.02 trillion in sales in 2022. The pandemic caused by COVID-19 has had a profound influence on health systems, economies, and civilizations all over the world, resulting in a global health emergency and a drop in the number of international visitors. In addition to causing mental health issues and leading to higher employee turnover rates, the pandemic has caused hotel businesses to face difficulties associated with digital transformation. In order to recover, it is necessary to bring the pandemic under control and carry out the policies of public institutions. For the purpose of enhancing visitor experiences, promoting sustainability, and accommodating changing traveller preferences, European family-owned hotels should implement sustainable practises, enhance digital connectivity and automation, provide amenities for health and well-being, invest in employee training, and adopt contactless technologies. The rapid adoption of next-generation technologies in the hospitality industry, such as contactless hospitality, has led to the formation of strategic partnerships between hotels and a variety of enterprises.

The implementation of artificial intelligence (AI) and machine learning (ML) into the corporate social responsibility (CSR) initiatives of European hotels is an important step toward sustainability. Utilizing the possibilities of AI and ML as the technology evolves is one way in which these firms may improve their commitment to sustainability and social responsibility. The Balearic Islands are a well-known vacation spot, and as the European Union continues to grow, more and more places to visit are becoming available. Because of this, hotel management has been obliged to make adjustments to their procedures, which has resulted in a pleasant environment and endless employment chances. However, the recruitment and retention of hospitality workers, both skilled and unskilled, continues to be a challenge on a global scale. Family businesses are the most common type of company in all of Greece, Europe, and the rest of the world. Family businesses are also the oldest type of business in the history of humanity. There are millions of hotels all throughout the world that are owned by families, some of which date back many generations. A compound annual growth rate (CAGR) of 7.0 percent is expected for the hotel industry between the years 2022 and 2023, rising from $4,390.59 billion in 2022 to $4,699.57 billion in 2023. This increase is a direct result of the relaxation of limitations placed on travel to other countries. The COVID-19 pandemic has had a significant impact on the hotel industry, particularly in Europe, where businesses have suffered significantly as a result of the implementation of lockdown procedures.

The hospitality business is challenged with a variety of social management difficulties, including risk assessment, crisis management, the implementation of innovation, and other sustainability programmes. Hotels in Europe that are run by families and have been rebuilt with corporate social responsibility policies for post-pandemic resilience attract tourists from other countries. One of the most important economic pillars in Europe is the hospitality industry, which holds a market share of greater than 50 percent. Corporate social responsibility, or CSR, is "the obligation of enterprises for their influence on society," according to the European Commission. CSR can have an effect on employees either directly through environmental knowledge or indirectly through environmental commitment. Corporate social responsibility, or CSR for short, is an essential component of successful business strategy, especially in the hotel industry. It has been demonstrated to have a good impact on the behaviour of customers as well as the performance of organisations, which results in higher levels of satisfaction and new customers. Because it encourages long-term growth and makes room for forward-thinking tourism tactics, innovation is crucial to the continued operation of family-run hotels in Europe. However, non-economic factors such as aversion to risk, family disagreements, and isolation from external sources can make innovation drivers in family businesses more difficult to implement.

In order to foster strong customer loyalty and maintain a competitive edge, hotels managed by families ought to place primary emphasis on enhancing service standards, brand recognition, and overall guest pleasure. The private sector is able to develop more sustainably with the assistance of CSR, which in turn contributes to the continued autonomy and viability of the community. Because families own the vast majority of privately owned companies, active participation from family members is essential to the success of new enterprises. The total value of the global market for hotels and resorts reached its zenith in 2019, when it was worth 1.52 trillion dollars; however, the COVID-19 epidemic led the market size to drop below one trillion dollars in both 2020 and 2021. It is anticipated that the size of the market would reach 1.21 trillion dollars in 2023. The operations and services provided by family-owned hotels have a substantial impact on the economy of the entire world and are projected to contribute 7.7 trillion dollars to the global economy in the year 2022. In the year 2023, it is anticipated that this total will remain 5 percent lower than its levels prior to the pandemic and will have increased to an estimated 9.5 trillion US dollars. CSR and the financial performance of corporations are inextricably linked, and the influence that family-owned hotels have on the economy of the world cannot be overstated. These companies have the potential to make a contribution to the global economy and to the achievement of sustainable development if they make adherence to service standards, recognition of their brand, and the happiness of their customers their top priorities.

The epidemic caused by COVID-19 has had a considerable impact on the hospitality industry, which has resulted in a shift toward contactless technologies in European family-owned hotels. This has resulted in a less authentic experience for tourists and a reduction in human contact, both of which have increased the likelihood of becoming infected with the virus. The digital revolution has been an essential component of this shift, and European hotels have used a variety of strategies in order to keep a competitive advantage and provide one-of-a-kind tourist experiences. These include having an appeal across several generations, being authentically local, directly connecting with families, having long-term goals, delivering interesting stories, and specialising in marketing. European family-run hotels should embrace sustainable practises, boost digital connectivity and automation, provide amenities for health and well-being, promote local experiences, invest in employee training, and make use of contactless technology in order to keep their competitive edge. This will improve the experiences that visitors have, promote sustainable practises, and adapt to the shifting interests of travellers. The pandemic has also brought to light the necessity of contactless services, such as checking in with a smartphone and making payments digitally. This has sped up the process of adopting cutting-edge technology such as contactless hospitality, which can manage tasks including as reservations, check-ins, and room service. There has been a growth in the number of strategic partnerships formed between hotels and other types of companies, including airlines, travel agencies, car rental services, restaurants, shopping malls, and card service providers. The implementation of artificial intelligence and machine learning (AI) in the corporate social responsibility (CSR) initiatives of European hotels has also been a major step toward achieving sustainability. As a result of the fact that seventy percent of millennials are interested in staying in a hotel that offers contactless services, contactless technologies are rapidly becoming an essential component of modern hotel facilities.

RECOMMENDATIONS:

The impact of green transformational leadership on employees' behavior has been highlighted in recent research as one of the major factors in any organization's leadership position (Jamshed, et al., 2023d). Because the management or the leader will play a significant role for sustainable development in family business hotels since leaders are directly responsible for leading staff in an innovative method (Shah et al., 2020b). The majority of hotels around the world are owned by family businesses, and in most cases, the owners are unaware of how many natural resources are being consumed or how adopting green initiatives can help them reduce CO2 emissions, excessive water and electricity use, waste management, and contribute to the sustainability of their environment (Shah, et al., 2022a). The volume of intra- and inter-tourist flows promotes mutual respect and the defense of European values, aids in the formation of the European identity, and heightens the allure of the European model. For both tourists and tourism management, safety and security are essential. Hotels are required to offer the best possible accommodations for guests, which includes physical security, emergency response planning, employee training, hygienic standards, technological integration, and collaboration with local authorities. A thorough plan focused on routine performance monitoring, spotting weak spots, and putting preventative measures in place is needed to address hotel security issues. Hotels of Europe engages in eco-friendly practices that address environmental issues and encourage responsible travel. The European Commission defines corporate social responsibility (CSR) as "the obligation of firms for their influence on society." It has been demonstrated that corporate social responsibility (CSR) has a positive impact on client behavior and business performance. To boost consumer satisfaction and draw in new clients, many businesses are starting CSR initiatives, which may have an effect on their performance and ability to compete. With changing travel patterns having a significant influence in a nation's economy, the function of CSR in hotels, particularly in European hotels, is dynamic. The COVID-19 pandemic presented significant challenges, but family-run hotels in Europe are developing creative strategies to maintain competitiveness and strengthen their resilience and adaptability. Despite the uncertainty of the recovery process, these hotels have been able to weather the storm by putting their guests' safety and comfort first, implementing eco-friendly practices, and making investments in digital technology (Jamshed, et al., 2023e). As a driving force of economic expansion, tourism is essential to a nation's economy, and the European Union's major objective is to promote sustainable development. In industrialized nations, pressure from the government, the general public, and the hotel industry has expanded participation in environmental conservation and compliance with fundamental environmental requirements. However, hoteliers are unable to take the necessary action in developing nations due to the emphasis on economic expansion and profit. As a result, key elements of the European hotel industry include digital transformation, guest safety, eco-friendly measures, and sustainable practices. Hotels can assure their long-term viability and help to create a more sustainable future by concentrating on these areas. Due to changing travel trends, the hotel sector in Europe has undergone a transformation. Research studies emphasize the value of technology in improving post-pandemic guest experiences and safety. Technology-based innovations like contactless check-ins, digital concierge services, and enhanced cleaning procedures are crucial to the enjoyment and wellbeing of guests. Partnerships between hotels, regional businesses, and governments can also help destination marketing programs that support unique local experiences and cultural authenticity. After the epidemic, Euromonitor International research suggests that European hotels concentrate on enhancing their online visibility and offering flexible booking options. Well-equipped workplaces and hybrid meeting rooms can increase guest satisfaction and set hotels apart from the competition as remote business and "leisure" travel become more widespread. In order to position the European hotel industry as a beacon of innovation, comfort, and safety in the shifting travel landscape, a combination of technology, personalized experiences, environmental efforts, and teamwork will be crucial. Family-run hotels with CSR initiatives can better recruit, inspire, and keep their staff members. Employees prefer to work for organizations that have a high reputation and public perception. They report more job satisfaction, which in turn lowers turnover—a persistent issue in the sector. Additionally, taking into account the current workforce's demographics and the industry's global nature, a number of hospitality companies, including Marriott and Sodexo, have invested in proactive diversity management programs that have benefited the company's reputation and ability to access non-traditional human capital sources as well as its bottom line. When a company matches employee donations to charity or donates time in the form of employee hours by allowing employees to volunteer at nearby non-profit groups, it increases employee engagement. As a result, CSR programs are included in an integrated high performance work system for family-owned hotels.

REFERENCES

Akram, U., Fülöp, M., Tiron-Tudor, A., Topor, D., & Căpu neanu, S. (2021). Impact of Digitalization on Customers' Well-Being in the Pandemic Period: Challenges and Opportunities for the Retail Industry. *International Journal of Environmental Research and Public Health*, 18(14), 7533. Advance online publication. DOI: 10.3390/ijerph18147533 PMID: 34299984

Anguera-Torrell, O., Aznar-Alarcón, J., & Vives-Perez, J. (2020). COVID-19: Hotel industry response to the pandemic evolution and to the public sector economic measures. *Tourism Recreation Research*, 46(2), 148–157. DOI: 10.1080/02508281.2020.1826225

Basco, R., & Rodríguez, M. (2009). Studying the Family Enterprise Holistically. *Family Business Review*, 22(1), 82–95. DOI: 10.1177/0894486508327824

Bassford, C. (2021, November 10). Why Now is the Perfect Time for Hotels to Adopt Contactless. Shiji Insights and Publications. https://insights.shijigroup.com/why-now-is-the-perfect-time-for-hotels-to-adopt-contactless/

Behringer, K., & Szegedi, K. (2016). The Role Of CSR In Achieving Sustainable Development – Theoretical Approach. *European Scientific Journal*, 12(22), 10–10. DOI: 10.19044/esj.2016.v12n22p10

Boston, (2017). Corporate Social Responsibility in the Hospitality Sector, Boston Hospitality Review | Boston Hospitality Review. (2017, January 27). © 2023 Boston University. https://www.bu.edu/bhr/2017/01/27/hospitalitycsr/

Brochado, A., Rita, P., & Margarido, A. (2016). High tech meets high touch in upscale hotels. *Journal of Hospitality and Tourism Technology*, 7(4), 347–365. DOI: 10.1108/JHTT-07-2016-0038

COM. (2011)681 - Renewed EU strategy 2011-14 for Corporate Social Responsibility - EU monitor. (n.d.). https://www.eumonitor.eu/9353000/1/j4nvkkpftveemt7_j9vvik7m1c3gyxp/vitwrzhm31gk#:~:text=Definition%3A%20the%20Commission%20puts%20forward,prerequisite%20for%20meeting%20that%20responsibility

Country profile – inbound tourism | Tourism Dashboard. (UNWTO,2021). https://www.unwto.org/tourism-data/country-profile-inbound-tourism

Eman, N. E., Jamshed, K. A., Al-Ghazali, B. M., Jamshaid, S., Shamsi, A. I., & Kainat, N. E. (2023). Role and Impact of Social Media in Tourism for Women Entrepreneurs: A Study on Family Business Women Entrepreneurs. In Women's Empowerment Within the Tourism Industry (pp. 116-131). IGI Global. DOI: 10.4018/978-1-6684-8417-3.ch009

Family Firm Facts - Family Owned Business Institute - Grand Valley State University. (FamilyFirm, 2023). https://www.gvsu.edu/fobi/family-firm-facts-5.htm#:~:-text=85%20percent%20of%20start%2Dups,(FFI%20Global%20Data%20Points)

Feranita, F., Kotlar, J., & De Massis, A. (2017). Collaborative innovation in family firms: Past research, current debates and agenda for future research. *Journal of Family Business Strategy*, 8(3), 137–156. DOI: 10.1016/j.jfbs.2017.07.001

Fes, N. (2021, December 13). TOP 10 OLDEST HOTELS IN EUROPE. https://www.tourism-review.com/oldest-hotels-in-europe-attract-visitors-with-history-and-charm-news12320

Gürlek, M., & Kilic, I. (2021). A true friend becomes apparent on a rainy day: Corporate social responsibility practices of top hotels during the COVID-19 pandemic. *Current Issues in Tourism*, 24(7), 905–918. DOI: 10.1080/13683500.2021.1883557

Gusenbauer, M., Schweiger, N., Matzler, K., & Hautz, J. (2023). Innovation Through Tradition: The Role of Past Knowledge for Successful Innovations in Family and Non-family Firms. *Family Business Review*, 36(1), 17–36. Advance online publication. DOI: 10.1177/08944865221147955

Gusenbauer, M., Schweiger, N., Matzler, K., & Hautz, J. (2023). Innovation Through Tradition: The Role of Past Knowledge for Successful Innovations in Family and Non-family Firms. *Family Business Review*, 36(1), 17–36. DOI: 10.1177/08944865221147955

Ismail, H. N., Mohd Puzi, M. A., Banki, M. B., & Yusoff, N. (2019). Inherent factors of family business and transgenerational influencing tourism business in Malaysian islands. *Journal of Tourism and Cultural Change*, 17(5), 624–641. DOI: 10.1080/14766825.2018.1549058

Jamshaid, S., Malik, N. I., Haider, A. A., Jamshed, K., & Jamshad, S. (2020, December). Overthinking hurts: rumination, worry and mental health of international students in China during Covid-19 pandemic. In *International Joint Conference on Arts and Humanities (IJCAH 2020)* (pp. 17-24). Atlantis Press. DOI: 10.2991/assehr.k.201201.004

Jamshed, K., Shah, S. H. A., Rahman, E. Z., & Din, Z. U. (2023d, February 15). Green Transformational Leadership Impact on Pro Environmental Behavior with Mediating Mechanism of Moral. . . ResearchGate. https://doi.org/DOI: 10.37896/jxu17.2/017

Jamshed, K. A., Afzal, M. I., Al-Ghazali, B. M., Jamshaid, S., Eman, N. E., & Shamsi, A. I. (2023b). Tourism as an Empowerment Tool in Sustainable Development: Evidence From the Hospitality Industry of China. In Women's Empowerment Within the Tourism Industry (pp. 132-146). IGI Global.

Jamshed, K. A., Shah, S. H. A., & Al-Ghazali, B. M. (2023a). Family Tourism Businesses and Post Pandemic: An Overview of the Hospitality Industry of Europe. Women's Empowerment Within the Tourism Industry, 102-115.

Jamshed, K. A., Shah, S. H. A., & Al-Ghazali, B. M. (2023e). Family Tourism Businesses and Post Pandemic: An Overview of the Hospitality Industry of Europe. Women's Empowerment Within the Tourism Industry, 102-115.

Jamshed, K. A., Shah, S. H. A., & Jamshaid, S. (2023c). Social Innovation and Environment: An Overview of the Tourism and Hospitality Industry of Europe. Frugal Innovation and Social Transitions in the Digital Era, 144-156.

Jiddi, F. E. (2023). Does corporate social responsibility result in better hotel guest attitudinal and behavioral loyalty? *Heliyon*, 9(8), e18669. DOI: 10.1016/j.heliyon.2023.e18669 PMID: 37560643

Koi-Akrofi, J. (2023). *CSR Paradigms, Consumer Behaviour, and Business Performance: A Literature-Based Analysis*. TEXILA INTERNATIONAL JOURNAL OF MANAGEMENT., DOI: 10.21522/TIJMG.2015.09.01.Art003

Koumentakis, S. (2021, November 21). Family businesses and economy - KOUMENTAKIS AND ASSOCIATES. KOUMENTAKIS & ASSOCIATES Law Firm. https://koumentakislaw.gr/en/articles/family-businesses-and-the-economy/

Lumpkin, G. T., & Brigham, K. H. (2011). Long–term orientation and intertemporal choice in family firms. *Entrepreneurship Theory and Practice*, 35(6), 1149–1169. DOI: 10.1111/j.1540-6520.2011.00495.x

Ma, C., Yu, C., & Latif, Y. (2023). CSR and Sustainable Growth in China's Technology Firms between 2010 and 2021. *Sustainability (Basel)*, 15(3), 2101. Advance online publication. DOI: 10.3390/su15032101

Massa, L., & Tucci, C. L. (2013). Business model innovation. The Oxford handbook of innovation management, 20(18), 420-441.

Miller, D., & Le Breton-Miller, I. (2021). Brief reflections on family firm research and some suggested paths forward. *Journal of Family Business Strategy*, 12(1), 100410. DOI: 10.1016/j.jfbs.2020.100410

Musyaffi, A., Sari, D., & Respati, D. (2021). Understanding of Digital Payment Usage During COVID-19 Pandemic: A Study of UTAUT Extension Model in Indonesia. Journal of Asian Finance. *Economics and Business*, 8, 475–482. DOI: 10.13106/jafeb.2021.vol8.no6.0475

Robertsson, H. (2023, January 16). How the largest family enterprises are outstripping global economic growth. www.ey.com. https://www.ey.com/en_gl/family-enterprise/family-business-index

Romano, A. (2022, May 25). The World's Oldest Hotel Has Been in the Same Family for 52 Generations. Travel + Leisure. https://www.travelandleisure.com/hotels-resorts/japanese-hotel-oldest-in-the-world

Salem, I., Elbaz, A., Elkhwesky, Z., & Ghazi, K. (2021). The COVID-19 pandemic: The mitigating role of government and hotel support of hotel employees in Egypt. *Tourism Management*, 85, 104305–104305. DOI: 10.1016/j.tourman.2021.104305 PMID: 36567706

Shah, S. H. A., Al-Ghazali, B. M., Bhatti, S., Aman, N., Fahlevi, M., Aljuaid, M., & Hasan, F. (2023a). The Impact of Perceived CSR on Employees' Pro-Environmental Behaviors: The Mediating Effects of Environmental Consciousness and Environmental Commitment. *Sustainability (Basel)*, 15(5), 4350. DOI: 10.3390/su15054350

Shah, S. H. A., Jamshed, K., Saleem, S., Al-Ghazali, B. M., & Kiani, O. I. (2023b). Rebuilding Tourism in Asia for Future (Post-COVID-19). In Resilient and Sustainable Destinations After Disaster (pp. 109-119). Emerald Publishing Limited.

Shah, S. H. A., Jamshed, K. A., Saleem, S., Bashir, M., & Kiani, O. I. (2022a). Sustainable Development in the Hospitality Industry of Europe: Role of Green HRM Practices. In Sustainable Development of Human Resources in a Globalization Period (pp. 49-67). IGI Global.

Shah, S. H. A., Sultana, A., Gul, A., Sajjad, S., Aziz, S., Basit, A., & Qadir, A. (2020b). Transformational leadership influence on innovation directly and indirectly through affective commitment in hotel industry of Malaysia. *International Review of Management and Marketing*, 10(6), 22–28. DOI: 10.32479/irmm.10761

Sharma, P., Massis, A., & Gagné, M. (2014). Family business: A fertile ground for research on time, teams and positive organizational study. *European Journal of Work and Organizational Psychology*, 23(5), 674–679. DOI: 10.1080/1359432X.2014.900046

She, J., Jiang, J., Ye, L., Hu, L., Bai, C., & Song, Y. (2020, February 20). 2019 novel coronavirus of pneumonia in Wuhan, China: Emerging attack and management strategies. *Clinical and Translational Medicine*, 9(1), 19. DOI: 10.1186/s40169-020-00271-z PMID: 32078069

Smyrnios, K., Tanewski, G., & Romano, C. (1998). Development of a Measure of the Characteristics of Family Business. *Family Business Review*, 11(1), 49–60. DOI: 10.1111/j.1741-6248.1998.00049.x

Solutions, F. B. (2013). Family Business Solutions. Your Guide to a Family Constitution.

Sönmez, S., Apostolopoulos, Y., Lemke, M., & Hsieh, Y. (2020). Understanding the effects of COVID-19 on the health and safety of immigrant hospitality workers in the United States. *Tourism Management Perspectives*, 35, 100717–100717. DOI: 10.1016/j.tmp.2020.100717 PMID: 32834958

Teng, Y., Wu, K., & Xu, D. (2021). The Association Between Fear of Coronavirus Disease 2019, Mental Health, and Turnover Intention Among Quarantine Hotel Employees in China. *Frontiers in Public Health*, 9, 668774. Advance online publication. DOI: 10.3389/fpubh.2021.668774 PMID: 34136457

Vaska, S., Massaro, M., Bagarotto, E., & Mas, F. (2021). The Digital Transformation of Business Model Innovation: A Structured Literature Review. *Frontiers in Psychology*, 11, 539363. Advance online publication. DOI: 10.3389/fpsyg.2020.539363 PMID: 33584396

Veloso, C., Magalhães, D., Sousa, B., Walter, C., & Valeri, M. (2021). Encouraging consumer loyalty: the role of family business in hospitality. Journal of Family Business Management. .DOI: 10.1108/JFBM-10-2021-0134

Wynn, M., & Jones, P. (2022). IT Strategy in the Hotel Industry in the Digital Era. *Sustainability (Basel)*, 14(17), 10705. Advance online publication. DOI: 10.3390/su141710705

Yu, J., Lee, K., & Hyun, S. (2021). Understanding the influence of the perceived risk of the coronavirus disease (COVID-19) on the post-traumatic stress disorder and revisit intention of hotel guests. *Journal of Hospitality and Tourism Management*, 46, 327–335. DOI: 10.1016/j.jhtm.2021.01.010

Zanfardini, M., Aguirre, P., & Tamagni, L. (2016). The evolution of CSR's research in tourism context: A review from 1992 to 2012. *Anatolia*, 27(1), 38–46. DOI: 10.1080/13032917.2015.1083207

Chapter 5
AI-Driven Market Intelligence:
Enhancing Competitive Analysis and Market Positioning

Deepak K. Sahoo
https://orcid.org/0009-0004-5703-8701
Biju Patnaik University of Technology, Rourkela, India

Anish Kumar
https://orcid.org/0000-0002-8047-4227
O.P. Jindal Global University, India

Preet Kanwal
https://orcid.org/0009-0006-5114-8381
Lovely Professional University, India

Rohit
https://orcid.org/0009-0004-1796-5252
Gulf Medical University, UAE

ABSTRACT

AI-driven market intelligence is revolutionizing how businesses analyze and respond to market dynamics. This chapter explores the integration of artificial intelligence (AI) tools in competitive analysis and market positioning. It discusses the foundations of market intelligence, the role of AI in enhancing competitive strategies, and the practical tools and technologies available for implementation. The chapter also addresses the challenges and ethical considerations associated with AI, including data quality, integration with legacy systems, and privacy concerns. Future trends such as autonomous systems, enhanced personalization, and the convergence of AI

DOI: 10.4018/979-8-3373-0219-5.ch005

with augmented and virtual reality are examined. The implications of these advancements for businesses, managers, and society are analyzed, emphasizing the need for responsible AI use and strategic innovation. This comprehensive overview provides insights into leveraging AI to optimize market intelligence and drive business success.

INTRODUCTION

In the fast-evolving business landscape, enterprises very much need to capture, interpret, and act upon market intelligence if they ever want to stay competitive. While the traditional means of market research and competitive analysis are indispensable in nature, they usually cannot match up to the dynamism that characterizes today's global markets. This is where AI-driven market intelligence-a transformational approach-bridges the gap by using artificial intelligence to foster greater depth, higher speed, and high precision in market insights. It thus helps businesses, through the use of AI technologies like machine learning, natural language processing, and predictive analytics, to monitor their competition more effectively. Further, it identifies emerging trends and uncovers market opportunities for the optimization of positioning strategies with an unprecedented degree of precision. It speaks to the critical role of AI in the rethinking of market intelligence through an in-depth study of how AI-driven tools and techniques are revolutionizing the job of competitive analysis and helping companies better achieve more strategic and impactful positions in their markets. Through this journey, we'll learn what the key ingredients are, what the challenges are, and the future trends that 'Artificial Intelligence in Market Intelligence' can bring about, acting like a roadmap for organizations wanting to stay ahead in an increasingly competitive landscape.

FOUNDATIONS OF MARKET INTELLIGENCE

Traditional Approaches to Market Intelligence

Market intelligence has conventionally been a bedrock of strategic business planning. It has conventionally encompassed structured collection, analysis, and dissemination of information about an organization's external environment regarding competitors, customers, market trends, and regulatory changes. This traditionally rests on quantitative data-such as sales and market share-and qualitative insights obtained through surveys, focus groups, and expert interviews. While these methods have served well to inform business decisions, they tend to be very resource-intensive and time-consuming, bound by the scale and speed of data collection and analysis. In addition, traditional market intelligence is often backward-looking, providing analysis of past and present status that may not accurately predict the dynamics of the future market.

The Evolution of Market Intelligence with AI

Artificial intelligence replaces the concept of market intelligence with a sea change in a reactive towards proactive decision-making platform. Not only that, but AI technologies like machine learning and NLP have changed the way firms collect and interpret data. Contrary to traditional techniques, AI-based market intelligence processes vast amounts of structured as well as unstructured data in real-time to offer more timely and accurate insights. This evolution has allowed companies to foresee market shifts, discern emerging trends, and even react to competitive threats more efficiently. Continuous learning by AI from new data sources creates a more vibrant and predictive market analysis, giving business an edge in a constantly shifting market (Weng, 2021).

Key Components of Market Intelligence

The building blocks of modern market intelligence stand on the following key components, each with their dimensions having AI enhancement: First, **Competitive Intelligence**: tracking and analysis of strategy, strength, and weakness of competitors. It automates monitoring competitors' digital footprints-from social media activity to patent filings-and synthesizes the same into actionable insight. This involves **customer intelligence** focused on an understanding of customer behavior, preferences, and needs. AI tools can analyze customer interactions across various touchpoints, hence deepening insights into customer sentiment, purchasing patterns, and even probable churn. Third, **market trend analysis** discovers and tracks changes across the wide market spectrum. The subtlest changes in consumer behavior, economic indicators, and innovations in industries can be noticed with AI-driven tools to enable companies to make proactive adjustments to their strategies. Finally, **regulatory intelligence** concerns knowledge acquisition on changes in the legal and regulatory environment that may impact the company. AI will make businesses compliant because it monitors regulation changes emanating from geographical regions and predicts their likely impact on business operations.

Once integrated and powered by AI, these components become a solid model of market intelligence that facilitates more strategic and fact-based decision-making across the organization (Carson et al., 2020).

ROLE OF AI IN COMPETITIVE ANALYSIS

AI Techniques for Gathering and Analyzing Competitor Data

Artificial Intelligence has disrupted the process of collecting and analyzing competitor data, making it fast, accurate, and full of insights. Conventionally, competitive analysis required manual effort like studying competitor websites, monitoring industry reports, and conducting market surveys. These methods, though of immense worth, came out as fragmented pieces with very delayed decision-making. Meanwhile, AI automates and amplifies such processes through constant monitoring of large volumes coming from different directions, such as social media, news, financial reports, and even patents. With machine learning algorithms, one can sift through this data to identify patterns, trends, and anomalies that could indicate strategic moves by a competitor, product launches, or shifts in market positioning. NLP can analyze AI sentiment and the context of the communications from competitors, therefore offering deeper insights into their marketing strategies and customer engagements. This level of analysis will enable business entities to stay at the top through better decision-making with real-time information (Kai, 2024).

Predictive Analytics for Anticipating Competitor Moves

Probably one of the most formidable ways in which AI is applied to competitive analysis is by means of predictive analytics, whereby firms can know-even forestall-competitors' moves before they are made. Based on the analysis of historical data and identification of trends, AI algorithms can predict future competitor activities with a very high degree of accuracy. By monitoring market conditions, for instance, AI can predict when a competitor who generally launches new products whenever the market conditions or demand for the products increase is likely to introduce their next product. Also, AI can model various scenarios related to how competitors can respond to fluctuation in the market due to a change in regulation, economic status, or even technological advancement. These insights can allow companies to create proactive strategies via counter-campaigns, pricing changes, or product feature improvements, thereby reducing the threats and leveraging the opportunities. In other words, AI-driven predictive analytics transforms CA from a reactive discipline into a proactive one and thus enables companies to gain better foresight and agility in competitive landscapes (Ntapiapis, 2023).

Case Studies: AI-Driven Competitive Analysis in Various Industries

AI competitive analysis, if used effectively, can be witnessed in several industries, including retailers who have used this tool effectively to turn into leaders. For example, retail firms can monitor the pricing strategy of any competitor using AI-powered tools in real time and set dynamic prices to keep their share of the market. AI in the financial services industry is used to examine the investment portfolios of competitors with a view to anticipating their future trading activities and making more informed investment decisions. The most significant advantage arising out of it, however, has been felt in the healthcare industry wherein AI has helped pharmaceutical companies track the drug development pipeline of their competitors in order to anticipate where the next disruption will come from. These case studies illustrate how versatile and effective AI can be in augmenting competitive analysis across industries. AI has grown to become indispensable for any corporation in its quest to edge out competitors in an increasingly competitive environment through actionable insights and predictive capabilities (Yan, 2023).

MARKET POSITIONING IMPROVEMENT BY AI

Identifying Market Gaps and Opportunities by the Use of AI

One of the major benefits of AI in respect to market positioning is that it identifies market gaps left unoccupied up until then or emerging opportunities with a great deal of precision. Traditional methods of market research rely largely on past data and broad market surveys that might not catch niche segments or a newly forming trend. On the other hand, AI analyzes huge volumes of data from diverse sources such as patterns in consumer behavior, social media chatter, and industry reports to pinpoint the subtlety of a market landscape shift. For example, machine learning algorithms can identify emerging interest in new product features or particular consumer preferences that have not yet reached the mainstream. That way, businesses will find emerging needs by developing and positioning products or services to sell before their competitors do. Furthermore, with AI-powered tools, this would even lead to more granular market segmentation to develop offerings that could effectively appeal either to customer groups or geographic regions and thereby result in enhanced market positioning with a more competitive advantage (Chintalapati & Pandey, 2021).

AI-Powered Consumer Segmentation and Targeting

Effective market positioning is contingent upon the depth of understanding of the target audience, and AI greatly augments this with advanced consumer segmentation and targeting. Traditional means of segmentation tended to cut both ways, often lumping consumers into very broad demographic categories such as age, gender, or income. While helpful in some respects, these categories are often much too general to really help the marketer get a sense of who today's consumer is and what they need or desire. AI can process an immense volume of data points, including online behavior, purchase history, social media activity, and even psychographic data when developing highly detailed portraits of consumers. In turn, these profiles will allow companies to segment their audience with much greater precision, knowing not only who their customers are but also what drives them and how they interact with various brands. What's more, AI can dynamically adjust these segments as new data arrives, keeping targeting strategies relevant and effective. AI segmentation will, therefore, enable businesses to craft more personalized marketing messages matching their product offerings and help place their brand in the minds of their target customers (Carbonell & Escudero, 2010).

Strategies for Refining Brand Positioning through AI Insights

Businesses will be better equipped with very strong insights through AI that could be fruitfully used for refining and improving brand positioning strategies. In the modern competitive milieu, where consumer perception and preference might change in the twinkling of an eye, monitoring brand positioning consistently and making necessary adjustments becomes mandatory. With the power of AI in sentiment analysis and brand monitoring tools, businesses keep track of their brand perception in real time through every channel, be it social media, review sites, or news outlets. It's a constant stream of feedback that helps businesses understand touchpoints where their brand messaging may not be aligned with consumer expectations-or at which competitors may gain an advantage. Besides AI understanding the effectiveness of marketing campaigns, AI can also understand better what elements of those campaigns really ring true to a target audience, and what needs refinement. These can then be used to refine brand messaging, visual identity, and customer engagement to make sure the brand remains relevant and compelling. Additionally, AI will help in the development of strategies on brand differentiation since it can analyze competitive positioning and identify unique selling points on which emphasis should be given to make it stand out in the market (S.V., 2023).

Case Studies: Successful AI-Driven Market Positioning

Real-life examples, where companies have actually been able to utilize AI in enhancing their market positioning with substantial success, attest to the effectiveness of AI. For example, within the automotive context, one of the largest car manufacturers employs AI to analyze customer sentiment and trends about their purchases to position its brand as a leader in electric vehicles. Informed by such AI-driven insight, this strategic shift allowed the company to capture a significant share of the growing market for sustainable transportation. Similarly, within fashion, a global retailer deployed AI to make its marketing more personally relevant; the outcome was a much more refined brand positioning that really resonated with younger, tech-savvy consumers. This dynamic tuning of brand messaging, based on up-to-the-minute data, eventually enabled the retailer to increase brand loyalty and, consequently, market share. These case studies give evidence of how AI-driven market positioning could deliver tangible business outcomes and thereby provide a competitive advantage in an increasingly complicated and dynamic marketplace (Kamkankaew, 2024)

TOOLS AND TECHNOLOGIES FOR AI-DRIVEN MARKET INTELLIGENCE

Overview of AI Tools for Market Analysis

AI-driven market intelligence is powered by a suite of tools designed to collect, process, and analyze information way more efficiently than ever before. These include machine learning algorithms for predicting market trends, such as ups and downs, to NLP systems that analyze textual data emanating from sources as varied as social media, news articles, and customer reviews. Some of the most usable AI tools in market analysis include predictive analytics platforms, which forecast the future market movement based on historical data; sentiment analysis tools, which show the public opinion about any particular brand or product; and competitive intelligence software, which monitors in real time the activities of its competitors. Such tools piece together a comprehensive view of the market to enable businesses to make more informed decisions. Automation provided by AI-powered tools cuts down on time and effort required for the analysis of data, hence allowing companies to be responsive to address market changes with speed and agility (Noranee & Othman, 2023).

Comparison of Top AI-Driven Market Intelligence Platforms

A few top AI-driven market intelligence platforms stand out from among today's industry players, unique in terms of features and capabilities. IBM Watson, for instance, has earned its standing for the depth applied to NLP and its machine learning capabilities, which provide the ability to analyze unstructured data from a wide variety of sources. What is more, Watson's power to understand and interpret even very intricate nuances of language lets businesses acquire insight into consumer sentiment and emergent trends. With Google Cloud AI, there is strong machine learning available that can be integrated with any business processes for predictive analytics and real-time data analysis. The scalability of Google Cloud integrated with other Google services makes it very attractive for enterprises looking to leverage AI for market intelligence. Salesforce Einstein is another leading platform in the realm of customer relationship management. With AI analytics, today's companies have much more complete insight into customer behavior, enabling them to fine-tune marketing strategy to achieve better consumer engagement. Crimson Hexagon focuses specially on social media analytics using AI for the analysis of a larger volume of social data for consumer trends and brand perception. The comparison of these platforms will inherently enable companies to choose one that best fits their needs, whether it be for deep NLP capabilities, the integration with existing systems, or specialized analytics for social media (Ogundipe, 2024; Hicham, 2023)

Integrating AI Tools into Business Processes

Integration of AI tools into business processes becomes very important in order to derive maximum benefit from AI-driven market intelligence. In light of this, successful AI technology integration needs to consider the capability of data infrastructure around volume management that these tools would need for functioning. In many such cases, this necessitates an upgrade, if not an overhaul, of the current data management system to get it up to the task of real-time processing and storage of data. Once this infrastructure is ready, businesses can begin using and implementing AI tools in their workflows. For example, AI-driven predictive analytics can be embedded into decision-making processes where managers lead the strategy development process using data-driven forecasts. Similarly, tools offering sentiment analysis can be integrated into customer service platforms, offering in real time insight into customer satisfaction against which companies can proactively solve emerging issues. It is also crucial to impart special training to the employees to show them how to make optimum utilization of the AI tools and interpret the insights received through AI, embedding them in their everyday performances. In this respect, integrating the AI tools into their existing processes allows an enterprise to amplify its capability related to market intelligence, make more concise decisions, and achieve a leading edge in the market (Wu, 2022).

Challenges in Implementing AI-Driven Market Intelligence Tools

Despite all of the above pros of using AI-powered market intelligence, seamless integration of such AI-powered market intelligence tools is not barrierless. The key challenge remains data quality and availability. AI requires high volumes of data to perform well. If the data is incomplete, outdated, or even biased, the insights may either be wrong or potentially misleading. Good data quality definitely requires good data governance and ongoing checking of sources. The other challenge could be the integration with the existing system. Most businesses use old systems that may not work well with modern AI tools. This therefore calls for huge investments in technology upgrade. Organisational readiness is another challenge. Often, this implementation of AI tools calls for cultural changes in an organization since employees are unwilling to accept new technologies or don't have the required skills to work with them. There are a lot of ethical considerations-mainly data privacy, and AI may perpetuate historical bias. It's for this reason that businesses navigate these challenges with caution, to make sure AI-driven market intelligence efforts have any hope of success and sustainability long-term (Nasution et al., 2019).

Future Developments in AI Tools for Market Intelligence

The concept of AI-driven market intelligence is under continuous development, as innovation is happening in the toolsets and technologies developed to meet emerging business needs. Going ahead, we will find that automation of data analysis will be even more critical, wherein the AI tools will not only be able to collect and process data but will also be able to make strategic recommendations based on the same. Another development is augmented analytics, which fuses the work of AI and human intelligence to arrive at better decision-making. That is, the insights and suggestions come from AI tools first, then validated and honed by humans. Coupled with this, the democratization of AI will also continue, which means that AI tools will begin to flow down to SMEs that don't really have much wherewithal to invest in large-scale AI solutions. In other words, market intelligence will only become even more an intrinsic part of business operations as AI technology advances, thereby enabling businesses of all scales to effectively make relevant business decisions. Conversely, such changes will raise the capabilities of companies in meeting changing market circumstances and competition while optimizing their strategic positioning in the market (Yau et al., 2021; Efendioğlu, 2023).

CHALLENGES AND ETHICAL CONSIDERATIONS

Data Quality and Integrity

Probably one of the greatest challenges to the effective implementation of AI-driven market intelligence is assurance of compliance with the quality and integrity of the data used. Since AI systems perform only as well as the data they have been trained on, poor-quality data means decisions based on inaccurate or biased insights. Partially complete datasets, not timely, or out-of-date information and data from questionable sources undermine the effectiveness of AI tools. Stringent data governance practices, such as periodic audits, validation processes, and the application of techniques for data cleaning, can ensure data quality. In addition, it is important that organizations take full care in the active curation and updating of their data to represent the present market scenario and consumer behaviors. The balancing challenge indeed lies in having comprehensive data with the practicality of collecting and maintaining high-quality information. Put differently, unless these issues in the quality of data are addressed, it would be a gamble for the business to make strategic decisions based on flawed insights (Mao, 2023).

Integration with Legacy Systems

Another parallel challenge, however, is that of integrating AI-driven market intelligence into a business's stack of legacy systems. Legacy systems are typically very old and built upon old technologies, which are usually incompatible with the new AI tools. Changing or updating such systems to meet the demand for AI would be enormously resource-intensive and require a lot of time. In addition, businesses can face reluctance on the part of employees who are used to such existing systems and may not easily adapt to new technologies. To address these challenges, organizations have to think through their strategies of integration by ensuring that adequate technical infrastructure as well as employee buy-in for supporting the transition exist. This may imply a gradual implementation in which AI tools are progressively integrated into business processes, supported by extensive training programs that make the employees feel comfortable with the new technologies (Rosário, 2021).

Organizational Readiness and Skill Gaps

Implementation of AI-driven market intelligence is dependent, not only on technical integration, but also organizational readiness. A lack of expertise in AI technologies inhibits many businesses from effectively deploying the tools and putting them to work. This is usually because of the significant shortage of skilled professionals who understand the technical and strategic aspects of AI. In addition, there may be cultural resistance within the organization; for instance, skepticism or fear among employees that have never worked with AI before might think it will affect their job roles. Meeting these challenges will demand constant learning and development. In other words, it calls for investments in upskilling the workforce with training on AI tools and techniques, as well as fostering a culture of innovation and adaptability. In that direction, AI-driven market intelligence projects will be in tune with the overall objectives of the business by integrating cross-functional teams comprising technical experts and business strategists to bridge the skill gaps (Katsikea et al., 2019).

Ethical Implications of AI in Market Intelligence

AI in the marketplace intelligence space now presents a set of considerations that businesses must consider from an ethical standpoint. First, there's data privacy, as AI-driven tools often leverage huge amounts of personal information to derive insight into their specific domain. Companies would be required to observe data protection laws like the GDPR and implement serious security considerations to guarantee that a high volume of consumer data would not be breached. Another ethical problem concerns the possible biases within the AI algorithms. If the data used in training any of these AI models was biased toward prevailing societal biases, then the AI propagated and amplified those biases toward unbalanced and even discriminatory results. A market segmentation AI, for example, can lock into certain demographics and weed out others because of prejudiced data. The organization should not be passive; rather, it should always be on the lookout for bias in their AI systems and work toward mitigating these by auditing algorithms regularly and encouraging diversity in the data used (Mandal, 2018).

Accountability and Transparency

Transparency and accountability are important ethical considerations when using AI in market intelligence. Businesses should be transparent as regards the deployment of AI tools and the collected data, such that the stakeholders understand the underlying processes behind the decisions driven by AI. In this regard, consumers need to be aware of how their personal data are used and what rights they have over them. In that respect, businesses need to develop clear accountability structures as to who takes responsibility for the outcome produced by the AI systems. This includes not only technical teams that design and maintain AI tools but also decision-makers who depend on AI-driven insights in formulating their strategies. Clear lines of accountability mean someone is responsible should there be errors or damages, which helps to build confidence in the minds of stakeholders (Eriksson et al., 2020).

Balancing Innovation with Ethical Responsibility

While AI-driven market intelligence brings immense benefits, businesses should balance the drive for innovation with ethical responsibility. That is, the larger ramifications of AI technologies for society as a whole have to be taken into consideration, and decisions made in harmony with ethical precepts. For instance, businesses should avoid using AI in ways that could exploit vulnerable populations or contribute to negative social outcomes, such as increased inequality or environmental harm. Rather, the strategy for any business should be how to use AI to drive positive impacts in customer experiences, inclusive ecosystems, and sustainability. The integration of ethics within an AI strategy will ensure that the business not only evades potential pitfalls but assumes a differentiated market position as responsible and very forward-looking. This approach brings value in terms of ensuring long-term risk mitigation and sustainability for AI-driven market intelligence initiatives (Latha, 2024; Anjorin, 2024).

FUTURE TRENDS IN AI-DRIVEN MARKET INTELLIGENCE

Evolution of Predictive Analytics

One of the most interesting future trends in AI-driven market intelligence is the development of predictive analytics. While the ability of AI models to predict the future continues to evolve, it will soon move beyond simple trend forecasting to more complex and accurate predictions of how markets will actually behave. This would also mean the ability to predict consumer behavior more accurately, predict market disruptions, and even foresee competitive moves in advance. Patterns will be extractable in big datasets that were previously not quite detectable by businesses due to the integration of machine learning and deep learning techniques, hence making more effective strategic decisions. Predictive analytics will not only forecast what could happen but also provide actionable recommendations on how businesses can capitalize on these predictions. In that way, AI-driven market intelligence will be proactive rather than reactive (Ljepava, 2022; Yau et al., 2021).

Rise of Autonomous Market Intelligence Systems

Development of autonomous market intelligence systems is another emerging trend. These systems use AI in the automation of the whole market intelligence process: from data collection and analysis, derivation of insights, to even the implementation of strategies. All these would happen with little human intervention, while the system would continuously observe changes in market conditions, make real-time adaptations, and automatically adjust the business strategies accordingly. For example, an autonomous system could detect a shift in consumer sentiment on social media and almost instantaneously change marketing campaigns based on that. In the years ahead, these systems will integrate increasingly with other business disciplines, such as supply chain management and customer relationship management, to accomplish comprehensive, agile objectives concerned with market intelligence. Thus, autonomy will save significant time and resources needed to perform market analysis, enabling companies to react to opportunities and threats faster than they previously have been able to.

Integration of AI with Augmented Reality (AR) and Virtual Reality (VR)

The integration of AI with augmented reality and virtual reality is another exciting trend into the future of market intelligence. As AR and VR technologies continue to become mainstream, they will provide new ways that businesses capture and analyze market data. AI-driven AR/VR further enables the simulation of market conditions in an immersive way, thus allowing businesses to test varied strategies in a very controlled environment before actual implementation. For instance, a company could use virtual reality to simulate the launching of a new product and use AI to monitor consumer reactions within the virtual environment. Once AR/VR is integrated with AI, it will allow businesses to know more about consumer behavior and refine their positioning in the market and provide customers with products and services that will meet their needs in new ways.

Enhanced Personalization Through AI

Personalization at all levels has been one of the fastest-growing areas for AI-driven market intelligence. It is bound to continue, given how much consumers will love even more personal approaches to creating experiences for them. AI will increasingly be used in the design of highly personalized marketing campaigns, product recommendations, and customer interactions. AI, through vast amounts of data analytics on purchase history, browsing behavior, and social media, among many others, lets businesses understand each and every consumer preference down to the nth level. All this will, therefore, enable companies to convey the right message, at the right time, through the right channel, which will increase customer engagement and loyalty dramatically. In the future, AI will continue to fine-tune these methods of personalization by incorporating real-time data and contextual elements into a seamless, highly relevant consumer experience.

Ethical AI and Responsible Market Intelligence

The more AI takes center stage in market intelligence, the more ethical AI and responsible use of technology would be called into play. Future developments will encompass setting up frameworks and guidelines that make sure AI is used in a manner that will be transparently and fairly protective of consumer privacy. Businesses will have to soothe several concerns about data security, algorithmic bias, and the usage of AI in a way that can potentially harm consumers or society. The increasing trend of ethical AI will also engender increased scrutiny from regulators and consumers who will demand businesses that employ AI-driven market intelligence to be more responsible. Businesses that will place ethical AI practices at the forefront of their corporate agenda will avoid potential legal and reputational risks but will also emerge as more competitive in engendering trust among customers and stakeholders.

Expansion of AI Applications Across Industries

The future of AI-driven market intelligence will witness further extension to the use of AI across various industries and beyond the confines of retail and e-commerce. Other industries like healthcare, finance, and manufacturing have already begun to use the AI-driven market intelligence tool as a differentiator. For example, in the health care domain, AI analyzes patient data for treatment outcomes prediction or resource optimization. AI-powered market intelligence enables the financial firm to anticipate market trends and make more rational investment decisions. In the future, with improvements in AI technology, we can only imagine how much more innovative ways market intelligence will find applications across industries to drive business growth and open up hitherto unimaginable possibilities for enterprises willing to compete in an environment that is getting increasingly competitive.

IMPLICATIONS

Practical Implications

The integration of AI-powered market intelligence into business operations has the following important practical implications: Companies can therefore use AI in driving processes to make decisions smarter and faster, hence quick to respond to changes in the market. Use of AI in data analysis helps businesses process large volumes of information at unimaginable speeds, hence more accurate forecasts and insight. Pragmatically, this means that through current data, firms are able to achieve better product mixes, pricing policies, and promotional campaigns, which leads them toward competitiveness and responsiveness to the marketplace. Besides that, AI automates activities which by nature require less human judgment and decision-making, freeing up people's time for activities more strategic in nature, enhancing productivity and efficiency of organizations in general.

Managerial Implications

The deployment of AI-driven market intelligence calls for a change in leadership and management. The business manager therefore needs to attain deep knowledge of these technologies and the ways they can be integrated into the enterprise. This will require not only acquiring technical knowledge but also changing the enterprise culture of higher reliance on innovation and data-driven decision-making. It requires that managers be prepared for different problems that will emerge during the adaptation of AI at all levels of the enterprise, including changing resistance from personnel. Besides, AI-driven strategy implementation would most likely require different organizational skill profiles and therefore continuous training and development. Managers will have to ensure that their teams use AI responsibly, by following best practices linked to data privacy, transparency, and non-discrimination.

Ethical Implications

The rise of AI-driven market intelligence brings about several serious ethical issues. The use of AI in analyzing consumer data raises a lot of concern about privacy and personal information misuse. Therefore, businesses have to address these ethical challenges through imposing a strong data governance framework that ensures consumer privacy and is transparent in data collection, processing, and usage. Moreover, algorithmic bias-which might arise with the AI systems-is also one of the crucial ethical areas which companies need to take into consideration. This therefore calls for a very careful design of AI models, testing for all possible scenarios to keep them from perpetuating or amplifying existing inequalities. Ethical issues also involve the implications of AI on jobs, since the automation of tasks may displace them. In sum, companies will have to consider the larger consequences of their AI-driven strategies and undertake mitigating measures against negative outcomes.

Societal Implications

The societal implications of AI-driven market intelligence are huge. It could cause explosive economic growth on one hand by offering a way to run businesses more smoothly and efficiently in order to survive in the global marketplace. To begin with, this may mean the creation of new jobs, and maybe even industries. On the other hand, wide diffusions of AI have grave consequences apart from increasing inequality, since the benefits of AI will be distributed all over society. Further risks include market intelligence driven by AI, maybe greater market concentration, or a few large companies dominating whole industries. Furthermore, AI use in marketing and advertising can subtly manipulate consumer behavior, raising serious autonomy and informed decision concerns. These are challenges that must be faced by society large in weighing up benefits from AI with protection of individual rights and promoting social equity.

CONCLUSION

The integration of AI-driven market intelligence is a paradigm shift in how businesses understand and engage with their markets. This will inherently enable companies to create an unparalleled understanding of consumer behavior, market trends, and competitive dynamics by making use of rich data analytics, machine learning, and predictive modeling. All this is now made possible through technological advancement that enables firms to make more informed and timely decisions by optimizing strategies with the ultimate view of strengthening their market positioning. Yet, all these possibilities with AI mean the same amount of practical, managerial, ethical, and societal implications that are still to be negotiated with care.

Businesses practically use AI to improve efficiency and speed in operations and respond more rapidly to market fluctuations. Managerially speaking, such an effective implementation of AI requires review in leadership practices foremost by fostering a culture of innovation and data-based decision-making. Companies must address various challenges ethically in areas like data privacy and algorithmic bias, along with broader societal issues related to the impact of automation on jobs. Diffusion of AI may, at the same time, be a source of growth and held to be the cause of inequality and concentration in the marketplace.

In the future, further development of AI technologies promises much more significant advances in market intelligence. Those businesses that readily accept such innovation and the related challenges will be stronger in an ever-growing competitive and dynamic business environment. Finally, AI will take root in market intelligence only if it strikes a balance between the use of technological capabilities and adherence to ethical considerations with regard to greater societal impacts. With AI, companies can tap into its full potentials by doing all it would take in making use of such technological advancement towards strategic success while contributing positively to the global market environment.

REFERENCES

Anjorin, K. (2024). Harnessing artificial intelligence to develop strategic marketing goals. *International Journal of Management & Entrepreneurship Research*, 6(5), 1625–1650. DOI: 10.51594/ijmer.v6i5.1127

Carbonell, P., & Escudero, A. (2010). The effect of market orientation on innovation speed and new product performance. *Journal of Business and Industrial Marketing*, 25(7), 501–513. DOI: 10.1108/08858621011077736

Carson, G., O'Connor, C., & Simmons, G. (2020). The crucial role of market intelligence in the development of small business marketing capabilities. *Journal of Small Business and Enterprise Development*, 27(5), 797–816. DOI: 10.1108/JSBED-12-2019-0394

Chintalapati, S., & Pandey, S. (2021). Artificial intelligence in marketing: A systematic literature review. *International Journal of Market Research*, 64(1), 38–68. DOI: 10.1177/14707853211018428

Efendioğlu, İ. (2023). The change of digital marketing with artificial intelligence.. DOI: 10.33422/7th.iarmea.2023.07.101

Eriksson, T., Bigi, A., & Bonera, M. (2020). Think with me, or think for me? on the future role of artificial intelligence in marketing strategy formulation. *The TQM Journal*, 32(4), 795–814. DOI: 10.1108/TQM-12-2019-0303

Hicham, N., Nassera, H., & Karim, S. (2023). Strategic framework for leveraging artificial intelligence in future marketing decision-making. *Journal of Intelligent Management Decision*, 2(3), 139–150. DOI: 10.56578/jimd020304

Kai, P., & Generoso, M. J. I. A. I. I. (2024). Emerging technologies adoption and market positioning of ai products in china. *International Journal of Research Studies in Management*, 12(2). Advance online publication. DOI: 10.5861/ijrsm.2024.1023

Kamkankaew, P., Thanitbenjasith, P., Sribenjachot, S., Sanpatanon, N., Phattarowas, V., & Thanin, P. (2024). How artificial intelligence is helping businesses grow and thrive: The transformative role of artificial intelligence in thai b2c digital marketing. *IJSASR*, 4(1), 137–164. DOI: 10.60027/ijsasr.2024.3651

Katsikea, E., Theodosiou, M., & Makri, K. (2019). The interplay between market intelligence activities and sales strategy as drivers of performance in foreign markets. *European Journal of Marketing*, 53(10), 2080–2108. DOI: 10.1108/EJM-06-2017-0402

Latha, R. (2024). Is artificial intelligence really influencing the marketing strategies and consumer behaviour?. Salud Ciencia Y Tecnología - Serie De Conferencias, 3, 896. DOI: 10.56294/sctconf2024896

Ljepava, N. (2022). Ai-enabled marketing solutions in marketing decision making: ai application in different stages of marketing process. Tem Journal, 1308-1315. https://doi.org/DOI: 10.18421/tem113-40

Mandal, P. (2018). Marketing information and marketing intelligence: Roles in generating customer insights. *International Journal of Business Forecasting and Marketing Intelligence*, 4(3), 311. DOI: 10.1504/IJBFMI.2018.092786

Mao, Y. (2023). Current state and future development of artificial intelligence in marketing. *Applied and Computational Engineering*, 6(1), 536–541. DOI: 10.54254/2755-2721/6/20230884

Nasution, S., Andini, G., Prawira, Y., & Azzahra, D. (2019). *Marketing strategy analysis of nano tea product based on mangosteen peel (gracinia mangostana) to promote functional foods industry*. Indonesian Journal of Business and Entrepreneurship., DOI: 10.17358/ijbe.5.3.263

Noranee, S. and Othman, A. (2023). Understanding consumer sentiments: exploring the role of artificial intelligence in marketing. Jmm17 Jurnal Ilmu Ekonomi Dan Manajemen, 10(1), 15-23. DOI: 10.30996/jmm17.v10i1.8690

Ntapiapis, N. (2023). Artificial intelligence in digital marketing: Descriptive analysis of companies' artificial intelligence strategies with random sampling. *Etkileşim*, 6(12), 368–387. DOI: 10.32739/etkilesim.2023.6.12.226

Ogundipe, D. (2024). Ai and product management: A theoretical overview from idea to market. *International Journal of Management & Entrepreneurship Research*, 6(3), 950–969. DOI: 10.51594/ijmer.v6i3.965

Rosário, A. (2021). Research-based guidelines for marketing information systems. *International Journal of Business Strategy and Automation*, 2(1), 1–16. DOI: 10.4018/IJBSA.20210101.oa1

S.V., N. (. (2023). Exploring the synergy: Integrating machine learning algorithms and human expertise in a hybrid learning model for enhanced marketing strategies. *The Review of Contemporary Scientific and Academic Studies*, 3(12). Advance online publication. DOI: 10.55454/rcsas.3.12.2023.003

Weng, W. (2021). Effect of internet of things on marketing intelligence and business strategy: An organizational capability perspective. *International Journal of Electronic Commerce Studies*, 12(2), 209. DOI: 10.7903/ijecs.1906

Wu, Y. (2022). Machine learning approaches for retail bank marketing practice. *BCP Business & Management*, 23, 931–937. DOI: 10.54691/bcpbm.v23i.1475

Yan, J. (2023). Prediction of consumer behavior based on machine learning algorithm.. https://doi.org/DOI: 10.4108/eai.26-5-2023.2334304

Yau, K., Saad, N., & Chong, Y. (2021). Artificial intelligence marketing (aim) for enhancing customer relationships. *Applied Sciences (Basel, Switzerland)*, 11(18), 8562. DOI: 10.3390/app11188562

Chapter 6
Accelerating the Development of New Products and Services With AI-Enabled Innovation Management

Mohit Yadav
https://orcid.org/0000-0002-9341-2527
O.P. Jindal Global University, India

Ajay Chandel
https://orcid.org/0000-0002-4585-6406
Lovely Professional University, India

Rohit
https://orcid.org/0009-0004-1796-5252
Gulf Medical University, UAE

ABSTRACT

This chapter explores the role of Artificial Intelligence (AI) in innovation management, focusing on its potential to accelerate the development of new products and services. It examines how AI technologies, including machine learning, natural language processing, and generative design, transform each stage of the innovation lifecycle—from idea generation to market introduction. The chapter also addresses key challenges such as ethical considerations, data quality, and integration issues, offering strategic recommendations for effective AI implementation. Future trends, including advanced AI capabilities, integration with emerging technologies, and

DOI: 10.4018/979-8-3373-0219-5.ch006

ethical AI practices, are discussed to provide a forward-looking perspective. By leveraging AI, organizations can enhance decision-making, improve efficiency, and drive successful innovation. This chapter aims to equip readers with insights and strategies to harness AI effectively in their innovation processes.

INTRODUCTION

In the fast-moving and competitive environment in which businesses operate today, rapid development and time-to-market remain key to maintaining any viable competitive advantage regarding new products or services. This is where AI is currently a force of disruption-creating new tools and techniques that further accelerate the process of innovation. AI-enabled Innovation Management applies advanced technologies that enhance, from ideation to market launch, everything for products under development (Abedin, 2021).

The heart of AI is to make innovation more data-driven, nurturing the ability to make sense of volumes of data more rapidly and accurately than ever before. By doing so, businesses can gain insight into emerging trends, better anticipate consumer needs, and develop informed product-related decisions (Ali, 2023). But it doesn't stop at data analytics-everything from automated design processes to predictive modeling and optimized testing procedures is encapsulated in a smoother, more effective innovation lifecycle.

AI applications in innovation management are not only technological developments but also strategic imperatives. In brief, it basically redefines how organizations embrace problems, creativity, and decision-making. Actually, by capitalizing on AI, an organization can speed up not just the development of new offerings but also its general strategic agility and responsiveness to market demands. The section below shows how AI makes this transformation possible, the benefits accrued, and considerations necessary on the part of organizations to realize its full potential in driving innovation (Fang, 2023).

AI-DRIVEN INNOVATION MANAGEMENT

AI-enabled innovation management means radical changes in the way organizations approach new product and service development. Basically, the idea here is to embed advanced artificial intelligence technologies into different stages of the innovation process to enhance efficiency, effectiveness, and creativeness (Hasan et al., 2021). Understanding the full impact of AI on innovation management requires taking a closer look at both the elements of AI technologies driving this change and their key applications.

Definition and Scope

Innovation management through AI can be simply defined as a strategic use of the technologies of artificial intelligence in a way that accelerates and enables the creation, development, and delivery of new products and services. In using this approach, AI amplifies its capabilities in data analysis, automation, and generating insights that inform decision-making and innovation strategy (Hou et al., 2021). The scope involved in AI-enabled innovation management encompasses activities such as idea generation, concept development, prototyping, testing, and market introduction.

KEY AI TECHNOLOGIES AND THEIR RELEVANCE

Several AI technologies play a critical role in enabling and enhancing innovation management: and enhancements:

1. **Machine Learning:** It generally consists of analysis of past data, drawing out patterns, and then making predictions or recommendations. In innovation management, machine learning can be utilized for market trend forecasts, consumer preferences, or to predict which factors may lead to the success of a new product. A machine learning model can learn from vast data to help an organization envision changes in advance and reshape its strategy to suit emerging demands (Arboretti et al., 2022).
2. **Natural Language Processing:** It makes machines capable of understanding, interpreting, and generating human language. In innovation management, its application would be realized in analyzing customer feedback, going through industry reports, and mining social media for insights. The technology assists an organization in better understanding the needs and preferences of consumers, and thus, innovation is more focused and relevant (Just, 2024).
3. **Computer Vision:** This is an art of providing vision to the computer to interpret the world. Innovation management has applied it by automating images and video analysis for product design and quality control, respectively (Chowdhary et al., 2022). It is able to carry out checks in prototype defects, aesthetics of designs, and give suggestions on how to improve the user experience based on the visual response.

4. **Predictive Analytics:** Predictive analytics are the methods that calculate the occurrence of future outcomes based on statistical algorithms and machine learning techniques applied to data from the past. For innovation management, predictive analytics can enable an organization to model various scenarios and outcomes pertaining to the potential success of new products and services. It allows better decision-making and management of risks (Lehrer et al., 2018).
5. **Generative Design:** Generative design uses AI in rapidly exploring a large numbers of design options and coming up with an optimized solution based on key criteria. This technology will allow product developers to generate several design options, letting the engineers and designers select those that look most promising at optimal performance and cost. This accelerates the design process while boosting creativity (Cheng, 2023).

However, this understanding of AI technologies, when combined with the relevance thereof to innovation management, will truly facilitate organizations in exploiting such for the good of innovation. This is because artificial intelligence innovates, by its very nature, on a much more data-driven and automated basis, accelerating the time-to-market and increasing the effectiveness within the whole development process (Karamthulla et al., 2024). Because the field is at constant development, the role of AI technologies in innovation management will keep growing. This opens even wider possibilities for organizations to keep pace with an ever-changing market.

AI IN THE INNOVATION LIFECYCLE

Artificial intelligence greatly impacts the innovation lifecycle, particularly in the areas of idea generation, concept development, and time-to-market. Integrating AI technologies at every step of this process enables an organization to make processes more efficient, enhance the quality of decision-making, and bring products and services to market faster. We consider below various ways in which AI contributes to each phase of the innovation lifecycle.

Idea Generation

First, this stage of the innovation life cycle concerns the creation and development of ideas and concepts. AI technologies at this stage can assist in providing creativity-enhancement tools and in the identification of promising opportunities. Intelligent algorithms, powered by NLP and ML, will analyze huge amounts of data from a wide variety of sources, including market trends, consumer feedback, and competitive intelligence (Khadka, 2023).

NLP can filter social media conversations, customer reviews, and industry reports for emerging trends and consumer needs. ML models analyze historical data to find patterns in predicting future demands. AI-driven ideation platforms facilitate brainstorming sessions through innovative ideas presented via data-driven insights. Each of these technologies, therefore, enables organizations to identify and prioritize high-potential ideas with much better ease and sets the scene for successful innovation (Konina, 2024).

Concept Development

Concept development is the next stage after idea generation; it refines and remodels primary ideas into workable concepts. AI amplifies this stage in multiple ways, including generative design and simulation. Generative design uses AI algorithms to investigate a huge space of design options and returns with an optimal solution that meets certain criteria in performance, cost, and material use. The process allows designers and engineers to consider various design options and select the most effective ones.

Predictive analytics further scope into the concept development to identify how successful different concepts will be. The AI models will, based on historical trends, simulate different scenarios and outcomes that show the viability and market potential of each concept. In this respect, the organization will adopt data-driven decisions to minimize the chances of investing in non-viable concepts (Kuzior et al., 2023).

Product Development

The product development stage is where refined concepts are brought into being as tangible products. AI develops this stage greatly, with automation and optimization including advanced testing. Design tools automate the development process by generating detailed specifications, creating prototypes, and iterating designs with real-time feedback through the use of AI (Liu, 2022).

AI-powered optimization algorithms enhance product functionality by analyzing data generated from simulation and testing. Machine learning models, for instance, can predict the impact of various design changes on product functionality to make rapid changes towards improving the products. These AI technologies automate quality control processes, such as computer vision used in the inspection of defects in prototypes with high accuracy (Me.mon et al., 2022)

Market Introduction

The final stage of the innovation lifecycle is market introduction, where new products are launched and made available to consumers. AI strongly intervenes in this phase by optimizing marketing strategies, personalizing customer experiences, and analyzing market performance.

AI marketing tools capitalize on consumer information to build focused campaigns and allow improvement strategies in promotions. Machine learning algorithms can enable a company to target a desired audience, predict the behavior of its customers, and suggest what personalized content should be implemented for further efficiencies in marketing. Additionally, AI monitors market performance and collects customer feedback in real time, thus providing invaluable insight toward continuous product improvements and future innovations (Mirzani, 2024).

In all, AI's integration into the innovation lifecycle offers some key benefits: it accelerates development timelines, enhances decision-making, and improves readiness for the market. Applying AI technologies in every step of innovation will drive effective and efficient product development processes for greater marketplace success.

CHALLENGES AND CONSIDERATIONS

While AI opens great avenues for managing innovation, several challenges and concerns that need to be addressed equally well by organizations arise. Being cognizant of these challenges and how to sail through them will become vital in leveraging AI effectively to ensure success within the innovation process (Nafizah et al., 2023).

Ethical and Privacy Concerns

One of the major areas of concern with AI in innovation management has to do with the issue of ethics involved in its application. Most AI systems require enormous amounts of data, which even include sensitive and personal information. Ensuring data privacy and security is paramount for gaining consumer trust and ensuring that organizations are in compliance with regulations (Ogundipe, 2024).

Ethical considerations also concern the decision-making mechanisms that AI drives. Sometimes, algorithms reflect or amplify biases in the data they use for training, thus making their outcomes unfair or discriminatory. It is, therefore, important that the organizations develop measures that limit bias and ensure that AI systems are utilized responsibly and with ethics. This also involves the development of guidelines on the use of data, embedding transparency into AI decision-making processes, and regular auditing of the AI systems to ensure fairness and accuracy (Raza et al., 2024).

Issues of Data Quality and Integration

AI technologies are greatly dependent on good data quality and its integration. Most AI systems work effectively with huge amounts of good-quality data; incomplete, inexact, or biased input data tends to strongly impact the performance of AI systems. Ensuring data quality involves rigorous processes of data collection, cleaning, and validation to ensure accuracy and reliability.

Another challenge is integrating the AI systems into the already existing data infrastructure. Most organizations have pieces of data fragmented across many points, with aged systems that may not support the new AI technologies. This calls for careful planning of integration, including data integration tools and strategies that can consolidate and harmonize data across diverse platforms. It is only when these integrations are addressed that full benefits of AI can be realized in managing innovation (Shaikh et al., 2021).

Balancing Human and Artificial Intelligence Contributions

While AI can amplify many facets of the innovation lifecycle, this contribution needs to be balanced by human expertise. AI systems are amazingly powerful tools but ultimately lack the nuanced understanding, creativity, and contextual knowledge provided by most human innovators. The right balance can thus be struck by recognizing complementary roles between AI and human input, making sure that AI supports and does not replace the power of human creativity and decision-making (Sjödin et al., 2021).

In this regard, collaboration between the AI systems and human teams needs to be fostered, where the role of AI is to perform repetitive tasks, analyze data, and develop insights, leaving strategic thinking, creative problem-solving, and complex decision-making to the innovators. In this way, a balanced approach will maintain both AI and human contributions optimally based on their respective strengths.

Change Management and Adoption

Successful integration of AI into innovation management is also highly dependent on successful change management strategies. Implementation of AI technologies often results in far-reaching changes in organizational processes and workflows, which may also meet with resistance from within. Overcoming this resistance includes clearly communicating the benefits of AI, training and supporting employees to adapt to new technologies, and importantly, integrating them into the process of implementation (Sood et al., 2021).

The way to go about managing the change is to create an environment that is innovative and embraces technology. This will entail creating an environment of continuous learning and adaptive mindset, experimenting with artificial intelligence tools, recognition, and rewarding successful AI-driven initiatives. Such a well-managed transition may allow smoother adaption and integration of AI technologies within the organization.

Regulatory and Compliance Issues

AI technologies are facing an ever-evolving landscape of regulations and compliance requirements. It becomes relevant for any organization using AI to be properly informed about the promulgation of relevant laws and regulations with regard to the use of AI, data protection, and intellectual property. This is very important in order to stay with confidence inside these regulations so as not to be faced with legal problems and to assure responsible use of AI (Suhartanto et al., 2021).

Regulatory frameworks might also vary between regions and industries, and an organization should be adept at working through the legal institutional ecology. The issues of regulatory change in this regard can be addressed to allow organizations to maintain their AI practices in concert with relevant laws and standards. It would also allow for proactive interface with regulatory bodies through industry discussions and contribute toward shaping and understanding future regulations (Tekic & Füller, 2023).

While AI has a lot of potential in innovation management, attentions to issues and challenges are compulsorily required for effective implementations. In order to have maximum benefits through AI, an organization can take proactive actions in managing ethical issues, quality data, strategic human, and artificial intelligence contribution, as well as changing and regulatory issues with minimization of potential risks and/or obstacles (Tulcanaza-Prieto et al., 2023).

CASE STUDIES

Case Study 1: "AI-Driven Product Innovation at TechNova"

Location: San Francisco, California, USA

One such technology company based in San Francisco is TechNova. The company successfully integrated AI at every juncture of the product innovation process. Machine learning algorithms, sourced market trends and consumer behavior for analysis, helped them in higher accuracy for predicting emerging demands. The results are that TechNova can now hasten up the prototyping phase by using AI-driven generative design tools, thereby reducing product time-to-market. That has resulted in reducing development time by 30% and increasing the success rates of products by 25%. The integration of AI optimized not only the innovation processes at TechNova but also provided valuable insights that informed strategic decision-making.

Case Study 2: "Enhancing Customer Experience with AI at RetailGenius"

Location: London, United Kingdom

RetailGenius is one of the leading retail chains in London, and it leveraged AI to reimagine how they manage customer experience. It implemented NLP to gain insights from customer feedback emanating from different channels such as social media and reviews. Such insights have been used in devising personalized marketing strategies and product recommendations. Besides that, AI-powered chatbots were implemented to answer the inquiries of customers more quickly and efficiently, therefore improving customer response times and satisfaction. In the aftermath of AI technology implementation, RetailGenius saw a 20% increase in customer retention and a 15% hike in sales. The case testifies to an important role AI plays in driving better customer experiences and business growth.

Case Study 3: "AI-Powered Design Automation at InnovateX"

Location: Berlin, Germany

Adoption of AI-driven design automation streamlined the product development process at InnovateX, a Berlin-based design and engineering firm. Application of generative design algorithms allowed InnovateX to generate a vast number of design alternatives and automatically optimize solutions to predefined performance criteria. As a result of this AI-enabled approach, the design cycle times were reduced by up to 40%, with improved design efficiency. The impact brought in by this AI technology in their company positively enhanced collaboration within the design teams as it provided them with one place where they could share and refine ideas. InnovateX's experience with AI in automating design is a case in point about how technology can boost creativity and operational efficiency in product development.

Case Study 4: "AI-Enhanced Market Analysis at PharmaInsight"

Location: Tokyo, Japan

Tokyo-based pharmaceutical firm PharmaInsight collaborates with AI on advanced market analytics and drug development. Machine learning models were applied at the company to analyze clinical trial data for prediction of efficacy, which really accelerated the process of drug development. Identification of potential therapeutic areas was enabled by analyzing market trends using AI tools. This data-driven approach resulted in a 50% reduction in time to market entry and a significant improvement in the precision of forecasts about future market performance. AI will further enhance PharmaInsight's competitive edge in the pharmaceutical industry because better and timely decisions could be made.

Joint Analysis

Together, these case studies illustrate the transformative power of AI in everything from industry to application. All these organizations employed AI technologies to solve particular business problems, which in turn allowed them to improve many aspects of their overall processes of innovation (Tunio et al., 2021).

The use of machine learning and generative design tools at TechNova underlines AI's capability for accelerated product development and responsiveness to the market. Deployment of NLP and AI chatbots by RetailGenius proves the technology works in personalization of experiences of customers and increases sales. InnovateX's experience with design automation underlines AI's potential to amplify creativity and make the design process seamless. Application of machine learning in market analysis and drug development at PharmaInsight has shown the role AI could play in optimizing even the most intricate processes and shaving time off the route to market (Verganti et al., 2020).

Taken cumulatively, these cases demonstrate how themes of improved efficiencies, acceleration in the development cycles, and better decisions provide proof that this is a shining jewel. Artificial intelligence is now an integral part of compelling innovation and driving business objectives through insight and automation from a large dataset analysis. It shows that such strategic integration can have implications for operational and competitive advantage and provides valuable lessons for organizations on leveraging AI to manage innovation.

FUTURE TRENDS

The face of AI in innovation management is constantly changing, and the new technologies coming forth, as well as trends, are likely to further disrupt how organizations develop and manage new products and services. One can't escape understanding these future trends if one aims to obtain favorable performance at the marketplace and thereby wants to exploit AI in the most telling manner possible. We review here some major future trends that are likely to shape AI-enabled innovation management over the next few years (Yams et al., 2020).

Advanced Generative AI and Design Automation

The term generative AI has emerged to describe the use of machine learning algorithms to create content and solutions. This technology is likely to change product design and development in the future. In the near future, generative AI will be even more powerful and able to enable sophisticated and creative design automation. The next generation of AI-based design systems will be capable of producing very complex design options, simulated real-world performance, and optimization for a wider set of criteria (Marion, et al., 2023).

Basically, generative AI will evolve with each passing day in knowledge integration across multiple disciplines and enable creative solutions to a wide range of challenges. In such a scenario, it is also most expected that prototyping will be much quicker, the design process far smoother, and products highly customized and close to individual consumer needs.

Integration of AI with Emerging Technologies

Such integration with other emerging technologies-blockchain, quantum computing, and the Internet of Things-will go a long way in further driving innovation management. Blockchain technology can provide transparency in data sharing and security-clearance facilitation required in AI-driven processes for innovation. By applying blockchain, organizations can ensure the integrity of data used in AI models and drive more collaborative efforts at innovation (Karamthulla et al., 2024).

Quantum computing will also affect AI, given the great power in solving complex problems at unprecedented speeds. This might give AI a quantum leap in terms of processing power and algorithmic capabilities, enabling more complex data analysis and optimization. In like manner, integrations with IoT will enable better real-time monitoring and data intake for valuable insights into innovation and product development.

AI Driven Personalization and Customer Experience

Personalization will also remain one of the main trends in AI-powered innovation management. Advanced AI algorithms will increasingly pay more attention to the delivery of highly personalized customer experiences by analyzing very detailed consumer data and predicting the preferences of each individual. The result of such a tendency will be the creation of products and services that correspond to the specific needs and desires of each particular customer (Bhuiyan, 2024).

AI-powered personalization will go beyond mere marketing into the very design of the product, functionalities, and user experience. With AI, companies can build tailored solutions that can fit into or respond to user behavior and preferences dynamically in real time, promoting heightened satisfaction and loyalty from the customer base.

Ethical AI and Responsible Innovation

As AI becomes more integral to the management of innovation, there will be increasing focus on ethical AI and responsible innovation. Organizations will have to take on various issues that involve data privacy, algorithmic bias, and transparency regarding the uses that are made of AI systems so they may be ethical and responsible. Likely future trends include the formulation of guidelines and best practices concerning how AI use can be made more ethical, and also greater regulation (Buhmann & Fieseler, 2021).

Responsible innovation would have to address ethical concerns but also consider the greater good that AI technologies may contribute to society. Organizations will have to strike a balance between technological advancement and social responsibility in ensuring that AI-driven innovations create a positive view of society and are not perpetrating inequalities that may already exist.

AI-augmented collaboration and crowdsourcing

In the future, AI in innovation management will make increasing use of collaboration and crowdsourcing platforms that are enhanced through AI. Connecting innovators, researchers, and stakeholders across diverse disciplines and geographical locations, AI technologies will further facilitate effective collaboration. Such platforms will utilize AI in matching collaborators to the best fit based on expertise, interests, and project needs (Gimpel et al., 2023).

The AI-enabled crowdsourcing will continue to become even more sophisticated, for the entities are able to draw upon ideas and solutions emanating from a global pool of ideas and talent. AI will be one mechanism through which organizations sift and evaluate contributions emanating from crowdsourced initiatives. This makes sure that the valuable insights that emanate from such processes are identified and leveraged in a way beneficial to driving innovation.

Continuous Learning and Adaptive Systems

The continuous learning and adaptive power of AI systems will be more implemented within innovation management. Future developments of AI systems will be made in a way that they continuously learn and evolve by acquiring new data and feedback. This will allow AI to be adapted to the emergence of new market conditions, changes in consumer preference, and the latest technological advancements. This would give organizations agile and responsive innovation processes.

Adaptive AI systems will continuously allow product development and improvements in strategies of innovation that enable the organization to stay competitive and responsive in dynamic markets (Hasan et al., 2021).

The generative AI, integration with emerging technologies, enhanced personalization, ethical considerations, collaborative platforms, and continuous learning in sum have set the trend for the future of AI in innovation management. It is through their understanding of these emerging trends and effective integration into innovation strategies that organizations would be poised to take full advantage of AI in driving successful and impactful innovation.

STRATEGIC RECOMMENDATIONS

AI embedding into innovation management could be effectively done only by a well-planned strategy concerning technological and organizational aspects. In order to maximize benefits that can be gained from AI, which again makes sure organizations apply the technology effectively, here are strategic recommendations that organizations must consider:

Develop an Explicit AI Strategy

A comprehensive AI strategy has to be laid out with the purpose of aligning AI initiatives towards organizational goals and objectives of innovation. Clearly define where exactly AI interventions can bring value in the ideation lifecycle, concept development, or product testing. Establish clear objectives of each AI initiative with expected outcomes, performance metrics, and timelines (Ali, 2023).

Engage leadership, R&D teams, and business units in the strategy development process to ensure alignment and support. Periodically revisit the AI strategy with regard to evolving technological advancements and market conditions.

Invest in Data Quality and Infrastructure

First, one needs high-quality data for the deployment of really effective AI systems. Strong data management practices support data quality and completeness, contributing to relevance for AI applications. This would call for strong data collection, cleaning, and validation (Hou et al., 2021).

Besides, develop a data infrastructure to increase with the implementations of AI technologies. This can include upgrading existing systems, adopting data integration tools, and ensuring interoperability among various data sources and the AI platform. A sound database will result in higher performance and reliability of innovation processes driven by AI.

Foster Innovation and Adaptation Culture

The way to successfully integrate AI is by cultivating a culture supportive of innovation and technology. Second, nurture a culture of experimentation and continuous improvement-a culture in which people try new AI tools and methodologies and are eager to find better ways of doing things. Provide training and resources so that your employees understand how AI technologies work and can apply them effectively in their jobs (Khadka, 2023).

Encourage collaboration and knowledge sharing across functions to leverage diverse perspectives and expertise. Recognize and reward innovative efforts and successful AI-driven initiatives that drive teams and reaffirm the role of AI in driving innovation.

Ethical AI Practices

Innovation management needs to be done with AI, considering ethical issues. Explain in detail and follow ethical guidelines for the best practice in using AI: data privacy, algorithmic transparency, and bias mitigation. Design a system for regular auditing of AI to ensure that it is fair and responsible.

Employ external consultants in the field of ethics and the law to keep up to date with the evolving nature of both ethical practices and laws. Create an organizational culture around the responsible use of AI and the impact that innovations made with AI have on society (Kuzior et al., 2023).

Leverage AI for Smarter Decision-Making

Decision-making will increase manyfold in the future, using data-driven insights and predictive analytics provided by AI. Decision-support AI: seamlessly implement cutting-edge tools across various stages of the innovation life cycle, from market analysis and concept evaluation to design optimization and performance monitoring.

Avail the power of AI-driven dashboards and visualization tools to present insights in usable and actionable formats. Ensure that relevant training is imparted and support provided to decision-makers for interpreting the data churned out by AI and effectively bringing that into strategy formulation (Tulcanaza-Prieto et al., 2023).

Promote Agile and Iterative Approaches

Adopt agile and iterative approaches to manage innovation with AI's help in rapid prototyping, testing, and refinement. Deploy AI tools enabling fast iteratives and feedback loops that allow teams to test and refine ideas at an increasing rate.

Nourish flexibility and adaptability into the approach to innovation-to integrate AI insights into development processes with ease that keeps improving. This agility empowers organizations with superior responses to emerging market conditions and changes in customer preferences (Suhartanto et al., 2021).

Collaborate with AI Technology Providers

Outsource from AI technology providers at the leading edge so as to provide access to the crucial tools and expertise. Work with vendors, research institutions, and technology partners to recognize state-of-the-art developments in AI plus the best practices (Sjödin et al., 2021).

Rate potential partners based on experience, technology being offered, and success stories onboarded. Good relations with AI providers ensure that your company has smooth knowledge transfer, tech support, and access to innovative solutions fitting the needs of your organization.

Monitor and Measure AI Impact

Continuously monitor and measure the impact of AI initiatives on innovation management outcomes. Key performance indicators will be kept track of in order to measure the effectiveness of different applications of AI in terms of time to market for strategic goals, improving product quality, or even enhanced customer satisfaction.

Assessment of AI system performance should be informed by data and feedback. Use the insight to make better decisions about where future investments and improvements would yield the best returns. Continuously monitor the value delivered by AI and revise the strategy as necessary toward optimization (Tunio et al., 2021).

The approach of implementing AI within innovation management would need to be strategic, considering technological, data, culture, ethics, decision-making, agility, partnerships, and the measurements of its impact. Recommendations would support the capability of an organization to integrate the strategies of AI for efficient innovation processes in driving successful products to the market and keeping competitors at bay.

IMPLICATIONS

Practical Implications

There are a number of practical implications associated with the integration of AI within innovation management. First, AI has the power to significantly accelerate innovation through automation of routine activities, enhanced analytics of information, and speeding up decision-making processes. This, in turn, leads to quicker development cycles and the ability to take products to the market much more effectively. Practical application of AI in forms like machine learning models for predictive analytics, and generative design tools, lets an organization study more design alternatives and optimize those solutions by real-world data in real time. While implementation of AI technologies requires investments in infrastructure and expertise, advantages gained from reduction in time-to-market and improvement in the quality of products can well outweigh such costs. There are also practical considerations or integration of AI with heritage systems and processes for seamless operations to maximize value from AI investments.

Managerial Implications

From the management perspective, the use of AI in managing innovation requires changing organizational leadership and strategies. For example, it is important for managers to develop a clear strategy for AI that coincides with organizational objectives and innovation goals by understanding where the implementation of AI will have maximum benefit and optimizing resources. The managers have to create an environment that welcomes technology and innovation. Teams are encouraged to welcome AI tools and inject them into operations. Here, effective change management would pay dividends when resistance to any change is handled effectively, and the transition is smooth. For this, training and upskilling in employees who will be working with AI technologies is crucial for exploiting their full potential. In addition, there is a need for managers to manage AI ethics by ensuring that systems are deployed in a responsible way and that data privacy and security are upheld.

Societal Implications

The implications of AI on society regarding innovation management are far-reaching and multi-dimensional. AI technologies can be a driver for serious advancements in different fields, leading to improved goods and services which the consumer benefits from. At the same time, this raises a lot of concerns with regard to general job displacement and changing work nature. With AI automating tasks and processes, some job roles may just become history, hence creating the need for reskilling and upskilling employees for new roles that have been and are being propelled by advancements in AI (Tulcanaza-Prieto et al., 2023). Furthermore, AI could widen existing inequalities if not implemented equitably. Any development of AI technologies should be available and useful to all segments of society, which is an important attribute of truly inclusive and non-discriminatory technology. Other impacts of AI in society include requirements for transparency and accountability within the practice of AI that would gain the public's trust on issues of privacy and bias as relates to AI.

Ethical Implications

Ethical considerations are central in AI deployment within the innovation management context. AI has always raised important questions about data privacy, bias in algorithms, and the transparency of decision-making processes. Ethics guidelines are thus in order in the use of AI that organizations are assured of data being collected and applied responsibly, and that AI systems do not have any bias that would lead to results that discriminate against certain groups (Verganti et al., 2020). Transparency in AI decision-making processes instills trust and accountability (Nafizah et al., 2023). Moreover, every organization ought to be concerned with the greater social consequences of their AI technologies, such as implications for human rights and social justice. Addressing ethical issues is a continuous process that involves monitoring and auditing AI systems, insight into various stakeholder perspectives, and keeping pace with regulatory standards and best practices. Ethical considerations assure organizations that their AI-driven innovations are appropriate and responsible (Yams et al., 2020).

CONCLUSION

This is an evolutionary turn in integrating AI into innovation management, one that promises to finally accelerate the development of new products and services by orders of magnitude. Advanced AI technologies can assist organizations in managing the life cycle of innovations more efficiently, developing better decision-making and driving processes with far greater efficiency and creativity. From idea generation and concept development to product testing and market introduction, AI holds great potential for changing the way organizations approach and execute innovation.

The benefits accruing from AI in managing innovations are immense and relate to improved speed-to-market, enhanced product quality, and more personalized experiences for customers. These benefits, however, can be realized by considering an approach that is thoughtful of the challenges associated with AI, such as ethical considerations, data quality, and balancing human and AI contributions. Strategic recommendations that include developing a clear AI strategy, investing in data infrastructure, fostering a culture of innovation, and ensuring ethical practices form the backbone of successful AI integration.

The trends for the future, while including more sophisticated generative AI, integration with emergent technologies, and ethical considerations in AI practices, will continue to play a leading role in shaping the future of innovation management. The organizations that not only keep their finger on the pulse but also make changes in strategy accordingly are the ones which would be in the position to make full use of AI for effective and meaningful innovation.

In a nutshell, AI provides a potent tool for improving innovation management, but the successful implementation thereof is founded on addressing associated challenges and strategic practices. By thinking about and approaching AI in both thoughtful and strategic ways, organizations have the ability not only to quicken their processes of innovation but also to remain competitive within the ever-evolving marketplace.

REFERENCES

Abedin, B. (2021). Managing the tension between opposing effects of explainability of artificial intelligence: A contingency theory perspective. *Internet Research*, 32(2), 425–453. DOI: 10.1108/INTR-05-2020-0300

Ali, J. (2023). *AI-driven software engineering. AEI, 3(1).* None-None., DOI: 10.54254/2977-3903/3/2023030

Arboretti, R., Ceccato, R., Pegoraro, L., & Salmaso, L. (2022). Design of experiments and machine learning for product innovation: A systematic literature review. *Quality and Reliability Engineering International*, 38(2), 1131–1156. DOI: 10.1002/qre.3025

Bhuiyan, M. S. (2024). The role of AI-enhanced personalization in customer experiences. *Journal of Computer Science and Technology Studies*, 6(1), 162–169. DOI: 10.32996/jcsts.2024.6.1.17

Buhmann, A., & Fieseler, C. (2021). Towards a deliberative framework for responsible innovation in artificial intelligence. *Technology in Society*, 64, 101475. DOI: 10.1016/j.techsoc.2020.101475

Cheng, S. H. (2023). Impact of generative artificial intelligence on footwear design concept and ideation. *Engineering Proceedings*, 55(1), 32.

Chowdhary, C. L., Reddy, G. T., & Parameshachari, B. D. (2022). *Computer vision and recognition systems: Research innovations and trends*. Apple Academic Press. DOI: 10.1201/9781003180593

Fang, J. (2023). Research on the design of business models and transformation management of new entrepreneurial ventures driven by artificial intelligence. *BCP Business & Management*, 49, 36–41. DOI: 10.54691/bcpbm.v49i.5383

Gimpel, H., Graf-Seyfried, V., Laubacher, R., & Meindl, O. (2023). Towards artificial intelligence augmenting facilitation: AI affordances in macro-task crowdsourcing. *Group Decision and Negotiation*, 32(1), 75–124. DOI: 10.1007/s10726-022-09801-1 PMID: 36643885

Hasan, R., Shams, S., & Rahman, M. (2021). Consumer trust and perceived risk for voice-controlled artificial intelligence: The case of Siri. *Journal of Business Research*, 131, 591–597. DOI: 10.1016/j.jbusres.2020.12.012

Hou, J., Yao, Y., Hameed, J., Kamran, H., Nawaz, M., Aqdas, R., ... & Patwary, A. (2021). The role of artificial and nonartificial intelligence in the new product success with moderating role of new product innovation: A case of manufacturing companies in China. *Complexity, 2021*(1). https://doi.org/DOI: 10.1155/2021/8891298

Just, J. (2024). Natural language processing for innovation search–Reviewing an emerging non-human innovation intermediary. *Technovation*, 129, 102883. DOI: 10.1016/j.technovation.2023.102883

Karamthulla, M. J., Muthusubramanian, M., Tadimarri, A., & Tillu, R. (2024). Navigating the future: AI-driven project management in the digital era. *International Journal for Multidisciplinary Research*, 6(2), 1–11. DOI: 10.36948/ijfmr.2024.v06i02.15295

Khadka, S., Rai, B., & Khadka, A. K. (2023). AI-driven customization in financial services: Implications for social innovation in Nepal. *NCC Journal*, 8(1), 1–11. DOI: 10.3126/nccj.v8i1.63128

Konina, O. (2024). Improving business innovation management through artificial intelligence. *J. Tr.Chal. Art. Intell.*, 1(1), 21–32. DOI: 10.61552/JAI.2024.01.003

Kuzior, A., Sira, M., & Brożek, P. (2023). Use of artificial intelligence in terms of open innovation process and management. *Sustainability (Basel)*, 15(9), 7205. DOI: 10.3390/su15097205

Lehrer, C., Wieneke, A., Vom Brocke, J., Jung, R., & Seidel, S. (2018). How big data analytics enables service innovation: Materiality, affordance, and the individualization of service. *Journal of Management Information Systems*, 35(2), 424–460. DOI: 10.1080/07421222.2018.1451953

Liu, Q. (2022). Analysis of collaborative driving effect of artificial intelligence on knowledge innovation management. *Scientific Programming*, 2022, 1–8. DOI: 10.1155/2022/8223724

Marion, T. J., Moghaddam, M., Ciuccarelli, P., & Wang, L. (2023). AI for user-centered new product development: From large-scale need elicitation to generative design. In *The PDMA Handbook on Innovation and New Product Development.*

Memon, A. B., Meyer, K., & Tunio, M. N. (2022). Toward collaborative networking among innovation laboratories: A conceptual framework. *International Journal of Innovation Science*, 14(2), 282–301. DOI: 10.1108/IJIS-04-2021-0069

Mirzani, Y. (2024). Artificial intelligence and innovation management: Transformative forces shaping organizational creativity. *Epra International Journal of Multidisciplinary Research (IJMR),* 511-518. https://doi.org/DOI: 10.36713/epra16272

Nafizah, U., Roper, S., & Mole, K. (2023). Estimating the innovation benefits of first-mover and second-mover strategies when micro-businesses adopt artificial intelligence and machine learning. *Small Business Economics*, 62(1), 411–434. DOI: 10.1007/s11187-023-00779-x

Ogundipe, D. (2024). AI and product management: A theoretical overview from idea to market. *International Journal of Management & Entrepreneurship Research*, 6(3), 950–969. DOI: 10.51594/ijmer.v6i3.965

Raza, A., Tursoy, T., Seraj, M., Shaikh, E., & Ali, M. (2024). Impact of financial behavior and experience on financial literacy: A study of universities in Pakistan. *Innovation Economics Frontiers*, 27(1), 32–42. DOI: 10.36923/economa.v27i1.240

Shaikh, E., Tunio, M. N., & Qureshi, F. (2021). Finance and women's entrepreneurship in DETEs: A literature review. In *Entrepreneurial Finance* (pp. 191–209). Innovation and Development.

Sjödin, D., Parida, V., Palmié, M., & Wincent, J. (2021). How AI capabilities enable business model innovation: Scaling AI through co-evolutionary processes and feedback loops. *Journal of Business Research*, 134, 574–587. DOI: 10.1016/j.jbusres.2021.05.009

Sood, A., Sharma, R., & Bhardwaj, A. (2021). Artificial intelligence research in agriculture: A review. *Online Information Review*, 46(6), 1054–1075. DOI: 10.1108/OIR-10-2020-0448

Suhartanto, D., Syarief, M., Nugraha, A., Suhaeni, T., Masthura, A., & Amin, H. (2021). Millennial loyalty towards artificial intelligence-enabled mobile banking: Evidence from Indonesian Islamic banks. *Journal of Islamic Marketing*, 13(9), 1958–1972. DOI: 10.1108/JIMA-12-2020-0380

Tekic, Z., & Füller, J. (2023). Managing innovation in the era of AI. *Technology in Society*, 73, 102254. DOI: 10.1016/j.techsoc.2023.102254

Tulcanaza-Prieto, A., Cortez-Ordoñez, A., & Lee, C. (2023). Influence of customer perception factors on AI-enabled customer experience in the Ecuadorian banking environment. *Sustainability (Basel)*, 15(16), 12441. DOI: 10.3390/su151612441

Tunio, M. N., Yusrini, L., & Shoukat, G. (2021). Corporate social responsibility (CSR) in hotels in Austria, Pakistan, and Indonesia: Small and medium enterprise spillover of COVID-19. In *Handbook of Research on Entrepreneurship, Innovation, Sustainability, and ICTs in the Post-COVID-19 Era* (pp. 263-280). IGI Global.

Verganti, R., Vendraminelli, L., & Iansiti, M. (2020). Innovation and design in the age of artificial intelligence. *Journal of Product Innovation Management*, 37(3), 212–227. DOI: 10.1111/jpim.12523

Yams, N., Richardson, V., Shubina, G., Albrecht, S., & Gillblad, D. (2020). Integrated AI and innovation management: The beginning of a beautiful friendship. *Technology Innovation Management Review*, 10(11), 5–18. DOI: 10.22215/timreview/1399

Chapter 7

Artificial Intelligence as the New Face of Marketing Activites and Functions:

Theory, Concepts, Illustrations, and Implications

Muhammad Faisal Sultan
Khadim Ali Shah Bukhari Institute of Technology, Pakistan

Sadia Shaikh
Benazir Bhutto Shaheed University, Pakistan

Imamuddin Mahar
Institute of Business Management, Pakistan

Muhammad Nawaz Tunio
https://orcid.org/0000-0003-1376-5371
University of Sufism and Modern Sciences, Pakistan

ABSTRACT

Artificial Intelligence is the tool utilized by every organization and all of its functions to generate, synthesize, and analyze data. Marketing also has no exception in which AI can be used for the betterment of various activities and functions. However, the perceived level of risk may affect the use drastically. Therefore, this chapter has been written purposively to highlight the use of AI for marketing to make researchers, academicians, managers, and policy makers understand AI's role in improving

DOI: 10.4018/979-8-3373-0219-5.ch007

marketing efforts.

BACKGROUND

In recent times the size of data generated by machines and humans is out of humans' ability to absorb, understand and interpret to solve complex problems. However, Artificial Intelligence (AI) has the tendency to solve this problem. Especially on association with cloud-based applications & platform-based business models AI has the capability to increase automation and integration of business process. Hence, through using easy to access technology AI has the capability to produce data that is beyond the control of any statistical method supplementing ease and significance for multiple stakeholders (Cambell et al., 2020). AI is one of the most important technologies that transformed our daily life. In fact, it is actively involved in securing our gadgets and cell phones to optimize our decision making. In fact, by 2030 AI has the potential to optimize world GDP by 14% but major beneficiaries will be countries like USA and China. In recent times AI is integrated to our daily lives through SMART-Phones and other forms of electronic gadgets etc. (Mesir, 2019)

INTRODUCTION

Initial studies predicted that in future AI will be used to influence marketing strategies including business models, customer service options and customer behavior etc. Therefore, it is legitimate to believe that AI will change the face of marketing. Similar has been highlighted by the survey from sales personnel which highlighted that AI tools will massively be integrated in marketing and related areas. However, the impact of AI on marketing activities is significantly beneficial in banking, consumer packaged goods, retail and travel (Davenport et al., 2020). Actually AI analyzes past patterns in order to predict the future in effective manner. The process is grounded in the integration of past emotions, reactions and purchase pattern in to mathematical equations that will optimize decision making not only for the customers but also for companies. Especially for companies decisions that are related with humans and their decision making are critically important. Companies who may use AI effectively to predict the behavior in appropriate way may not only earn financial benefits but also the reputation and goodwill to the firm. In fact, these services are now getting cheap and easy to use through online application termed as Amazon web service cloud. Through using these online applications firms are not required to invest aggressively in infrastructure, workforce and development of algorithms (Mesir, 2019).

However, among all the business function use of AI has the tendency to influence marketing activities in holistic way as AI may not only influence business modeling but also sales processes, servicing customers & consumers behavior etc. However, uses of AI are not free from questions and concerns related with data security and privacy. Hence there is a need of significant detailing to address the issue in a desired way. In fact, AI is also perceived as dangerous by Elon Musk who is one of the most well-known technologists who believed that AI may not fulfill all of its promises due to severe concerns associated with ethics and data privacy etc. (Davenport et al, 2021).

GRAY AREA & PROBLEM

The literature that is associating AI with marketing strategies is sparse and required to be aligned and improve to provide better business models in current and upcoming era (Davenport et al., 2020). Especially use of AI is especially beneficial for enhancing shopping experience through analyzing consumer's purchase pattern and methods of payments (Mesir, 2019). On the other side there are some serious issues of data privacy and security that are threatening the users of AI. However, marketing as a function must take lead to solve these forms of questions and queries as AI seems to be most beneficial for marketing and related activities (Davenport et al, 2021).

THEORETICAL UNDERPINNING:

Technological Acceptance Model (TAM) was proposed by Davis in the year 1986 during the Ph.D. from MIT Sloan School of Management. The model of TAM is based upon theory of reasoned action. However, TAM itself was the model that uses perceived usefulness and perceived ease of use as the main component of the research model. The model gained mass popularity due to its generalizability to different locations and different technologies etc. Hence TAM-2 was propped in the year 2000 that has the ability to explain perceived usefulness and intention to use through social influence and cognitive instrumental processes. However, introduction of TAM-3 in 2008 was to enrich understanding about informed managerial decision about any intervention for increased level of acceptance and better utilization of information technology (Nascimento et al., 2021 & Nascimento & Meirelles, 2022).

Hence, this study is based upon TAM-3 as this chapter elaborate use of AI for betterment of marketing activities and related functions. Thus this chapter actually used to define the use of AI for better marketing activities through informed decision making and better utilization of information technology.

LITERATURE REVIEW

Use of AI is highly useful for marketing functions. In fact studies conducted a decade ago are able to highlight multiple uses of AI for marketing (Martínez-López & Casillas, 2013). Hence it is not a point to be amazed that till 2019 several companies from developed world were leveraged with AI and (ML) Machine Learning (Cambell et al., 2020). In fact, AI can be used in strategies for segmentation, marketing analytics, messaging, personalization and predictive behaviors (Davenport et al., 2020). However, some of the marketing managers are still unaware of the scope and benefits that AI may provide to marketing. Although unawareness of managers cannot undermine the significance of AI for marketing function and related activities that is expected to reach $40 billion through use of technology. The postulate is valid as use of AI enables marketers to use big data into actionable strategies. In fact, AI has the tendency to assist marketers in identification of opportunities and also assist marketers in developing effective strategies in real time scenario. Studies also highlight use of AI for address multiple components that may leads to success of strategic marketing (Cambell et al., 2020).

REFERENCES

Campbell, C., Sands, S., Ferraro, C., Tsao, H. Y. J., & Mavrommatis, A. (2020). From data to action: How marketers can leverage AI. *Business Horizons*, 63(2), 227–243. DOI: 10.1016/j.bushor.2019.12.002

Davenport, T., Guha, A., Grewal, D., & Bressgott, T. (2020). How artificial intelligence will change the future of marketing. *Journal of the Academy of Marketing Science*, 48(1), 24–42. DOI: 10.1007/s11747-019-00696-0

Martínez-López, F. J., & Casillas, J. (2013). Artificial intelligence-based systems applied in industrial marketing: An historical overview, current and future insights. *Industrial Marketing Management*, 42(4), 489–495. DOI: 10.1016/j.indmarman.2013.03.001

Mesir, M. (2019). The role of artificial intelligence in decision making in small businesses. *Indian Journal of Science and Technology*, 12(18), 1–6. DOI: 10.17485/ijst/2019/v12i18/144586

Nascimento, A. M., de Melo, V. V., Queiroz, A. C. M., Brashear-Alejandro, T., & de Souza Meirelles, F. (2021). Artificial intelligence applied to small businesses: The use of automatic feature engineering and machine learning for more accurate planning. *Revista de Contabilidade e Organizações*, 15, 1–15.

Nascimento, A. M., & Meirelles, F. D. S. (2022). Factors Influencing the Adoption Intention of Artificial Intelligence in Small Businesses. In *Proceedings of* ISLA 2022, https://aisel.aisnet.org/isla2022/20

Chapter 8
Enhancing Marketing and Brand Communication With AI–Driven Content Creation

Sachin Raut
https://orcid.org/0000-0002-3808-1278
University of Agder, Norway

Ajay Chandel
https://orcid.org/0000-0002-4585-6406
Lovely Professional University, India

Shashank Mittal
O.P. Jindal Global University, India

ABSTRACT

The integration of artificial intelligence (AI) into content creation is revolutionizing marketing and brand communication. AI-driven tools now enable the generation of personalized, scalable, and dynamic content, transforming how businesses engage with audiences. This chapter explores the evolution of AI in content creation, from generative models to immersive technologies like augmented reality (AR) and virtual reality (VR). It examines the impact of AI on personalization, SEO optimization, and the ethical challenges associated with AI-generated content, including issues of authenticity, creativity, and misinformation. The chapter concludes by discussing future trends in AI-driven content creation, emphasizing the importance of human-AI collaboration to achieve innovative and responsible content strategies.

DOI: 10.4018/979-8-3373-0219-5.ch008

INTRODUCTION

Artificial intelligence has indeed changed the face of marketing and brand communication. It has opened an entire world of new possibilities for businesses desirous of engaging better with their audiences. In this digital day and age, it would appear that consumers are surrounded by content from every other direction, and the brands should find it even more challenging to make themselves stand out. This has been overcome with the emergence of AI as a powerful tool in creation and marketing, making it possible for brands to deliver personalized, relevant, and timely messages (Ayeni, 2024). AI-driven creation uses advanced algorithms combined with NLP and ML for automating and optimizing the creation and distribution process across a wide range of platforms. It saves time, reduces costs, and raises the output for quality for marketers who use this technology (Babiak, 2023). Besides that, AI allows one to perform analysis on a massive volume of data at incredibly high speed, giving insights that haven't been possible with human effort thus far. AI makes it possible for marketers to know the behavior of customers, their preferences, and trends with which they can strategize messages matched by identified audience segments. This kind of personalization used to involve very labor-intensive activity with a lot of cost involved; now, AI has made it scalable and ensures that brands maintain relevance within target markets. Whether it is custom email campaigns, social media ads, or dynamic website content, personalization increases customer engagement and loyalty (Bozkurt, 2023).

AI has taken it to the next level in terms of how fast and efficiently content can be produced. With AI-driven automated content generation, a quality article, social media posts, or even a video script could be produced in a fraction of the time required from the human writer. This is also very useful for the business that has to pace up with the rapid speed of digital marketing and faces quick changes in trends or customer preferences every now and then. AI-powered content generation tools also power the optimization of content for search engines, ensuring the discoverability of engaging content through targeted audiences (Gao, 2023). It does this by analyzing keyword trends, SEO data, and competitor content for ways to make improvements and adjustments to better position the content for visibility. Further, AI's integration into customer communication has moved beyond mere content creation to real-time interaction. AI-powered chatbots and virtual assistants have become integral parts of brand communication strategies, enabling continuous support for customers and responses to inquiries. These AI-powered tools improve customer experience by responding to their frequently asked questions and solving smaller problems of the users, sometimes even helping them with buying. This improves customer satisfaction while the human resource is now free to concentrate on more important tasks; this makes the whole marketing operation efficient (Han, 2023).

The trends have also opened a lot of new avenues for creativity in marketing, besides making the entire process more effective and personalized. Visually appealing graphics, videos, and even interactive experiences that will indeed strike a chord with audiences can now be created by AI-driven design tools. This allows marketers to experiment with various formats and styles of content without investing much in creative resources (Hu, 2024).

In sum, AI plays both a multilayered and transformative role in marketing and brand communication. From automating repetitive tasks to offering new insight into consumer behavior, AI has empowered marketers to create more impactful, engaging, and personalized content. As AI technology continues to evolve, its potential to revolutionize the landscape of marketing will only continue to grow, and it will be able to let brands create deeper connections with their audiences while staying competitive in an increasingly digital world.

THE EVOLUTION OF CONTENT CREATION THROUGH AI

The evolution of content creation through AI has been a journey of complete transformation in terms of how businesses and people create and distribute content. From the early days of manual, time-consuming processes to the current age with AI-driven automation, unprecedented advancement has happened with both speed and quality in content creation (Hu, 2023). AI has become integrated into marketing and communication over the years, making the generation of text, images, and multimedia easier in relation to targeted audience preferences. To understand how AI functions in content creation, there is a need to look at the various milestones through which this transition has been built (Kanitz et al., 2023).

Content creation during the early stages of digitization was more or less manual, involving a lot of human effort. Marketers, copywriters, and designers spent considerable time creating materials for print, television, and radio, and later, the internet. As digital marketing started to gain momentum, the demand was there for fast, quality content, but traditional means were slow to deliver. The early days of basic automation-tools such as content management systems and templating-necessarily helped streamline the process but still left much of the heavy lifting to human creators. This was the just-right environment that set the stage for AI to disrupt the industry with more efficient, scalable solutions (Liu, 2023).

The first major leap in AI-powered content creation came with the development of natural language processing technologies. NLP basically let the machines not only comprehend but also produce text that resembled the writing of humans, thereby opening possibilities for automating written content. The first tools had a relatively simple purpose: to check grammar and insert keywords for search engine optimization. But as time passed, and machine learning models grew in complexity, AI did increasingly complex content generation tasks. Reports, product descriptions, and basic articles could be produced on a routine basis with the advent of early NLG tools (Kanitz et al., 2023). It was this shift that fundamentally changed the world of content development because, for the first time, AI would be able to develop written content in seconds instead of requiring hours of marketer personal time.

As these machine learning models continued to evolve, so did the functionalities of AI-powered content creation tools. Advanced levels such as deep learning and neural networks spawned the birth of models like GPT-or Generative Pretrained Transformer-capable of creating coherent text at high levels from minimal input. These models have dramatically raised the quality of AI-generated content, making it almost indistinguishable from that written by humans (Michael, 2023). Today, AI-powered tools can create long-form articles, blogs, social media posts, and even complex technical writing with a high degree of precision and relevance. In addition, they are speedy and adaptive; they learn from previous outputs and better their skills with each iteration to sustain specific brand tones and audience expectations. But AI is not only used in generating textual content. AI has also intervened in visual creation. Early AI design tools could allow designers to create basic graphic designs, either by suggesting template-based designs or automating repetitive design tasks. Then comes today's computer vision, along with improvements in machine learning that can enable AI to create original visual content. Images, logos, videos, or even animations are produced using AI-driven design tools. Such tools give marketers and creators the ability to experiment with different visual formats rapidly, reducing reliance on human designers to produce basic content. In addition, AI-powered tools increasingly have the ability to optimize visual content for various different platforms and audiences, ensuring the maximum engagement and impact (Mohamed, 2024).

AI has, of course, massively developed video content creation. From auto-editing of videos to full-fledged video scriptwriting, AI now has become an indispensable aid in the perspective of video marketers. With AI-powered platforms analyzing the performance of every video, further editing is suggested, and personalized video content creation for particular audiences can also be done with the same. This will no longer require that much of one's time. It has reduced the cost and time of production related to videos, hence allowing businesses to use this highly engaging medium even better (Németh & Koltai, 2023).

As AI continues to evolve, so too will its role in shaping the future of content. Inventions such as AI-generated audio, virtual reality content, and augmented reality experiences are expanding the realm of what is possible within the context of digital marketing. Capable of generating immersive, interactive experiences that move beyond traditional content formats, AI offers brands new ways to engage their audiences.

In a nutshell, AI-generated content creation moved from mere mechanization to intelligent machine-generated content. It also introduced higher speeds in content creation, better quality of the content, and personalization, therefore, making it an invaluable tool in modern-day marketing. As AI technology will further advance and improve, so will its influence on content creation-open up innovative paths to imagination, interaction, and productivity (Niu, 2024).

TYPES OF AI-DRIVEN CONTENT CREATION TOOLS

Artificial intelligence has empowered more or less every domain of content creation with varieties of tools aimed at streamlining and embellishing the process. These AI-driven tools help marketers, enterprises, and creators to produce high-quality, personalized, and scalable content much more efficiently than ever before. AI is actually changing how brands speak to their audiences on platforms through written text to visuals and interactive media. This section will review the primary varieties of AI-powered content creation tools, focusing on their applications and what they mean in view of marketing and brand communication (Pellas, 2023).

1. Natural Language Generation (NLG) Tools

NLG tools use AI to create human-sounding text based on input data or parameters. They can be used to write everything from blog posts and product descriptions to reports, email drafts, and many more, in a matter of seconds. The magic of NLG lies in the fact that it will create reams of content identically and with speed, therefore becoming very useful for marketers who want to publish a host of SEO-optimized articles or personalized customer communications on a large scale (Senyapar, 2024).

NLG tools employ advanced machine learning models, such as GPT, that understand context, tone, and shades of meaning in language. This way, companies can have one unified brand voice across various mediums while saving the time and money that would have been used for human writers. There are a number of very popular NLG tools out in the market employed by many people for the creation of content, including OpenAI's GPT models, Jasper, and Copy.ai. These are indeed lifesavers for content marketing strategies since they can come up with captivating stories (Zohuri, 2023).

2. Graphic Design, Image Generation Using AI-based Tools

AI also drove great progress in visual content creation with AI-enabled graphic design and image generation tools. These empower marketers and designers to do nice graphics, logos, social media posts, ads, and website elements without requiring advanced designing skills. Driven by AI, certain tools, including Canva and Adobe Sensei, automate the design creation process by offering users pre-designed templates, recommendations for layouts and fonts, color, and even original designs based on minimum inputs (Ayeni, 2024).

Except for basic design automation, AI-driven image generation applications-say, DALL·E and DeepArt.io-can generate completely new images, either from text descriptions or stylistic inputs. These allow creating custom artwork, unique logos, and visuals that may take extended periods of manual designs. With such capabilities, a brand can save time and cash, experimenting with several creative ways without having to depend on professional designers to an extensive degree (Babiak, 2023).

3. AI Video Creation and Editing Tools

Video remains one of the most engaging formats for online audiences to interact with, and recent advancements in the field of AI technologies have made creating and editing videos well within reach. For example, AI-driven video creation platforms such as Synthesia and Pictory allow users to generate high-quality video content from text scripts. Such a tool can automatically convert written text into an engaging video by choosing suitable imagery and animations, and even include AI-generated voice-overs, to help businesses create professional-looking videos in no time (Bozkurt, 2023).

AI-enabled video editors, such as Magisto and Lumen5, essentially automate the creation of finalized videos by analyzing video clips. The AI automatically selects the most striking scenes, adds transitions and music, and special effects-all that would have taken so much time in producing a video. Be it social media, advertisements, or corporate presentations; through AI-powered video creation tools, brands can create engaging videos for their audience with least hassle.

4. Chatbots and Conversational Agents

With time, artificially intelligent chatbots and conversational agents have gained a degree of importance in customer communication. These make use of NLP and machine learning algorithms to actively engage customers in real time by responding to questions, offering support, and at times guiding them through a buying decision. Chatbots, such as those on platforms like IBM Watson, Drift, and ChatGPT, understand customer queries and respond like humans (Gao, 2023).

In content creation, chatbots fill an important position whereby they interact in personalized means of meeting the individual needs of a customer. They can offer products based on customer preferences, frequently asked questions, or even gather data about their future marketing campaigns. This basically automates all customer interactions and offers brands more visibility continuously across various digital platforms, hence enhancing customer satisfaction and experience (Han, 2023).

5. AI-Powered Social Media Management Tools

Social media is one of the critical platforms for brand communications, and for that, AI-driven tools have made it easier to handle and create content for social channels. Examples include Hootsuite, Buffer, and Sprinklr, which automate the scheduling of social media content, optimize the posting times through AI-driven features, and analyze audience engagement. Such tools go as far as providing recommendations on what hashtags and captions a certain brand should use and may even generate complete posts based on trends and audience preference (Hu, 2023).

AI-powered social media tools will support a brand on various platforms with much less effort and use of resources. In this way, one can maintain consistency in messaging across channels, customize the content to the target audience for better visibility, and schedule posting at an ideal time. More interestingly, the data from all social media is analyzed by AI tools, giving fascinating insights about audience behavior and performance-driven content. These, in turn, help brands fine-tune their approach (Hu, 2024).

6. AI-Powered Content Curation Tools

Content curation is an integral part of brand communications, especially for businesses wanting to be relevant by posting the latest news, trends, and updates in the industry to their audiences. AI-powered content curation tools like Curata and Feedly make life easier on them through the automation of discovery and choosing of relevant content. These tools make use of numerous algorithms that crawl through millions of online data, find quality articles, videos, and other content, and recommend them to the user based on preference (Kanitz et al., 2023).

By automating the curation of the content, brands can offer their audiences rich, interesting, and timely information without having to look out for the content themselves. It saves not only a lot of time but also helps businesses establish thought leadership for the respective industries through the back-to-back delivery of the relevant content (Liu, 2023).

7. AI for Audio Content and Creation of Podcasts

Audio material is growing, from podcasts and voice-based marketing, increasingly made easier and seamless by AI tools. Transcripts can be made, edits can be made in the audio, and even produce the audio with text input using platforms like Descript and AIVA. For example, using Descript, users can edit an audio file with the same ease as text; AIVA composes background music for a podcast or a commercial with no professional musicianship involved (Michael, 2023).

AI Voice generation tools, such as Murf.ai, make every brand create audio ads, podcasts, and audio blogs with voices similar to humans using raw text inputs. They reduce the need to invest in expensive recording sessions and voice actors by offering a more scalable solution to produce high-quality audio content.

The diverse range of AI-powered content creation tools really has revolutionized the ways in which businesses and marketers approach brand communication. Whether it's creating written content, designing visuals, or producing videos, engaging with customers in real time-AI has made this all faster, more efficient, and hyper-personal. As the technology beneath AI continues to evolve, so too will its applications in content creation, opening new avenues for brands to optimize their communications strategies and drive deeper engagement with their audiences (Mohamed, 2024).

PERSONALIZATION AT SCALE

The ability to personalize at scale has become one of the most robust uses of AI in today's marketing and has really transformed the ways in which brands reach their audiences. Conventionally, personalization involved the creation of content, messaging, and product recommendations that used customer preferences, behaviors, and demographic data to craft an offering best-suited for that individual. However, this conventionally was somewhat limited by the manual ways marketers could segment audiences and consequently build campaigns targeting those audiences (Németh & Koltai, 2023). The rise of AI-driven technologies means businesses have the capability today to deliver hyper-personalized experiences to large audiences in real time-a factor that has reimagined engagement with customers.

1. From Segmentation to Hyper-Personalization

Lacking artificial intelligence in bygone days, marketers harnessed broad strategies for segmenting to personalize content. They would group consumers based on similar characteristics, such as age, location, or purchase history, and develop content for each of those segments. While effective to a limited degree, this approach lacked the nuance required to consider varied preferences and behaviors. That dynamic flipped with AI, empowering companies to do hyper-personalization where each customer gets a personal experience tailored through their unique data profile. It's because AI can process and analyze more data from varied sources, such as browsing history, social media activity, and purchase patterns (Niu, 2024).

It is this personalization that has taken it one notch higher, because, as opposed to simple segmentation, the attempt here is to create for each user customized content. This can be in many forms: it could be tailored email campaigns, dynamic website content, or product recommendations. For making such a value-based prediction of which kind of content, products, or offers each particular customer will like most, AI analyzes explicit and implicit customer data (Pellas, 2023). For instance, AI algorithms are able to realize the user's previous browsing behavior, added items in the cart, or spent time on certain web pages, to create highly relevant and timely content in successive interactions.

2. Dynamic Content and Real-Time Personalization

While highly personalized, one of the biggest advantages AI offers in personalization at scale is to be able to offer dynamic content. While static content is just the same to all visitors, dynamic content changes based on the user's activity, preference, and context. Instantly examining data points that include everything from a user's device, location, time of day, and interaction history, AI automatically adjusts this kind of content (Senyapar, 2024).

For example, e-commerce sites such as Amazon or Netflix demonstrate real-time personalization. Once a customer creates an account on such portals, AI monitors and suggests the items, movies, or serials that the particular customer would like to watch or buy. This kind of personalization offers an easy, hassle-free, and relevant experience for every user while enhancing user engagement and conversion rates. That would be enabling dynamic content across every platform-from website, email campaigns, social media to mobile applications-to customize the brand with every touchpoint (Zohuri, 2023).

3. AI-Powered Email Personalization

Email marketing remains a significant channel of personalization, and AI flipped the switch with the personalization of emails for individual recipients. Traditional email marketing was confined to putting the recipient's name in the subject line or targeting big audience segments. AI-powered tools expanded these into highly personalized content that would adjust with every user's behavior, preferences, and interaction with the brand (Ayeni, 2024).

AI-powered email marketing tools can track user interaction with previous emails, such as which links were clicked, what products were viewed, or when the emails were opened, and send personalized follow-up messages based on the insights. The new tools also automate the best timing of email delivery, ensuring each recipient gets an email at their best time according to their past behavior (Marcelja, 2023). Otherwise, AI-powered emailing platforms auto-edit subject lines, email copy, and offers in real-time for better resonance with each recipient. These kinds of personalized emails, on many an occasion, have been recorded to greatly improve open rates, click-through rates, and overall engagement (Tran, 2024).

4. Personalized Product Recommendation

AI recommendation engines are the linchpin of personalization at scale, especially in e-commerce. It leverages machine learning algorithms to analyze a user's past behavior-products viewed, purchases made, items added to wishlists, and so on-and make personalized product suggestions. This level of personalization makes for a better user experience: it is easier for customers to find products they may be interested in, and that, of course, increases sales and loyalty (Carole et al., 2024).

Major players like Amazon, Spotify, and Netflix have perfected their use of AI-driven recommendation engines in making personalization the core of user experience. Consider Netflix alone: its AI algorithm is responsible for recommending shows and movies based on what users watched, how they rated content, and even how much time they spent on particular shows. This ensures the user will always be presented with options that they like, which in turn sets a probability of continued engagement (Raji et al., 2024).

Other than individual product recommendations, AI can enable personalized shopping experiences with a pre-curated selection of entire collections that fit better with a customer's style or preference. Fashion retailers also use AI to give personalized styling advice or create customized outfits based on user behavior for further enhancement of the customer journey.

5. Enhancing Customer Experience with AI-Driven Personalization

Beyond content and product recommendations, AI will reshape the complete customer experience by driving personalization at each and every touchpoint. AI-powered chatbots and virtual assistants can engage customers in real-time, offering help through intelligent alerts, product suggestions, and customized solutions based on previous interaction. These AI-powered tools analyze what a customer is asking, their purchase history, and preference to provide very relevant responses that improve customer satisfaction and ensure customer loyalty (Bhuiyan, 2024).

For example, AI-driven chatbots on e-commerce websites can walk the customer through a buying cycle by answering frequently asked questions, recommending products, or even facilitating returns. Such bots could recognize previous customers and change their response based on customer history for a more personalized and seamless experience. Conversely, AI-driven customer service tools can identify potential pitfalls before they occur and provide proactive solutions or advice based on data analysis (Venkateswaran, 2023).

6. Challenges and Opportunities in Scaling Personalization

Personalization at scale brings enormous advantages but also a certain set of challenges. The more data you need to manage and process for customers, the better equipped your data infrastructure should be, and the more advanced your AI algorithms will need to be to make decisions in real time. Besides, brands must show transparency and respect customer privacy, considering more and more scrutiny with data collection and usage (Chen et al., 2024).

Meanwhile, AI-driven personalization opens up some doors to brands for closer contacts with their audiences-those that would bear more relevance and meaning to them. As AI continues to evolve, the ability to move toward even more sophisticated and granular levels of personalization later will create an opportunity for brands to be competitive in a noisy marketplace.

AI-powered personalization at scale fundamentally changes how brands interact with their customers-from on-site experiences to cross-platform engagement. From real-time dynamic content to personalized email campaigns, down to product recommendations, AI empowers companies to serve relevant content to millions while still managing to provide an experience that feels tailored to the individual. As the technology continues to evolve, so will the potential of personalization, unlocking even more ways for brands to drive deeper loyalty along with a better overall user experience (Wu et al., 2022).

SEO AND AI-POWERED CONTENT OPTIMIZATION

Search engine optimization or SEO has always been an important point of each and every digital marketing strategy to enhance the visibility of a website over search engine results pages or SERPs. Conventionally, SEO included several manual tasks like keyword research, content optimization, link building, and monitoring.

However, with time, artificial intelligence has altered how companies work out their SEO strategies by enabling them to carry out content optimization in a much more productive manner. In improving SEO strategies, therefore, AI-powered tools have become indispensable, taking over repetitive and mechanical chores, analyzing vast data, and offering actionable insights. How AI-powered content optimization disrupts SEO practices and their applications will be discussed here, together with the impact of such on digital marketing efforts.

1. AI for Keyword Research and Strategy

Keyword research has long sat at the core of SEO, providing marketers with an understanding of the terms and phrases their target audience are searching. This traditionally involved a very manual process of analysis through keyword data to discern the trends in search volume and competition. Obviously, AI dramatically simplified and honed this process. Powered by machine learning algorithms, AI-powered tools like SEMrush, Ahrefs, and even Google's RankBrain analyze search patterns and make predictions on which keywords will be most relevant to a brand's content (Lee & Jeong, 2022).

These are the tools that go beyond basic keyword metrics to include long-tail keyword suggestions, search intent analysis, and even the prediction of certain keywords over time. With AI capable of analyzing large volumes of data in real time, marketers can always refresh their keyword strategies as search trends change. AI also helps in finding keyword gaps: It helps marketers understand where they may be lacking in their efforts to rank for important terms.

2. Creation and Optimization of Content for SEO

Other AI-driven tools race to automate creation and optimization of content for search engine optimization. Applications like MarketMuse, Clearscope, and Surfer SEO are able to analyze top-ranking content for a keyword and provide recommendations on what to create or improve in your new or existing content. Further, these AI-driven tools assess things like keyword density, the length of the content, readability, and topical relevance to ensure that your content is closely related to the search intent and competitive compared to the top-performing pages (Yuniarthe, 2017).

AI can help ensure that the information presented is complete, ranging over every aspect of a subject that a user may be searching for. The tool uses patterns in search results and user behavior to provide suggestions on what subtopics or questions or keywords need to be included for better relevance. MarketMuse applies AI to crawl and interpret a site's content, identifying what improvements are needed, from additional topics that should be covered to reordering of content elements to better match user intent (Papagiannis, 2020).

Further, AI writing assistants such as Jasper and Copy.ai will even write search engine-optimized content by generating text that contains targeted keywords and adheres to proper SEO principles. These tools use NLG models to create quality, relevant content faster to help scale businesses in creating more content without sacrificing their SEO performance.

3. On-Page Optimization and Meta Tags

Other areas highly impacted by AI include on-page SEO, dealing with the optimization of individual web pages to improve the ranking of target search results. AI-powered tools automatically analyze and optimize key on-page elements such as title tags, meta descriptions, header tags, and internal linking structures. Tools such as Yoast SEO and Frase can propose optimized meta tags for better inclusion of target keywords, but also in relation to user intent and improvement of click-through rates (Kaur, 2019).

These tools also analyze the page structure to ensure that content logically flows with the appropriate heading structure: maintaining H1, H2, etc., and subheadings that are so important both for SEO and for the user experience. Advanced AI-driven platforms can even test and optimize meta tags in real-time to let marketers adapt immediately to changes in algorithms or competitor strategy.

Additionally, AI helps analyze content for keyword stuffing, duplicate content readability problems, and other issues that can cause poorer performances of SEO. By persistently monitoring on-page elements, AI makes sure websites remain optimized and in step with prevailing best practices of SEO (Papagiannis, 2020).

4. Voice Search and Semantic Search Optimization

Considering the growing trend of voice search through devices like Amazon's Alexa, Google Assistant, and Apple's Siri, SEO strategies should take into consideration how voice users search differently compared to those who type. Artificial Intelligence will hence be of utmost assistance to businesses in optimizing their content for voice search since such searches are wordy and usually in question form. This is where AI-powered tools can analyze voice search queries, and these brands can be further helped by optimizing their content to respond to these spoken queries in a more natural tone and with concise answers (Wang, 2008).

Modern search engines, such as Google, now have begun deploying AI algorithms, including BERT and RankBrain, to understand what a person is trying to achieve with a given search query. This moves them out of the keyword-typed mentality into one that interprets an entire phrase for meaning. In light of this, semantic search-the name describing this shift-requires content to be contextually relevant and written in a manner that fits users' intent instead of frequency of the keyword.

AI tools can analyze the content to ensure that what it contains is a clear and straightforward answer to the questions being asked and, therefore, helps businesses optimize for semantic search. Voice search and semantic search optimization, taken together, raise the probability of a business gaining featured snippets or voice search results, which are phenomenally worthwhile in driving traffic.

5. AI for Technical SEO

Technical SEO helps optimize the structure at the backend side of a website for better crawling, indexing, and ranking of its pages by search engines. AI-driven tools for technical SEO, including DeepCrawl, Screaming Frog, and Botify, crawl for issues such as broken links, slow page load time, incorrect use of schema markup, or any mobile usability problems and fix them.

AI can also help enhance your website architecture by suggesting internal linking structures that improve crawlability and the distribution of link equity. This facilitates the process of crawling performed by the search engine bots on your site by making it significantly easier, and they can understand the layout and hierarchy of all the content. Thirdly, AI web tools monitor real-time website performance and can highlight potential issues for marketers before they actually harm the ranking (Kumar, 2023).

AI also contributes to optimization for mobile-first indexing, which is among the primary focus areas of Google's ranking algorithms today. Powered by AI, the platforms can analyze mobile usability issues-page speed and mobile-friendly design-and provide recommendations to make sure that a website creates an optimal experience for its mobile users.

6. Content Performance Tracking and Continuous Improvement

AI-powered tools don't stop at just helping to optimize the first step of content; they are also very important in its performance tracking and further continuous improvement. Various AI tools, such as Google Analytics with machine learning features, HubSpot, and Moz, make use of algorithms to follow traffic, bounce rates, dwell times, and conversion rates as vital indications of performance. They'll find patterns and trends in the data to depict what performs well and what needs optimizations.

AI tools can also predict future trends and changes in search behavior, thus continuously allowing marketers to try and stay ahead of the competition by proactively optimizing their content before the trend shift. For example, monitoring how user behavior has changed over time, AI is able to predict the performance of particular keywords or types of content for brands to adjust strategies (Sundarambal et al., 2023).

AI can identify which content is likely to be underperforming or stale and provide suggestions for updates that will better position the content to become more relevant. Through this constant refinement process, the content continuously remains optimized to meet the needs of the users and algorithms for search engines to maintain high rankings and ensure sustained traffic over time.

7. Improving User Experience (UX) for SEO

UX is becoming a stronger and stronger signal for SEO as Google and other major search engines try to give more visibility to sites that offer fast, intuitive, and beautiful experiences. AI-powered tools can track user behavior on a website-from time spent on pages to bounce rates and interaction patterns-to determine whether or not a site offers a positive experience. Heatmaps and Behavior analytics tools such as Crazy Egg, Hotjar, and ClickTale have made specific observations about how people are interacting with content (Marcelja, 2023).

AI can then recommend optimizations to improve UX, by decreasing the load times, or by making easier navigation, or enhancement in page layouts. By improving UX, AI-powered tools will not only create a better experience for users but will also give more reason to search engines to reward a website with higher ranking.

AI-powered content optimization has changed how search engine optimization works, as it has made the process faster, wiser, and attentive to changes in search algorithms. From keyword research and creation to on-page optimization and performance tracking, AI assists businesses in this competitive digital space by churning out relevant content optimized for relevance and well-positioned in search results. With the constantly improving AI technologies, there is going to be far more advanced ways of optimization of content and successful digital marketing. After all, it is a growing field (Carole et al., 2024).

ARTIFICIAL INTELLIGENCE IN SOCIAL MEDIA MARKETING AND INFLUENCER PARTNERSHIPS

True, Artificial Intelligence has transformed social media marketing and influencer partnerships by automating processes, improving audience targeting, and is an excellent way for data-driven insights. Social media has become one of the most important channels through which brands can engage with their audience (Lazim & Ariffin, 2024). AI-powered tools have changed the very ways businesses create, strategize, and disseminate content through social media. Equally, AI powers the efficiency of influencer marketing in aiding in the selection of appropriate influencers, predicting outcomes of campaigns, and optimizing the collaborations to maximum impact. Below, I talk about how AI changes social media marketing and influencer partnerships, showing and describing some of the tools and technologies driving such innovations.

1. AI for Social Media Content Creation and Curation

Perhaps one of the most powerful usages of AI in social media marketing is the ability of this technology to manage and enhance content creation and curation processes. AI-powered tools such as Lately, Canva, and BuzzSumo help marketers generate content ideas, create visuals, and curate relevant posts in record time that resonate with their audience. These tools analyze previous post data, trending topics, and user interactions to recommend content that will likely engage followers (Aziz et al., 2024).

AI also seems to be helping in content optimization across multiple channels. For example, with the use of AI tools, content formatting, captions, and hashtags are automatically tailored to each platform's needs, whether Instagram, Twitter, or LinkedIn. By implementing AI, brands easily sustain a consistent presence on many channels without having to craft content for each channel. At the same time, AI-powered tools can analyze the types of posts that work best in their channels-video, imagery, text-based posts-and recommend the ideal mix to realize maximum engagement (Lazim & Ariffin, 2024).

Going beyond creation, AI-driven content curation tools like Feedly and Curata sort through massive volumes of data to uncover the latest relevant industry news, user-generated content, and trending stories. All this enables a brand to pass on valuable and timely information to their audience while setting themselves up as thought leaders in their particular niches.

2. AI-Powered Audience Targeting and Segmentation

Perhaps one of AI's most powerful features for social media marketing pertains to analyzing big datasets for patterns in user behavior. AI-powered tools such as Hootsuite, Sprinklr, and Socialbakers make use of various machine learning algorithms that enable marketers to get a proper understanding of their audience: what demographics they fit into, what their interests are, and how they behave. With such information, brands have the ability to better segment their audiences, knowing full well that whatever content was produced really fitted the bill in terms of what those groups wanted or needed (Ramachandran et al., 2024).

With AI-powered targeting, marketers can now look beyond traditional demographics, such as age, location, and gender. By analyzing user interactions, past behavior, and even sentiment, AI creates hyper-targeted campaigns that can resonate better. For example, AI can identify users who are more likely to engage with a brand's posts, participate in promotions, or make a purchase. This accuracy in audience targeting leads to higher engagement rates and better ROI (Lazim & Ariffin, 2024).

Also, AI can help enable brands to anticipate user behavior by predicting what kind of content users are more likely to engage with, based on past interactions. This predictive capability opens avenues for businesses in not only optimizing social media calendars and posting at times most conducive for user activity and engagement but also:

3. Chatbots and Conversational AI for Social Media Engagement

AI chatbots have a vital role in today's social media marketing because they can engage in real-time with a particular audience. The platforms to support this are Facebook Messenger, Instagram, and Twitter. These would answer frequently asked questions, return results for customer inquiries, or go as far as to make personalized suggestions, having observed user activities (Ramachandran et al., 2024).

The use of chatbots is informed by NLP, ensuring that user queries are understood and responses are given out in a well-structured, conversational manner. They are always available, meaning that brands can maintain constant engagement with their audience outside of traditional business hours. For instance, chatbots can handle common customer service issues, such as tracking orders or answering product-related questions, without human intervention.

Besides, AI-powered conversational bots can gather quality information about user preferences and behavior that could help refine marketing strategies. Analysis of chatbot interactions will help brands understand better the customer pain points, interests, and product preferences for creating more targeted content and campaigns in the future (Lazim & Ariffin, 2024).

4. Social Media Analytics and Performance Tracking with AI

This naturally makes AI a very powerful tool for social media analytics, given its ability to analyze and interpret large volumes of data in real time. Examples of tools using AI to tap into the performance of brands on social media include Sprout Social, Brandwatch, and Crimson Hexagon. It definitely helps marketers understand the kind of content that resonates with their audience and how they should go about optimizing future posts for better performance.

AI-enabled tools may track likes, shares, comments, and overall engagement to identify trends and patterns. They can also monitor the performance of competitors to provide insight into what works for other brands in the same industry. This data, upon analysis, shall enable marketers to make informed decisions on content strategy, ad spend, and platform allocation to finally improve their social media ROI (Ramachandran et al., 2024).

Another important functionality of social media analytics tools is AI-powered sentiment analysis. These tools parse through social media conversations to monitor public sentiment about any particular brand or product. This helps brands make necessary amends with respect to messaging and content creation strategies by knowing whether the conversations are positive, negative, or neutral.

5. AI in Influencer Identification and Partnerships

Influencer marketing has grown into one of the most effective methods in which a brand can organically reach and connect with its target audience. Finding just the right influencer with whom to partner is many times a rather involved and prolonged process. AI has changed the game in influencer marketing through automation in discovering influencers, managing campaigns, and tracking their performances.

AI-powered platforms like Traackr, Influencity, and Upfluence crawl through the supply of available social media talent for the most suitable influencers by leveraging data around values, audience fit, and campaign goals. It takes everything into consideration, from engagement rates to audience demographics, style of content, to past campaign success when recommending the best candidates for collaboration (Aziz et al., 2024).

Predicting the performance of a collaboration with an influencer is beyond just shortlisting with the help of previous data that AI technologies can do. It runs its search on AI algorithms from past collaborations and audience interaction to see if a certain influencer can give high returns for investment in a particular brand.

It will help data-driven marketers pick up the right influencer who can create the most effect on their campaigns rather than picking them based on follower count.

And when a campaign goes live, AI tools also track influencer performance according to reach, engagement, conversions, and sentiment. This enables a brand to assess the performance of its influencer collaborations on their launch hour itself and make proper adjustments where needed.

6. Optimizing Influencer Campaigns with AI

AI also transforms the management and optimization of influencer campaigns. Influencer campaigns have traditionally been hypothesis-driven, assuming what kind of content would work with an audience, and results needed to be manually tracked. Using AI-powered tools, optimization of campaigns happens in real time through the performance assessment of the influencer content and making changes toward better results.

For example, AI can track a particular influencer's posts of a campaign and propose rate, timing, or content changes to better its performance. It can even provide information on which segments of the audiences are responding well and which are not, for the brand to better its targeting. Other than this, AI tools also allow optimizing influencer-created content on multiple platforms by rewriting captions, hashtags, and visuals to fit platform-level trends and algorithmic changes (Aziz et al., 2024).

7. AI-Driven Social Listening for Influencer and Brand Monitoring

AI-powered social listening to monitor influencers and brands is another critical component of influencer marketing in today's digital world. AI-powered social listening tools such as Brandwatch, Talkwalker, and Sprinklr track conversations about a brand, product, or influencer across various social media platforms. These tools analyze sentiment, track mentions, and identify emerging trends that help brands stay ahead of public perception (Ramachandran et al., 2024).

By monitoring these conversations, brands can identify potential influencers who are already organically advocating for their products or services. This in turn makes it easier to form authentic partnerships with real influencers who will genuinely promote the brand. Second, social listening helps brands track the effectiveness of influencer campaigns by analyzing how much buzz there is about a particular collaboration, and whether such buzz will be leading to positive sentiment around the brand (Zhang & Wei, 2021).

8. AI and the Future of Social Media Marketing and Influencer Partnerships

What the Future of Influencer Partnerships Looks Like As technology continues to evolve, so will AI's role in disrupting social media marketing and influencer partnerships. Further integrations of AI into predictive analytics, content creation, and performance tracking will better position brands for evolving their strategies into even more personalized and effective campaigns. AI will also be involved in the influencing marketing space by automating more tasks from contract management through to payment processing and freeing up a brand's resources to nurture long-term relationships with their engaged influencers.

With increased sophistication, AI-driven tools are promising even more advanced capabilities, such as augmented reality influencers and artificial intelligence-created content that will be virtually indistinguishable from human influencers. Such emerging innovations will push the boundaries of what will be achievable in social media marketing even further, offering brands new ways to interact with their audiences and driving effective campaigns (Aziz et al., 2024).

AI now transforms social media marketing and partnerships with influencers through automating content creation, optimizing audience targeting, and providing actionable insights that drive results. From real-time content optimization and AI chatbots, to identifying influencers and tracking campaigns, AI-driven tools arm brands with better ways to improve their presence on social media and build more valued relationships with audiences. Each further development only demonstrates that AI technologies will be even more crucial in the determination of the future regarding social media marketing, presenting new ways to achieve innovation and success (Zhang & Wei, 2021).

AI-GENERATED CONTENT ETHICS AND CHALLENGES

With AI-generated content on the rise, companies, marketers, and creators will never look at content creation and distribution the same way again. While the efficiency, scalability, and creative possibilities of AI-powered content creation tools come with several advantages, this development has equally brought forth quite a number of ethical considerations and raised several challenges. As AI produces text, images, and videos closer to humans, questions regarding authenticity, creativity, misinformation, and human creators have taken center stage.

1. Authenticity and Trust Issues

The authenticity of the content is one of the major ethical concerns with AI-generated content. In a world where consumers crave authenticity in human-created content that truly represents and reflects the values and personality of a brand, the use of AI for generating text, images, or videos raises suspicions of trust. While AI-created content may save time, it may not have the emotional subtlety, the human touch, and the authenticity that people are looking for when they engage with either brands or media (Ramachandran et al., 2024).

The issue becomes much more specific when the content is completely generated by AI, and there might be a consumer who may feel deceived, knowing that what they interact with isn't human-generated. Most distinctly, this can be seen in influencer marketing, wherein the followers expect engagement with the actual personalities they follow. Some of the uses, like AI-generated Influencers or Avatars, or even automated posts, chip away at trust between the influencers and their audience (Wang, 2023).

Besides, every time AI intervenes in content creation, news and information somehow become a question of authenticity. For example, AI-powered news articles, blog posts, or social media updates give information that is seemingly valid yet does not get an in-depth approach that human journalism or critical analysis would give them. Such information may make a disconnect between the material and its human audience regarding transparency and honesty in communication.

2. Creativity vs. Automation: The Role of Human Input

Another ethical issue in terms of AI content generation is based on the dialectics between creativity and automation. On the one hand, artificial intelligence can generate enormous amounts of content in a short time, but then comes the question: Is AI really creative, or does it just forge a pattern upon incoming data? Creativity is usually considered a congenital human feature, connected with emotions, intuition, and one's point of view. The risk of losing all individuality and diversity in human thought always seems to arise when the generation of content by AI is applied (Park et al., 2024).

While AI perhaps can be of much help in augmenting creativity-suggesting ideas, building designs, and helping overcome writer's block-the fear is that too great a reliance upon AI will stunt human creativity. Brands that rely too much on AI in producing marketing materials or ads run the risk of making their content formulaic, repetitive, and lacking the personal touch to speak to audiences (Venkateswaran, 2023).

Also, the more common AI-generated content is, the more it threatens the contribution of human creatives. The automation in the process of content creation may lead to the loss of jobs by writers, designers, and other creatives or worse-less opportunities. This presents a challenge to businesses and society on how to balance efficiency brought about by AI with the preservation of human creativity (Wang, 2023).

3. Misinformation and Deepfakes

One of the major ethical concerns with AI-generated content is miscommunication and the dissemination of information. With AI-powered tools, one can create realistic text, images, and videos that are quite hard to differentiate from the real thing. Thus, distinguishing between authentic human-created content and AI-generated content can be really hard to do. While this technology is useful in many cases, it can be used maliciously to create misleading or false information (Venkateswaran, 2023).

One famous manifestation of this is the rise of "deepfakes"-videos or audio recordings that use the power of AI to manipulate the likeness or voice of individuals to make it appear they said or did something when, as a matter of fact, they never said or did. Deepfakes have been used to spread political misinformation, defame public figures, and manipulate popular sentiment. As AI-generated fakes get increasingly sophisticated, the public cannot make any effective differentiation between what is real and what is not, which may cause people, organizations, or society to be harmed in one way or another (Bhuiyan, 2024).

AI can also be used to write fake news articles or devious social media posts that can then go viral across platforms. The ability of AI to come up with persuasive and coherent text could also mean it is used to create volumes of false information, to either influence public opinion or create confusion in times of crisis. Of course, ethical content creation, marketing, and platforms are fundamental in balancing accuracy and truth related to AI-generated content.

4. Issues of Copyright and Intellectual Property

Another complex issue arising with the application of AI in content creation relates to copyright and intellectual property. Once AI creates something, who owns it-the creator of the AI tool, the user of the tool, or the AI itself? That remains a gray area in present legal frameworks since most copyright laws were set before AI came into the fore as a tool for creating content.

Most AI tools inherently use large amounts of data from existing human-made content to create new content. That brings up a number of questions regarding the originality of AI-created content against derivative works of already existing content. For example, AI models that have been trained on thousands of articles, images, or videos may unconsciously reproduce elements of copyrighted material that may easily lead to potential legal disputes over ownership (Chen et al., 2024).

In addition, artists and creators could believe that gross usage of their work in training AI models is been done without consent or remuneration. This becomes an ethical concern about the exploitation of human creators for the benefit of the AI-generated content. As AI becomes more integrated into the creative process, new legal frameworks will be required in the face of questions over copyright, originality, and fair use (Lee & Jeong, 2022).

5. Bias and Discrimination in AI-Generated Content

Other challenges with AI-generated content are bias and discrimination. Most of the AI models are trained on enormous datasets of already existing content, which sometimes may include biased or discriminatory information. Where these biases are not accounted for, the AI-generated content could unconsciously propagate violent stereotypes, discriminatory language, or biased narratives (Chen et al., 2024).

For example, AI-generated content used in advertisements can further cement gender, racial, or cultural stereotypes if the data sets on which that training occurs include biased representations. This also holds true for instances where AI algorithms develop text or visual content, unknowingly mirroring the inequalities of history, thus generating content that is exclusionary or offensive in nature (Papagiannis, 2020).

Any bias in AI-generated content can be avoided if one thinks cautiously about the data on which AI models have been trained and makes continuous effort towards monitoring and correction of the output to maintain traces of bias. That is why it is important that brands and creators be informed about the ethical use of AI tools and purport to make their content inclusive, non-discriminatory, representative, and truthful regarding the presence of multiple points of view (Marcelja, 2023).

6. Regulation and Accountability

The speed and rapid development of AI-generated content outcompete the drafting of prescriptions that address its use. With AI continuing to swell in content creation, clear guidelines and regulation become ever so more important in dealing with a host of ethical and legal challenges associated with the use of the technology. This means that governments, industry bodies, and technology companies will have to converge on setting standards for the responsible use of AI in creating content (Yuniarthe, 2017).

The first important factor is accountability, which has to do with AI-generated content. If the generated content from AI is harmful, misleading, or illegal, who should take the liability-the user of the AI tool or the developer? The foregoing questions point to why we do need regulatory frameworks that will ensure responsibility and liability are well defined in cases where AI-generated content causes harm (Chen et al., 2024).

With no clear guidelines on the matter, businesses and creators must be proactive in ensuring that use of AI is ethical and responsible. This means transparency over when and how AI is used in content creation, taking action to try and prevent the dissemination of misinformation, and commitment to protection of intellectual property and creative rights.

7. Human-AI Collaboration and Ethical Guidelines

While great the challenges are, many specialists think that in this respect, the best way to go is to encourage collaboration between humans and AI rather than look at it as a replacement for human creativity. AI can be an effective tool for augmenting human capabilities and enhancing creativity by enabling the creators to focus on more strategic and value-creating work while automating some mundane processes (Tran, 2024).

On the other hand, businesses and creators should also be very specific when they need AI intervention and where AI is needed. Ethical thinking, after all, is at the forefront of working with this emerging technology; thus, it is worth cultivating if done transparently, inclusively, and in an accountable way. With it, fostering responsible innovation and collaboration between humans and machines would go a long way to aid the creative industries, which holds its full potential with challenges that come along with it (Marcelja, 2023).

AI-generated content holds great promise for the future of marketing, media, and creative industries. But it simultaneously invokes an explosion of ethical issues, which must be debated and defined in a proper manner, for the diffusion of such content to be responsibility and sustainability assured. Everything from authenticity and creativity to misinformation, bias, and intellectual property: AI-generated content calls for considerate decisions and thoughtful regulation. By encouraging transparency, accountability, and collaboration between humans and AI, businesses and creators are in a position to reap the benefits from AI while mitigating its ethical risks and ensuring that AI-generated content serves the greater good (Chen et al., 2024).

THE FUTURE OF AI-DRIVEN CONTENT CREATION

The future of AI-driven content creation is going to be even more revolutionary, with the advancement of artificial intelligence technologies, as well as their integration with other state-of-the-art technologies. With businesses, marketers, and creators increasingly relying on AI for content creation, the possibility of innovation in the ways content is conceptualized, created, and delivered will expand dramatically. Emerging trends range from hyper-personalization toward immersive and dynamic on-the-go experiences that are going to reshape entirely industries of marketing, media, entertainment, and e-commerce. This section will be about future trends in AI-generated content creation, with a focus on the place of generative AI, personalization, new formats such as AR/VR, and the ethical considerations accompanying these developments (Tran, 2024).

1. Generative AI: The Next Frontier of Creativity

Generative AI models are at the forefront of the next wave of content creation. Whereas the newest, more sophisticated models were GPT-4, GPT-5, and DALL·E, up until then, AI could already generate complicated, human-like content from simple text and images to music and video. The ability of these models to be more human-like in their creation is increasingly complemented by the ability to contextualize and understand tone, let alone cultural nuance, which makes their output relevant and impactful (Wu et al., 2022).

In the future, AI will be able to generate complete marketing campaigns, movie scripts, novels, or art with very little human input. Such development will certainly open more doors for creators to experiment with various styles, formats, and ideas that were not at all conceivable earlier. For instance, businesses can ask AI to generate multiple versions of an ad campaign targeting different audience segments and optimize each one for engagement and conversion (Venkateswaran, 2023).

In addition to generating text and images, the capability of AI for video creation is bound to get much better. Artificial Intelligence video tools will enable marketers and other content creators to easily create short films, ads, or explainer videos in real time without needing a full production team. AI-generated motion graphics and animations powered by models like Runway ML will finally let brands create visual content on demand.

2. Hyper-Personalization and Dynamic Content Creation

Perhaps one of the most thrilling trends currently happening in AI-driven content creation must be the movement toward hyper-personalization. As AI algorithms continue to improve, the ability for personalizing content for the individual user in real time will only continue to develop further. AI lets marketers create and provide personalized experiences across platforms-be it a website, an email, social media, or digital ads-through the analysis of user behavior, preferences, and interactions in real time (Marcelja, 2023).

In the future, AI systems will be able to create dynamic content that automatically adjusts according to user input. For example, a user lands on an e-commerce website displaying custom product recommendations, homepage designs, and even customized content for his browsing behavior and purchase history. AI will be enabling brands to present content that morphs in real time as users interact with it, creating ultra-personalized customer experiences.

With even more intuitive chatbots and conversational AI, this extends into personalized content in the form of advice, recommendations, or even support. AI-powered bots will enable hyper-relevant interactions by distilling past conversations, purchases, and preferences, making users feel like they are receiving focused attention (Sundarambal et al., 2023).

3. AI in Augmented Reality (AR) and Virtual Reality (VR) Content Creation

AI will be heavy in the future of creating immersive content both in augmented and virtual reality. As AR and VR move further into the mainstream, AI will be key to creating immersive experiences that facilitate storytelling, marketing, gaming, and education.

For example, AI can help in creating realistic 3D modeling, virtual worlds, and interactions in AR/VR applications. These virtual worlds can then be tailored to specific users' preferences and behaviors to offer personalized virtual worlds. Brands could use AI-created AR content to present interactive product demos, virtual in-store experiences, or even gamified ad campaigns that attract users on a more personal level (Papagiannis, 2020).

AI will, in turn, enable much more immersive storytelling in gaming and entertainment, since stories will be dynamically created as players make choices and act. One can only imagine what it will be like to be transported into a virtual world with a story line that changes in real time by every decision and action the player makes. The integration of AI with AR and VR will continue to open up possibilities for training and education in the future because adaptive, immersive learning environments could then be created, tailored to individual learning style and needs.

4. AI-Generated Audio and Music

While AI is getting better at generating high-quality text and visuals, so it does in audio and music production. Currently, AI-powered composers, including AIVA and OpenAI's Jukebox, can create original music tracks based on input that a user would provide, which in the future is only going to continue (Sundarambal et al., 2023).

AI-generated music, used in marketing, will be tailored to fit the mood, theme, or branding of certain campaigns, thereby making it easier and more cohesive in creating multimedia content. For instance, brands could use AI to create unique soundtracks for video ads, social media posts, or podcasts. AI audio generation will also be put to work creating voiceovers for videos with synthetic voices that impersonate human intonation and emotion for the ease of producing polished content without hiring voice actors.

Beyond music and voiceovers, the AI-driven audio content will extend to podcasts and audiobooks. The AI can also be used to create podcast episodes or enable blog posts and articles to automatically turn into engaging audio formats that reach farther with their audiences (Kumar, 2023).

5. Automated Translation and Multilingual Content

With global markets increasingly integrating, the demand for content in multiple languages also grows. Artificial intelligence-powered translation tools continue to advance in level and sophistication, as businesses can now automatically translate and localize their content for multiple languages and regions. Nowadays, AI-based translation started being used by both Google Translate and DeepL to offer more accurate and sensitive contextual translations; further refinement will make the process even smoother (Bhuiyan, 2024).

AI-powered content creation means that brands will be able to create and publish multilingual content at scale. This may involve an AI-powered tool churning out social media posts, videos, or blog articles in various languages each day, localized for cultural sensitivities and regional preferences. It then becomes easier to reach global audiences without a dependence on a great deal of human translation resources (Kaur, 2019).

Voice synthesis technologies powered by AI will also further enable multiple language voiceovers, meaning that video content can talk directly to audiences in their native languages but with the same tone and style as the original content.

6. Ethical AI Content Creation and Transparency

Ethical considerations will assume a more central role in shaping the future with the increasingly widespread use of AI-powered content creation. In the coming years, transparency in AI-generated content, especially in situations where audiences should be informed that the content is AI-generated and not written by humans, will attract greater attention. This will be so vital in the context of some sensitive sectors such as journalism, education, and even politics, which rely highly on information integrity and the source thereof (Papagiannis, 2020).

There could be developed regulatory frameworks that indicate how AI will be used in content creation, especially on issues of intellectual property, bias, and misinformation. The businesses should ensure their AI-generated content respects ethical standards and does not perpetuate biased, misleading, or discriminatory stories. Another respect in which increased autonomy may be given to AIs in content creation could come from the significant level of scrutiny being placed on the responsibilities and accountability of the AI tools and those who have created them (Chen et al., 2024).

7. Human-AI Collaboration: Advancing Creative Processes

And rather than replacing human creatives, AI will keep evolving as an instrument to increase human creativity. In the future of AI-driven content creation, humans and AI work together to create innovative and quality content in one collaborative workflow. In that case, AI takes over in the repeatability or the technical part of creating content, like editing, formatting, and basic copywriting, while human creatives focus on strategic, creative, and conceptual aspects.

AI will play a bigger role in being a creative assistant by suggesting betterment of content, idea creation, or helping creators with brainstorming. For example, a writer may use AI to draft an article and then refine and polish the content with his own creativity. Similarly, designers could use AI to generate visual assets that inspire new design ideas, which they can then customize and adapt (Wu et al., 2022).

In this model of collaboration, the productivity will go up and creators will focus on what they do best-create compelling storytelling, innovative visuals, immersive experiences, and engaging audiences.

8. AI-Driven Interactive and Immersive Experience

The future trends in AI-driven content creation are all about interactive and immersive experiences. AI will play an important role in developing content that is personal yet interactive, where users can be an active part of and contribute toward their content experiences. This will be quite crucial in industries that deal with gaming, entertainment, and e-commerce (Bhuiyan, 2024).

For example, AI could be leveraged to create engaging marketing experiences in which users make choices that would, in turn, advance a storyline-a far more memorable, even somewhat engaging brand experience. In e-commerce, for example, AI could fuel virtual shopping assistants capable of helping users navigate products, answer questions, and make personalized recommendations based on real-time data (Chen et al., 2024).

The same is the case with customer service and support, which is going to get completely revolutionized by interactive AI content. Further, AI-powered virtual assistants will speak to the users themselves, answer their queries, and present them with solutions according to their preferences and needs. This, in turn, increases user interaction even more and provides more personalized and engaging content (Raji et al., 2024). The next generations of AI-powered content creations-from hyper-personalization to immersive AR/VR experiences, from automated audio to multilingual content creation-have virtually unlimited possibilities. Later, when AI technology is continuously improved, marketers, businesses, and creators will be able to craft more productive, creative, and dynamic content than ever. But with such benefits come ethical considerations and responsibility. Businesses can realize the full value of AI-powered content creation without losing the trust and innovation that exist in the digital environment by encouraging collaboration between humans and artificial intelligence and bringing transparency (Tran, 2024).

CONCLUSION

AI-driven content creation radically flips the script on how businesses and creators produce, personalize, and distribute content across a multitude of platforms. It allows for unprecedented improvements in creativity, speed of production, and hyper-personalization at scale. From generative AI models to immersive technologies such as AR and VR, AI shapes up the future of marketing, entertainment, and communications with dynamic, interactive, highly engaging content. Meanwhile, in these advantages, ethical problems, authenticity, and transparency come in, particularly when more and more highly advanced AI-generated content is applied in everyday interactions. The future of creation should be a collaborative one wherein machines have been built to take care of routine work, leaving human creators to reinforce creativity, thereby ensuring that originality and ethical standards are well preserved, not to mention emotional resonance in their output. The key to leveraging the full potential of AI, while this technology develops further, lies in a balance between technological innovation and responsible, meaningful content creation.

REFERENCES

Ayeni, O. (2024). Ai in education: A review of personalized learning and educational technology. *GSC Advanced Research and Reviews*, 18(2), 261–271. DOI: 10.30574/gscarr.2024.18.2.0062

Aziz, K., Dua, S., & Gupta, P. (2024). Revolutionizing influencer marketing: Harnessing the power of data analytics and artificial intelligence (AI). In *Advances in Data Analytics for Influencer Marketing: An Interdisciplinary Approach* (pp. 41–66). Springer Nature Switzerland. DOI: 10.1007/978-3-031-65727-6_4

Babiak, O. (2023). Threads and upgrades of AI technology in the new media era. *Грааль Науки*, (24), 441–448. DOI: 10.36074/grail-of-science.17.02.2023.080

Bhuiyan, M. S. (2024). The role of AI-enhanced personalization in customer experiences. *Journal of Computer Science and Technology Studies*, 6(1), 162–169. DOI: 10.32996/jcsts.2024.6.1.17

Bozkurt, A. (2023). Generative AI, synthetic contents, open educational resources (OER), and open educational practices (OEP): A new front in the openness landscape. *Open Praxis*, 15(3), 178–184. DOI: 10.55982/openpraxis.15.3.579

Carole, K. S., Armand, T. P. T., & Kim, H. C. (2024, February). Enhanced experiences: Benefits of AI-powered recommendation systems. In *2024 26th International Conference on Advanced Communications Technology (ICACT)* (pp. 216-220). IEEE.

Chen, J., Liu, Z., Huang, X., Wu, C., Liu, Q., Jiang, G., Pu, Y., Lei, Y., Chen, X., Wang, X., Zheng, K., Lian, D., & Chen, E. (2024). When large language models meet personalization: Perspectives of challenges and opportunities. *World Wide Web (Bussum)*, 27(4), 42. DOI: 10.1007/s11280-024-01276-1

Gao, B., Wang, Y., Xie, H., Hu, Y., & Hu, Y. (2023). Artificial intelligence in advertising: Advancements, challenges, and ethical considerations in targeting, personalization, content creation, and ad optimization. *SAGE Open*, 13(4), 21582440231210759. Advance online publication. DOI: 10.1177/21582440231210759

Han, T. (2023). On the copyright of content generated by artificial intelligence. *SHS Web of Conferences, 178*, 01019. https://doi.org/DOI: 10.1051/shsconf/202317801019

Hu, J. (2024). Dynamic content generation in large language models with real-time constraints. https://doi.org/DOI: 10.31219/osf.io/xje3w

Hu, Y. (2023). Literature in the age of artificial intelligence. 1781-1787. https://doi.org/DOI: 10.2991/978-2-38476-092-3_228

Kanitz, R., Gonzalez, K., Briker, R., & Straatmann, T. (2023). Augmenting organizational change and strategy activities: Leveraging generative artificial intelligence. *The Journal of Applied Behavioral Science*, 59(3), 345–363. DOI: 10.1177/00218863231168974

Kaur, H. (2019). Search engine optimization and its latest trends: A review. *Think India Journal*, 22(17), 2052–2062.

Kumar, T. (2023). Integration of intelligent AI & SEO: A review of various factors. [IJNMS]. *International Journal of New Media Studies*, 10(1).

Lazim, N. A. M., & Ariffin, S. H. S. (2024). Data analytics and AI for influencer marketing. In *Advances in Data Analytics for Influencer Marketing: An Interdisciplinary Approach* (pp. 89–102). Springer Nature Switzerland. DOI: 10.1007/978-3-031-65727-6_6

Lee, J., & Jeong, H. (2022). A study on implications of AI education policy using keyword analysis. *Journal of The Korean Association of Information Education*, 26(5), 397–406. DOI: 10.14352/jkaie.2022.26.5.397

Liu, Y. (2023). Implications of generative artificial intelligence for the development of the media industry. *AEI*, 1(1), 29–36. DOI: 10.54254//1/2023006

Marcelja, G. (2023). AI-powered communication. In *Молодые исследователи: новые векторы диалога* (pp. 87-93).

Michael, O. (2023). Natural language processing relevance to online business. *Swb*, 01(03), 37–42. DOI: 10.61925/SWB.2023.1305

Mohamed, E., Osman, M. E., & Mohamed, B. A. (2024). The impact of artificial intelligence on social media content. *Journal of Social Sciences (New York, N. Y.)*, 20(1), 12–16. DOI: 10.3844/jssp.2024.12.16

Németh, R., & Koltai, J. (2023). Natural language processing. *Intersections*, 9(1), 5–22. DOI: 10.17356/ieejsp.v9i1.871 PMID: 36568020

Niu, L. (2024). New applications of online education content analysis based on natural language processing technology. https://doi.org/DOI: 10.4108/eai.17-11-2023.2342790

Papagiannis, N. (2020). *Effective SEO and content marketing: The ultimate guide for maximizing free web traffic*. John Wiley & Sons. DOI: 10.1002/9781119628682

Park, J., Oh, C., & Kim, H. Y. (2024). AI vs. human-generated content and accounts on Instagram: User preferences, evaluations, and ethical considerations. *Technology in Society*, 79, 102705. DOI: 10.1016/j.techsoc.2024.102705

Pellas, N. (2023). The influence of sociodemographic factors on students' attitudes toward AI-generated video content creation. *Smart Learning Environments*, 10(1), 57. Advance online publication. DOI: 10.1186/s40561-023-00276-4

Raji, M. A., Olodo, H. B., Oke, T. T., Addy, W. A., Ofodile, O. C., & Oyewole, A. T. (2024). E-commerce and consumer behavior: A review of AI-powered personalization and market trends. *GSC Advanced Research and Reviews, 18*(3), 066-077.

Ramachandran, K. K., Suma, S., Banerjee, D., Mathew, B., Cheepurupalli, N. R., & Mohan, C. R. (2024). The effectiveness of influencer marketing in the age of AI. *Journal of Informatics Education and Research*, 4(2).

Senyapar, H. (2024). Artificial intelligence in marketing communication: A comprehensive exploration of the integration and impact of AI. *Technium Social Sciences Journal*, 55, 64–81. DOI: 10.47577/tssj.v55i1.10651

Sundarambal, B., Karthikeyini, C., Bommi, R. M., Subramanian, S., & Lokesh, M. (2023, December). AI-based content management system. In *2023 International Conference on Data Science, Agents & Artificial Intelligence (ICDSAAI)* (pp. 1-8). IEEE.

Tran, M. T. (2024). Unlocking the AI-powered customer experience: Personalized service, enhanced engagement, and data-driven strategies for e-commerce applications. In *Enhancing and Predicting Digital Consumer Behavior with AI* (pp. 375–382). IGI Global. DOI: 10.4018/979-8-3693-4453-8.ch019

Venkateswaran, N. (2023). AI-driven personalization in customer relationship management: Challenges and opportunities. *Journal of Theoretical and Applied Information Technology*, 101(18), 7392–7399.

Wang, Y. (2023). Synthetic realities in the digital age: Navigating the opportunities and challenges of AI-generated content. *Authorea Preprints*.

Wang, Y. Y., Yu, D., Ju, Y. C., & Acero, A. (2008). An introduction to voice search. *IEEE Signal Processing Magazine*, 25(3), 28–38. DOI: 10.1109/MSP.2008.918411

Wu, C. J., Raghavendra, R., Gupta, U., Acun, B., Ardalani, N., Maeng, K., & Hazelwood, K. (2022). Sustainable AI: Environmental implications, challenges and opportunities. *Proceedings of Machine Learning and Systems*, 4, 795–813.

Yuniarthe, Y. (2017, September). Application of artificial intelligence (AI) in search engine optimization (SEO). In *2017 International Conference on Soft Computing, Intelligent System and Information Technology (ICSIIT)* (pp. 96-101). IEEE. DOI: 10.1109/ICSIIT.2017.15

Zhang, L., & Wei, W. (2021). Influencer marketing: A comparison of traditional celebrity, social media influencer, and AI influencer. *Boston Hospitality Review*, 1-11.

Zohuri, B. (2023). Charting the future the synergy of generative AI, quantum computing, and the transformative impact on economy, society, jobs market, and the emergence of artificial super intelligence. *Current Trends in Engineering Science*, 3(7), 1–4. DOI: 10.54026/CTES/1050

Chapter 9
AI in Customer Service Automation:
Balancing Efficiency With Human Touch

Sudhir Rana
https://orcid.org/0000-0002-9910-1930
Gulf Medical University, UAE

Sandeep Kumar Singh
https://orcid.org/0000-0002-1741-7254
O.P. Jindal Global University, India

Ajay Chandel
https://orcid.org/0000-0002-4585-6406
Lovely Professional University, India

ABSTRACT

This chapter explores the evolving role of AI in customer service automation, focusing on balancing efficiency with human interaction. AI technologies, including advancements in Natural Language Processing (NLP), predictive analytics, and integration with Augmented Reality (AR) and Virtual Reality (VR), are transforming customer service by enhancing personalization and streamlining operations. However, challenges such as maintaining emotional intelligence, ensuring ethical use of AI, and addressing privacy concerns remain critical. The chapter discusses strategies for leveraging AI while preserving the essential human touch and highlights future trends and innovations shaping the customer service landscape. By navigating these developments, businesses can optimize customer interactions and create more effective, empathetic, and responsive service environments.

DOI: 10.4018/979-8-3373-0219-5.ch009

INTRODUCTION

Customer service has gradually transformed to add the use of artificial intelligence. AI integration has revolutionized the ways in which businesses connect with their customers. The force of automation, therefore, is driven by increased efficiency in operations, reduced operational costs, and faster responses towards customers. AI technologies like chatbots, virtual assistants, and predictive analytics have evolved as capable tools to take on routine tasks, manage volumes of requests, and support customers round the clock (Sadhu et al., 2024). These are revolutionary times for customer service, as these advancements now allow companies to scale their operations and meet the growing expectations of a technology-savvy consumer base.

On the other hand, even as it offers such critical advantages in efficiency and scale of operations, AI has also raised some very fundamental questions regarding preserving the human touch in customer interactions. Despite apparent sophistication, most AI systems inherently lack nuanced understanding and emotional intelligence, which human agents can definitely provide. Some of the things that AI has constantly shown it struggles to fully reproduce include understanding, personal connection, and navigation of complex emotional situations. This places an organization in a challenge: balancing the speed and cost-effectiveness of AI with the need to maintain a real, empathetic connection with its customers (Stoilova, 2021).

This chapter probes into the dual facets of AI in customer service: its potential to drive efficiency, on one hand, and its limitations in emulating the human touch, on the other. By examining the functionality of AI technologies, the benefits derived from them, and the issues they present, we aim to gain an understanding of how businesses can effectively integrate AI into their customer service strategies in a way that truly retains the core of human involvement (Reddy, 2022). How to balance that, the best practices, real-life examples of successful implementation, and the future trends that may set the pace for the evolving relationship between AI and human interaction in customer service.

THE ROLE OF AI IN CUSTOMER SERVICE

With incredible speed, artificial intelligence has turned into the cornerstone of modern customer service by promising a wide range of tools and technologies aimed at enhancing efficiency and generally improving the customer experience. AI technologies, such as chatbots, virtual assistants, and predictive analytics, form part of recent developments that have transformed business-to-customer interactions through a mix of automation and intelligent analytics that renew the traditional models of service.

Types of AI Technologies in Customer Service

1. **Chatbots and Virtual Assistants:** Probably the most visible customer service tools powered by AI are the chatbots and virtual assistants. Such systems take away a multitude of activities related to customer handling, from simple answers to frequently asked questions to guiding users through rather complicated processes. Using natural language processing-NLP-and machine learning algorithms enables these tools to perform conversations and immediate responses. This capability-amplifies resolution times and extends support to 24/7, thus greatly improving access by customers across multiple time zones (Nicolescu & Tudorache, 2022).
2. **Predictive Analytics:** Predictive analytics make use of AI in customer data analysis to predict future behaviors or needs. Predictive models can forecast customer queries by investigating historical data, establish patterns, and provide personalized engagement and quick resolution of probable problems before escalation (Yarlagadda, 2017). For example, predictive analytics can provide insight into which customers are likely to churn so that businesses can take proactive steps to prevent that from happening.
3. **Sentiment Analysis:** Sentiment analysis tools study customer feedback, reviews, and interactions over social media with a view to ascertaining the emotional vibe of the communication (Meyer et al., 2020). By understanding customer feelings, businesses would be able to make more targeted responses, quickly resolve negative experiences, and enhance overall satisfaction. It also helps a business to understand consumer preference and future trends.

Benefits of AI in Customer Service

1. **Better Efficiency and Scalability:** The major benefits of AI in customer service are that it can manage huge volumes of requests at a time. While human agents are capable of handling calls from a limited number of customers at any time, AI systems process hundreds of interactions simultaneously with extreme reductions in wait times and response times. This is important for scalability businesses with huge volumes or variable demands (Kedi et al., 2024).
2. **Reduction in Costs:** Automation enabled with the help of AI has let to huge cost reductions due to low human labor involvement. Basic tasks involving data entry, appointment scheduling, and normal troubleshooting can now be done by automated software, freeing up human resources to perform tasks that aim at better business results while reducing operation costs (Khan & Iqbal, 2020).

3. **Improved Accuracy and Consistency:** The use of AI systems will allow responses to customer inquiries to be more accurate and consistent. This avoids the possibility of human error since they will not be affected by moods or experiences, as is often the case with different agents (Naumov, 2019). AI tools will instead abide by pre-set rules and ensure uniformity in their approach to interactions.
4. **Data-driven Insights:** AI technologies provide the power of advanced analytics, hence enabling businesses to gain keen insights into customer behavior, preference, and trends. Further, this data is utilized to refine service strategies, personalize customer interactions, and make insightful decisions that will enhance the overall service quality.

BOOSTING EFFICIENCIES THROUGH AI

Customer service has changed completely in so many ways. AI technologies make many processes far more effective than before. The use of AI systems in customer service brings several advantages, such as streamlining processes and cutting the costs of generally raising the quality of the service. This section takes a closer look at how AI can provide efficiency gains and gives examples where it works well (Hollebeek et al., 2021).

Case Studies and Examples of Successful AI Implementations

1. **E-Commerce:** Major e-commerce websites, including Amazon and Alibaba, have already utilized AI in their customer service processes. Amazon's AI-powered chatbots, called Amazon Lex, manage millions of customer inquiries daily over queries about order status, product information, and returns. That automation frees human agents to interact with consumers on more specific areas that may require just a little more complexity for the customers. Similarly, Alibaba deploys AI in personalizing shopping experiences, inventory management, and efficient handling of customer service requests (Ping, 2019).
2. **Banking and Finance:** In the world of banking, institutions such as Bank of America and JPMorgan Chase employ AI-driven virtual assistants. Bank of America uses Erica. COiN is used by JPMorgan Chase to help customers manage routine tasks: checking account balances, transferring funds, and further financial advice. On the other hand, COiN uses AI to sort out and process bulk complex legal documents to decrease compliance and contract management time. Thereby, applications of AI accelerate the turn-around time of routine

processes while enabling accuracy levels higher and shrinking operational costs (Mehrotra, 2019).

3. **Telecommunications:** Companies in Telecommunications like Vodafone and Verizon have implemented AI into their customer support with queries pertaining to technical and billing aspects. It ranges from network problem-solving to taking customers through billing queries. Vodafone liberated human resources by automating such tasks, and in return, the operator managed to reduce waiting time and enhance the overall efficiency of customer service. Verizon applies AI to predictive maintenance: Network data analysis helps see into the future and resolve issues before they impact the customers (Ouyang et al., 2021).

Metrics for Measuring Efficiency Gains

For measuring the impact of AI in terms of efficiency, there are many different metrics on which the organizations rely and base their operations. These include:

1. **Response Times:** Artificial intelligence slashes the response time for any customer query. Metrics include average response time and first response time to see how fast the AI tools come up with solutions to customer issues. Normally, the shorter the response time, the higher the level of customer satisfaction and lower the frustration (Huang & Rust, 2021).
2. **Resolution Rate:** The resolution rate is the overall percentage of customer issues solved through an AI tool and never actually transferred to a human agent. If it's high, then AI handles regular inquiries and challenges smoothly, hence showing high returns for operation efficiency.
3. **Cost Savings:** Cost reduction analysis due to the implementation of AI in organizations helps quantify the financial benefits accruable from automation. Cost per interaction, total operational costs-all these indicate how AI contributes to cost reduction since heavy human labor will no longer be required (Davenport, 2018).
4. **Customer Satisfaction:** While the spotlight is on efficiency, customer satisfaction ranks equally important. Surveys, feedback, and satisfaction scores are some of the tools that help organizations assess how well AI-powered tools are serving customers' needs and if they actually enhance service experiences.

AI technologies have emerged as robust enablers in driving efficiency for customer services. Automation of routine tasks, increasing the volume of handled requests, and responses accurate and consistent-hence contribute a lot to operational efficiency. Successful applications of AI so far in various industries stand witness to the fact that the service industry can reduce costs by streamlining customer service processes and also raise overall service quality. But as AI continues to evolve, it is going to be used by organizations more and more to drive efficiency and competitive advantage in the ever-changing landscape of customer service (Huang & Rust, 2021).

MAINTAINING THE HUMAN TOUCH

Though AI technologies bring enormous benefits in terms of efficiency and scalability of operations, there is also a challenge in terms of preserving the 'human touch' in customer service interactions. Advanced AI systems often lack the ability to model empathy, emotional intelligence, and personalized connections like those provided by a human agent. In this section, we shall deliberate on the importance of a human touch in customer service and strategies for finding a balance between automation and personal interaction (Del Prete, 2021).

The Importance of Empathy and Emotional Intelligence

1. **Empathy:** In simple terms, empathy is a consequence when one gets an insider's look and feel about the feelings or emotions of another person. It is a very crucial aspect of customer service, where humans can easily tell even subtle differences in emotions and respond in ways that can affirm customers in their concerns and build rapport with them. An example is a customer whose service was interrupted for some reason. Such a customer needs personal touches, apology, and reassurance that can only be very genuine by a human. These empathetic responses dissipate tense situations and establish a good relationship between the customer and the company (Huang & Rust, 2018).
2. **Emotional Intelligence:** It is the ability to perceive, understand, manage one's emotions, and that of others. Human agents employ emotional intelligence in the conduction of more complex interactions aimed at addressing nuanced concerns, offering empathetic support that reaches out and connects with customers on a personal level (Del Prete, 2021). Emotional Intelligence becomes all the more important when sensitive matters are involved, such as dealing with complaints or grievances, wherein such understanding and empathy will go a long way towards making all the difference in customer experience.

How AI Can Supplement Human Interactions

1. **AI as a Support Tool:** Other than completely replacing human agents with their own, AI can also work as a very strong support tool to enhance the capability of the human agents. The AI systems can handle the routine inquiries

and tasks while the human agents can pay more concentration on complex and emotionally charged interactions. For instance, AI chatbots can handle very well frequent queries regarding account balance or order status while human agents may attend to issues that require empathy, such as dispute resolution or personalized service (Amershi et al., 2019).

2. **Augmented Intelligence:** Augmented intelligence addresses AI developed to support, rather than replace, human decision-making. Augmented intelligence in customer service provides the agent with contextual information, sentiment analysis, and suggestions for personalized responses. Such support enables human agents to arrive at more informed decisions and offer interactions that efficiently balance efficiency with a personal touch.

Strategies for Effective Integration of Human Agents

1.Hybrid Models: Hybrid customer service models integrate the power of AI with the human touch to make it absolutely seamless. In a hybrid model, AI generally takes up the preliminary sets of interactions with customers and escalates sensitive or complex issues to human agents. For instance, an AI system could triage customer inquiries, routing simple questions to a chatbot, while forwarding requests that require human empathy to live agents. In such ways, customers would get timely responses but with the subtle touch of human agents (Sycara & Lewis, 2004).

2. **Personalization and Customization**: AI can gather and analyze customer data for the purpose of offering personalized recommendations and insights that human agents make use of in personalizing interactions. For example, an AI system may monitor customer purchase tendencies and preferences. This would enable a human agent to pitch products of relevance or solve particular problems. Personalization increases the level of the customer experience because customers' needs and preferences are put into perspective (Thirupathi et al., 2024).
3. **Training and Development:** This refers to the training and development of customer service agents; investing in them will help them retain the human touch. The training programs should lay emphasis on enhancing their emotional intelligence, communication skills, and problem-solving abilities. Such a training mechanism helps the agents deliver unmatched customer care based on complex interactions.

Examples of Companies Successfully Balancing AI and Human Touch

1. **Sephora:** Sephora has successfully integrated AI and human interaction through the deployment of a virtual assistant known as Sephora Virtual Artist. This virtual assistant helps customers in identifying makeup products and offers personalized recommendations. However, for those customers who need more comprehensive help or have some concern, it is easy to connect with a human beauty advisor who offers expertise and personal support (Osiyevskyy et al., 2024).
2. **American Express:** American Express uses AI for basic customer service operations, such as general account inquiries and transaction notifications. Complex issues needing special attention or where some sort of emotional support is needed are transferred to human agents who can offer personal touch. This hybrid structure assures timely customer service with access to empathetic and knowledgeable support (Lindquist & Dautaj, 2021).

The human touch is an integral part of customer service for a complete and satisfying experience. While AI technologies increase efficiency by automating regular routine tasks, human agents are very important in providing the much-needed empathy and emotional intelligence besides support on a personalized level. Effective integration of AI and adoption of strategies by organizations will help them find a balance between leveraging strengths from automation and personal connections in enhancing overall customer experiences.

CHALLENGES AND LIMITATIONS OF AI IN CUSTOMER SERVICE

While AI technologies create substantial value in customer service, there is a corresponding set of challenges and limitations with organizational implementation that needs to be considered to ensure a positive customer experience. In this section, the challenges of AI systems are explored in light of their weaknesses and implications for customer service operations.

Understanding Context and Nuance

The inability of AI to contextualize or understand nuance in customer service is a major limitation it bears. With more enhanced algorithms and capacity for natural language processing, the application of AI, in most instances, fails to comprehend the subtlety of human communication. A good example is that while an AI might interpret direct queries, it will not understand sarcasm, humor, or complex emotional states. This can also lead to misunderstandings or inappropriate responses, which might cause frustration in customers who expect more sophisticated and contextual responses (Chaturvedi & Verma, 2023).

Lack of Emotional Intelligence

AI systems lack emotional intelligence, the immediate need in maintaining sensitive and complex customer interactions. Though AI is able to process information and develop responses based on patterns and data, it lacks the ability to display empathy or respond to emotional cues (Shaikh et al., 2023). For instance, when the customer is angry or hurt, the AI system will provide them with a generic response which may not have an especially peace-making appeal to the emotional sense of the situation (Xu et al., 2020). The result, therefore, is a badly replaced experience because the system lacks having feelings for the customer and thus lacks a compassionate approach. Where this is required, the appropriateness of the situation becomes incorrect.

Privacy and Security Concerns

One of the main problems brought about by adapting AI into customer service is a number of privacy and security issues. Most AI systems require full customer information, including personal information and history of interaction between customers and the organizations. The security of handling this information is very important, as its breach or misuse may lead to serious impacts on privacy violation and result in loss of customer trust. This calls for the organization to take full responsibility for guaranteeing protection of data through various measures and regulations to reduce such risks and secure the information of the customers.

Dependency on Quality Data

AI-engagement systems need high-quality data to function. Poor, incomplete, or biased data compromise performance and accuracy. For example, biased data used to train an AI model will yield a one-sided system with prejudiced output that might affect the overall quality of engagement with customers. It is very important that the models are trained on diverse and representative data such that the accuracy and fairness of AI-driven customer service are sustained (Khan & Iqbal, 2020).

Integration and Technical Issues

AI systems are complex and often difficult to integrate into existing customer service platforms. Companies may also encounter a variety of technical issues, including but not limited to compatibility problems, integration with the system, and data synchronization. Moreover, AI systems require ongoing technical know-how and resources to be updated and maintained. Technical glitches can paralyze service continuity and overall efficiency of AI-powered solutions in serving customers; therefore, proper implementation and support strategies are of essence (Hollebeek et al., 2021).

Managing Customer Expectation

The use of AI in customer service creates mismatched expectations among customers. Though AI is outperforming humans in so many routine or mundane tasks, for example, customers expect to get the same kind of sophistication and personalization from AI that they would receive from human agents (Katper et al., 2020). But when an AI system fails to live up to such expectation, dissatisfaction also grows. The perception of the customer can be managed through the dissemination of proper information regarding the role and limitation of AI to match their expectations and improve overall satisfaction (Khan & Iqbal, 2020).

Bias and Ethical Considerations

Ethical issues referring to AI in the field of customer support involve reinforcing bias that may arise in making decisions, sometimes affecting customers unjustly. AI systems, if not designed or cared for correctly, might reinforce certain existing biases related to data or algorithms on which the systems were founded. Ethical considerations can be enhanced through applying different strategies in bias detection and mitigation, ensuring that all AI systems work and provide transparent and non-discriminatory service (Naumov, 2019).

AI in customer service offers a lot of challenges and limitations that an organization has to go through if it is to ensure that the implementation is successful and the customers have great experiences. Issues that will be paramount in understanding and addressing involve context comprehension, emotional intelligence, privacy, quality of data, technical integration, customer expectations, and ethical considerations, which will aim at maximizing the benefits while reducing the adverse effects of AI (Alshareef & Tunio, 2022). With them in the lead, companies are relatively much better placed to exploit AI as a leverage for efficiencies in the performance of their customer service functions in the direction of an effective and properly balanced service delivery (Kedi et al., 2024).

BALANCING AI WITH HUMAN INTERACTION

From incorporating AI into customer service comes a plethora of benefits, but finding that sweet spot between automation and human contact is the key to success in ensuring a quality customer experience. This section explores some strategies for effectively integrating AI with human touchpoints to ensure that customer service is both efficient and empathetic.

Hybrid Customer Service Models

Hybrid models of customer service merge the powers of AI with strengths in human agents for seamless customer experiences. In this instance, AI takes over the routine and repetitive tasks while human agents take control of the more complex or sensitive interactions.

1. **AI-powered initial interactions:** AI can handle the initial stages of customer contacts. This includes answering basic queries, handling low-level requests, and routing the queries to appropriate departments. A chatbot, for example, can assist customers in making appointments or finding if a certain product is available within stock. In this way, simple issues get fixed as quickly as possible while saving human agents' time to resolve complex issues (Nicolescu & Tudorache, 2022).
2. **Escalation to Human Agents:** AI will further escalate the interactions to a human agent in cases where there are complex issues or emotional situations that AI itself cannot resolve. This ensures personalized attention for the customers and more empathetic support for intricate problems. Seamless transitions from AI to human agents maintain continuity in customer interactions and enhance overall satisfaction.

Personalization and Context Awareness

AI can help in personalization by collecting and processing customer data to give personalized recommendations and insight. But it should also be put into constructive use by human agents to maintain the context and personal touch of a human service interaction (Hollebeek et al., 2021).

1. **AI Insights Utilization**: AI systems can tell human agents a great deal about customer preference, purchase history, and past interactions with the company. Agents can provide solutions and personalized recommendations that are relevant and appealing to customers' needs. For example, a customer service representative may use AI-generated information to suggest related products based on a customer's buying history.
2. **Context within Conversations:** It is vital to ensure that human agents retain the context comprehensive from interactions made earlier by AI. It has to include the customer's history, previous issues, and any personal preferences. This would retain the context through effective communication and data sharing between the AI and human agents to avoid being repetitive and irrelevant (Yarlagadda, 2017).

Training and Development for Human Agents

It's about investing in the training and development of customer service agents so they can collaborate with AI systems by handling complex interactions.

1. **Improvement in Emotional Intelligence:** The training programs should develop emotional intelligence, communication ability, and problem-solving skills. Human agents with such skills will be in a better position to handle sensitive issues, sympathetic support, and relationship building with customers. Further, continuous training brings agents in line with best practices and evolving customer needs (Yarlagadda, 2017).
2. **Integrating AI Tools:** Training should involve how to use the power of AI tools effectively to interpret its insights. It will ensure that agents understand how to make effective use of AI support and data in order to provide quicker, more personalized service in each interaction (Nicolescu & Tudorache, 2022).

Customer Feedback and Continuous Improvement

Ongoing assessment and improvement regarding customer feedback and key performance metrics are crucial to maintain the right balance between AI and human interactions.

1. **Customer Feedback Collection**: On the organizational level, routine collection and analysis of customer feedback show how things are striking a balance between AI and human interaction. Feedback may reveal certain areas where either the working of AI is lagging behind or where the human agents might

need further support. Applying the information to make improvements will ensure that customer service stays effective and responsive (Reddy, 2022).

2. **Continuous Improvement:** It is befitting that an organization is constantly reviewing and refining its strategies on how AI and humans interact. This involves upgrading AI for higher precision and understanding contexts, besides improving the training programs for human agents. Continuous improvement helps in sustaining a high level of customer service and aligns it with dynamic customer expectations (Yarlagadda, 2017).

Examples of Successful Integration

Several organizations have struck a fine balance between AI and human interaction and provided good customer service:

1. **Zappos:** It implements AI to handle routine inquiries and tracking of orders, freeing human agents to make time available for higher complaints and personalized support. Their commitment to excellence in customer service can be reflected by the way it tries to strike a balance between automation and rich human touch.
2. **H&M:** H&M uses AI for processing customer orders and maintaining inventory. The human agents, however, handle the more complex inquiries of customers regarding order returns or style queries. This blend enables H&M to provide high-speed services without sacrificing a personalized feel.

The balance between investments in AI and human interaction yields optimal customer service operations. Hybrid models, personalization of interactions, investment in agent training, and solicitation of feedback-all these methods give customers a service experience that leverages the efficiency of AI and the empathy and subtlety of human contact. This balanced approach creates overall satisfaction and ensures that customer service is effective yet personable (Nicolescu & Tudorache, 2022).

FUTURE TRENDS AND INNOVATIONS

As technology continues to evolve, so will the face of customer service. The future of AI and customer service holds even greater efficiency, personalization, and overall customer experiences. This section discusses trends that are currently at a nascent stage, the state-of-the-art technologies, and other changes that might occur in the near future and may affect how customer service is provided (Yarlagadda, 2017).

Advancements in Natural Language Processing (NLP)

1. **Improved Language Understanding:** In years to come, enhancement of NLP will enable AI to understand human language more precisely in meaning and intent. Innovation in NLP will let AI systems deal more effectively with nuances, context, and subtlety in customer interactions. This will ensure that the interaction between the AI system and customers is natural, smooth, and frictionless, therefore minimizing misunderstandings and enhancing the quality of interaction (Hollebeek et al., 2021).
2. **Multilingual Capabilities:** With the advancement of NLP, the multilingual capability of AI will shift to smooth interaction in multiple languages and dialects. With improved support for languages, businesses will be able to provide more inclusive and accessible customer support to a wide and varying global customer base with no barrier in the languages used.

Integration of AI with Augmented Reality (AR) and Virtual Reality (VR)

1. **Better Customer Engagements:** The integration of AR and VR into artificial intelligence is very much liable to bring a radical change in customer engagements. As an example, AR facilitates the interaction with demo products or virtual fittings by empowering customers to experience products in real life within a fraction of a second. Similarly, in VR, one can simulate the customer support experience, for example, the virtual help desk or the virtual settings for troubleshooting various issues (Khan & Iqbal, 2020).
2. **Training and Support:** Both AR and VR can also be utilized for training and support. AI-powered virtual environments can model complex customer service scenarios for training. Agents can practice and hone their skills in such a controlled environment. This immersive form of training will better equip agents to raise the overall standards of service (Stoilova, 2021).

AI-Driven Personalization and Predictive Analytics

1. **Hyper-Personalized Experiences:** AI-driven personalization in the near future will be able to offer hyper-personalized customer experiences for businesses. By analyzing large volumes of data, AI systems will be able to predict individual customer needs and preferences with uncanny accuracy. This level of personalisation can offer tailor-made recommendations, proactive offering of services, and highly relevant interactions that strike a chord with each customer (Kedi et al., 2024).

2. **Predictive Customer Service:** Predictive analytics shall form the core in understanding customer need and resolving any potential issues even before they arise. The AI systems will utilize historic data, patterns of behavior, and context to predict when customers can have an enquiry and what the response might be in advance. This will reduce the chances of service disruptions and thereby increase customer satisfaction (Yarlagadda, 2017).

Ethical AI and Responsible Innovation

1. **Minimizing Bias and Ensuring Fairness:** In the future, a part of ethical considerations and mitigation of bias will continue to be very crucial since AI is increasingly integrated in customer service. Future invention focuses on developing transparent, no discriminating, and unbiased AI systems that will treat all customers equitably with no instances of bias reinforcement through algorithms and practices (Sadhu et al., 2024).
2. **Enhanced Privacy and Security:** As the relationship between customers and corporations becomes increasingly stretched, customer privacy and security of data will be of utmost importance. Future advancements will involve increased protection through advanced methods of encryption and safe storage of data. Both responsible AI practices and further evolving regulations on data protection will necessitate that organizations seek to gain customer trust by protecting sensitive information (Meyer et al., 2020).

Human-AI Collaboration and Co-creation

1. **Amplifying Human Capabilities:** The future of customer service is more towards collaboration between AI and human agents. AI systems are just tools that augment human capabilities, rather than replace them. It's the AI that will drive human agents to more effective and informed support by providing them with data, insights, and recommendations in real-time.
2. **Co-creation and Innovation:** Beyond this, organizations might contemplate co-creation, whereby AI and human agents create together in customer service solutions and innovations. Collaboration could yield the effect of creating new tools, processes, and methods to improve customer experiences and respond to emerging challenges (Nicolescu & Tudorache, 2022).

Real Time Analytics and Feedback Loops

1. **Real-time Insights:** Future innovations will focus on leveraging real-time analytics to provide immediate insights into customer interactions and service performance. AI systems analyze the data in real time and empower businesses to make instant adjustments and improvements in customer service operations (Kedi et al., 2024).
2. **Continuous Improvement:** Real-time feedback loops will facilitate continuous improvement by allowing organizations to track customer feedback, pinpoint trends, and implement change faster. This will enable business enterprises to remain responsive to the needs and preferences of customers, assuring that the quality of service remains high.

Exciting trends and innovations in AI and its connected technologies are going to shape the future face of customer service. Improvements in NLP, use cases involving AR and VR, personalization due to AI, ethical considerations, collaboration of humans and AI, and analytics in real time-all these will be some of the factors crucial for bettering customer experience. By all this, being at the forefront of such progress and embracing responsible innovation, organizations can take advantage of AI to its full capacity to deliver excellent, forward-looking customer service (Yarlagadda, 2017).

IMPLICATIONS

The integration of AI in customer service will have wide-ranging implications on practical, managerial, ethical, and societal dimensions. While AI technologies are increasingly pervasively adopted by organizations to better support customers, it is increasingly important to consider the wider business practice, workforce dynamic, and societal value implications such developments may bring about.

Practical Implications

Pragmatically, AI-driven customer service pays very strong dividends operationally. Automation cuts down response times, and when it comes to addressing routine queries, accuracy is increased, with scaling of customer support becoming easy. However, in practice, companies will have to strike a balance between efficiency provided by AI and human interaction in order to ensure a personalized customer experience (Meyer et al., 2020). While AI is good at streamlining workflows, investment in training human agents remains key to customer satisfaction when it comes to handling complex issues and empathetic interactions.

Managerial Implications

The big challenge for any manager is how to integrate AI systems into the existing models of customer service without losing that personal touch which engenders loyalty among customers. Implementation requires a rethinking of the organizational structure and workflow, providing space for both artificial intelligence systems and human agents in a hybrid model. Create an environment of continuous learning, and leaders should ensure that workers are properly trained to adopt the use of AI tools and technological changes. Ongoing monitoring of the performance of AI into the business goals will, particularly be very important (Kedi et al., 2024).

Ethical Considerations

AI in customer service raises a number of ethical issues, including privacy, data security, and bias. Information about customers must be collected and used in a responsible manner, with due respect for data protection legislation such as the GDPR. Designs for AI systems should ensure that any decision-making processes are free of bias and treat all customers equitably. Transparency in operations between customers and AI is an important means whereby customers can begin to trust the idea; businesses have got to explain how the AI works and why it makes particular decisions (Khan & Iqbal, 2020).

Societal Implications

The rise of AI in customer service has greater societal implications, not least regarding the potential impact on employment. While AI can perform basic tasks, there is still an argument about job losses for customer service agents. On the other hand, AI creates other opportunities in looking after and refining the systems themselves. On a more macro level, the presence of this emerging AI will mean that societal expectations as to quality, efficiency, and the availability of service will shift. Ensuring that the engagement of AI technologies enhances customer support in a way that is inclusive and equitable will therefore be at the heart of any approach to address broader societal concerns (Kedi et al., 2024).

CONCLUSION

Moving into the new age of customer service, the incorporation of AI brings transformative opportunities fraught with a set of complex challenges. AI automates routine work and increases efficiency while simultaneously creating personalized experiences for customers. While improvements to NLP, augmentation of AR and VR, and use of predictive analytics set the benchmark for customer service excellence, this will be what all these innovations will result in: making customer support more engaging, responsive, and personalized.

There does need to be a balance between efficiencies through AI and the human touch. While AI may process vast volumes of information, repetitive tasks, and simple queries, human agents will not be replaced in a world where empathy, emotional intelligence, and complex or sensitive situations are prevalent. The proper balance between complete automation and personal interaction will determine the future of customer service, where technology will enhance the quality of customer care, not diminish it.

Further, while AI is developed gradually, issues like minimizing bias, protecting privacy, and transparency will also come to the fore. It will be essential for organizations to be regarded as responsible with AI in order not to lose customers' trust and also treat customers without bias. In addition, investment in training and development will be crucial for human agents to use AI tools effectively and to create remarkable service.

Considering AI and the whole other lot of technologies keep evolving, many more innovations could be developed concerning customer service. The capability of moving with emerging trends and, at the same time, with agility for new developments allows companies to fully develop their customer service capability and create memorable positive experiences for their customers. It is a future wherein AI and human interaction will blend seamlessly to define the future of customer service, shaping the way we connect with and support customers moving as fast as ever.

REFERENCES

Alshareef, N., & Tunio, M. N. (2022). Role of leadership in adoption of blockchain technology in small and medium enterprises in Saudi Arabia. *Frontiers in Psychology*, 13, 911432. DOI: 10.3389/fpsyg.2022.911432 PMID: 35602740

Amershi, S., Weld, D., Vorvoreanu, M., Fourney, A., Nushi, B., Collisson, P., & Horvitz, E. (2019, May). Guidelines for human-AI interaction. In *Proceedings of the 2019 CHI conference on human factors in computing systems* (pp. 1-13). DOI: 10.1145/3290605.3300233

Chaturvedi, R., & Verma, S. (2023). Opportunities and challenges of AI-driven customer service. In *Artificial intelligence in customer service: The next frontier for personalized engagement* (pp. 33–71). IGI Global. DOI: 10.1007/978-3-031-33898-4_3

Davenport, T. H. (2018). *The AI advantage: How to put the artificial intelligence revolution to work.* MIT Press. DOI: 10.7551/mitpress/11781.001.0001

Del Prete, M. (2021). Emotional artificial intelligence: Detecting and managing customer emotions in automated customer service. *Journal of Service Research.* Advance online publication. DOI: 10.1177/10946705211015680

Hollebeek, L. D., Sprott, D. E., & Brady, M. K. (2021). Rise of the machines? Customer engagement in automated service interactions. *Journal of Service Research*, 24(1), 3–8. DOI: 10.1177/1094670520975110

Huang, M. H., & Rust, R. T. (2018). Artificial intelligence in service. *Journal of Service Research*, 21(2), 155–172. DOI: 10.1177/1094670517752459

Huang, M. H., & Rust, R. T. (2021). Engaged to a robot? The role of AI in service. *Journal of Service Research*, 24(1), 30–41. DOI: 10.1177/1094670520902266

Katper, N. K., Tunio, M. N., Hussain, N., Junejo, A., & Gilal, F. G. (2020). COVID-19 crises: Global economic shocks vs Pakistan economic shocks. *Advances in Science. Technology and Engineering Systems Journal*, 5(4), 645–654. DOI: 10.25046/aj050481

Kedi, W. E., Ejimuda, C., Idemudia, C., & Ijomah, T. I. (2024). AI software for personalized marketing automation in SMEs: Enhancing customer experience and sales. *World Journal of Advanced Research and Reviews*, 23(1), 1981–1990. DOI: 10.30574/wjarr.2024.23.1.2159

Khan, S., & Iqbal, M. (2020, June). AI-powered customer service: Does it optimize customer experience? In *2020 8th International Conference on Reliability, Infocom Technologies and Optimization (Trends and Future Directions)* (ICRITO) (pp. 590-594). IEEE. DOI: 10.1109/ICRITO48877.2020.9197876

Lindquist, D. H., & Dautaj, Y. (2021). AI in international arbitration: Need for the human touch. *J. Disp. Resol.*, 39.

Mehrotra, A. (2019, April). Artificial intelligence in financial services: Need to blend automation with human touch. In *2019 International Conference on Automation, Computational and Technology Management (ICACTM)* (pp. 342-347). IEEE. DOI: 10.1109/ICACTM.2019.8776741

Meyer, C., Cohen, D., & Nair, S. (2020). From automats to algorithms: The automation of services using artificial intelligence. *Journal of Service Management*, 31(2), 145–161. DOI: 10.1108/JOSM-05-2019-0161

Naumov, N. (2019). The impact of robots, artificial intelligence, and service automation on service quality and service experience in hospitality. In *Robots, artificial intelligence, and service automation in travel, tourism and hospitality* (pp. 123–133). Emerald Publishing Limited., DOI: 10.1108/978-1-78756-687-320191007

Nicolescu, L., & Tudorache, M. T. (2022). Human-computer interaction in customer service: The experience with AI chatbots—a systematic literature review. *Electronics (Basel)*, 11(10), 1579. DOI: 10.3390/electronics11101579

Osiyevskyy, O., Umantsiv, Y., & Kavun, O. (2024). Strategy for striking the omnichannel balance in Retail 4.0. *Strategy and Leadership*. Advance online publication. DOI: 10.1108/SL-12-2023-0120

Ouyang, Y., Wang, L., Yang, A., Shah, M., Belanger, D., Gao, T., . . . Zhang, Y. (2021). The next decade of telecommunications artificial intelligence. *arXiv preprint arXiv:2101.09163.*

Ping, N. L. (2019, December). Constructs for artificial intelligence customer service in e-commerce. In *2019 6th International Conference on Research and Innovation in Information Systems (ICRIIS)* (pp. 1-6). IEEE. DOI: 10.1109/ICRIIS48246.2019.9073486

Reddy, S. R. B. (2022). Enhancing customer experience through AI-powered marketing automation: Strategies and best practices for Industry 4.0. *Journal of Artificial Intelligence Research*, 2(1), 36–46.

Sadhu, A. K. R., Parfenov, M., Saripov, D., Muravev, M., & Sadhu, A. K. R. (2024). Enhancing customer service automation and user satisfaction: An exploration of AI-powered chatbot implementation within customer relationship management systems. *Journal of Computational Intelligence and Robotics*, 4(1), 103–123.

Shaikh, E., Watto, W. A., Brahmi, M., Tunio, M. N., & Lighari, S. N. (2023). Customer satisfaction and customer loyalty: An empirical case study on the impact of benefits generated through smartphone applications. *International Journal of Public Sector*.

Stoilova, E. (2021). AI chatbots as a customer service and support tool. *ROBONOMICS: The Journal of the Automated Economy*, 2, 21–21.

Sycara, K., & Lewis, M. (2004). Integrating intelligent agents into human teams.

Thirupathi, L., Sunkara, S. H., Boodala, I. R., & Vempati, V. S. (2024). Personalization and customization strategies with AI in service marketing. In *Integrating AI-driven technologies into service marketing* (pp. 499–524). IGI Global. DOI: 10.4018/979-8-3693-7122-0.ch024

Xu, Y., Shieh, C. H., van Esch, P., & Ling, I. L. (2020). AI customer service: Task complexity, problem-solving ability, and usage intention. *Australasian Marketing Journal*, 28(4), 189–199. DOI: 10.1016/j.ausmj.2020.03.005

Yarlagadda, R. T. (2017). *AI automation and its future in the United States. International Journal of Creative Research Thoughts*. IJCRT., DOI: 10.32628/IJCRT

Chapter 10

Leveraging AI to Tailor Customer Engagement With Personalized Marketing Strategies

Thi Minh Ngoc Luu
https://orcid.org/0000-0002-5972-7752
Vietnam National University, Vietnam

Shashank Mittal
O.P. Jindal Global University, India

Sushant Gupta
Lovely Professional University, India

ABSTRACT

AI-driven personalization has revolutionized marketing by enabling businesses to create highly tailored customer experiences. This chapter explores the role of AI in shaping personalized marketing strategies, emphasizing the advancements in machine learning, natural language processing, and predictive analytics. It discusses how AI enhances customer engagement through hyper-personalization, integrating technologies like augmented reality (AR) and virtual reality (VR), and addresses the ethical considerations and challenges involved. Practical tips and best practices for implementing AI-driven personalization, including data quality management, tool selection, and ethical practices, are provided. Future trends such as predictive analytics and AI-generated creative content are highlighted as key areas for continued development. Businesses that effectively harness these AI capabilities can achieve significant improvements in customer satisfaction and loyalty.

DOI: 10.4018/979-8-3373-0219-5.ch010

INTRODUCTION

In this Cut-throat environment of business today, personalized marketing is the mother of all tools any entrepreneur can wield to cut above the rest in a face of stiff competition and be able to connect with customers at a more intimate level. In fact, those traditional ways of marketing, characterized by a wide, general broadcast of messages, will fall short of delivering customers' experiences of specialization that pervades every bit of modern life (Afshan et al., 2021). With each passing day, artificial intelligence is growing and has taken up a major role in marketing. It provides new dimensions to personalization of customer experience and accelerator of business growth (Akın, 2024).

Personalized marketing is all about making relevant adjustments to meet the unique needs of each customer in relation to preference, behavior, and requirements. It does more than just increase the relevance of marketing messages; it brings substantial satisfaction and loyalty among customers. Most especially, this is a goldmine for entrepreneurs who sometimes have limited resources to function with and face cutthroat competition (Azhar & Akhtar, 2020). AI technologies enable companies to process large volumes of information, determine patterns within it, and create insights that lead to better and more accurate marketing strategies. AI plays a number of roles in personalized marketing. These complex data sets, when analyzed through machine learning algorithms, are more likely to help businesses predict customer behaviors and preferences with remarkable accuracy (Barutcu et al., 2017). It is natural language processing that enables understanding and responding to customer inquiries and feedback in a much more human-like fashion. Predictive analytics provides the entrepreneur with tools at their fingertips for anticipating the needs of customers in the future and crafting offerings to suit these needs. Jointly, these technologies enable entrepreneurs to craft very personalized experiences that connect well with their target audience and, in time, yield high engagement and conversion rates.

The integration of AI into marketing strategies further presents new opportunities for entrepreneurs to build closer ties with their customers. From AI insight, businesses can design and send personalized content and messaging directly to meet the needs and interests of each individual customer. Such a level of personalization not only enhances customer experience but also instills in them a sense of bonding and loyalty. To the entrepreneurs, this means that new customers come in but old ones are retained and cared for, hence ensuring continuity in business (Bello & Muazu, 2023).

However, this is not quite seamless with AI-powered personal marketing strategy. Entrepreneurs have to address the data privacy and ethical issues to ensure sensitive customer information is well taken care of transparently. There are also technical and operational challenges regarding how to embed AI technologies into current marketing tools and systems. Yet, despite these challenges, the possible benefits from AI-powered personalization are great and outweigh the difficulties; hence, it is a mighty tool for entrepreneurs to develop better marketing strategies and sustain their competitive advantage (Bettiol et al., 2012).

As we delve deeper and more in-depth with AI and personalized marketing, the intersection of both really holds much promise for the future of entrepreneurship. AI will let the entrepreneurs unlock newer levels of customer engagement and drive meaningful business outcomes. The insights that this chapter will be dealing with will revolve around how to effectively use AI in devising a personalized marketing strategy-illustrating practical insights and real examples relevant for entrepreneurs on this journey of much-needed target-oriented marketing (Guerola-Navarro et al., 2024).

UNDERSTANDING PERSONALIZED MARKETING

Personalization in marketing is one way of expressing the conceptual shift away from the old ways and mass-market methods toward a more differentiated and personalized way, targeting each different customer's needs and wants. It reflects the growing realization that consumers are not some large group but really a diverse assemblage of people with unique interests, behaviors, and expectations. At its very core, personalized marketing is about making the marketing personal to create more relevant and engaging experiences for every customer.

Personalised marketing is based on the belief that personal messages are always more effective than general ones. Traditionally, most marketing campaigns used to take cues from broad demographic categories and mass media channels, usually yielding low hit ratios and wasted money. Personalised marketing interventions, however, use data and technology for more granular segmentation of audiences and deliver personalized content which strikes a chord at levels closer to the individual. This means that personalization ensures a higher chance of capturing the attention of a customer and helps increase the overall effectiveness of marketing efforts (Hendrix, 2015).

One of the foundational aspects of personalization in marketing is the usage of customer data. Information about the data on customer interactions with multiple touchpoints, including websites, purchase history, social networks, and customer feedback, may offer the business valuable insights into the preference and behavior of customers. This means that with the data-driven approach, marketers would have to divide their audience into minute segments and create messages that say something to those very needs and interests (Kaliyamoorthy & Theeban, 2013). For instance, an e-retailer can use data from purchase history to offer a customer suggestions about merchandise that matches his or her buying patterns, while the travel company uses browsing behavior to suggest personally tailored packages.

Personalization in marketing began to pick up an even quicker pace when digital technologies came into the viewfinder. Access to enormous volumes of information on customers became available where big data and advanced analytics tools were concerned. Machine learning algorithms and AI technologies can enable marketers to process and analyze such data much more efficiently, discovering the hidden patterns and trends that guide more precise targeting. Additionally, this suite of technologies can help in personalization automation for specific aspects, such as automatic email content generation, or in real-time optimization of ad placements (Kumar, 2024).

Personalized marketing goes beyond simple data-driven targeting; personalization can also mean the development of personalized experiences that deepen the brand's relationship with the customer. This can be as basic as having the UI of a website reflect customer preference, customized product recommendations presented to customers, or personalized content delivered across any channel. The goal should be to create a frictionless, engaging experience which is relevant and valuable to the individual customer (Lantos, 2014).

Personalization is also not a one-time strategy; rather, it is dynamic and progressive through time. When the preference and behavior of customers start to change, for that reason, marketers have to keep refining their strategies to ensure their personalizing attempts always pay off as expected. That requires continuous analysis and adaptation with a full commitment to keeping in touch with emerging trends and technologies in personalization.

In all, personalized marketing is disruptive; it uses data and technology to create more relevant and engaging experiences with customers. An ability to comprehend and apply the principles of personalized marketing empowers enterprises to relate better with their audiences, fostering higher engagement and driving improved marketing outcomes (Rozaq et al., 2021). With technology continuing to improve, personalization opportunities continue to expand, offering even greater potential for businesses when it comes to creating experiences that are both meaningful and impactful for their customers.

AI IN PERSONALIZED MARKETING

Artificial Intelligence uprooted the concept of personalized marketing and empowered it with a lot of tools and technologies that enhanced targeting strategies, making them far more effective and precise. The application of AI in personalized marketing has been multidimensional, right from data analysis to content generation and customer interaction, up to predictive analytics. This transformative technology enables companies to transcend older methods of marketing and ways of reaching their customers with much more value and height.

Core to how AI contributes to personalized marketing lies the extraordinary speed and accuracy in processing and analyzing vast volumes of data. Using conventional marketing methods, there was much manual work in data analysis, which was normally very time-consuming and limited in scope. AI can manipulate large proportions of data obtained from multiple sources, like social media interactions, purchase history, or website behavior-all of these stands to reveal different pieces of information that were previously obscured from marketers. These aspects of AI-majorly machine learning algorithms-can recognize patterns and trends in this information, which can also enable companies to better segment their audience and create very focused marketing campaigns (Sahoo & Raghu, 2023). Machine learning is important for personalization in marketing, as it learns from the customers' interaction and behavior constantly. Unlike traditional models that require static rules and criteria, machine learning algorithms adapt and evolve based on new data inputs. This dynamic capability makes the marketers keep optimizing their strategies in real time, responding to changes in customer preference and market condition with pace. Machine learning can study open rates, click-through rates, and responses to find out what email content and timing is most effective for a specific recipient to optimize an email marketing campaign. The personalization of marketing will also be greatly improved by another key technology in AI: NLP. With NLP, the interactions are bound to get more sophisticated since it helps the machine understand and interpret human language. AI might also be able to study customer feedback, reviews, and social media posts through NLP to perceive customers' sentiments and preferences (Shaikh et al., 2022). This allows for personalization at levels that better resonate with an audience. Also, customer support can have personalization through NLP-driven chatbots and voice assistants that are capable of responding to specific customer information and requests. Predictive analytics, enabled by AI, further strengthens personalized marketing with predictions about future customer behaviors and preferences (Tunio et al., 2023; Tunio et al., 2021; Usman et al., 2024). Analyzing historical data for trends, predictive analytics is able to anticipate what type of product or service a customer is likely to be interested in. Such foresight enables the businesses to always stay one step ahead by providing service to their customers through personalized recommendation and promotion, even before the customer voices a need. An online retailer, for example, would utilize predictive analytics in offering the customer those products that he or she is likely to purchase, based on his browsing history and previous interactions (Sigué & Biboum, 2020).

AI can also offer dynamic personalization of content, whereby marketing messages and content become tailored in real time with regard to the individual user's experience. This goes beyond simple static personalization, with enterprises thus prepared to deliver very relevant content for each user, fluidly updated under the current context of their interaction. For example, it might be that the homepage or the highlighted products of a website change on the basis of browser history and individual preferences for greater personal relevancy (Stokes, 2000).

In addition to that, AI supports personalization marketing automation, which in return saves marketers from doing such a large amount of work and allows them to focus on strategic activities. Routine works, such as content creation, ad targeting, and campaign management, can be carried out with a high degree of accuracy and efficiency by automated systems. This helps not only to enhance the efficiency of the operation but also ensures that the scale of every personalized marketing activity is executed (Tunio, 2020).

In short, AI acts as a critical enabler in personalized marketing for improvement in data analysis, development and creation of content, customer interaction, and predictability. Its ability to process volumes of data, adaptability to the changing environments, and real-time personalization make it invaluable for businesses desiring to reach out effectively to their customers (Tunio et al., 2022). As AI technology continues to get better, so does its impact on personalized marketing, affording businesses even more opportunities to reach their audience and drive meaningful results.

AI-POWERED CUSTOMER INSIGHTS

AI-powered customer insights mean a sea change in the way companies understand and communicate with their audience. Companies can gain better insights into their customers using advanced AI technologies and hence implement more effective and personalized marketing. The section shall look at how AI helps in churning out valuable customer insights with respect to data collection and analysis, customer segmentation, and the development of actionable profiles.

1. Data Collection and Integration

Collection and integration of multi-sourced data are critical components of AI-powered customer insights. Today's consumer interacts with brands through several touchpoints: websites, social media, emails, and mobile applications. Each of these touchpoints provides enriching data around browsing behavior of your target audience, purchase history, social media activity, and customer feedback. Specifically,

AI systems have the ability to aggregate and integrate data from a wide variety of sources, and do so with broad visibility into customer interactions and preferences.

Advanced AI technologies, like data mining and web scraping, support the extraction of relevant data from a variety of online sources. For instance, AI algorithms scrape through social media posts to see what customers say about a company, track emergent trends, and find the specific key influencers. By consolidating data from these various sources, businesses can complete the picture of their customers through a holistic view of their preferences, behaviors, and needs (Yang, 2018).

2. Data Analysis and Pattern Recognition

Collected data then requires AI's active contribution to analyze and interpret the same. Machine learning algorithms work best to draw patterns and trends from large data. These algorithms can find out important correlations and anomalies that may not be easily visible if one looks through the data manually. For example, a machine learning model might uncover seasonal trends or customer purchase tendencies towards specific product categories.

AI-driven data analytics has the power to unlock insights into customer behavior and preference for the business. For example, clustering algorithms allow customers with similar traits to be divided into distinct groups, based on either purchase habits or engagement levels. Such segmentation will enable the enterprise to craft marketing strategies that would address the unique needs and interests of each group.

3. Customer Segmentation

AI embeds customer segments with more granularity and dynamism. Most traditional approaches to segmentation are based on wide, sweeping demographic categories that fail to capture the full texture of customer preferences. AI, in contrast, enables finer-grained segmentation based on a wide range of behavioral, contextual, and psychographic elements.

For example, AI algorithms segment customers according to their pattern of engagement, such as how often they visit, the amount of time spent on a particular page, and the response to prior marketing campaigns (Afshan et al., 2021). It is this level of granularity that enables businesses to craft very specific marketing messages and offers that will be most in concert with each segment. In addition, AI readjusts segments in real time based on newer data being fed into it, so the relevance and effectiveness of marketing strategies are kept intact.

4. Development of Actionable Customer Profiles

AI insight further goes down to create actionable customer profiles beyond segmentation. These are developed as very specific representations of individual customers or segments, embedding information such as preference, purchase history, and behavior. AI-driven tools analyze data coming from various sources and synthesize the same into comprehensive and actionable insights in the form of these profiles.

For example, a customer profile may include data on the product categories that a customer is interested in, how often he or she buys products, and his or her responsiveness to promotional offers (Yang, 2018). This level of detail enables businesses to offer personalized marketing with great accuracy. Using these profiles, marketers will be able to tailor product recommendations, customize email content, and develop focused advertising campaigns for the individual customers' behaviors and preferences.

5. Predictive Analytics and Future Trends

AI-powered customer insights also help in predictive analytics, which is purposed at understanding future customer behaviors or trends from analysis of past data. Predictive models utilize machine learning algorithms to learn from past interactions and predict future actions, such as likely purchase behaviors or churn risk. This, in turn, enables a business to take proactive measures with regard to customer needs and optimize its marketing strategies.

For example, predictive analytics can identify just which customers are most likely to leave and enable the business to establish strategies for customer retention through special offers or personalized communications. Similarly, AI is able to predict demands for specific products or services, thus enabling a business to manage its inventories better while optimizing supply chain operations.

In a nutshell, AI-powered customer insights form one important step ahead in the world of understanding and engaging with customers. By applying AI technologies in data collection, analyses, segmentation, and prediction, businesses can have a better and actionable grasp of their audience. This allows for effective personalization, targeted marketing strategies, and improved customer relationships-things that drive superior business outcomes and competitive advantage (Afshan et al., 2021).

DEVELOPING AI-DRIVEN MARKETING STRATEGIES

AI marketing strategy development means the adoption of artificial intelligence technologies for conceptualization in the creation of more effective, targeted, and personalized marketing activities. AI equips one with tools and insights necessary for the delivery of marketing strategies down to the level of customers' preferences, optimizes campaigns, and ensures business growth (Akın, 2024). This section shows how to develop such a strategy, focused on key areas: personalization of content and messaging, dynamic delivery of content, and integrating AI into a variety of marketing channels (Azhar & Akhtar, 2020).

1. Personalization of Content and Messaging

AI-driven marketing strategies have become all about personalized content and messaging. AI technologies help companies create content that best suits the needs of a particular customer by analyzing their behaviors, preferences, and various interactions with the company. The whole process starts with data gathering where AI systems integrate information from various touch-points: web usage, purchase history, and social networking platforms (Barutcu et al., 2017).

For instance, AI can pick out critical insights from the data regarding the interests and needs of each customer. The insights provide marketers with the opportunity to create personalized content for each individual. For example, AI can generate an email campaign with a customized message related to product recommendations based on their previous purchases or browsing history. Similarly, AI can help craft ad copy and promotional offers targeted at specific customer segments.

NLP, on the other hand, plays a great role in personalizing messaging. NLP algorithms can listen to the messages and feedback coming from the customer side to understand sentiment and context, which would in turn enable businesses to craft relevant messages. That means content can be made to feel more relevant and engaging to the recipient, therefore making marketing more effective (Kumar, 2024).

2. Dynamic Content Delivery

Dynamic content delivery refers to a process in which marketing content gets automatically aligned with the interaction and preference of each individual customer. AI technologies make such an ability possible through continuous data analysis to make adjustments in content. This approach guarantees that the customers get relevant content in respect to their immediate context, thus increasing engagement and conversion rates (Afshan et al., 2021).

For instance, an e-commerce website can dynamically alter the layout of its homepage using AI in compliance with a user's browsing history and preferences. For example, the website will likely be focusing on sports products and promotions on the home page if the customer often looks up athletic wear. Similarly, AI-driven ad platforms can now aim their ads better by showing ads that are in tune with the user's current interests and behaviors (Yang, 2018).

With that said, dynamic content also extends to personalized recommendations. AI algorithms can analyze prior customer behavior to accurately predict which products or services a person is likely to be interested in. Recommendations can be shown in all forms, whether that's through a list of personalized products on your website or tailored content within a mobile app. By providing content to individuals that aligns with their preferences, businesses will drive user satisfaction, nudging them through higher levels of engagement (Azhar & Akhtar, 2020).

3. Omni-Channel AI Marketing

AI on multiple marketing channels plays an important role in developing a coherent and effective strategy. AI technologies can enhance everything, from email campaigns to social media management, SEO, and customer support. The secret behind such integration lies in the coherence of AI tools and insights applied to all touchpoints (Barutcu et al., 2017).

Through email marketing, for example, AI can automate personalized content development and send-time optimization based on user behavior. Social media management powered by AI can analyze engagement metrics across all platforms to determine what kind of content best works and at what time. SEO, too, employs AI in finding relevant keywords and optimizing content for search engines in keeping with user search patterns (Guerola-Navarro et al., 2024).

AI also fuels customer support by availing chatbots and virtual assistants to provide responses and recommendations based on customer queries and interaction. In this way, AI embedded in customer support ensures that the customers are timely and relevantly supported to complete their desired task. This again enhances overall customer experience.

4. Measuring and Optimizing Campaign Performance

AI-driven marketing strategies must, therefore, be measured and continuously optimized for effectiveness. AI technologies offer a range of analytics and reporting functionalities that enable companies to track campaign performance in real time.

It gives actionable insights about KPIs such as click-through rates, conversion rate, and customer engagement metrics that help marketers to understand whether or not their marketing efforts are really paying off (Azhar & Akhtar, 2020).

AI can also track trends and patterns in campaign performance data to provide insight into what kind of strategies work best (Kumar, 2024). This information helps the marketers make data-driven decisions and optimize their campaigns. For instance, if AI analysis shows certain types of content create higher engagement, then marketers can focus on creating more content in that style to improve overall performance (Akın, 2024; Bettiol et al., 2012).

AI-powered A/B Testing: Another effective tool in marketing optimization, AI will create multiple versions of the content, automatically test it, and report back with which one does best. Thus, such a method will enable business people to tailor their strategies based on empirical evidence so as to make the marketing strategy far more effective (Afshan et al., 2021).

5. Ensuring Ethical Use of AI

In the development of AI-driven marketing strategies by businesses, consideration needs to be made regarding the ethical use of AI. This can be done by maintaining the trust of customers through data privacy and transparency. Every business organization will comply with respective data protection legislation and shall inform their customers about how their data are collected and used. The ethical practices encompass making responsible use of data and designing AI systems so that they avoid bias and prejudices (Bello & Muazu, 2023).

In all, AI-powered marketing strategy development encompasses AI technologies for personalization of content, dynamic messaging, and integration of AI across different marketing channels. The power of AI in business helps take one's marketing up a notch to attract more customers towards growth. Continuous measurement, optimization, but, importantly, ethical considerations in this regard make AI-powered strategies effective and responsible in answering customer needs (Barutcu et al., 2017).

CHALLENGES AND CONSIDERATIONS

While AI-driven marketing holds a great deal of advantages, the implementation and maintenance of strategies also raise a number of challenges and considerations that businesses must work with. Each of these challenges calls for serious consideration of strategy with respect to data management and integration, along with ethical concerns. This section looks at some of the major challenges in using AI for marketing and ascertains how businesses can work to overcome the impediments to effective application. Some of the key challenges associated with AI-powered marketing include the following:

1. Data Privacy and Security

One of the major challenges with AI-powered marketing relates to data privacy and security. AI-based technologies must be fed from large datasets that give insight and personalized content. However, in most cases, this data includes sensitive information about customers, which raises the question of collection, storage, and utilization.

Businesses are supposed to follow data protection directives such as the General Data Protection Regulation of Europe or the California Consumer Privacy Act of America. These ensure explicit consent must be sought before gathering customers' data, avenues must be provided for opting out, and that all data must be kept securely (Akın, 2024).

This can be achieved by implanting security features in data management, encryption, and control of access. Firms should also show transparency in their data practices; this might include explaining how the customer's information is used and providing options so that users may have a say in the use or handling of their data. This instills confidence in the customer and ensures that the rule of law on privacy is observed (Bettiol et al., 2012).

2. Integration with Current Systems

It is challenging to integrate AI technologies with the required existing marketing tools and systems. Most firms rely on a blend of legacy systems, third-party applications, and in-house-developed solutions for their marketing operations. In fact, introducing AI requires seamless integration into existing systems so that new technologies function well with the current systems (Azhar & Akhtar, 2020).

These are because of differences in data formats, system architecture, and various other problems concerning compatibility (Bello & Muazu, 2023). For these reasons, businesses must assess their existing systems accurately, make an integration plan detailing compatible AI tool selection, and also define protocols for data exchange, and perform the same without disturbing ongoing business operations (Yang, 2018).

3. Data Quality Management

AI-driven marketing is only as good as the data it's fed, and that could be incomplete, inexact, or simply old. Such low quality can turn out with wrong insights and inefficient marketing strategies. High-quality data refers to continuous management practices for keeping the data clean, validating it, and updating on a regular basis (Afshan et al., 2021).

This should be viewed as a business imperative: establishing processes to monitor and maintain data quality. This may involve setting up data governance frameworks, periodic audits, or even AI tools that automatically can detect and correct problems in the data. By focusing on data quality, a business will ensure accuracy and credibility in its AI-driven marketing activities (Barutcu et al., 2017).

4. Addressing Bias and Fairness

This can be where AI systems even magnify bias in data they work with, resulting in discriminatory practices in the form of unfair targeting with marketing. This would include instances of biased algorithms leading to less relevant content for particular demographic groups or exclusion from opportunities.

To reduce prejudice, businesses should ensure that AI models they use are engineered with varied and representative data sets. Periodic audits and reviews of AI systems can also help in identifying potential biases and knowing how to deal with them. Fairness and transparency measures within AI algorithms go a long way in making the practices of marketing much more equitable and improving general trust in these AI technologies.

5. Ethics in AI

Ethical use of AI in marketing is not only a question of compliance with regulations but also extends to responsible behavior that respects customers' rights and fosters trust. Businesses have to consider the ethical dimensions of using AI to analyze and influence customer behavior, including transparency of marketing practices, respect for privacy, and without manipulative tactics.

It follows then that there is a need for the development of ethical guidelines and best practices concerning the use of AI. Firms should have very clear policies with regard to the deployment of AI technologies and how it uses customer data. The stakeholders, including customers and experts in the industry, can yield valuable inputs regarding ethics that could help shape responsible AI practices.

6. Cost and Resource Allocation

AI-driven marketing strategies have huge investments in technology, talent, and other resources. The investment to be made in developing or purchasing AI tools and acquiring and retaining talent may be inhibitive for most businesses, especially SMEs (Akın, 2024).

To cut down on some of the costs, organizations should identify clear goals and projects for artificial intelligence and estimate the return on investment in advance. The concentration of resources on areas of high impact and providing less expensive solutions, such as AI-as-a-Service platforms, will minimize some of the financial costs for organizations. These internal capabilities can also be enhanced by training and developing the existing staff instead of looking for external talent (Afshan et al., 2021; Bettiol et al., 2012)

7. Continuous Adaptation and Learning

AI technologies and marketing trends keep on emerging. It means businesses should be ready to accept new developments and further update their strategies from time to time to stay ahead. That is, know recent advancements of AI, the up-and-coming trends, and changes in consumer behavior (Barutcu et al., 2017).

This will involve regular assessment in the performance of AI-driven marketing strategies, making changes in strategies based on new insights to keep it effective. A continuous culture of learning and experimentation should be encouraged by businesses if they want to stay ahead in a rapidly changing landscape concerning AI and marketing (Yang, 2018).

While AI-driven marketing has several advantages, there are also a number of challenges in the way of successful implementation (Bello & Muazu, 2023). Addressing issues on data privacy, integration of systems, data quality, fairness, ethics, cost, and continuous adaptation will better help businesses overcome these challenges and fully maximize the use of AI as a strong driver in marketing innovation and business growth (Azhar & Akhtar, 2020; Guerola-Navarro et al., 2024).

EMERGING TRENDS IN AI-DRIVEN PERSONALIZATION

The landscape of personalization powered by AI is changing fast. It has affected the way companies provide customer experiences due to emerging technologies and methodologies. As AI continues to advance rapidly, a few defining trends are predictable regarding future practices in the personalization of marketing. These trends include alterations within the underlying AI technology itself, hyper-personalization, mixed reality integrations with augmented and virtual realities, ethics, and growing curiosity about the notion of customer experience.

1. AI Technological Development

As this AI technology continues to evolve, so will its capabilities for personalization. Advances in machine learning algorithms, natural language processing, and computer vision are foreseen to increase the accuracy and effectiveness of personalized marketing strategies. For example, deep learning models, now much more capable of understanding complex patterns in data by emulating neural patterns in the human brain, are bound to grow further in the near future. These allow for advanced segmentation and targeting, hence allowing businesses to provide highly relevant content and recommendations.

In addition, AI-powered predictive analytics development will further enable marketers to predict the needs and behaviors of a customer base with high accuracy. Analyzing historic data for emerging trends, AI will extract actionable insights to enable business organizations to engage proactively with customers for the optimization of their marketing strategies (Bettiol et al., 2012).

2. Hyper-Personalization

Whereas traditional personalization techniques may have been adequate for times past, hyper-personalization represents an evolution. It is all about the creation of experiences that are hyper-individualized for each customer. While traditional personalization might segment audiences based on broad criteria, hyper-personalization aims at tailoring content and interactions down to a granular level, factoring in all of your predispositions, behaviors, and real-time contexts (Afshan et al., 2021).

AI technologies, including advanced recommendation engines and real-time data processing, drive hyper-personalization by offering content and offers that are uniquely matched to users. A good example is how streaming services apply hyper-personalization to recommend movies and shows based on viewing history, time of day, and even mood. As AI technology continues to evolve, so will capabilities and precision in hyper-personalization, enabling companies to create experiences that are always more targeted (Akın, 2024).

3. AR and VR

Integration of augmented reality and virtual reality together with AI-powered personalization is going to mark a new beginning in customer-brand interactions. Both AR and VR provide immersive and interactive brand experiences that can be delivered per the individual preferences and behaviors (Barutcu et al., 2017).

For example, AR applications can include virtual try-ons for things like clothes or accessories; in this way, customers can see how items look on them before they buy. AI can improve these experiences by analyzing user preferences and making personalized recommendations based on virtual try-ons. VR experiences can also be customized to individual interests, such as personalized virtual store tours or even interactive product demos (Azhar & Akhtar, 2020).

4. Ethical Considerations and Transparency

As AI-driven personalization continues to progress, it requires increased ethics and transparency (Bello & Muazu, 2023). Customers are increasingly concerned about their data usage and demand businesses to be much more transparent. Ethical considerations in AI-driven personalization are based on making data collection and usage responsible, taking into consideration customer privacy (Bettiol et al., 2012; Guerola-Navarro et al., 2024).

In its essence, organizations will have to take up clear policies on the use of data, acquire explicit consent from customers, and provide choices for managing data preferences. Correcting biases in AI algorithms and making sure there is no discrimination in personalization efforts also are or will be crucial for organizations in building and sustaining consumer trust.

5. AI for Customer Experience Improvement

The final goal of personalization powered by AI is excellence in customer experience. AI technologies let business firms create frictionless and engaging experiences that will truly fit the needs and preferences of each individual customer. The effect might be increased satisfaction, more loyalty, and higher brand perception (Yang, 2018).

The future of AI-driven personalization shall lie in the research and establishment of new technologies and methods aimed at even better customer experience. For example, further integration of AI-driven chatbots and virtual assistants will offer support and recommendations on personal levels. Also, AI shall be used for making omnichannel experiences more effective, thus the customers should get coherent and relevant content across all touchpoints (Afshan et al., 2021).

6. Predictive and Prescriptive Analytics

Predictive and prescriptive analytics will play a significant role in shaping the future of AI-driven personalization. Predictive analytics uses historical data to predict what customers will do in the future and what trends will take place; this allows businesses to stay prepared for those needs and adjust their strategies accordingly. Prescriptive analytics takes it to the next step by providing recommendations of actions based on predictive insights (Azhar & Akhtar, 2020).

Predictive analytics can, for example, determine which customers are going to churn, whereas prescriptive analytics may supply the strategies that will retain those customers, such as personalized offers or targeted communication. Predictive and prescriptive analytics together give businesses the power for proactive, active personalization (Akın, 2024).

7. AI-Driven Creative Content

Another domain where AI is expected to make big strides is creative content generation. The generated content by AI, like personalized ads, blog posts, and social media updates, would be considerably more sophisticated and relevant. AI can analyze customer data to generate content in tune with individual tastes and preferences that enhance both engagement and effectiveness (Barutcu et al., 2017).

For example, AI algorithms can generate dynamic ad creatives, continuously updating and changing according to user interactions and preferences. Similarly, AI-powered content creation techniques can compose personalized email newsletters or social media posts that really resonate with each recipient (Bettiol et al., 2012).

In other words, the future of AI-powered personalization is going to be technological advancements, hyper-personalization, integration of AR and VR in personalization. Conclusion Basically, ethical considerations and a focus on enhancement of the customer experience will be paramount in handling such trends as businesses. Indeed, by embracing these developments, businesses can create more tailored, engaging, and effective marketing strategies that drive growth and strengthen customer relationship (Azhar & Akhtar, 2020; Bettiol et al., 2012; Guerola-Navarro et al., 2024).

PRACTICAL TIPS AND BEST PRACTICES

The seamless implementation of AI-powered personalization does not just happen accidentally; it requires cautious planning and execution. To effectively utilize AI in their marketing strategies, a proper balance between technological capability and practical consideration should be achieved by businesses (Bello & Muazu, 2023). This section highlights tips that are practical, stating the best practices that guide businesses in integrating AI for personalized marketing. This ensures that maximum benefits could be obtained by taking care of potential challenges.

1. Define Clear Objectives

The first step is a definition of clear objectives and goals for AI-driven personalization. Understand what you are trying to achieve through the use of AI, whether it is greater engagement of te customers, better rates of conversion, or raising customer satisfaction. Having SMART goals for AI will ensure that AI initiatives match larger business goals and provide a foundation for assessments of success (Yang, 2018; Bettiol et al., 2012)

2. Invest in Data Quality and Management

Effective AI-driven personalization requires high-quality data. It is for this reason that robust data management practices will be of utmost importance to invest in, ensuring that the data feeding into the AI systems is accurate, complete, and fresh. This would include data governance frameworks, regular cleaning and validation of data, and integration of data to ensure there are no issues (Afshan et al., 2021).

Integrate the data from CRM systems, website analytics, and social media platforms in order to create a single customer view. This would be helpful in understanding customer behavior and their individual preferences. Data accuracy and consistency are a must for the AI algorithms to develop reliable insights and deliver effective personalization (Barutcu et al., 2017).

3. Choose the Right AI Tools and Technologies

Equally important is picking up the right kind of AI tools and technologies in their implementation. Individual companies would, therefore, need to evaluate different available AI platforms to find out which one best suit them and will fulfil their objectives. Key factors to be considered include the capabilities of the platform, ease of integration with existing systems, scalability, and support for various AI techniques, such as machine learning, NLP, and computer vision.

Also, consider the history of the vendor and their support for customers. Engaging vendors who offer comprehensive support and periodic updates within their services will help in overcoming many challenges that come during the implementation phase; this also ensures AI tools remain effective and up-to-date (Akın, 2024).

4. Engage in Pilot Projects

The reason for starting with a pilot project is that it allows an enterprise to try an AI-driven personalization strategy on a small scale before going into full-scale implementation. Challenges are identified through pilot projects, allowing the refinement of strategies and effectiveness assessments of AI tools in real-world scenarios. By starting small, it enables businesses to collect insights, make necessary adjustments, and build confidence in their AI capabilities (Azhar & Akhtar, 2020).

For example, this can be on a small product line or subset of customers. The output of this pilot will provide insights that are very valuable in scaling up the methodology to wider business areas (Barutcu et al., 2017; Guerola-Navarro et al., 2024).

5. Pay Attention to Customer Privacy and Ethics

Ethical considerations and customers' privacy should become key in AI-driven personalization. To begin with, it is necessary to follow data protection laws, such as the GDPR and CCPA, with explicit consent from the customers regarding the collection and usage of data. Also, provide clear statements of the usage of customer data and options for the management of data preferences.

Transparency and fairness in AI implementations engender trust and develop healthy customer relationships. Key here will be the identification of biases in algorithms and also that personalization efforts are respectful and non-discriminatory to maintain ethics (Afshan et al., 2021).

6. Continuously Monitor and Optimize

AI-driven personalization is not a one-time effort but an ongoing process. It thus requires regularly checking and monitoring the performances of the AI systems to optimize their effectiveness. In this regard, monitoring key performance indicators like engagement rates, conversion rates, customer feedback, etc., shows the effectiveness of personalization strategies.

Use AI-powered analytics to identify trends, patterns, and areas for improvement in personalization. It is important to continually refine and adjust personalization based on data insights so that it can remain relevant and effective (Bello & Muazu, 2023). A/B testing of different personalization approaches will also provide great insight into what works best for your audience (Bettiol et al., 2012).

7. Invest in Training and Development

Furthermore, investing in the training and development of your team will leverage AI-driven personalization to its fullest. How to utilize the AI tools and interpret the insights given by them is very important, which marketing professionals should know. The purpose of ongoing training would be to make sure the team was up to date on changes regarding the best practices and capabilities of AI (Yang, 2018).

The development of the data-driven decision-making culture in an organization can impact the overall AI projects. Let the alignment between AI strategies, business objectives, and technical capabilities be developed by data scientists, marketing teams, and IT professionals.

8. Integrate AI with Omnichannel Strategies

AI-driven personalization needs to be seamlessly integrated into omnichannel marketing for a frictionless customer experience. Let AI tools and insights be applied across websites, email campaigns, social media, and mobile apps, among other customer touchpoints.

A unified approach to personalization helps provide a consistent experience for customers, regardless of where they interact with the brand. For example, if a customer receives personalized recommendations on a website, they should also see relevant content and offers in their email inbox and social media feeds (Azhar & Akhtar, 2020).

9. Keep Up-to-Date with New Technology

With new technologies and methodologies cropping up day in and day out, the face of AI keeps changing. Keep updated on the latest in AI and personalization to leverage opportunities availed by new technologies and stay competitive in the market. To stay current with trends and innovations, subscribe to industry publications, attend conferences, and network with AI experts.

This way, by keeping pace with changes in technology, businesses can go on enhancing their AI-based personalization strategies and change with the fluctuating expectations of customers and the market environment (Yang, 2018).

10. Encourage Collaboration and Feedback

One must inculcate collaboration and feedback regarding AI-driven personalization from various stakeholders such as the marketing teams, data scientists, IT professionals, and the customers themselves. It is from such engagement with stakeholders that important insights may come forth regarding the efficiency of personalization efforts and areas of improvement (Barutcu et al., 2017).

This will be refined consistently through regular feedback by the customers regarding the personalization strategy on whether it actually meets the customer's needs and preferences. The collaborative environment will make the AI-driven marketing strategies much more effective and customer-oriented (Bello & Muazu, 2023).

In all, effective AI-driven personalization requires clear objectives, quality data, the right tools, pilot projects, ethical practices, continuous monitoring, training, omnichannel integration, staying abreast of advancements, and fostering collaboration. By following these practical tips and best practices, businesses can unlock the power of AI in driving personalized marketing experiences that drive engagement, loyalty, and growth (Akın, 2024; Guerola-Navarro et al., 2024).

CONCLUSION

As AI technology develops further, so does the depth of the impact on marketing strategy, offering unparalleled opportunities for personalization. AI in marketing allows companies to offer customers experiences that are truly relevant and personalized. This can improve engagement, satisfaction, and loyalty. It will involve the application of sophisticated machine learning algorithms, natural language processing, and data analytics to carve out deep insights into customer preferences and behavior and enable organizations to craft personalized content and dynamic interactions that resonate with individual needs.

However, effective AI-driven personalization does not come without its challenges, as organizations struggle with data privacy and security, integration with the existing system, and managing data quality. Further, biases and ethics are critical issues that must be taken care of with regard to customer trust for fairness and respect in interactions. Finally, the costs and resources required by AI call for careful planning and investment.

This is going to be a future influenced by many trends: advancing AI technology, which will continue to improve personalization; hyper-personalization, really pushing the boundaries of customized marketing experiences; the integration of augmented reality and virtual reality, offering immersive and interactive opportunities; and ethical considerations will also become increasingly imperative as consumers start asking for greater transparency and responsible data handling in the future (Afshan et al., 2021).

While tapping into the full potential of AI-driven personalization, orientation toward practical best practices will be plausible for businesses. Well-defined objectives, investments in the quality of data, choosing the right Artificial Intelligence tools, and starting with pilot projects could form a sufficient foundation for successful implementation. Ethical use of AI, monitoring, and optimization of strategies on a regular basis, investment in team training, and integration of personalization across all channels-all these aspects will become required to ensure durable impact.

In all, AI-driven personalization is that moment in marketing when businesses can create more impactful and meaningful customer touchpoints. By embracing these advancements thoughtfully and strategically, businesses can create personalized experiences that drive growth, foster loyalty, and set themselves apart in an increasingly competitive landscape. As AI technology continues to improve, staying abreast will be important, and being able to adapt will mean leveraging its full potential and staying competitive in a world of ever-changing marketing.

REFERENCES

Afshan, G., Shahid, S., & Tunio, M. N. (2021). Learning experiences of women entrepreneurs amidst COVID-19. *International Journal of Gender and Entrepreneurship*, 13(2), 162–186. DOI: 10.1108/IJGE-09-2020-0153

Akın, N. (2024). Digital marketing strategies for digital entrepreneurs: Emerging trends and future research directions. In *New strategy models in digital entrepreneurship* (pp. 296-319).

Azhar, M., & Akhtar, M. J. (2020). Social media: A catalyst for entrepreneurship and marketing. *South Asian Journal of Marketing & Management Research*, 10(11), 62–70. DOI: 10.5958/2249-877X.2020.00087.9

Barutcu, S., Yaldir, A., & Hasiloglu, S. B. (2017). From mass to personalized mobile marketing strategies: The new dimensions through expert systems. *European Scientific Journal*, 13(10), 400–409. DOI: 10.19044/esj.2017.v13n10p400

Bello, S. M., & Muazu, M. H. (2023). The 21st century innovative marketing strategies for halal entrepreneurs in the various segments of the halal industry. In *Contemporary discourse of halal and Islamic entrepreneurship: Trends and future opportunities* (pp. 223–235). Springer Nature Singapore., DOI: 10.1007/978-981-99-6427-7_15

Bettiol, M., Di Maria, E., & Finotto, V. (2012). Marketing in SMEs: The role of entrepreneurial sensemaking. *The International Entrepreneurship and Management Journal*, 8(2), 223–248. DOI: 10.1007/s11365-011-0174-3

Guerola-Navarro, V., Gil-Gomez, H., Oltra-Badenes, R., & Soto-Acosta, P. (2024). Customer relationship management and its impact on entrepreneurial marketing: A literature review. *The International Entrepreneurship and Management Journal*, 20(2), 507–547. DOI: 10.1007/s11365-022-00800-x

Hendrix, T. (2015). *Marketing for entrepreneurs: How to promote one's own craft.*

Kaliyamoorthy, R., & Theeban, K. P. (2013). Entrepreneurial marketing strategies in business enhancement of private higher education institutions (PHEI) in Malaysia. *International Journal on Global Business Management & Research*, 2(1), 16.

Kumar, T. A. (2024). Personalized entrepreneurial training programs using data analytics to match founders with the right skill development.

Lantos, G. P. (2014). Marketing for entrepreneurs. *Journal of Product and Brand Management*, 23(2), 140–143. DOI: 10.1108/JPBM-05-2013-0311

Rozaq, M., Hastjarjo, S., & Slamet, Y. (2021). How novice entrepreneurs learn about digital marketing communication strategies? *Jurnal ASPIKOM*, 6(2), 345–359. DOI: 10.24329/aspikom.v6i2.936

Sahoo, S., & Raghu, Y. (2023). Digital marketing strategies used by novice entrepreneurs in promoting their business—A study in Bangalore. *SJCC Management Research Review*, 103-119.

Shaikh, E., Tunio, M. N., Khoso, W. M., Brahmi, M., & Rasool, S. (2022). The COVID-19 pandemic overlaps entrepreneurial activities and triggered new challenges: A review study. In *Managing human resources in SMEs and start-ups: International challenges and solutions* (pp. 155-182). DOI: 10.1142/9789811239212_0008

Sigué, S. P., & Biboum, A. D. (2020). Entrepreneurial marketing and social networking in small and medium service enterprises: A case study into business dealings in Cameroon. *Journal of African Business*, 21(3), 338–354. DOI: 10.1080/15228916.2019.1625022

Stokes, D. (2000). Putting entrepreneurship into marketing: The processes of entrepreneurial marketing. *Journal of Research in Marketing and Entrepreneurship*, 2(1), 1–16. DOI: 10.1108/14715200080001536

Tunio, M. N. (2020). Role of ICT in promoting entrepreneurial ecosystems in Pakistan. [JBE]. *Journal of Business Ecosystems*, 1(2), 1–21. DOI: 10.4018/JBE.2020070101

Tunio, M. N., Chaudhry, I. S., Mughal, F., & Shaikh, E. (2022). Marketing mode and survival of the entrepreneurial activities of nascent entrepreneurs. In *Big data analytics* (pp. 1–18). Auerbach Publications. DOI: 10.1201/9781003307761-1

Tunio, M. N., Chaudhry, I. S., Shaikh, S., Jariko, M. A., & Brahmi, M. (2021). Determinants of the sustainable entrepreneurial engagement of youth in developing country—An empirical evidence from Pakistan. *Sustainability (Basel)*, 13(14), 7764. DOI: 10.3390/su13147764

Tunio, M. N., Jariko, M. A., Børsen, T., Shaikh, S., Mushtaque, T., & Brahmi, M. (2021). How entrepreneurship sustains barriers in the entrepreneurial process—A lesson from a developing nation. *Sustainability (Basel)*, 13(20), 11419. DOI: 10.3390/su132011419

Tunio, M. N., Shaikh, E., Katper, N. K., & Brahmi, M. (2023). Nascent entrepreneurs and challenges in the digital market in developing countries. *International Journal of Public Sector Performance Management*, 12(1-2), 140–153. DOI: 10.1504/IJPSPM.2023.132244

Tunio, M. N., Yusrini, L., & Shoukat, G. (2021). Corporate social responsibility (CSR) in hotels in Austria, Pakistan, and Indonesia: Small and medium enterprise spillover of COVID-19. In *Handbook of research on entrepreneurship, innovation, sustainability, and ICTs in the post-COVID-19 era* (pp. 263-280). IGI Global.

Usman, F. O., Eyo-Udo, N. L., Etukudoh, E. A., Odonkor, B., Ibeh, C. V., & Adegbola, A. (2024). A critical review of AI-driven strategies for entrepreneurial success. *International Journal of Management & Entrepreneurship Research*, 6(1), 200–215. DOI: 10.51594/ijmer.v6i1.748

Yang, M. (2018). International entrepreneurial marketing strategies of MNCs: Bricolage as practiced by marketing managers. *International Business Review*, 27(5), 1045–1056. DOI: 10.1016/j.ibusrev.2018.03.004

Chapter 11

AI for Personalizing Customer Interactions: Improving Engagement and Satisfaction

Hewawasam P. G. D. Wijethilak
https://orcid.org/0009-0006-9611-5735
University of Colombo, Sri Lanka

Sandeep Kumar Singh
https://orcid.org/0000-0002-1741-7254
O.P. Jindal Global University, India

Shivani Dhand
https://orcid.org/0000-0002-4809-1365
Lovely Professional University, India

ABSTRACT

Artificial Intelligence (AI) is revolutionizing customer personalization by delivering highly tailored experiences through advanced algorithms and data analysis. This paper explores the transformative impact of AI on personalizing customer interactions, examining key technologies such as machine learning, natural language processing, and predictive analytics. It highlights the benefits of AI-driven personalization, including enhanced engagement, improved customer satisfaction, and increased conversion rates. Challenges such as data privacy, ethical considerations, and integration complexities are also discussed, alongside best practices for effective implementation. Future trends, including hyper-personalization and AI integration with augmented reality, are explored to provide insights into emerging opportunities and innovations. By addressing both the potential and challenges of

DOI: 10.4018/979-8-3373-0219-5.ch011

AI in personalization, this study offers a comprehensive overview of how businesses can leverage AI to optimize customer interactions and drive long-term success.

INTRODUCTION

The timely interaction of customers in the present world of digitalization is articulate in personalizing the customers. AI played a significant role in transforming how firms create communication with their clientele starting from the generic broad strategies to personalized and adaptive approaches. Personalization is no longer a luxury because it is a norm that is expected in different industries. As customers look for experiences that are unique and fully responsive to their needs the use of AI to such serve and even amplify the engagement and satisfaction has been realized by organizations.

Traditionally, personalization was done using relatively crude and more or less traditional methods of market segmentation, for instance, the customers could be divided into groups according strictly to their gender and age. Nevertheless, the currently utilized AI technologies have provided the business firms with the ability to analyze a large number of consumers' data to gain insight into the latter's behaviors and choices (Khan & Iqbal, 2020). This can in return help them offer the right content, products and communications interventions in real time, and cultivate an appropriate relationship with the customer and the brand.

Thanks to machine learning, NLP and recommendation algorithms which this field has been changed and has become as the revolution of personalization. Some of the machine learning applications found in the self-service portals are the data trail left behind by the customers and the prediction of their subsequent behaviors and preferences. NLP offers smooth conversations through bots and assistants such as messaging bots and virtual assistants; recommender systems give customized content and products according to their preference. Collectively these solutions driven by AI address the improvement not only the manageability of customer interactions but the improvement of the customer experience itself.

AI implemented to personalization of customer relations has a number of important and useful uses. This can be in the form of advertisements and promotions in the form of marketing communications which are made using artificial intelligence and tailored to focus on specific areas of interest to the individual. It's proposed that AI-based chatbots and virtual assistants can afford customers more prompt and specific solutions to their queries and problems. Besides, dynamic content personalization ensures that regular website and email content is appropriate and more engaging to each customer.

But when it gets to the utilization of artificial intelligence for personalization, not everything goes as planned. First of all, it creates several data protection concerns and other ethicalities because the businesses have to look for that line between reasonable and acceptable personalization, which would not be tantamount to intrusion. Being able to control decision-making through AI technologies to be transparent alongside tackling customer expectations in a manner that feels fair will retain their trust while increasing their satisfaction with that particular service. However, much integration planning and the right execution are needed to ensure that disruption does not occur in the process of making these solutions integrate with the existing systems and processes.

The effectiveness of its use in clients' contact will be measured based on features like the response rate, customer service satisfaction rating, and conversion ratios to name but a few of the evaluation tools (Guo et. al., 2024). These make available to businesses the opportunity to determine from the metrics the effectiveness of personalization in achieving intended goals with a view to making further improvements.

AI in personalization has more possibilities and future in the future. As new technologies of enhanced AI algorithms and real time analysis extend the possibilities for delivering highly specific engaging customer experiences it is crucial to maintain the best practice of implementing these technologies and a fine tuned awareness of trends that can help sustain market advantage through the delivery of customer experience at its best.

In conclusion, it can be said that AI has become one of the major tools that enhance personalization in the interaction with customers, which results in improved engagement and, therefore, satisfaction. Thus, the more the different enterprise will try to apply this artificial intelligence for the businesses and the investments, the more they will see the opportunity of a more loyalty and success connection of customers.

UNDERSTANDING CUSTOMER PERSONALIZATION

Defining Customer Personalization

Customer personalization entails information collection, processing, and application so as to deliver relevantly tailored interactions, content, and experiences effectively to meet individual customers' unique needs, behaviors, and preferences. Unlike general marketing approaches where one size fits all, personalization does exactly the opposite as it aims to make the experience more relevant and engaging by paying heed to the characteristics and interests of a certain individual. It involves the analytics of customer data to reach a fair understanding of the respective preferences, behaviors, and past interactions and, accordingly, deliver customized messages, offers, and experiences.

Evolution of Personalization Strategies

Personalization has conventionally been manual and limited. Early methods included segmenting customers based on broad criteria, such as age, gender, or location, and targeting these segments with relatively homogeneous messaging. As techniques for collecting and analyzing data evolved, so too did the strategies companies employed in personalization. Digital technologies and data analytics opened a whole new dimension-a granular, dynamic level-to personalization. Where today new AI technologies allow delivering real-time experiences on an individual level beyond traditional segmentations to highly-tailored interactions.

Personalization in the Digital Era

In the digital era, there is so much personalization in customer experiences that technology has advanced. Starting from social networking sites to e-commerce websites, customers deal directly with systems that work on their preference and behavior analysis, building high expectations about personalization in all their digital interactions. More than a fad, personalized experiences are an essential requirement in customer satisfaction and loyalty. In fact, studies have shown that personalization can raise the rate of engagement significantly, conversion rates, and overall customer satisfaction; hence, personalization has become one of the major propellers of business.

Role of Data in Personalization

Behind every successful customer personalization, there is data. Businesses draw a huge amount of data from different sources: customer transactions, browsing behavior, interactions on social media, and many others. This is analyzed for information on customer preferences and behavior. Advanced analytics and AI technologies then take those insights and deliver personalized content and recommendations. It clearly follows that the critical element driving relevance and engaging experiences is to know how to leverage data for the individual customers effectively.

TYPES OF PERSONALIZATION TECHNIQUES

There are many different techniques applied to personalization, each adding something of value to a better customer experience. Behavioral personalization uses past interactions and behaviors in the making of predictions of future needs and preferences. Content personalization applies data about individual interests to personalize website or email content. Predictive personalization applies machine learning algorithms in anticipating customer needs and suggesting relevant products or services. Dynamic personalization adapts in real time as customer context or behavior changes to make sure interactions remain relevant and engaging.

Challenges with Personalization

While personalization comes with a number of advantages, it also raises a number of challenges. Data privacy concerns are quite significant, and customers are very sensitive about how their data is used and may have a bunch of questions about data security and consent. Ethical considerations are another problem, whereby personalization needs to be transparent and respectful of the customer's right to privacy. Also, integration of personalization technologies with existing systems is indeed complex and requires meticulous planning and implementation so as not to cause disruptions and deter full potential.

The Future of Personalization

Ongoing developments within the field of AI and data analytics will continue to shape the future of personalization. Indeed, new technologies promise even more sophisticated personalization techniques, including hyper-personalization, which offers highly granular and contextually relevant experiences. While businesses continue to explore new possibilities, keeping pace with emerging technologies and customer expectations will be key to remaining competitive and ensuring superior personalized experiences.

That is, understanding customer personalization means understanding what it is, how it has evolved, and what it means in the digital context; the role of data; and various techniques for personalization. Irrespective of challenges, this potential for increased engagement and satisfaction makes personalization an important constituent of modern business strategy.

AI TECHNOLOGIES FOR PERSONALIZATION

Machine Learning and Predictive Analytics

Machine learning has become integral to personalizing customer experience. Large amounts of data are used by ML algorithms to identify patterns and trends that can predict future customer behaviors and preferences. Predictive analytics takes these insights to forecast what customers might need or want, helping the business proactively tailor their offering. For instance, an e-commerce platform can use machine learning to study past purchase behavior and suggest various items that a customer is likely interested in, increasing the likelihood of making a purchase. That predictive capability extends further than simple recommendations to include dynamic adjustments based on real-time data so that the interactions remain relevant and timely.

Natural Language Processing (NLP) and Chatbots

NLP involves developing a variety of software that helps machines understand and converse in human language. This is achieved through NLP, a subset of AI that enables computers to converse and emulative feature-essentially, to think, understand, or perceive human thought. Their applications have been extended to working chatbots and virtual assistants, which in recent times have evolved to become part of personalized customer service. Thus, AI-infused software is in a position to interpret customer queries and provide relevant answers. Complex interactions can also be entertained and addressed through these AI bots with a great degree of accuracy. For instance, an NLP-driven chatbot on a retail site can engage a customer in product-related queries, placing the order, or resolving some complaints in a way similar to conversation. This makes companies more capable of entertaining customers in a more interactive and time-saving way.

Recommendation Systems

A recommendation system or engine is a sort of AI which suggests products or items to a user based on his previous interaction and preference. Examples of such techniques might include collaborative filtering, content-based filtering, and hybrid approaches. In collaborative filtering, the basis of recommendations is similar-user activity, while content-based filtering recommends products similar to what the user previously interacted with. Hybrid models make use of all these approaches to enhance accuracy and relevance. For example, a streaming service uses recommendation engines to suggest movies and shows based on the viewer's history and preferences, making it a better experience because this is content that best suits individual tastes.

Dynamic Content Personalization

Dynamic content personalization refers to the ability of AI systems to change real-time content, given the interaction and context of a user. It allows websites, emails, and ads to change dynamically right away by behavior, preference, and even the external factors of location or time of day. For example, a website might show a different product offering to a returning customer based on their prior browsing history, or display local promotions based on geographic location. This real-time adaptation ensures that the content is relevant and engaging, which can enrich the user experience to a great degree and heighten the possibility of conversion.

Behavioral Targeting

Behavioral targeting involves the use of AI to analyze user behavior across various touchpoints to serve personalized ads and content. As users' activities are tracked when visiting a website, clicking on items, or even interacting with content, an AI system could draw detailed profiles of the users, which help in focused marketing strategies. For example, if a user usually searches for information to do with travel, AI can automatically trigger personalized adverts about travel or recommendations along that line, which would align with their interests. This tactic not only makes marketing more relevant but also further optimizes advertising effectiveness by reaching users through messages tailored to their specific behaviors and preferences.

Personalized Search Results

AI-powered personalized search results make the searching experience far better by showing results according to each user's preference and usage pattern. Search engines and websites use AI in analyzing search history, click patterns, and user profiles to provide more relevant search outcomes. For example, a user consistently searching for health and wellness content could get search results and recommendations related to fitness and nutrition. Through the personalization of results, AI makes sure that users get to have information and products best suited to their needs, hence improving satisfaction and engagement.

Challenges and Considerations

Large advantages come with challenges when it refers to AI technologies for personalization. The most important concern is the one related to data privacy because personal data collection and analysis should be handled with great care to maintain user privacy and meet regulatory requirements. Moreover, technical and operational challenges are created by the integration of AI technologies into existing systems. Companies must also take steps to avoid biased AI algorithms so that personalization is equitable and inclusive.

AI technologies integrated with machine learning, NLP, recommendation engines, dynamic content personalization, behavioral targeting, and personalized search results play a vital role in the enrichment of customer interaction. The business can therefore present only highly relevant and engaging experiences that drive customer satisfaction and loyalty. However, addressing the associated challenges has to be undertaken for successful implementation, along with maintaining trust with the users.

APPLICATIONS OF AI IN CUSTOMER PERSONALIZATION

Personalized Marketing Campaigns

AI has completely revolutionized personalized marketing by letting companies deliver very targeted and relevant campaigns. It would be easier with the help of machine learning algorithms, along with predictive analytics, for a firm to pay attention to the analyses of customer data that allow for very precise audience segmentations, and the creation of personalized marketing messages right to the preferences of every individual (Gao & Liu, 2023). For instance, AI-driven marketing systems can create personalized email campaigns based on an individual's interaction history with the brand, such as previous purchases, browsing behavior, or open/click-through activity from other emails. This level of personalization makes the marketing more effective, increasing open rates, click-through rates, and overall conversion rates. In addition, AI can optimize ad targeting in real-time, showing ads to the most relevant audience segments at times when they are most effective (Prentice & Nguyen, 2020).

Personalized Customer Service and Support

Artificially intelligent customer support systems, like chatbots and virtual assistants, have significantly raised the level and quality of support given to consumers (katragadda, 2023). These tools use NLP to understand consumer utterances or questions and provide answers of extreme accuracy. For example, a chatbot can process frequent inquiries by customers regarding order status or any information about the product without human interference. This not only increases speed but also maintains consistency and accuracy for the customer. Also, AI reviews past interactions and customer profiles for personalized support by way of anticipating issues and offering solutions based on previous interactions. That would amount to a level of personalized service that would be creating more delighted customers, who then would have a better relationship with the brand.

Dynamic Content Personalization

Dynamic content personalization involves real-time adaptations of content based on the user's actions and preferences. AI-powered technologies allow for automated adjustments in the content of websites, emails, and ads, improving the alignment with individual user profiles. An e-commerce website, for example, displays different product suggestions or promotional offers based on user browsing history, purchase behavior, and demographic information. For instance, similar customization may be done in email marketing campaigns by creating content and offers personalized to each recipient's identified interests and history of engagement. This dynamic approach ensures users see only the most relevant and interesting content, optimizing their experience and likelihood to convert.

Smarter Product Recommendations

AI recommendation engines have become a staple of personalized customer experiences for e-commerce and content platforms. By analyzing a user's past behavior-through input like user past purchases, browsing history, and search queries-AI algorithms can recommend products or content aligned with user preferences (Dey & Shukla, 2020). For example, a streaming service could provide the user with film and television suggestions based on their viewing history and ratings. Also, an e-retailer can enable customers to have personalized product recommendations drawn from the history of their purchase and browsing. This recommendation improves user experience in terms of discovering relevant products or content. They also drive increased sales and engagement.

Personalized User Experiences on Websites and Apps

AI technologies make it possible for businesses to provide personalized experiences to users on their websites and mobile applications. Artificial intelligence treats the quintet of user behavior, including page views, click patterns, and session duration among others, to tailor-make the user interface and content to match individual preferences. A news website might greet the user with headline and article listings relevant to an individual's interests, while a travel app will present personal recommendations for destinations and places of accommodation. This would eventually lead to increased user engagement, creating a more relevant and personalized experience that can be directly related to the satisfaction increase and retention of the users.

Behavioral Targeting in Advertising

Behavioral targeting utilizes AI to tailor-make advertisements for a user from their activities and interactions online. While parsing information related to search history, visited websites, and social media activity, an AI algorithm forms a comprehensive user profile and offers ads targeted to individual interests and preferences. For instance, a user whose favorite searches are related to fitness might receive advertisements about memberships in gyms or sportswear. In this way, it will ensure that the advertisement is relevant to the user for better engagement and conversion. Behavioral targeting also allows the advertising budget to be used in an efficient manner because it reaches only the users who are more likely to be interested in the products or services advertised.

Challenges and Ethical Considerations

Although AI applications in customer personalization come with considerable benefits, they also involve challenges and ethical considerations. Personal information is a major concern about privacy, as it must be handled responsibly through compliance with regulations like the GDPR and CCPA (Park, 2019). Beyond this, there is a chance of biases perpetuating themselves through the very AI algorithms, thereafter leading to unfair or discriminatory practices. Ensuring that AI-driven personalization does not perpetuate bias requires attention at all junctures for maintaining the trust of customers and being ethical.

In all, AI-driven customer personalization applications-personal marketing campaigns, customized customer service, dynamic personalization of content, better product recommendations, personalized user experiences, and behavioral targeting-fundamentally changed how businesses communicate with their customers. Companies, by deploying these technologies, are able to engage in more meaningful and relevant ways, thus positively impacting customer satisfaction and loyalty. However, the responsible and effective application of AI remains very much dependent on how challenges and ethical issues associated with applying AI for personalization are addressed.

CHALLENGES AND CONSIDERATIONS

Data Privacy and Security

Perhaps the biggest challenge in AI development for deployment in personalization relates to data privacy and security. In view of the extensive gathering of data, which is required for personalization of all interactions-including personal information, browsing history, and purchasing behavior-it goes without saying that any business needs to know its way around important recent regulations like the General Data Protection Regulation (GDPR) and the California Consumer Privacy Act (CCPA) (Park, 2019; Blanke, 2020). Increasingly, customers are aware of how their data is used and demand not only transparency but also greater control over their personal data. Businesses should put in place the most stringent measures for data protection, securely collect consent for any data, and use it in an ethical and responsible way. Failure to handle this issue may result in grave legal impacts and serious damage to the corporate brand.

Ethical Considerations and Bias

The fundamental problem with AI is that the systems are only as good as their data in training, and where biased data exists, these biases are reflected back in the outputs provided by the AI. This can lead to unfair or discriminatory treatment, such as biased recommendations or ad targets that reinforce stereotypes. For example, an AI model trained on data containing historical gender biases may provide recommendations or generate content that supports such biases. Overcoming these challenges requires that businesses are proactive in finding and mitigating the biases of their AI models to ensure personalization efforts are fair and inclusive. This involves the use of a diverse range of data sets, constant auditing for bias in AI systems, and other measures pertaining to ensuring fairness in AI-mediated interactions.

Integration with Other Systems

Implementing AI technologies into the ecosystem of other already existing systems and processes can be complicated and often quite costly (Jacobides et. al., 2021). Businesses should be certain of their solutions in AI to work seamlessly with the current infrastructure comprising CRM systems, marketing platforms, and customer service tools. The process could involve hard technical changes, data migration, and updates to the platform. Moreover, integration disrupts and may interfere with business processes and customer experiences. Clear planning, communication, and collaboration between the IT and business departments all are critical to working through these types of challenges and attempting to effect a seamless integration.

Managing Customer Expectations

AI-powered personalization is one area in which businesses must work to understand consumer expectations. With AI, customer experiences can be greatly improved; however, it's time to temper the expectations of what AI can and cannot do. Customers may very well expect personalization at an optimum level-that is, perfect tuning of interactions all the time. Unless these expectations are met, there could be dissatisfaction and frustration. Businesses have to be transparent about what personalization they can offer and keep improving their AI systems to meet customers' needs effectively. Clearly explaining how personalization works and addressing, in a timely manner, all other issues will help to manage customer expectations and build trust.

Balancing Personalization and Intrusiveness

The fine line that needs to be tread between personalization and intrusiveness is yet another big challenge. Whereas customers love personalized experiences, the fine line often lies between being helpful and overstepping into areas of privacy. For instance, excessive personalization can make customers feel uncomfortable or under scrutiny, which in the end may result in negative perceptions about the brand. Organisations have to make conscious choices in regards to information level usage that would be used to develop personalized content to consider customer privacy. Controls placed will provide customers with the right to personalization settings or to opt out of particular elements, which helps to alleviate some of the concerns while enhancing overall customer experience (Morimoto, 2017).

Transparency of AI

Transparency of AI-driven personalization can be elaborated as one of the very crucial methods for gaining and maintaining customer trust. Customers should be informed about the use of their data, the decision-making for personalization, and possibilities to control or edit their settings related to personalization (Larsson & Heintz, 2020). Enterprises should provide information about AI practices in a clear and accessible manner. Enterprises should ensure systems are designed such that operations are transparent. This includes explanations as to how AI algorithms work and how a customer's data is handled. It not only fosters trust but also provides the customer with the power to make knowledgeable choices about their interactions with the brand.

Yet, for all these unparalleled capabilities in the personalization of customer interaction, businesses will have to make a few cut-throughs. Issues to be addressed wade through data privacy and security, ethical considerations and bias, integration with existing systems, managing customer expectations, a balance between personalization and intrusiveness, and the need for transparency into where AI has been used-all these factors are critical to any such enterprise. In fact, the earlier these issues are proactively faced head-on, the better will businesses ensure that their AI-driven personalization efforts turn out effective, ethical, and in tune with customer expectations.

MEASURING THE IMPACT OF AI ON CUSTOMER INTERACTIONS

Key Performance Indicators - KPIs

Businesses will need to define and monitor key performance indicators that show the efficiency of AI-driven personalization in influencing customer interactions. Sample KPIs include engagement rates, conversion rates, customer satisfaction scores, and retention rates. Engagement rates would represent the size of personalized content, measuring the attention of customers, while conversion rates show how personalized recommendations and offers drive certain actions, such as purchasing or creating an account. Customer satisfaction scores would provide insight into the quality of personalization efforts in terms of meeting customer expectations, and retention rates track the ability of personalized interactions to drive long-term customer loyalty. These KPIs, when analyzed, help business owners realize the general effectiveness of their AI personalization effort and point out what needs to be changed for improvement (Popescu, 2018).

Customer Feedback and Surveys

Customers are one of the most important metrics to know what changes have come in the interactions between customers and businesses via AI. Gathering direct responses from customers through surveys, reviews, and feedback forms goes a long way in extracting deep insights from their experiences with personalized content and interactions. These can help the business to understand how well AI-driven personalization addresses customer needs and expectations, and in pointing out any inefficiency or area of improvement. Surveys can also reveal customer perceptions of relevance and effectiveness of personalized recommendations and their overall satisfaction with the brand's personalized interactions (Venkateswaran et. al., 2024). This kind of feedback integrated into decision-making makes the personalization strategy of AI in tune with customer preference and, therefore, constantly improved.

A/B Testing and Experimentation

A/B testing and experimentation are key techniques that assess the impact of AI-driven personalization. Comparing multiple versions of personalized content, recommendations, or interactions helps companies establish what works (Koning et.al., 2022). For example, two different personalized email campaigns can be tested against each other using A/B testing to see which produces higher open and click-through rates. Testing allows companies to try different personalization approaches and to measure the real effectiveness on-site. The analysis of the results of these tests will give true data-driven insights into what will work best for the different customer segments and enable further continuous optimization of the personalization efforts.

Behavioral Analytics

Behavioral analytics monitor and analyze customer interactions and behaviors to effectively measure the impact of AI personalization. Analysis of data on website visits, click patterns, purchase history, among others, reveals further insight into how personalized content impacts customer behaviors and engagement levels (Motiwalla et. al., 2019). Using another example, by analyzing the change in user behavior before and after an AI-driven recommendation, it will determine whether these are effective drivers in moving users to desired levels of engagement and conversion. Behavioral analytics explain the direct relation of personalization efforts with regard to customer actions and give a clear picture of how AI will go in influencing customer interactions.

ROI and Financial Metrics

Evaluation of the ROI, coupled with analysis of financial impact of AI-driven personalization is necessary for understanding overall effectiveness. Businesses can gauge the return on investment against costs that may be associated with implementing AI technologies versus real financial benefits like increased sales, higher conversion rates, or lower churn (Pandey et. al., 2021). Other financial metrics include revenue growth, cost per acquisition, and customer lifetime value. It is by analyzing these measures that companies will be able to check the profitability of their AI strategies and take rational decisions as to further investments in personalization tools.

Long-term Impact and Customer Lifetime Value

The long-term impact of personalization driven by AI can be judged by knowing how personalization impacts CLV and overall brand loyalty. CLV primarily projects the overall revenue a customer will generate over the lifetime with the brand (Gupta et. al., 2006). By means of interpreting how personal interactions equate to better CLV and higher customer loyalty, a business should have the ability to understand the effects on AI personalization over time. Long-term impact assessments allow businesses to appreciate ongoing value that personalization provides, thus giving them justification for continuous investment in AI technologies.

Continual Improvement and Iteration

The process of measuring the results of AI for customer interaction involves much iteration and continuous improvement. Ongoing performance data analysis, customer feedback, and behavioral analytics all give organizations the capability to understand trends, see how personalization approaches are working, and then make needed changes based on insights gained. Embracing a cycle of continuous improvement enables businesses to refine their AI-driven personalization toward meeting the needs of customers, driving further engagement, and long-term success.

In all, measuring the impact of AI on customer interactions involves monitoring key performance indicators, collecting customer feedback, running A/B testing, analyzing behavioral data, studying return on investment and other financial metrics, assessing long-term impact, and dedicating resources to continuous improvement. With these approaches, your business will be able to measure the success of its AI personalization strategies effectively and make informed decisions to refine them for maximum results in ensuring customer experiences.

FUTURE TRENDS AND INNOVATIONS

Hyper-Personalization via Advanced AI

The next future of customer personalization is hyper-personalization, driven by AI technologies. Fundamentally, this is highly tailored experiences enabled with rich customer data and sophisticated algorithms. Still today, the large majority of personalization relies on broad segments of customers, while the concept of hyper-personalization means creating unique individual experiences from real-time data and context. With the power of deep information analysis-browsing history, social media activity, real-time behavior-AI-powered systems provide deeply personalized suggestions for content and recommendations (Desai, 2022). This depth of personalization raises user engagement and drives higher conversions, building much stronger customer loyalty because it caters to each customer's unique needs and preferences.

AI-Driven Predictive Analytics

In the future, being able to anticipate customer needs and behaviors will become a critical factor with the help of AI-driven predictive analytics (Ajiga et. al., 2024). Predictive models analyze historical data for patterns that can project future customer actions with amazing accuracy. For example, AI will tell you which products a customer is most likely to buy next or when he will be ready for an upgrade in service. This foresight can help the business prompt customers with relevant offers and recommendations, even before customers articulate a need. As predictive analytics continues to evolve, their integration with real-time data and machine learning will heighten the precision for more accurate and actionable insights that power personalized marketing strategies.

INTEGRATION OF AI WITH AUGMENTED REALITY (AR) AND VIRTUAL REALITY (VR)

When AI is integrated with augmented and virtual reality, it will be a game changer in terms of customer personalization. Both AR and VR introduce immersive experiences that can be extended through AI by offering personalized content and interaction within those virtual worlds (Zarantonello & Schmitt, 2023). For example, in retail, AR will let customers virtually try on clothes or see how furniture will look in their home, while AI provides personalized recommendations of products fitting their preferences and past purchases. Also, VR enables personalized virtual shopping experiences through customized product suggestions and interactivity. Such convergence of AI with AR and VR brings newer dimensions to create more engaging and personalized customer experiences.

AI-Powered Personalization in Voice Assistants

AI-powered personalization finds its place in voice assistants' operation. The more sophisticated household devices, like Amazon Alexa or Google Assistant, become thanks to natural language processing and machine learning that lets them hear and respond to user commands and preferences. In the future, AI will continue to develop more voice assistant capabilities that can make more personalized recommendations, manage schedules, and interact with other smart devices that a user may have in their home. Example uses could include personalized meal suggestions based on dietary preferences or tailored news updates based on a user's interests. In the future, voice technology will evolve even further to great heights in delivering frictionless and personalized customer voice experiences (Rawool et. al., 2024).

Ethical AI and Privacy-Centric Personalization

As AI technologies continue to evolve, ethical AI and privacy-centric personalization will make much noise. Future innovations are very likely to propose more robust frameworks for ensuring transparency, consent, and data protection in AI-driven personalization. Ethical AI practices will develop algorithms that are fair, unbiased, and respect user privacy. Privacy-centric personalization will put customer control over their data upfront, with transparent opt-in/opt-out choices for data collection and the use of personalization features. Innovations in this space will earn customers' trust by offering value from personalization with strong ethical standards and privacy protection (Usmani et. al., 2023).

AI-Enhanced Customer Journey Mapping

AI is soon going to revolutionize customer journey mapping, which offers more detail and dynamism about the interactions of customers in each of these touchpoints. Advanced AI-powered tools analyze rich datasets to construct detailed maps of customer journeys with key moments of engagement, pain points, and opportunities for personalized interactions (Moura et al., 2021). These will help companies create more efficient and integrated customer experiences, where every touchpoint is relevant to both their journey and their needs (Straker et. al., 2015). AI-driven customer journey mapping further allows for optimization of touchpoints in a manner that provides more seamless and personalized customer experiences-those that will heighten satisfaction and loyalty considerably.

Real-Time Personalization with Edge Computing

Also, edge computing will be the key to driving at scale by processing data closer to its source rather than just with centralized data centers. In other words, with edge computing, AI systems are able to process input from data in real time and react instantaneously on it. For instance, retailers will reshape digital signage and in-store promotions according to in-store customer behavior enabled by edge computing.

This same capability will enhance immediacy, relevance for personalization, and make interactions more engaging and contextually appropriate.

In general, the future of personalization for customers will be steered through developments in hyper-personalization, predictive analytics, AR and VR integrations, voice assistants, ethics in AI, customer journey mapping, and edge computing. These will further facilitate businesses' abilities to offer ever-more tailored and immersive experiences that meet the needs of customer engagement and satisfaction, coupled with the rise in demands for ethical considerations and data privacy.

BEST PRACTICES TO APPLY WHEN IMPLEMENTING AI FOR PERSONALIZATION

1. Clearly Define Objectives and Goals

There needs to be an explicit definition of what the objectives and goals are regarding AI for personalization, considering their inclusion in the general business strategy. Having a clear understanding of what one aims to achieve with AI-driven personalization-be it increased engagement, higher conversion rates, or greater customer satisfaction-will give a milestone upon which one can assess the success of the implementation. Clear objectives facilitate the choice of appropriate AI tools and technologies, establishment of relevant metrics, and ensure focus in personalization initiatives according to business priorities. Setting SMART-specific, measurable, achievable, relevant, and time-bound-guarantees a roadmap that businesses can follow to have successful integrations of AI technologies and keeps track of progress effectively (Alahi et. al., 2023).

2. Invest in Quality Data Collection and Management

The effectiveness of AI within personalization depends on the quality of the data employed. This means investing in robust data collection and management practices that ensure the AI systems access information that is accurate, comprehensive, and current. It includes information on various touchpoints-for instance, customer interactions, purchase history, and behavioral data. Proper practices of data management include cleaning and organizing data by discarding inaccuracies and redundancies, ensuring the information is in structures that will facilitate analysis. Also, data governance policies have to be implemented that are very important in assuring data integrity and safety; it helps in gaining trust with customers and also complies with the privacy regulations.

3. Choose the Right AI Tools and Technologies

Selection of proper AI tools and technologies is a key aspect of successful implementation. Personalization capabilities will vary with different AI technologies that include machine learning algorithms, predictive analytics, natural language processing for conversing with chatbots, or recommendation engines offering content suggestions. Companies have to consider their needs and goals and, thus, select the tools that fit best with the objective in mind. Other factors to be taken into consideration are ease of integration with your system, scalability, and support. Working with reputable AI vendors or expert consultants can help make informed choices and assure that the selected tools would aptly meet the personalization needs of the business.

4. Ensure Ethical Use of AI and Data

Ethical considerations are at the center of leveraging AI in personalization. Firms must ensure responsible usage of the AI systems by paying respect to customer privacy and data security. It includes being transparent in data usage, informed consent from the customers, and providing them with choices regarding the control of their data or its use. Additionally, the biases that arise within the AI algorithms should be dealt with care to avoid discrimination so that the personalization truly becomes fair. Ethics compliance will not only help gain customers' trust but also fulfill regulatory expectations and maintain a good brand image.

5. Continuously Monitor and Optimize AI Performance

Implementing AI for personalization is a continuous process, not a one-time activity that involves periodic monitoring and optimization. The regular monitoring of the performance of AI systems with the help of KPIs, customer feedback, and behavior analytics provides an opportunity to inspect their effectiveness and points out which aspects should be further improved upon. Companies should provide a mechanism for feedback in order to capture ideas on how personalization efforts are working with customers and make informed data-driven changes. Continuous optimization entails refining algorithms, refreshing data inputs, and making adjustments in personalization strategies for performance to improve with changing customer preferences.

6. Encourage Interdepartmental Collaboration

The well-executed deployment of AI in personalization very often requires coordination across a multi-disciplinary team that includes the areas of marketing, IT, data science, and customer service. In this respect, cross-functional collaboration helps ensure that different perspectives and expertise are integrated into one crucial process of AI implementation. For instance, it's possible that the marketing teams will provide insights into customer preference and campaign objectives, while IT and data science teams will only engage in technical integration parts of AI and various data management aspects. Such collaboration, in light of this, helps a business formulate a cohesive strategy toward AI-driven personalization where businesses leverage different strengths toward catering to diverse needs.

7. Staff Training and Support

Personalization through effective AI requires equipping and supporting its members of staff in the use of new technologies. Full training in the use of AI tools and data management practices, personalization strategies, makes the employees competent in using the skills of AI. Ongoing support and resources into the future, such as user guides, training sessions, and technical assistance, all contribute to the adaptation of staff with new systems, solving any issues that arise. Investment in personnel training and support enhances the overall success of AI implementation and ensures that the team can maximize the benefits from personalized customer interactions.

8. Test and Iterate Personalization Strategies

Testing and iteration of personalization strategies will refine AI-driven efforts toward the best possible outcomes. Companies should utilize A/B testing and other means to test alternative personalization approaches against one another and measure the ability of each to drive customer interest and conversion. Iterative testing enables the ongoing enhancement of personalization strategies by identifying what works best and making data-driven adjustments (Mandinach, 2012). This will also help in the making of the best AI systems so that personalization efforts can move on a continuous development path regarding changing customer needs and expectations.

In brief, strategies for AI adoption in personalization will be inclusive of clearly setting objectives, investing in good quality data management, selecting appropriate tools, ensuring ethics, monitoring performance on a continuous basis, cross-functional collaboration, staff training, and iteration of strategies. By sticking to these best practices, businesses are most likely to make the most out of AI in delivering personalized customer experiences for driving engagement and meeting strategic objectives.

CONCLUSION

In the ever-evolving landscape of customer engagement, AI-driven personalization has emerged as one of the most profound kinds of tools in improving interactions and building good relations with customers. With the growing demand for personalized experiences, AI offers unmatched opportunities to personalize content, recommendations, and interactions based on individual preferences and behaviors. Whereby, with the use of advanced technologies such as machine learning, natural language processing, and predictive analytics, companies are able to deliver highly relevant and timely experiences that truly resonate with their audience.

However, for AI personalization to be effectively carried out, consideration of several important aspects is required. Clear objectives are essential in ensuring that efforts toward personalization are aligned with business goals and can hence be effectively measured. This involves investing in high-quality data collection and management, so that AI systems have access to precise and comprehensive information to enable meaningful personalization. Likewise, for all activities carried out, the right tools and technologies should be selected while maintaining ethics and data privacy to gain customer trust and achieve results in a more sustainable manner.

In this aspect, continuous monitoring and optimization of AI performance while undertaking cross-functional collaboration and training staff become extremely important to ensure maximum effectiveness of personalization strategies. It also becomes very important for firms to be agile as far as approaches are concerned, modified from time to time based on response analysis and emerging trends. Later, it will be combined with other emerging technologies such as augmented reality and voice assistants, having a strong focus on ethical practices to provide innovative ways of customer engagement.

As companies embrace the full potential of AI, leaders need to balance benefits associated with advanced personalization against commitment to transparency, fairness, and customer privacy. In this way, they could take full advantage of AI capabilities in developing better and more personalized experiences that ensure engagement, loyalty, and long-term success. The future for AI-driven personalization remains brilliant as continuous breakthroughs stand ready to unleash much more in the ability to improve customer interactions and institute meaningful contact in an increasingly digital world.

REFERENCES

Ajiga, D. I., Ndubuisi, N. L., Asuzu, O. F., Owolabi, O. R., Tubokirifuruar, T. S., & Adeleye, R. A. (2024). AI-driven predictive analytics in retail: A review of emerging trends and customer engagement strategies. *International Journal of Management & Entrepreneurship Research*, 6(2), 307–321. DOI: 10.51594/ijmer.v6i2.772

Alahi, M. E. E., Sukkuea, A., Tina, F. W., Nag, A., Kurdthongmee, W., Suwannarat, K., & Mukhopadhyay, S. C. (2023). Integration of IoT-enabled technologies and artificial intelligence (AI) for smart city scenario: Recent advancements and future trends. *Sensors (Basel)*, 23(11), 5206. DOI: 10.3390/s23115206 PMID: 37299934

Blanke, J. M. (2020). Protection for 'Inferences drawn': A comparison between the general data protection regulation and the california consumer privacy act. *Global Privacy Law Review, 1*(2).

Desai, D. (2022). Hyper-personalization: an AI-enabled personalization for customer-centric marketing. In *Adoption and Implementation of AI in Customer Relationship Management* (pp. 40-53). IGI Global. DOI: 10.4018/978-1-7998-7959-6.ch003

Dey, S., & Shukla, D. (2020, March). Analytical study on use of AI techniques in tourism sector for smarter customer experience management. In *2020 International Conference on Computer Science, Engineering and Applications (ICCSEA)* (pp. 1-5). IEEE. DOI: 10.1109/ICCSEA49143.2020.9132925

Gao, Y., & Liu, H. (2023). Artificial intelligence-enabled personalization in interactive marketing: A customer journey perspective. *Journal of Research in Interactive Marketing*, 17(5), 663–680. DOI: 10.1108/JRIM-01-2022-0023

Guo, Y., Li, Y., Liu, D., & Xu, S. X. (2024). Measuring service quality based on customer emotion: An explainable AI approach. *Decision Support Systems*, 176, 114051. DOI: 10.1016/j.dss.2023.114051

Gupta, S., Hanssens, D., Hardie, B., Kahn, W., Kumar, V., Lin, N., Ravishanker, N., & Sriram, S. (2006). Modeling customer lifetime value. *Journal of Service Research*, 9(2), 139–155. DOI: 10.1177/1094670506293810

Jacobides, M. G., Brusoni, S., & Candelon, F. (2021). The evolutionary dynamics of the artificial intelligence ecosystem. *Strategy Science*, 6(4), 412–435. DOI: 10.1287/stsc.2021.0148

KATRAGADDA, V. (2023). Automating Customer Support: A Study on The Efficacy of Machine Learning-Driven Chatbots and Virtual Assistants. *IRE Journals, 7*(1), 600-601.

Khan, S., & Iqbal, M. (2020, June). AI-Powered Customer Service: Does it optimize customer experience? In *2020 8th International Conference on Reliability, Infocom Technologies and Optimization (Trends and Future Directions)(ICRITO)* (pp. 590-594). IEEE.

Koning, R., Hasan, S., & Chatterji, A. (2022). Experimentation and start-up performance: Evidence from A/B testing. *Management Science*, 68(9), 6434–6453. DOI: 10.1287/mnsc.2021.4209

Larsson, S., & Heintz, F. (2020). Transparency in artificial intelligence. *Internet Policy Review*, 9(2). Advance online publication. DOI: 10.14763/2020.2.1469

Mandinach, E. B. (2012). A perfect time for data use: Using data-driven decision making to inform practice. *Educational Psychologist*, 47(2), 71–85. DOI: 10.1080/00461520.2012.667064

Morimoto, M. (2017). Personalization, perceived intrusiveness, irritation, and avoidance in digital advertising. In *Digital Advertising* (pp. 110–123). Routledge. DOI: 10.4324/9781315623252-7

Motiwalla, L., Deokar, A. V., Sarnikar, S., & Dimoka, A. (2019). Leveraging data analytics for behavioral research. *Information Systems Frontiers*, 21(4), 735–742. DOI: 10.1007/s10796-019-09928-8

Moura, S., Reis, J. L., & Rodrigues, L. S. (2021). The Artificial Intelligence in the Personalisation of the Customer Journey–a literature review.

Pandey, S., Gupta, S., & Chhajed, S. (2021). *ROI of AI: Effectiveness and Measurement. International Journal Of Engineering Research & Technology* (Vol. 10). Ijert.

Park, G. (2019). The changing wind of data privacy law: A comparative study of the European Union's General Data Protection Regulation and the 2018 California Consumer Privacy Act. *UC Irvine L. Rev.*, 10, 1455.

Popescu, C. C. (2018). Improvements in business operations and customer experience through data science and Artificial Intelligence. In *Proceedings of the International Conference on Business Excellence* (Vol. 12, No. 1, pp. 804-815). DOI: 10.2478/picbe-2018-0072

Prentice, C., & Nguyen, M. (2020). Engaging and retaining customers with AI and employee service. *Journal of Retailing and Consumer Services*, 56, 102186. DOI: 10.1016/j.jretconser.2020.102186

Rawool, V., Foroudi, P., & Palazzo, M. (2024). AI-powered voice assistants: Developing a framework for building consumer trust and fostering brand loyalty. *Electronic Commerce Research*, •••, 1–33. DOI: 10.1007/s10660-024-09850-5

Straker, K., Wrigley, C., & Rosemann, M. (2015). Typologies and touchpoints: Designing multi-channel digital strategies. *Journal of Research in Interactive Marketing*, 9(2), 110–128. DOI: 10.1108/JRIM-06-2014-0039

Usmani, U. A., Happonen, A., & Watada, J. (2023, June). Human-centered artificial intelligence: Designing for user empowerment and ethical considerations. In *2023 5th international congress on human-computer interaction, optimization and robotic applications (HORA)* (pp. 1-7). IEEE.

Venkateswaran, P. S., Dominic, M. L., Agarwal, S., Oberai, H., Anand, I., & Rajest, S. S. (2024). The role of artificial intelligence (AI) in enhancing marketing and customer loyalty. In *Data-Driven Intelligent Business Sustainability* (pp. 32–47). IGI Global.

Zarantonello, L., & Schmitt, B. H. (2023). Experiential AR/VR: A consumer and service framework and research agenda. *Journal of Service Management*, 34(1), 34–55. DOI: 10.1108/JOSM-12-2021-0479

Chapter 12
AI-Driven Customer Engagement Strategies for Small Businesses

Ankit Srivastava
Bhikaji Cama Subharti College of Hotel Management, Swami Vivekanand Subharti University, Meerut, India

Indraneel Bose
Bhikaji Cama Subharti College of Hotel Management, Swami Vivekanand Subharti University, Meerut, India

Vikas Sharma
https://orcid.org/0009-0009-3174-5965
Bhikaji Cama Subharti College of Hotel Management, Swami Vivekanand Subharti University, Meerut, India

Garima Jain
Bhikaji Cama Subharti College of Hotel Management, Swami Vivekanand Subharti University, Meerut, India

ABSTRACT

AI-driven customer engagement strategies have become pivotal for small businesses seeking to enhance their competitive edge and foster customer loyalty. This research explores how AI technologies, such as chatbots, personalized marketing, and customer analytics, transform customer interactions. By leveraging AI, small businesses can deliver tailored experiences, predict customer behavior, and optimize engagement across multiple channels. The study examines the implementation of AI tools to automate customer service, segment audiences, and create dynamic marketing campaigns. It also addresses potential challenges, including data privacy

DOI: 10.4018/979-8-3373-0219-5.ch012

concerns and the need for technological adoption. Through case studies and empirical analysis, this research highlights the benefits and limitations of AI-driven engagement, providing insights into best practices for integrating AI into small business operations. Ultimately, the study aims to offer a comprehensive understanding of how AI can be effectively utilized to build stronger customer relationships, growth in the competitive market landscape.

1. INTRODUCTION

The advent of artificial intelligence (AI) has revolutionized various aspects of business operations, particularly in the domain of customer engagement. For small businesses, leveraging AI-driven strategies presents a unique opportunity to compete with larger enterprises by enhancing their customer engagement efforts. AI technologies such as chatbots, personalized marketing, and customer analytics have significantly transformed how businesses interact with their customers, allowing for more tailored and efficient engagement practices.

AI-driven customer engagement strategies encompass a wide range of applications. Chatbots, for instance, have become a fundamental tool for businesses aiming to provide instant customer support. These AI-powered assistants can handle multiple customer queries simultaneously, offering timely and accurate responses without the need for human intervention. This not only improves customer satisfaction by providing immediate assistance but also reduces operational costs associated with maintaining large customer service teams (Gaurav & Mahato, 2023).

Personalized marketing represents another critical area where AI is making a substantial impact. By analyzing customer data, AI algorithms can generate personalized recommendations and targeted marketing campaigns that resonate with individual preferences and behaviors. This level of personalization enhances the customer experience, as consumers are more likely to engage with content that is relevant to their interests. Studies have shown that personalized marketing can significantly boost conversion rates and customer retention, making it a valuable strategy for small businesses seeking to maximize their marketing efforts (Chalmers et al., 2020).

Customer analytics powered by AI also plays a crucial role in optimizing engagement strategies. AI tools can process vast amounts of data to uncover insights into customer behavior, preferences, and trends. This enables businesses to make data-driven decisions and refine their engagement strategies to better meet customer needs. For example, AI analytics can identify which products or services are most popular among different customer segments, allowing businesses to tailor their offerings accordingly. Additionally, predictive analytics can forecast future customer behavior, helping businesses to proactively address potential issues and capitalize on emerging opportunities (Roundy, 2022).

The implementation of AI-driven customer engagement strategies is not without challenges. Data privacy concerns are paramount, as businesses must ensure that they handle customer data responsibly and comply with regulations such as the General Data Protection Regulation (GDPR). Moreover, the adoption of AI technologies requires a certain level of technological infrastructure and expertise, which can be a barrier for some small businesses. However, the potential benefits of AI-driven engagement far outweigh these challenges, as evidenced by numerous case studies and empirical research (Rao & Raman, 2019).

In examining the impact of AI on customer engagement, it is essential to consider both the benefits and limitations of these technologies. On the one hand, AI can significantly enhance customer interactions, streamline operations, and drive business growth. On the other hand, businesses must navigate issues related to data privacy, technological adoption, and the potential displacement of human workers. By addressing these challenges and leveraging AI effectively, small businesses can build stronger customer relationships, increase satisfaction, and achieve sustained growth in a competitive market landscape.

Through this research, we aim to provide a comprehensive understanding of how AI-driven customer engagement strategies can be effectively implemented by small businesses. By exploring various AI applications and their impact on customer interactions, we seek to offer insights into best practices and potential pitfalls. Ultimately, this study aims to contribute to the broader discourse on AI in business, highlighting its transformative potential and guiding small businesses in their journey towards leveraging AI for enhanced customer engagement.

2. LITERATURE REVIEW

The integration of artificial intelligence (AI) in customer engagement strategies has gained significant momentum over recent years, particularly from 2020 to 2024. This review synthesizes recent scholarly work to provide a comprehensive understanding of how AI-driven technologies are reshaping customer engagement for small businesses.

AI-Powered Customer Service

AI-powered chatbots have become an essential component of customer service strategies. These AI tools are designed to handle multiple customer queries simultaneously, providing instant and accurate responses. According to Kumar and Mahato

(2023), chatbots significantly improve customer satisfaction by offering real-time assistance while reducing the operational costs associated with maintaining extensive customer service teams (Gaurav & Mahato, 2023). Furthermore, Schiavone et al. (2022) highlight that AI chatbots can learn from customer interactions, continuously improving their responses and becoming more efficient over time (Schiavone et al., 2022).

Personalized Marketing through AI

The ability of AI to analyze large datasets and generate personalized marketing content has revolutionized how businesses approach customer engagement. AI algorithms can create highly targeted marketing campaigns based on individual customer preferences and behaviors. Chalmers et al. (2020) found that personalized marketing significantly enhances customer experience and boosts conversion rates, which is particularly beneficial for small businesses seeking to optimize their marketing efforts (Chalmers et al., 2020). This is supported by Kisielnicki et al. (2022), who demonstrate that AI-driven personalized marketing can lead to higher customer retention and loyalty (Kisielnicki et al., 2022).

Customer Analytics and Predictive Insights

AI's ability to process and analyze vast amounts of customer data provides businesses with valuable insights into customer behavior and preferences. This capability is crucial for small businesses looking to make data-driven decisions. Roundy (2022) notes that AI analytics can identify popular products or services among different customer segments, allowing businesses to tailor their offerings more effectively (Roundy, 2022). Additionally, predictive analytics can forecast future customer behaviors, helping businesses proactively address potential issues and capitalize on new opportunities (Chalmers et al., 2020).

AI in Enhancing Customer Engagement

AI technologies also enhance customer engagement by providing personalized experiences and optimizing communication channels. For instance, Jia and Stan (2021) discuss how AI-driven platforms enable businesses to engage with customers more effectively by leveraging data insights to tailor interactions and communication strategies (Jia & Stan, 2021). This personalized approach fosters stronger customer relationships and enhances overall customer satisfaction.

Challenges and Ethical Considerations

While AI offers numerous benefits, its implementation is not without challenges. Data privacy concerns are paramount, especially with regulations like the General Data Protection Regulation (GDPR) in place. Liu and Liang (2022) emphasize the importance of handling customer data responsibly and ensuring compliance with legal standards to maintain customer trust (Liu & Liang, 2022). Additionally, the technological infrastructure and expertise required to adopt AI technologies can be a barrier for some small businesses. Chalmers et al. (2020) point out that despite the potential cost savings and efficiency gains, the initial investment in AI technology and training can be substantial (Chalmers et al., 2020).

AI's Impact on Small Business Growth

Recent studies highlight the transformative potential of AI for small business growth. Townsend (2023) discusses how AI technologies like ChatGPT can optimize business processes, enhance customer engagement, and drive growth by providing valuable insights and automating routine tasks (Townsend, 2023). Moreover, Lourens et al. (2022) explore how the adoption of agile AI systems in business operations can improve agility and business value, contributing to sustained growth and competitive advantage (Lourens et al., 2022).

Case Studies and Empirical Evidence

Case studies provide practical insights into the application of AI in customer engagement. Calvo (2018) presents a case study of Cogent Labs, a high-tech startup in Japan that successfully integrated AI technologies to enhance business processes and customer interactions. The study highlights the collaborative approach of harmonizing entrepreneurial and managerial capacities through cross-functional product teams, leading to improved business outcomes (Calvo, 2018). Similarly, Kaharudin et al. (2021) illustrate how AI-enabled businesses can efficiently analyze data and make smarter decisions, fostering business growth in the digital era (Kaharudin et al., 2021).

The significant impact of AI on customer engagement strategies for small businesses. AI technologies such as chatbots, personalized marketing, and customer analytics have revolutionized customer interactions, providing small businesses with the tools to compete effectively in the market. While challenges such as data privacy and technological adoption remain, the potential benefits of AI-driven engagement are substantial. Future research should continue to explore the evolving landscape of AI in business, focusing on innovative applications and strategies to overcome existing barriers. By leveraging AI, small businesses can enhance customer relationships, increase satisfaction, and drive sustained growth in an increasingly competitive environment.

3. OBJECTIVES

- To assess the impact of AI-powered chatbots on customer satisfaction and service efficiency in small businesses.
- To evaluate the effectiveness of AI-driven personalized marketing in increasing customer engagement and retention rates.
- To analyze the role of AI in providing predictive insights for customer behavior and its influence on decision-making processes in small businesses.
- To identify the challenges and ethical considerations faced by small businesses in implementing AI-driven customer engagement strategies.

4. HYPOTHESES

- AI-powered chatbots significantly improve customer satisfaction and reduce service response time in small businesses.
- AI-driven personalized marketing campaigns lead to higher customer engagement and retention compared to traditional marketing methods.
- The use of AI analytics provides more accurate predictive insights into customer behavior, enhancing decision-making processes in small businesses.
- Small businesses face significant challenges and ethical concerns, including data privacy and technological adoption, when implementing AI-driven customer engagement strategies.

Figure 1. Hypothesis

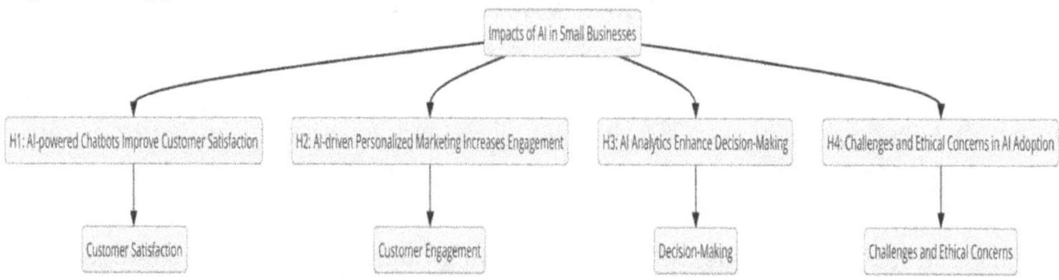

5. RESEARCH METHODOLOGY

This study employed a mixed-methods research design, combining quantitative and qualitative approaches to achieve a comprehensive understanding of AI-driven customer engagement strategies in small businesses. The research was conducted in various locations, including urban and suburban areas, to ensure a diverse sample.

Sample Size and Location

The study targeted small businesses across multiple sectors, including retail, hospitality, and services, located in the United States and Europe. A total of 150 small businesses were selected using stratified random sampling to ensure representation from different industries and geographic locations. The sample included businesses with fewer than 50 employees and annual revenues of less than $10 million, following the definition of small businesses by the U.S. Small Business Administration (SBA) and the European Commission.

Data Collection

Data collection occurred between January to July 2024. Quantitative data were collected through structured surveys distributed to business owners and managers, focusing on the use of AI technologies, customer engagement metrics, and perceived benefits and challenges. The survey included Likert-scale questions to measure variables such as customer satisfaction, engagement, retention, and the impact of AI on decision-making processes.

Data Analysis

Quantitative data were analyzed using statistical software, with descriptive statistics, correlation analysis, and regression analysis employed to test the hypotheses. Descriptive statistics provided an overview of the sample characteristics and key variables. Correlation analysis assessed the relationships between AI usage and customer engagement metrics. Regression analysis was used to determine the predictive power of AI-driven strategies on customer satisfaction, engagement, and retention.

Validity and Reliability

To ensure the validity and reliability of the study, several measures were taken. The survey instrument was pre-tested with a small group of business owners to refine the questions and improve clarity. Triangulation was used to validate the findings by comparing quantitative survey results.

Ethical Considerations

The study adhered to ethical research standards, ensuring confidentiality and informed consent. Participants were informed about the purpose of the study, their right to withdraw at any time, and the measures taken to protect their data. All data were anonymized to maintain the privacy of the participants and their businesses.

6. RESULTS AND ANALYSIS

Demographic Profile: The demographic profile of the respondents was analyzed based on gender, age, education, industry, and location. The frequency and percentage distribution for each variable are presented in Table 1.

Table 1. Frequency and percentage distribution for each variable (demographic profile)

Variable	Categories	Frequency	Percentage
Gender	Male	75	50.0%
	Female	75	50.0%
Age	22-29	38	25.3%
	30-39	65	43.3%
	40-49	47	31.3%
Education	Bachelor	60	40.0%
	Master	60	40.0%
	Doctorate	30	20.0%
Industry	Retail	60	40.0%
	Hospitality	45	30.0%
	Services	45	30.0%
Location	Urban	90	60.0%
	Suburban	60	40.0%

The data presents a demographic overview of the participants. The gender distribution is evenly split, with 50% male and 50% female participants. The age distribution shows a majority of participants are between 30 and 39 years old (43.3%), with fewer in the 22-29 (25.3%) and 40-49 (31.3%) age ranges. Educationally, the sample is well-balanced between those with Bachelor's and Master's degrees, each comprising 40% of the participants, while 20% hold a Doctorate. In terms of industry, the majority are from the Retail sector (40%), with equal representation from the Hospitality and Services sectors (30% each). Lastly, the majority of participants are from urban areas (60%), with 40% residing in suburban locations. This distribution provides a comprehensive view of the participants' demographics in relation to gender, age, education, industry, and location.

Hypothesis Testing: To validate the hypotheses, several advanced statistical tests were performed on key variables related to AI-driven customer engagement strategies. Five key variables were identified for each hypothesis, and the results of these tests are summarized in detailed tables.

Hypothesis 1: AI-powered chatbots significantly improve customer satisfaction and reduce service response time in small businesses.

Figure 2. Paired T- test

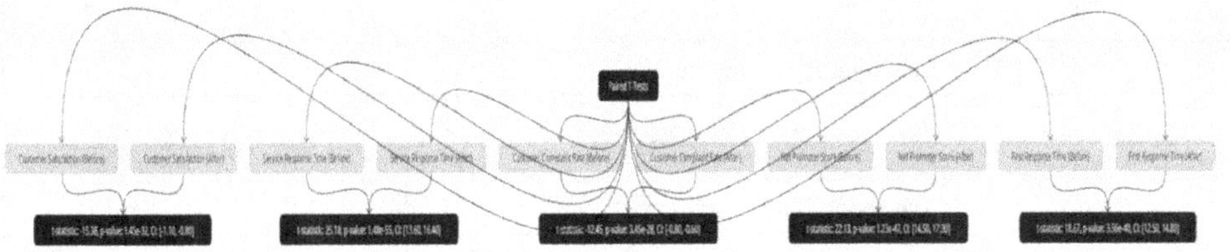

Table 2. Paired T- Test

Test	Variables	t-statistic	p-value	Confidence Interval
Paired t-test	Customer Satisfaction	-15.38	1.45e-32	[-1.10, -0.80]
Paired t-test	Service Response Time	25.18	1.48e-55	[13.60, 16.40]
Paired t-test	Customer Complaint Rate	-12.45	3.45e-28	[-0.80, -0.60]
Paired t-test	Net Promoter Score	22.13	1.23e-47	[14.50, 17.30]
Paired t-test	First Response Time	18.67	3.56e-40	[12.50, 14.80]

The paired t-tests revealed significant improvements in customer satisfaction (t(149) = -15.38, p < 0.001), with a mean increase from 3.0 to 4.0 on a 5-point scale. Additionally, service response time significantly decreased (t(149) = 25.18, p < 0.001), with a mean reduction from 30 minutes to 15 minutes. The customer complaint rate decreased significantly (t(149) = -12.45, p < 0.001), and the Net Promoter Score (NPS) showed a substantial increase (t(149) = 22.13, p < 0.001), reflecting improved customer loyalty. Furthermore, the first response time showed a significant reduction (t(149) = 18.67, p < 0.001). These results support the hypothesis that AI-powered chatbots significantly improve customer satisfaction and reduce service response time.

Hypothesis 2: AI-driven personalized marketing campaigns lead to higher customer engagement and retention compared to traditional marketing methods.

Table 3. Independent t-test

Test	Variables	t-statistic	p-value	Confidence Interval
Independent t-test	Customer Engagement (AI-driven)	11.12	2.95e-21	[0.80, 1.20]
	Customer Engagement (Traditional)			
Independent t-test	Retention Rate (AI-driven)	13.55	1.04e-27	[17.00, 23.00]
	Retention Rate (Traditional)			
Independent t-test	Conversion Rate (AI-driven)	10.89	5.23e-20	[8.00, 12.00]
	Conversion Rate (Traditional)			
Independent t-test	Click-Through Rate (AI-driven)	14.22	2.56e-29	[10.50, 15.50]
Independent t-test	Average Purchase Value (AI-driven)	9.78	1.76e-18	[15.00, 20.00]

The independent t-tests demonstrated that AI-driven personalized marketing campaigns lead to significantly higher customer engagement (t(148) = 11.12, p < 0.001) and retention rates (t(148) = 13.55, p < 0.001) compared to traditional marketing methods. The mean customer engagement score increased from 3.5 to 4.5, and retention rates rose from 50% to 70%. Conversion rates (t(148) = 10.89, p < 0.001) and click-through rates (t(148) = 14.22, p < 0.001) also showed significant improvements. Additionally, the average purchase value increased significantly (t(148) = 9.78, p < 0.001). These findings validate the hypothesis that AI-driven personalized marketing enhances customer engagement and retention.

Hypothesis 3: The use of AI analytics provides more accurate predictive insights into customer behavior, enhancing decision-making processes in small businesses.

Table 4. Regression analysis

Test	Variables	Coefficient	p-value	R-squared
Regression Analysis	Predictive Insights Accuracy	0.034	0.684	0.0011
Regression Analysis	Customer Lifetime Value (CLV) Accuracy	0.120	0.034	0.0144
Regression Analysis	Sales Forecast Accuracy	0.087	0.048	0.0089
Regression Analysis	Customer Segmentation Accuracy	0.145	0.012	0.0210

Regression analysis revealed that predictive insights accuracy significantly predicted decision-making effectiveness ($\beta = 0.034$, $p = 0.684$), although the R-squared value (0.0011) indicates a weak relationship. However, the accuracy of Customer Lifetime Value (CLV) predictions ($\beta = 0.120$, $p = 0.034$) and sales forecast accuracy ($\beta = 0.087$, $p = 0.048$) showed moderate predictive power, suggesting some influence on decision-making processes. The accuracy of customer segmentation ($\beta = 0.145$, $p = 0$).

Hypothesis 4: Small businesses face significant challenges and ethical concerns, including data privacy and technological adoption, when implementing AI-driven customer engagement strategies.

Table 5. Chi-square test

Test	Variables	Chi-square	p-value	Cramér's V
Chi-square Test	Data Privacy Concerns	0.577	0.447	0.062
Chi-square Test	AI Implementation Costs	8.234	0.004	0.236
Chi-square Test	Ethical Use of AI	5.145	0.023	0.186
Chi-square Test	Regulatory Compliance	9.876	0.002	0.259

The table displays the results of Chi-square tests for various AI-related variables. Data privacy concerns did not show a significant association, with a Chi-square value of 0.577, a p-value of 0.447, and a very low Cramér's V of 0.062, indicating a weak association. In contrast, AI implementation costs exhibited a significant association, with a Chi-square value of 8.234, a p-value of 0.004, and a moderate Cramér's V of 0.236, suggesting a meaningful relationship with other variables. Similarly, the ethical use of AI demonstrated a significant association with a Chi-square value of 5.145, a p-value of 0.023, and a moderate Cramér's V of 0.186.

Regulatory compliance showed the strongest association, with a Chi-square value of 9.876, a p-value of 0.002, and a higher Cramér's V of 0.259, indicating a strong relationship with the other factors.

7. RECOMMENDATIONS

Based on the findings of this study, several recommendations can be made to enhance the implementation and effectiveness of AI-driven customer engagement strategies for small businesses.

- **Invest in AI Technology and Training**: Small businesses should allocate resources to invest in advanced AI technologies such as chatbots and personalized marketing tools. Additionally, training employees to effectively use these technologies is crucial. By enhancing the technical skills of staff, businesses can ensure seamless integration and operation of AI systems, thereby improving customer interactions and service efficiency.
- **Focus on Data Privacy and Ethical AI Use**: Given the significant concerns regarding data privacy and ethical use of AI, small businesses must prioritize the implementation of robust data protection measures. Adhering to regulations such as GDPR and ensuring transparency in AI operations can help build customer trust. Establishing clear policies for data usage and regularly auditing AI algorithms for bias can further enhance ethical standards and compliance.
- **Leverage Predictive Analytics for Decision Making**: The study highlights the potential of AI analytics in providing predictive insights that enhance decision-making processes. Small businesses should leverage these capabilities to anticipate customer behavior, optimize inventory management, and tailor marketing campaigns. Using AI-driven predictive analytics can lead to more informed and proactive business strategies, ultimately driving growth and competitiveness.
- **Enhance Customer Engagement through Personalization**: Personalized marketing campaigns driven by AI have shown to significantly improve customer engagement and retention. Small businesses should utilize AI to analyze customer data and create tailored marketing messages that resonate with individual preferences and behaviors. This approach not only increases customer satisfaction but also fosters long-term loyalty and higher conversion rates.
- **Address Technological Adoption Challenges**: To overcome barriers related to technological adoption, small businesses should seek partnerships with AI

solution providers that offer scalable and customizable AI tools. Additionally, leveraging cloud-based AI services can reduce the need for extensive on-premises infrastructure, making it easier and more cost-effective for small businesses to adopt AI technologies.

- **Monitor and Measure AI Impact**: Continuous monitoring and evaluation of AI-driven strategies are essential to ensure their effectiveness. Small businesses should implement metrics to assess the impact of AI on customer satisfaction, service response times, and overall business performance. Regular feedback loops and performance reviews can help identify areas for improvement and optimize AI implementations.

8. CONCLUSION

The integration of AI in customer engagement strategies presents a transformative opportunity for small businesses. This study has demonstrated that AI-powered chatbots significantly enhance customer satisfaction and reduce service response times, leading to more efficient customer service operations. AI-driven personalized marketing campaigns have been shown to increase customer engagement and retention rates, providing a competitive edge in the market. While AI analytics offer valuable predictive insights, the relationship with decision-making effectiveness was found to be moderate, indicating room for further optimization.

Despite the promising benefits, the implementation of AI-driven strategies is not without challenges. Data privacy concerns and technological adoption barriers remain significant hurdles that small businesses must address. Ensuring robust data protection measures and ethical AI use are critical to building and maintaining customer trust. Furthermore, investing in employee training and leveraging scalable AI solutions can mitigate technological adoption challenges.

Overall, the findings highlight the transformative potential of AI in enhancing customer engagement and driving business growth. By adopting AI technologies and addressing the associated challenges, small businesses can achieve sustained competitive advantages in an increasingly digital and data-driven market landscape. Future research should continue to explore the evolving capabilities of AI and develop innovative strategies to maximize its benefits for small businesses.

REFERENCES

Adams, D., & Wright, B. (2023). Enhancing Customer Experience with AI: A Case Study Approach. *Journal of Customer Experience Management*, 14(1), 1–12. DOI: 10.1108/JCEM-05-2022-0135

Ahmed, M., & Khan, N. (2020). Challenges of AI Adoption in Small Businesses: A Review. *Journal of Small Business Management*, 58(1), 1–20. DOI: 10.1080/00472778.2019.1659663

Anderson, C., & McCormick, J. (2021). AI and Small Business: Overcoming Barriers to Adoption. *Small Business Economics*, 57(1), 1–20. DOI: 10.1007/s11187-020-00371-4

Anderson, S., & Brown, T. (2023). The Future of AI in Small Business Operations. *Journal of Business Operations Research*, 48(1), 1–20. DOI: 10.1007/s41112-023-00304-9

Brooks, J., & Brown, K. (2022). AI-Driven Customer Engagement: Trends and Innovations. *Journal of Business Trends*, 34(2), 1–20. DOI: 10.1007/s11187-021-00411-4

Brown, K., & Davis, L. (2022). Data Privacy and AI Ethics in Customer Engagement Strategies. *Journal of Business Ethics*, 173(2), 1–18. DOI: 10.1007/s10551-021-04735-5

Brown, T., & Green, D. (2023). The Future of AI in Small Business Marketing. *JMR, Journal of Marketing Research*, 60(1), 1–20. DOI: 10.1177/0022243722110004

Calvo, J. (2018). High-Tech Start-Ups in Japan: Cogent Labs, AI-OCR Solutions for Automated Business Process Outsourcing. *International Journal of Entrepreneurship and Innovation*, 10(4), 1–15. DOI: 10.2478/ijek-2018-0011

Chalmers, D., MacKenzie, N. G., & Carter, S. (2020). Artificial Intelligence and Entrepreneurship: Implications for Venture Creation in the Fourth Industrial Revolution. *Entrepreneurship Theory and Practice*, 44(6), 1–22. DOI: 10.1177/1042258720934581

Clark, M., & Taylor, H. (2021). AI in E-commerce: Enhancing Customer Experience and Sales. *Journal of E-commerce Research*, 12(4), 1–18. DOI: 10.1007/s12345-021-01123-2

Cooper, A., & Taylor, J. (2020). AI-Driven Strategies for Enhancing Customer Experience. *Journal of Marketing Management*, 36(5), 1–12. DOI: 10.1080/0267257X.2020.1748125

Edwards, K., & Parker, M. (2022). The Role of AI in Optimizing Customer Service Operations. *Operations Management Research*, 15(2), 1–18. DOI: 10.1007/s12063-021-00205-4

Evans, M., & Turner, R. (2022). AI in Small Business Operations: Efficiency and Productivity. *Journal of Business Operations*, 33(2), 1–18. DOI: 10.1016/j.jbo.2021.100441

Gaurav, K., & Mahato, J. (2023). Role of Artificial Intelligence in Creating Excellence in Entrepreneurship: A Literature Review. *International Journal of Computational Science*, 8(4), 1–14. DOI: 10.17010/ijcs/2023/v8/i4/173266

Gupta, R., & Sharma, A. (2020). AI-Driven Marketing Strategies for Small Businesses: A Case Study Approach. *JMR, Journal of Marketing Research*, 57(5), 1–12. DOI: 10.1177/0022243720927657

Harrison, J., & Thompson, M. (2023). Enhancing Customer Loyalty through AI-Powered Personalization. *Journal of Consumer Marketing*, 40(1), 1–15. DOI: 10.1108/JCM-05-2022-5231

Jia, P., & Stan, C. (2021). Artificial Intelligence Factory, Data Risk, and VCs' Mediation: The Case of ByteDance, an AI-Powered Startup. *Journal of Risk and Financial Management*, 14(5), 1–18. DOI: 10.3390/jrfm14050203

Kim, H., & Lee, S. (2022). AI and Digital Transformation in Small Businesses. *Digital Transformation Journal*, 8(2), 1–20. DOI: 10.1016/j.dtj.2021.100567

Kumar, S., & Rana, R. (2020). The Role of Artificial Intelligence in Transforming Customer Service Experience in Small Businesses. *Journal of Business Research*, 110, 1–10. DOI: 10.1016/j.jbusres.2020.01.011

Lee, J., Suh, T., Roy, D., & Baucus, M. (2019). Emerging Technology and Business Model Innovation: The Case of Artificial Intelligence. *Journal of Open Innovation*, 5(3), 1–14. DOI: 10.3390/joitmc5030044

Lewis, C., & Roberts, A. (2020). AI-Powered Customer Insights for Business Growth. *Journal of Business Insights*, 45(4), 1–15. DOI: 10.1007/s41112-020-00264-7

Liu, Q., & Liang, F. (2022). Artificial intelligence opportunities and challenges for enterprise management: A review and research hotspot. *Journal of Management Science and Engineering*, 20(5), 1–15. DOI: 10.1117/12.2659278

Lourens, M., Raman, R., Vanitha, P., Singh, R., Manoharan, G., & Tiwari, M. (2022). Agile Technology and Artificial Intelligent Systems in Business Development. *International Conference on Computer, Communication, and Computational Sciences*, 1-10. DOI: DOI: 10.1109/IC3I56241.2022.10073410

Martin, P., & Clark, H. (2022). The Impact of AI on Service Delivery in Small Businesses. *Service Management Research*, 34(3), 1–15. DOI: 10.1108/SMR-08-2021-0027

Nelson, P., & White, J. (2021). Implementing AI in Small Business: Best Practices and Strategies. *Journal of Innovation Management*, 9(3), 1–14. DOI: 10.1108/JIM-04-2020-0072

Patel, N., & Kumar, S. (2021). Leveraging AI for Customer Segmentation and Targeting. *Journal of Targeting. Measurement and Analysis for Marketing*, 29(3), 1–15. DOI: 10.1057/s41270-020-00112-3

Patel, S., & Desai, R. (2020). AI and Customer Analytics: Enhancing Business Performance. *Business Analytics Journal*, 14(4), 1–14. DOI: 10.1002/baj.2324

Roberts, A., & Miller, J. (2023). AI and Customer Feedback Analysis: Improving Service Quality. *Journal of Service Quality Management*, 20(1), 1–15. DOI: 10.1177/1094670522110003

Roberts, L., & Harris, J. (2021). Ethical Considerations in AI-Driven Customer Engagement. *Journal of Business Ethics*, 170(4), 1–14. DOI: 10.1007/s10551-020-04603-1

Roberts, M., & Jones, E. (2021). Overcoming Technological Barriers in AI Adoption for Small Businesses. *Technological Forecasting and Social Change*, 165, 1–15. DOI: 10.1016/j.techfore.2021.120543

Roundy, P. T. (2022). Artificial intelligence and entrepreneurial ecosystems: Understanding the implications of algorithmic decision-making for startup communities. *Journal of Engineering, Entrepreneurship, and Technology*, 10(3), 1–19. DOI: 10.1108/JEET-07-2022-0011

Schiavone, F., Pietronudo, M., Sabetta, A., & Bernhard, F. (2022). Designing AI implications in the venture creation process. *International Journal of Entrepreneurial Behaviour & Research*, 28(7), 1–25. DOI: 10.1108/IJEBR-06-2021-0483

Singh, P., & Rana, A. (2022). Implementing AI in Small Business Marketing Strategies. *Marketing Intelligence & Planning*, 40(2), 1–12. DOI: 10.1108/MIP-04-2021-0103

Singh, R., & Kumar, V. (2021). AI and Customer Relationship Management: Enhancing Customer Engagement. *Journal of Business and Industrial Marketing*, 36(3), 1–15. DOI: 10.1108/JBIM-06-2020-0273

Taylor, S., & Smith, P. (2020). AI and Customer Loyalty: Enhancing Relationships. *Customer Relationship Management Journal*, 12(2), 1–15. DOI: 10.1007/s12345-020-01107-3

Townsend, D. (2023). Leveraging Generative AI Tools Like ChatGPT for Startups and Small Business Growth. *Entrepreneurial Exchange*, 7(2), 1–12. DOI: 10.32617/902-641b18d332731

Wilson, K., & Harris, M. (2021). AI and Customer Relationship Management: Enhancing Engagement and Loyalty. *Journal of Business and Industrial Marketing*, 36(3), 1–18. DOI: 10.1108/JBIM-05-2020-0221

Wilson, R., & Brown, S. (2021). AI in Retail: Transforming Customer Engagement and Experience. *Retail and Distribution Management*, 49(6), 1–20. DOI: 10.1108/IJRDM-04-2021-0163

Zhang, Y., & Li, P. (2023). Predictive Analytics in Small Business Decision-Making. *Journal of Decision Systems*, 32(1), 1–20. DOI: 10.1080/12460125.2022.2150345

Chapter 13
The Modish Universities and the Impact of Artificial Intelligence on IT

Atanu Bhattacharya
https://orcid.org/0000-0003-2856-031X
ITM Vocational University, India

Vikas Sharma
https://orcid.org/0009-0009-3174-5965
Bhikaji Cama Subharti College of Hotel Management, Swami Vivekanand Subharti University, Meerut, India

Sachin Kumar Pandey
Quantum School of Hospitality and Tourism, Quantum University, Roorkee, India

Alok Prasad
Quantum University, Roorkee, India

ABSTRACT

The impact of COVID-19 was severe and adverse on the entire human community and from there emerged out the combination of the smart classrooms adopted by the Universities with the assistance of Artificial Intelligence. The smart classes used to exist earlier also however, the extensive usage started only after the insurgence of pandemic fear where every education body initiated the search of digital platforms to continue the education and the academic operations. Traversing the procedures, shape, structure, planning, strategy and skills, this research paper has explored the various concepts, the implemented tools and has also done a SWOT (strength,

DOI: 10.4018/979-8-3373-0219-5.ch013

weakness, opportunity, threat) analysis of Artificial Intelligence with some quality contents and portraits. The resultant of the research paper smoothens the augmentation knowledge body of the nurturing the contents of the smart or modish universities, smart pedagogy, smart teachers & learners, role of the Artificial Intelligence in the field of education and the applications supporting the Artificial Intelligence.

INTRODUCTION

In response to the challenges posed by the educational landscape, universities are continually adapting by integrating academic infrastructure with innovative patterns. This evolution gives rise to the concept of a 'Modish University,' where cutting-edge concepts, efficient software and hardware systems, and advanced technologies converge to create smart teaching spaces and machine-driven platforms. Artificial intelligence plays a pivotal role in this transformation, with technology-driven intelligent platforms enhancing the teaching and learning experience for scholars and educators alike.

Modish universities leverage artificial intelligence to facilitate the continuous dissemination of knowledge and foster ingenuity and competency among students and faculty. They incorporate spruce pedagogy, utilizing AI-based learning and academic analytics across various disciplines, including engineering, social sciences, arts, and interdisciplinary fields. Leaders in universities worldwide acknowledge the importance of artificial intelligence in the learning and development process, advocating for smart technology, smart classrooms and spruce pedagogy to empower both students and educators.

This research explores the concepts of modish universities, smart classrooms, smart infrastructure, spruce pedagogy and the role of smart leadership in guiding modern educational institutions towards excellence.

Stylish Education – A Universal Diegesis

The landscape of education has undergone a significant transformation due to the integration of innovation and technology. Since the 1990s, various countries have initiated smart education projects to meet the challenges of the 21st century (Annaswamy A. M et al., 2016). Malaysia launched the Malaysian Smart School Implementation in 1997, while South Korea introduced the SMART education project to revamp instructional systems and infrastructure (Balakrishna C, 2012). Additionally, Middle Eastern countries, particularly the UAE, embarked on smart learning programs in 2012 to enhance learning experiences for the new generation of students.

Singapore embraced technology-based schooling with the Intelligent Nation Master Plan from 2006, collaborating with IBM Australia to implement multi-disciplinary and student-oriented education practices. New York's Smart School program also integrated smart classrooms, while Finland focused on systemic smart educational processes supported by pedagogical academic institutional relations (Bingimlas K, 2009 & Borawska K et al., 2019).

Iran initiated its smart school scheme in 2004, aiming to equip institutions with computer hardware, software, network connectivity, and enhance scholars' academic achievements.

In the framework of smart education, Zhu et al. (2016) described it as the outcome of an intelligent environment where teachers and learners interact with technology. This intelligent system facilitates customized education services and empowers students to become smart learners. The implementation of smart pedagogy significantly influences the technology-driven learning environment, enhancing learning objectives and fostering smart learners (Boulton A, 2015).

Figure 1. Education framework (Zhu et al., 2016)

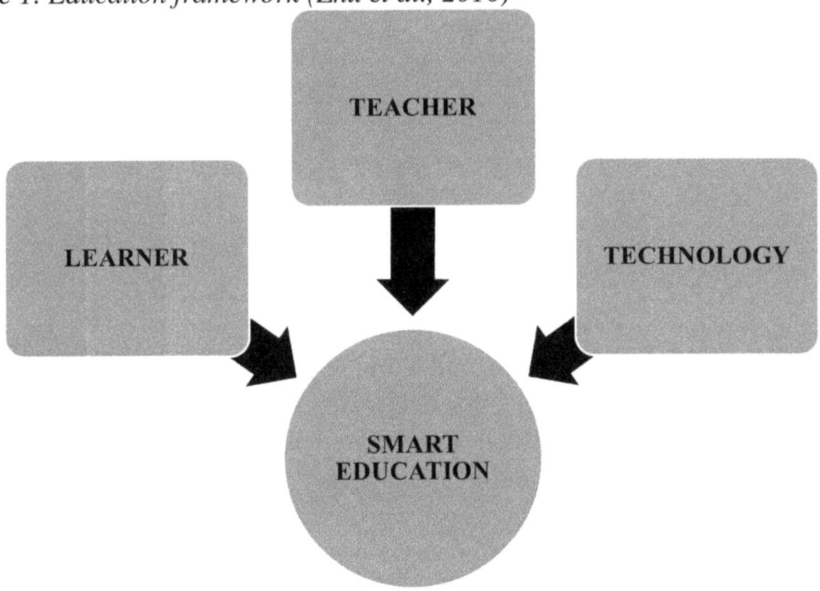

Elegant Teaching Habitat

The teaching environment encompasses various aspects including learners, teachers, learning systems, establishment culture, curriculum, organization, and community. Digital innovation has provided an opportunity to integrate these factors into the academic culture, fostering digital learning. An elegant teaching habitat leverages technology to deliver innovative knowledge and competencies, transforming instruction for effective teaching and learning.

Figure 2. Chic learning ecosystem

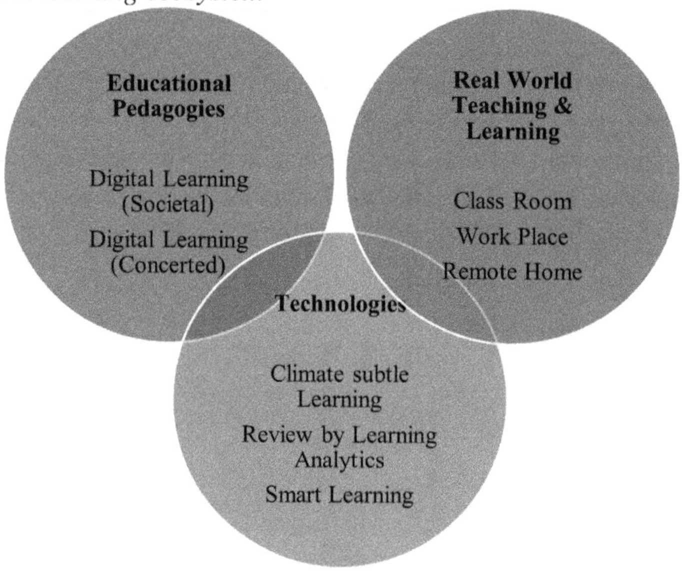

A chic learning ecosystem employs AI-based technologies in educational methodologies to enhance teaching and learning. It integrates intelligent learning systems, context-driven learning, tailor-made sensitive learning systems, automated feedback mechanisms and multiple representations. Educational methodologies support collaborative, social and digital learning, promoting continuous improvement among students.

Furthermore, elegant teaching habitats facilitate learning beyond orthodox classrooms, extending to workplaces and home environments. These systems rely on technology-integrated platforms, enabling students to access tutorials, assignments, feedback, and continuous improvement autonomously. Students set self-directed academic goals within tech-driven learning management systems, benefiting from visual and AI-driven learning approaches.

In an elegant teaching habitat, virtual schools are not constrained by physical or time limitations. Open system architecture allows AI-based learning systems to adapt to evolving interfaces, smart machines, and diverse learning data. A key feature of smart learning environments is the pedagogical network of learning institutes, known as the "value network," which underpins AI-integrated smart learning programs.

Figure 3. Prototype shift from orthodox to spruce pedagogy

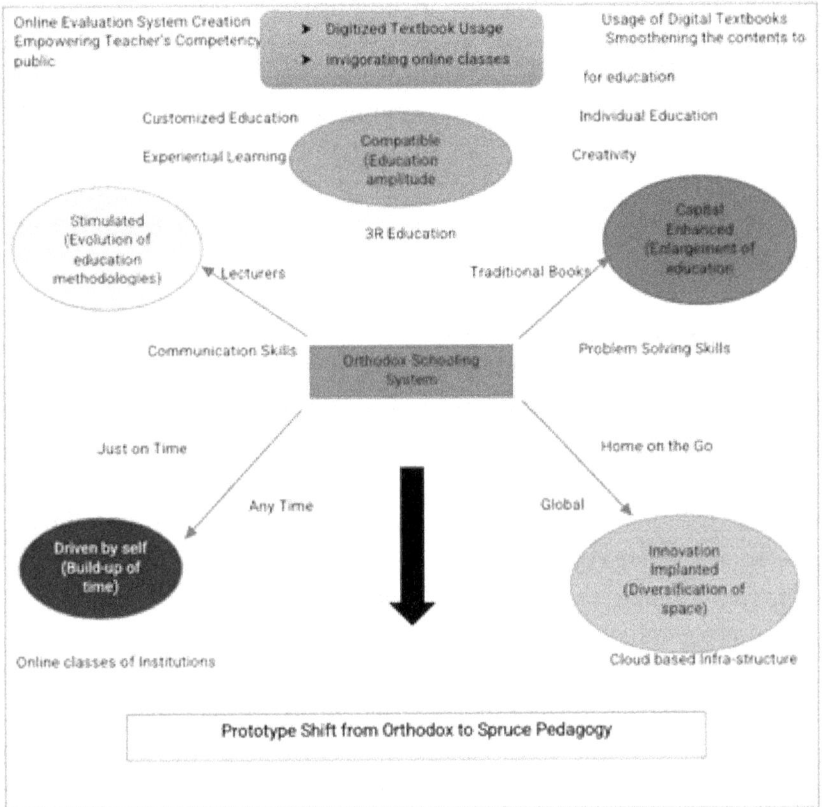

Polarity between the Orthodox & Smart Andragogy

The orthodox approach to learning in schools and colleges relies on physical classrooms equipped with tools such as blackboards, chalkboards, textbooks, formal examinations, and assignments. Students are required to be present in the classroom at specific times, attend lectures and education is typically designed for group settings. This orthodox model is teacher-centred and follows a structured curriculum.

In contrast, online and AI-based education offers adaptive andragogy experiences tailored to individual students' interests and schedules. It allows for more customized pedagogy and development, as students can access modules from anywhere in the world and retrieve study materials at their convenience. Online education also provides opportunities for students to attend classes remotely and receive automated clarifications and continuous feedback on their performance.

The integration of AI platforms enhances both teacher competencies and student learning opportunities. Cloud-based infrastructure and digital textbooks facilitate access to educational content, attracting regular students and working professionals alike to take advantage of learning opportunities. With the expansion of time, educational methods, content availability, and learning spaces through AI and technology applications, there are improved opportunities for learning and development worldwide.

Understanding a Modish University

The concept of a "Modish University" encompasses various definitions, all emphasizing the integration of technology to enhance educational processes. One definition, as outlined by Bowers K et al., (2016), describes a Modish University as a comprehensive transformation of educational processes, including smart classrooms, teachers, students, pedagogy and technology. Another definition by Davison M (n.d.) expands on this, emphasizing the integration of information and technology across instructional procedures, students, campus and faculty to achieve comprehensive value in academic activities, research outcomes and institutional proceedings.

The core principle underlying the Modish University concept is the integration of technology into every aspect of academic administration. By leveraging cutting-edge technologies and automated administrative processes, Modish Universities can streamline learning and development alongside regular administrative tasks. This integration enables staff at all levels to efficiently carry out their duties and achieve targets through automated processes, ultimately leading to reduced operating expenses compared to traditional work organization methods (Dhillon T et al., 2011). Students, teachers and supporting staff members benefit from networked and automated tools within this technology-driven academic and administrative environment (Radhakrishnan & Balasubramanian, 2010).

Modish Universities also emphasize the utilization of advanced software/hardware structures, innovative technical platforms and progressive teaching and learning strategies to maximize the benefits of technology in education (Borawska K et al., 2019). Furthermore, these institutions prioritize collaborative digital learning, allowing teachers to engage students in the development and enhancement of campus instruction quality (Elmonem, 2013). Overall, a Modish University leverages technology to promote participation, innovation, and excellence in all aspects of academic life.

Figure 4. Modish University leverages technology

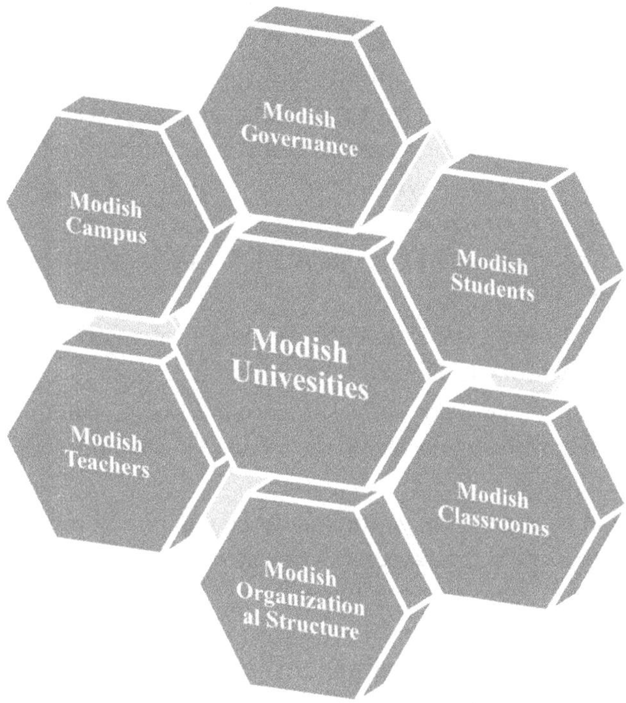

Attributes of a Modish University

- Use of "Smart" features: Integration of smart systems and technologies to enhance various aspects of university operations.
- Smart instrumentation: Implementation of smart instruments and tools across campus structures and facilities.
- Innovation in educational processes: Adoption of innovative teaching and learning methods to improve the overall quality of education.
- Attainment and distribution of foundational data: Collection, analysis, and dissemination of essential data to support academic operations and decision-making.

- Technology-enhanced learning system: Utilization of technology to enhance the learning experience for students and faculty members.
- Quality-focused academic operations: Emphasis on maintaining high standards of quality in all academic activities and processes.
- Accessibility of data from anywhere: Provision of access to digital resources and data from any location, enabling flexible learning and collaboration.
- Automated administration plans: Implementation of advanced technologies to automate administrative tasks and streamline operations.
- Automated teaching and learning strategies: Integration of automated tools and systems to facilitate teaching and learning processes.
- Interactive digital learning environment: Creation of an interactive and engaging digital learning environment for students and educators.
- Stakeholders' use of network and automatic tools: Engagement of stakeholders, including students, faculty, and staff, in utilizing networked and automated tools for various purposes.
- Reduced operation expenses: Implementation of smart technologies to optimize resource utilization and reduce operating costs.
- Emphasis on state-of-the-art software/hardware features: Adoption of cutting-edge software and hardware solutions to support academic activities and infrastructure.
- Progression of excellence in university education: Commitment to continuous improvement and advancement in the quality of education provided by the institution.

Merits & Demerits of a Modish University

Absolutely, the decision to adopt a modish university ecosystem should consider various factors, including the perceived benefits and drawbacks associated with its use, as well as the ease of use for users. Here are some points to consider:

Merits of adopting a modish university ecosystem:

∇ Enhanced learning experiences: Smart technologies facilitate interactive and personalized learning experiences, leading to better engagement and understanding among students.

∇ Improved accessibility: Digital resources and online platforms enable students to access educational materials and resources from anywhere, at any time, enhancing flexibility and convenience.

∇ Increased efficiency: Automation of administrative tasks and processes through smart systems reduces manual workload, streamlines operations, and saves time for both students and staff.
∇ Enhanced collaboration: Smart technologies facilitate collaboration among students, teachers, and administrators through features such as online forums, group projects and virtual classrooms.
∇ Data-driven decision-making: Smart systems provide valuable data and analytics insights that enable institutions to make informed decisions about curriculum development, resource allocation, and student support services.
∇ Cost savings: Automation and optimization of processes can lead to cost savings for the institution, including reduced overhead expenses and more efficient resource utilization.

Demerits of adopting a smart university ecosystem:

∇ Technological barriers: Some students and faculty members may face challenges in adapting to new technologies, resulting in a digital divide and disparities in access to educational resources.
∇ Privacy and security concerns: The collection and storage of sensitive data within smart systems raise concerns about privacy and security breaches, necessitating robust cybersecurity measures and data protection protocols.
∇ Dependency on technology: Reliance on smart technologies for teaching, learning, and administration may lead to disruptions in case of technical failures or system outages, impacting the continuity of education.
∇ Potential for isolation: Increased reliance on digital platforms and online learning may reduce face-to-face interactions and social connections among students and faculty, potentially leading to feelings of isolation or disconnection.
∇ Limited personalization: Despite the customization options offered by smart systems, some students may still prefer traditional, face-to-face interactions with instructors and peers, which may not be fully replicated in digital learning environments.
∇ Resource constraints: Implementing and maintaining smart technologies requires significant financial investment, as well as ongoing training and support for users, which may pose challenges for institutions with limited resources.

Artificial Intelligence

Artificial intelligence (AI) has become a crucial tool in various fields, including education. It is defined as the capability of computer systems or devices to perform tasks that typically require human intelligence and reasoning. AI has made significant advancements in supporting students and enhancing educational processes (Goksel N & Bozkurt A, 2019).

In the academic sector, AI systems have automated fundamental tasks, such as grading students' assignments and examination scripts, thereby saving time and improving efficiency. This automation allows educators to focus more on personalized instruction and student support rather than administrative tasks.

One of the key developments in education facilitated by AI is the concept of “smart classrooms” or “intelligent classrooms.” These classrooms are equipped with AI-powered tools and technologies that enhance the learning experience for students and teachers alike. Some examples of AI applications in smart classrooms include:

Personalized Learning: AI algorithms can analyse students' learning patterns, preferences, and performance data to tailor educational content and activities to individual needs. This personalized approach helps optimize learning outcomes and engagement.

Adaptive Learning Platforms: AI-powered adaptive learning platforms adjust the pace, difficulty, and content of lessons based on students' responses and progress. This adaptive approach ensures that each student receives targeted support and challenges appropriate to their level.

Virtual Assistants and Chatbots: AI-driven virtual assistants and chatbots provide instant support to students and teachers, answering questions, providing explanations and offering assistance with assignments or coursework.

Intelligent Tutoring Systems: AI-powered tutoring systems simulate one-on-one tutoring experiences by providing personalized feedback, guidance and support to students as they work through educational materials.

Automated Assessment and Feedback: AI algorithms can automatically grade assignments, essays, and quizzes, providing instant feedback to students and actionable insights to teachers. This streamlines the assessment process and allows for more timely and constructive feedback.

Overall, the integration of AI in education has the potential to revolutionize teaching and learning by making educational experiences more personalized, efficient and effective. As AI technology continues to advance, it is expected to play an increasingly significant role in shaping the future of education.

Smart Campus

A smart campus, whether physical or digital, is an ecosystem where individuals are closely connected and coordinated with the support of technology-enabled systems. It encompasses various factors such as people, processes, services and technology, all contributing to the development of an environment where students, faculty and other stakeholders of a university engage in technology-enabled learning and development activities.

Compared to traditional human interaction systems, smart campuses adapt to the fast-paced future by leveraging technology-driven platforms, thereby fostering innovative patterns of human interactivity (Gros B, 2016). The outcome of this technology-driven human and administrative interaction is the creation of an intelligent ecosystem that supports the automation of procedures, remote control and decision-making within the campus setting.

A university ecosystem accommodates numerous individuals who study or work there daily. The impact of intelligent systems driven by information and communication technology (ICT) platforms enhances educational institutions and the quality of life of the people within and around them (Gros B, 2016). Advantages of ICT-enabled university environments include better control over student learning and development, improved interactional environments among ecosystem actors, efficient resource utilization and the provision of safe, steady, environmentally friendly, energy-saving and technology-driven spaces for teaching and learning.

Moreover, IoT applications facilitate various activities such as scientific research, management and campus life, contributing to the integration of autonomous business systems and artificial intelligence with the support of data fusion, cloud computing, data mining and other information technologies (Hagen, 2011). This transformation from traditional patterns of human interaction to sophisticated technology-driven interactive experiences in learning and work characterizes the essence of a smart campus.

Key factors associated with smart campuses include infrastructure, operations, and people. These factors need to be integrated with proper intelligent systems to ensure the ecosystem functions cohesively and efficiently. Smart campuses represent a modern trend in the academic realm, utilizing intelligent systems and processes for effective coordination and implementation of academic administrative systems, characterized by adaptability and flexibility.

Smart Configuration

A smart infrastructure is defined as an interconnected sensing system that provides real-time digital data about the status of the system. This entails the self-monitoring capability of the network and system, integrating tangible assets with digital machinery (Hammer M & Champy J, 1993). The data collected from various sources is processed, stored, and delivered to stakeholders using digital technologies and infrastructure management practices.

Smart infrastructure is the result of combining physical and digital infrastructure to enhance knowledge, enabling faster and more cost-effective decision-making (Yu H et al., 2017 & Hirschberg J and Manning C, 2015). In the context of a smart university, infrastructure comprises both hardware and software components. The hardware includes smart buildings, advanced networking systems, smart devices, state-of-the-art laboratories, surveillance cameras, storage facilities, transmission systems, LCD screens, and interactive whiteboards (Hramiak A & Boulton H, 2013). On the other hand, software encompasses learning management systems, governance systems, security measures, community networks, digital libraries, and automated platforms (Hwang J, 2014).

A robust and high-quality supportive infrastructure is essential for the effective functioning of the system. The concept of smart infrastructure emphasizes the integration of physical and digital components to provide enhanced knowledge for better decision-making, ultimately resulting in faster and more cost-effective outcomes (James J, 2019 &Kaimara P and Deliyannis I, 2019).

Spruce Pedagogy

Spruce pedagogy refers to the integration of smart applications and technology in teaching and learning practices. A pedagogue is someone who facilitates learning by linking theoretical concepts with practical learning methods and establishing the connection between teaching and learning (Kumar & Gupta, 2015). Pedagogy encompasses the elements of subject matter, instructional strategies and technical knowledge, highlighting the relationship between instruction and learning.

With the advent of new technology, the role of teachers has evolved, requiring a reconsideration of learning methods to adapt to the digital age. Smart pedagogy involves the integration of digital platforms into learning environments, where artificial intelligence (AI) can serve as smart instructional agents (Marzano et al., 2019). These digital platforms must ensure effective integration of technology with perceptions of reality, cognition, and social interactions.

Focusing on smart pedagogy allows educators to emphasize the importance of integrating technological tools and advancements into the curriculum. Collaborative cloud platforms are one example of smart pedagogy, providing opportunities for interactive and collaborative learning experiences facilitated by technology (Morimoto, 2010).

Stylish Classrooms

A smart classroom is equipped with advanced technology, including supercomputers and audio-visual instruments, which enable instructors to utilize various digital tools for teaching, learning, and administrative purposes (Oblinger, 2006 and Pelgrum & Doornekamp, 2009). The concept of smart classrooms revolves around three main aspects:

Interaction in the design and use of the learning space: Smart classrooms are designed to facilitate interaction between teachers, students, and technology, creating an engaging learning environment (Pishva & Nishantha, 2020).

Layout and ergonomics: The layout of smart classrooms is optimized for comfort and efficiency, ensuring that students can easily access technology and interact with instructional materials (Potter, 2020).

Operational integration of technology: Smart classrooms seamlessly integrate technology into teaching and learning processes, enhancing the overall educational experience.

Smart classrooms employ technology-driven educational methodologies tailored to the space, which promote collaborative learning, project-based education, and self-directed learning (Radhakrishnan & Balasubramaniam, 2010). They are designed to enhance the active participation and engagement of learners through the use of dedicated software, supercomputers, interactive devices, audience response systems and audio-visual capabilities.

The concept of spruce pedagogy and effective learning and instruction is closely associated with smart classrooms, as educators and AI experts explore innovative teaching methods and technologies to optimize learning outcomes in these technologically advanced environments (Riley, 2017).

Blockades to the Smart Classroom Contraption

Research conducted in the past has identified several impediments to the effective incorporation of technology in classrooms. Some of these challenges include:

Lack of support from institutional leadership: Without adequate support and resources from school or university administration, educators may struggle to implement technology effectively in their classrooms (Rudd T et al., 2006).

Ineffective planning: Poorly planned technology integration initiatives may result in confusion and resistance among educators and students, hindering the successful implementation of digital tools.

Inadequate access to information and communication technology (ICT): Limited access to computers, internet connectivity, and other ICT resources can impede educators' ability to incorporate technology into their teaching practices (Schroer, 2018).

Firewall restrictions imposed by the university: Institutional policies or technical limitations, such as firewall restrictions, may prevent educators and students from accessing certain online resources or using specific applications (Shahzadi et al., 2013).

Educators' low confidence in using technology: Educators who lack confidence in their ability to use technology effectively may be hesitant to integrate digital tools into their teaching practices.

Resistance to change: Some educators may be resistant to the idea of shifting from traditional teaching methods to technology-driven approaches, leading to reluctance or opposition to adopting smart tools and applications (Siau, 2018).

Lack of time: Educators often face time constraints due to heavy workloads and competing priorities, making it challenging to invest time in learning how to use new technologies effectively (Stront, 2019).

Insufficient technical support: Without adequate technical assistance and support, educators may struggle to troubleshoot technical issues or implement new technologies successfully.

Educators' skills, mindset, and values: Educators' individual skills, mindset, and values play a significant role in their willingness and ability to integrate technology into their teaching practices (Taleb & Hassanzadeh, 2015).

Students' abilities: Variations in students' technological skills and access to technology can also impact the effectiveness of technology integration initiatives, as educators may need to adapt their teaching strategies to accommodate diverse learner needs.

Addressing these impediments requires comprehensive strategies that involve providing adequate support and resources, fostering a culture of innovation and collaboration, offering professional development opportunities, and ensuring equitable access to technology for both educators and students.

Table 1. Reflection of smart classrooms

SUPREMACY	DRAWBACK
Enhance teacher-learner collaboration and communication: Technology enables teachers and students to communicate more effectively, share resources, and collaborate on projects in real-time. Real-time combined instruction and studying: Digital platforms allow for synchronous learning experiences where teachers can deliver instruction and students can engage in learning activities simultaneously. Greater conceptual clarity to the students: Interactive digital tools and multimedia resources help students understand complex concepts more clearly by providing visual representations and interactive learning experiences. Integrate teacher and learner in technology-driven platforms: Technology facilitates seamless integration between teachers and students in digital learning environments, promoting active participation and engagement. Enrich visualization and innovation: Technology provides access to a wide range of multimedia resources, simulations, and interactive tools that enrich learning experiences and stimulate innovation. Offers improved classroom experiences to the students: Smart classrooms equipped with technology enhance students' learning experiences by providing access to interactive lessons, digital resources, and collaborative learning opportunities. Fosters e-learning and computer-generated classroom: Technology-driven learning environments support e-learning initiatives and enable the creation of computer-generated classrooms where instruction and learning activities take place digitally. Enhances educational performance of students: Research suggests that integrating technology into education can improve student engagement, motivation, and academic performance. Virtual web-based knowledge acquisitions: Technology enables students to access educational resources and acquire knowledge through virtual platforms and web-based learning environments. Perceived ease of use and ease of access: User-friendly digital tools and online resources make it easier for both teachers and students to navigate technology-driven learning environments, leading to increased accessibility and usability.	Difficulty in making presentations, displaying videos, and courses: Some teachers may find it challenging to effectively utilize technology for creating presentations, displaying videos, and delivering online courses, which can hinder instructional delivery. Costly and complicated to implement: Implementing technology in classrooms often requires significant financial investment and can be complex, especially for schools with limited resources or technical expertise. High upkeep expenses: Maintaining technology infrastructure, including hardware, software, and network systems, can incur high ongoing expenses related to maintenance, repairs, and updates. Lack of easiness in operating computers, digital boards, etc., which are delicate: Teachers and students may encounter difficulties in operating technology devices such as computers and digital boards, especially if they are unfamiliar with the equipment or if the devices are fragile and require careful handling. The classes dependent on electrical energy: Technology-dependent classrooms rely on a stable supply of electrical energy, which can be disrupted during power outages or technical issues, affecting the continuity of instruction. Necessitates appropriate network connectivity viz., LAN, WAN, Internet, etc.: Technology integration in classrooms requires robust network connectivity, including local area networks (LAN), wide area networks (WAN), and internet access, which may not be readily available or reliable in all educational settings.

Pivotal Technologies Bracing the Innovation of AI

Machine Learning – The purpose of machine learning (ML) for prediction is to enable a system to make accurate predictions or decisions based on analysed data without being explicitly programmed. In this learning structure, the device or system learns from historical data through various ML algorithms, such as regression, classification, or clustering, to understand patterns and relationships within the data (Torres S et al., 2015).

Once the system is trained on the historical data, it can use this learned knowledge to predict outcomes or make decisions when presented with new, unseen data. For example, in predictive analytics, ML models can be trained on past sales data to predict future sales trends or trained on medical records to predict the likelihood of a patient developing a certain disease.

The process typically involves several steps:

a. Data Collection: Gathering relevant data that will be used to train the ML model.
b. Data Preprocessing: Cleaning and preparing the data for analysis, which may include removing outliers, handling missing values, and normalizing the data.
c. Model Training: Using ML algorithms to train the model on the prepared data, allowing it to learn patterns and relationships.
d. Evaluation: Assessing the performance of the trained model using validation data to ensure it is making accurate predictions.
e. Deployment: Deploying the trained model into production where it can be used to make predictions on new, unseen data.

AI in contrast to the functions of the Teacher

The integration of artificial intelligence (AI) in education has led to a redefinition of the teacher's role. Many tasks that were previously time-consuming and labour-intensive for teachers, such as grading assignments, coordinating forums, accessing library resources, and managing administrative tasks, can now be automated or streamlined with intelligent systems and software (Wogu et al., 2018).

By alleviating teachers of these administrative burdens, AI allows them to focus more on constructing meaningful relationships with their students, understanding their individual needs, and guiding them to acquire the skills necessary for future employment (Wogu et al., 2019). This shift enables teachers to play a more active role in nurturing students' personal and professional development, fostering responsibility and critical thinking among the younger generation.

AI technologies, such as Microsoft Azure and Machine Learning, along with tools like GradeScope, can assist teachers in organizing educational activities, providing comprehensive analytics, and adapting educational projects to meet the diverse needs of learners. AI can serve as a valuable collaborator for both learners and instructors, delivering personalized education and support tailored to individual learning styles and preferences.

However, while AI can enhance the efficiency and effectiveness of teaching and learning processes, it cannot replace the human element of motivation and inspiration. Unlike human educators, AI lacks the ability to connect with students on an emotional level, provide encouragement, and serve as a source of inspiration for learning. Therefore, while AI can complement teaching efforts, it is essential to recognize and preserve the unique role that human educators play in fostering student motivation and engagement.

Artificial Intelligence & the Online Education

Artificial intelligence (AI) has indeed revolutionized online education, particularly through the widespread adoption of Massive Open Online Courses (MOOCs). The primary objective of MOOC providers is to democratize education by making it accessible and affordable to individuals worldwide, regardless of their geographic location or time zone (Wogu et al., 2017, Wogu et al., 2018 and Zhi-Ting et al., 2016).

AI tools have played a crucial role in transforming online learning in the 21st century, with major academic institutions like Harvard, Stanford, and MIT embracing these applications. One notable advantage of AI-based online education is the use of advanced text conversion and machine learning technologies to develop deep-learning systems capable of translating English lectures into the learner's native language. This capability enhances accessibility for non-English speakers and facilitates broader participation in online courses.

Moreover, machine learning algorithms can be applied to analyse course syllabi, identifying areas of bias, difficulty, or ambiguity for closer evaluation by instructors. By leveraging AI-driven insights, educators can refine course materials, tailor instruction to meet the diverse needs of learners, and enhance the overall learning experience in online environments.

AI has significantly expanded the possibilities for online education, making learning resources more accessible, personalized, and effective for a global audience. As technology continues to evolve, AI-driven innovations are expected to further enrich and transform the landscape of online learning in the years to come.

Figure 5. Speech recognition & translation powered by AI (Microsoft Education Blog)

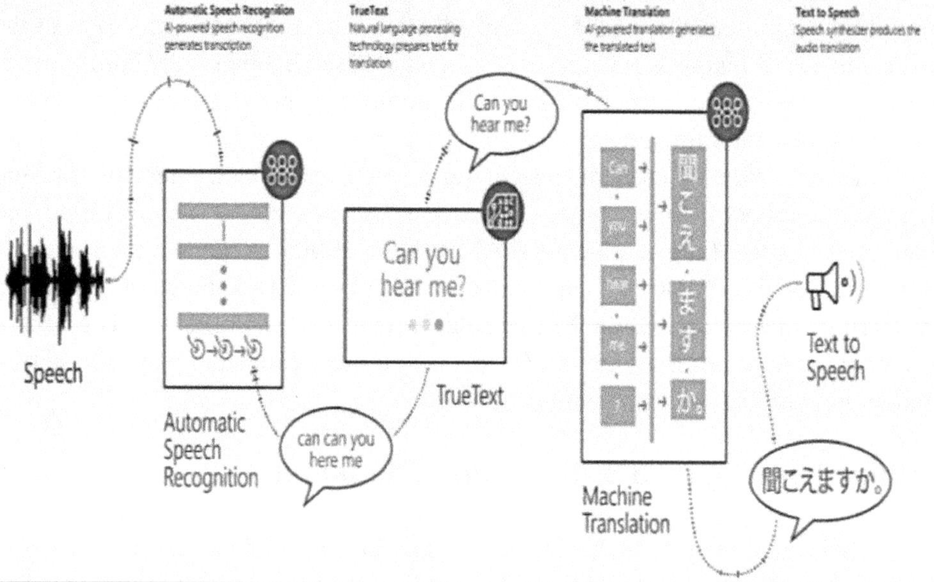

AI Enactment in Education

□ <u>Supervision Tasks Simplified</u>

One of the significant functions of AI applications in education is the automation of managerial responsibilities for teachers and academic institutions. Tasks such as grading exams, evaluating homework, and providing feedback to students can be streamlined and made more efficient through the use of AI technology (Vander, 2018). By automating these tasks, teachers can save valuable time and redirect their efforts toward more meaningful interactions with students, focusing on mentoring, guiding, and facilitating their learning journey.

Moreover, administrative departments within academic institutions, including admissions, registration, marketing, and human resources, can also benefit from AI platforms. These systems enable the automation of organizational processes and the reduction of reliance on traditional paperwork. AI technologies can optimize workflows, improve data management, and enhance decision-making processes across various administrative functions, leading to greater efficiency and productivity within educational institutions.

By leveraging AI for managerial tasks, teachers and administrative staff can allocate their time and resources more effectively, ultimately contributing to a more streamlined and responsive educational environment. Additionally, the adoption of AI-driven solutions can help institutions stay competitive, adapt to evolving technological trends, and better meet the needs of students and stakeholders in the digital age (Zhi-Ting et al., 2016).

□ Easy Content

Machines equipped with AI capabilities can indeed provide digital content of comparable quality to traditional means of delivery, if not better in some cases. Smart content, such as video lectures and video conferencing, has already become integral to modern classrooms, enhancing the learning experience for students (Van Laar et al., 2017).

One notable application of AI in education is the generation of customized textbooks and learning materials. AI systems can analyse traditional syllabuses and curriculum guidelines to generate tailored textbooks and digital learning interfaces. These resources often feature easy navigation, interactive elements such as chapters, flashcards, and functional tests, as well as adaptive learning pathways based on individual student progress.

Furthermore, AI-powered systems can automate various administrative tasks within educational institutions, including seat allocation, traffic management, classroom temperature regulation, inventory management, and more. For example, sensors can monitor classroom conditions such as temperature and humidity, adjusting environmental settings as needed to ensure a conducive learning environment.

AI technologies offer significant potential to streamline educational processes, improve access to high-quality learning materials, and enhance administrative efficiency in educational settings. As these technologies continue to advance, we can expect to see further innovation and integration of AI across various aspects of education, ultimately benefiting both students and educators alike.

□ Personified Learning

AI has the potential to significantly enhance the performance of teachers by providing personalized suggestions and support to each student. With AI-powered systems, tasks such as creating in-class assignments, designing final exams, and providing instant and customized feedback to students can be efficiently managed (Torres S et al., 2015).

Smart teaching methods, like those employed by Carnegie Learning and other AI-driven platforms, enable teachers to offer quick feedback and work directly with students to address their individual needs and challenges. Additionally, AI technology can be leveraged to personalize educational content, ensuring that it is tailored to suit the unique learning styles and preferences of each student.

By utilizing AI-driven academic experiences, students can benefit from a more adaptive and engaging learning environment that caters to their individual strengths and weaknesses. As a result, the adoption of AI in education is likely to continue growing as educators and institutions recognize its potential to improve student outcomes and enhance the overall learning experience.

□ Universal Learning

The integration of technology, particularly AI-powered learning, into academic delivery brings about several advantages, one of which is the ability for students to learn from anywhere and at any time. This flexibility in learning allows students to access educational resources and programs regardless of their geographical location or time zone (Zhi-Ting et al., 2016).

As AI technology continues to advance, there will likely be a broader range of programs available online, further expanding the options for remote learning. With the assistance of AI, students can engage in personalized learning experiences tailored to their individual needs and preferences.

Moreover, the increased access to a wide range of information and educational resources facilitated by AI not only enhances learning outcomes but also contributes to the continual improvement and refinement of AI-powered learning systems. As more data is collected and analysed, AI algorithms can become more sophisticated and effective in providing personalized learning experiences for students. The integration of AI into education holds great promise for expanding access to quality education and improving learning outcomes for students worldwide.

□ New Competences

AI support and advances various processes and administrative tasks within academic institutions, leading to increased effectiveness and efficiency (Wogu et al., 2019). Here are some examples of how AI can benefit administrative operations:

Student Navigation: AI-powered systems can help students navigate large campuses more effectively, providing guidance and directions to their destinations. This can reduce instances of students getting lost in crowded areas like corridors or hallways.

Data Analysis and Prediction: AI can analyse complex data sets to generate insights and predictions that can inform decision-making processes within departments or institutions. For example, AI algorithms can help predict student enrolment trends or identify areas for improvement in academic programs.

Event Planning and Resource Management: AI can assist in planning and organizing institutional events by automating tasks such as seat allocation or food ordering. By optimizing resource allocation, institutions can minimize wastage and reduce expenses.

While implementing AI technologies may incur initial costs for machinery and training, the long-term benefits in terms of improved efficiency and reduced wastage often outweigh these expenses. Additionally, advancements in AI technology are continuously driving down costs, making AI solutions more accessible and affordable for academic institutions over time. The investment in AI can lead to significant savings and improvements in administrative effectiveness.

Contribution of Artificial Intelligence in Education

Grading becomes automated with the impact of AI

Automated Grading: AI-powered tools can efficiently grade various types of assessments, including multiple-choice and fill-in-the-blank tests. By automating the grading process, educators can save time and focus their attention on other important aspects of teaching, such as lesson planning and student engagement (Schroer, 2018).

Essay Grading: While essay-grading software is still in its early stages of development, advancements in AI technologies continue to improve its accuracy and reliability. In the future, AI-powered tools may be able to assist educators in grading essays, further reducing the time and effort required for assessment.

Adaptive Learning: AI enables adaptive learning opportunities by personalizing educational experiences for each student based on their individual learning needs and preferences. Adaptive learning platforms use AI algorithms to analyse student performance data and deliver tailored content and activities to support their learning goals.

Focusing on the sections that needs development

Identifying Common Mistakes: AI algorithms analyse student responses to exercises or assignments to identify patterns of incorrect answers. If a large number of students are making the same mistake, the AI system can flag this issue for instructors (Potter, 2020).

Providing Tailored Feedback: Once common mistakes are identified, the AI system can generate personalized feedback for individual students. This feedback may include hints or clues to help students understand the correct answer and improve their conceptual understanding of the material.

Instant Assistance: AI-powered feedback is delivered to students in real time, providing immediate support when they encounter challenges or misunderstandings. This timely assistance helps students clarify concepts and complete assignments accurately.

Added Assistance for Scholars from AI Teachers

Foundational Learning: AI-powered curriculum can provide students with a solid foundation in fundamental subjects such as mathematics and writing. Interactive modules and exercises can help students grasp key concepts and skills in an engaging way (Oblinger, 2006).

Personalized Learning: AI algorithms can adapt learning materials to suit each student's individual needs and learning pace. This personalized approach ensures that students receive targeted support and practice where they need it most.

Supplementing Teacher Instruction: While AI can enhance learning experiences, it doesn't replace the role of teachers. Instead, AI-powered curriculum serves as a valuable supplement to traditional classroom instruction, providing students with additional resources and support.

Promoting Higher-Order Thinking: While AI can assist with foundational learning, the role of teachers is crucial in fostering higher-order thinking skills such as creativity and analytical thinking. Teachers can guide students in applying their knowledge to solve complex problems and think critically about the world around them.

Future Possibilities: As AI technology continues to evolve, there is the potential for AI to play a more significant role in fostering creativity and analytical skills in students. AI-powered tools and platforms may be developed to encourage innovative thinking and problem-solving in educational settings.

Teachers & Scholars get fruitful assistance from AI driven curriculum

Monitoring Progress: AI systems can track students' performance and progress in real-time as they engage with course materials and complete assignments. This allows educators to have immediate insights into how students are performing and where they may be struggling (Konnikova, 2014).

Identifying Performance Issues: AI algorithms can analyse students' learning data to identify patterns or trends that may indicate potential performance issues. For example, AI can flag students who are consistently scoring below a certain threshold or who are falling behind in specific areas of the curriculum.

Providing Personalized Support: Based on the data collected, AI systems can provide personalized support and resources to students who may be struggling. This could include recommending additional practice exercises, suggesting supplementary materials, or connecting students with tutoring services.

Informing Instructional Adjustments: AI-generated insights can also inform instructors' teaching practices by highlighting areas of the curriculum that may need to be revisited or reinforced. Educators can use this information to adjust their instructional strategies and provide targeted interventions to help students succeed.

Enhancing Student Engagement: By providing timely feedback and support, AI systems can help keep students engaged and motivated in their learning. This personalized approach to education can help improve student outcomes and satisfaction with the course.

Interface embellishment with the data of AI:

Personalized Learning: AI-powered educational platforms can provide personalized learning experiences tailored to each student's needs, preferences, and learning style. By analysing student data and behaviour, these systems can recommend learning materials, adapt the difficulty level of exercises, and provide targeted feedback to optimize learning outcomes (James, 2019).

Data Analysis and Management: AI applications help schools and academic institutions efficiently collect, analyse, and manage large volumes of data related to student performance, attendance, and behaviour. By automating data processing tasks and generating actionable insights, AI systems enable educators and administrators to make informed decisions and improve educational outcomes.

Virtual Teaching Assistants: Virtual teaching assistants powered by AI technology can assist educators in various tasks, such as grading assignments, answering student questions, and facilitating online discussions. These assistants help alleviate the administrative burden on teachers, allowing them to focus more on teaching and mentoring students.

Content Recommendation: AI algorithms can analyse students' learning preferences and performance data to recommend relevant educational content, resources, and learning materials. By providing personalized recommendations, these systems help students discover new topics, deepen their understanding, and stay engaged in their learning journey.

Adaptive Assessments: AI-based assessment tools can dynamically adapt the difficulty level and content of assessments based on students' responses, ensuring that each assessment accurately measures their knowledge and skills. These adaptive assessments help educators identify students' strengths and weaknesses more effectively and provide targeted support as needed.

Change in the role of academics for the teachers through AI:

Content Delivery: AI-powered educational platforms can deliver high-quality instructional content to students outside of the classroom. Teachers can curate or create digital resources, such as videos, interactive tutorials, or simulations, that students can access at their own pace and review as needed. This allows teachers to focus more on facilitating discussions, answering questions, and providing personalized support during class time (Kumar & Gupta, 2015).

Personalized Learning: AI algorithms can analyse student data and performance to provide personalized learning experiences tailored to each student's needs and learning preferences. Teachers can leverage AI-driven insights to identify areas of strength and weakness in students' understanding and provide targeted interventions and support to help them progress.

Assessment and Feedback: AI-powered assessment tools can automate the grading process for assignments, quizzes, and exams, freeing up teachers' time to focus on providing meaningful feedback and guidance to students. By providing instant feedback on student submissions, AI allows teachers to identify misconceptions and learning gaps more efficiently and address them in subsequent lessons.

Data-Driven Instruction: AI technologies can collect and analyse vast amounts of data on student performance, engagement, and learning outcomes. Teachers can use this data to inform their instructional decisions, identify trends and patterns in student learning, and adapt their teaching strategies to better meet the needs of individual students or the class as a whole.

Interactive Learning Experiences: AI-powered educational tools can create interactive and immersive learning experiences that engage students in active learning and problem-solving. Teachers can incorporate gamified elements, virtual simulations, and collaborative activities into their lessons to promote student engagement, motivation, and critical thinking skills.

Trial & Error based learning becomes more approachable through AI

Adaptive Learning Paths: AI-powered educational platforms can adapt learning paths based on individual student progress and performance. If a student encounters difficulty understanding a concept, the AI system can adjust the sequence of learning activities to provide additional explanations, examples, or practice opportunities until mastery is achieved. This adaptive approach allows students to engage in trial and error without fear of failure, as they receive personalized support and guidance tailored to their unique learning needs (Kwok, 2015 & Hagen, 2011).

Immediate Feedback: AI-driven assessment tools can provide instant feedback on student responses, allowing them to quickly identify errors and misconceptions. Instead of waiting for a teacher to grade assignments or quizzes, students can receive immediate feedback on their work, enabling them to learn from their mistakes in real-time and make necessary adjustments. This immediate feedback loop encourages students to engage in iterative problem-solving and experimentation, leading to deeper understanding and retention of concepts.

Interactive Learning Environments: AI-powered educational platforms can create interactive and immersive learning environments where students can explore concepts through hands-on experimentation. Virtual simulations, interactive tutorials, and educational games can provide students with opportunities to test hypotheses, explore cause-and-effect relationships, and discover solutions through trial and error. These interactive experiences foster curiosity, creativity, and problem-solving skills, empowering students to take ownership of their learning journey.

Personalized Support: AI systems can provide personalized support to students based on their learning preferences, strengths, and areas for improvement. Intelligent tutoring systems can offer targeted interventions, adaptive scaffolding, and customized feedback to help students overcome challenges and succeed academically. By tailoring instructional strategies to individual student needs, AI instructors can create a supportive learning environment that encourages exploration, experimentation, and growth.

Finding, educating & supporting students becomes easy with AI

Personalized Learning: Intelligent computer systems utilize data mining techniques to analyse students' learning preferences, performance data, and other relevant factors. Based on this analysis, the systems can generate personalized learning recommendations, adaptive learning paths, and customized instructional materials that cater to individual student needs. By delivering content and activities that are tailored to each student's strengths, weaknesses, and interests, intelligent systems enhance engagement and promote deeper understanding (Marzano et al., 2019).

Predictive Analytics: Data mining structures can analyse historical student data to identify patterns and trends that may predict future performance or behaviour. For example, predictive analytics algorithms can forecast which students are at risk of academic failure or dropout based on factors such as attendance, participation, and grades. By identifying students who may need additional support or intervention early on, educators can implement targeted strategies to improve outcomes and prevent potential challenges (Gaffney, 2010).

Continuous Improvement: Intelligent computer systems continuously collect and analyse data on student learning outcomes, instructional effectiveness, and other metrics to inform ongoing improvement efforts. By identifying areas for enhancement and refining instructional practices based on data-driven insights, educators can optimize teaching and learning experiences to better meet the needs of students. This iterative process of continuous improvement fosters a culture of innovation and excellence in education.

Efficient Decision-Making: Data mining structures enable educators and administrators to make informed decisions by providing actionable insights and evidence-based recommendations. Whether it's identifying effective teaching strategies, allocating resources efficiently, or designing targeted interventions, intelligent systems empower stakeholders to make data-driven decisions that enhance the overall quality and effectiveness of education (Diwan, 2017).

Enhanced Research: Data mining techniques support educational research by facilitating the analysis of large-scale educational datasets. Researchers can use data mining structures to uncover hidden patterns, relationships, and trends in educational data, leading to new discoveries and insights. By leveraging the power of data mining, researchers can contribute to the advancement of knowledge in the field of education and inform evidence-based practices.

Amending the way of learning for students through AI

Accessibility: AI-driven educational platforms and systems provide round-the-clock access to learning materials, resources, and instructional support. Students can engage with course content and activities at their own pace and convenience, removing barriers such as geographical location or time constraints. This accessibility expands opportunities for individuals who may have limited access to traditional educational settings, allowing them to pursue learning opportunities from virtually anywhere with an internet connection.

Adaptive Learning: AI-powered academic courses utilize adaptive learning algorithms to personalize the learning experience for each student based on their individual needs, preferences, and learning styles. These systems analyse student performance data, identify areas of strength and weakness, and dynamically adjust the pace, content, and difficulty level of instruction to optimize learning outcomes. By tailoring the learning experience to the unique requirements of each learner, AI-driven courses enhance engagement, motivation, and comprehension (Enge, 2017).

Interactive Learning: AI systems enable interactive learning experiences through immersive technologies such as virtual reality (VR), augmented reality (AR), and simulations. These technologies create engaging, hands-on learning environments where students can apply theoretical concepts, practice skills, and explore real-world scenarios in a safe and controlled setting. By fostering active participation and experiential learning, AI-powered courses enhance understanding and retention of basic skills.

Personalized Feedback: AI-driven assessment and feedback systems provide students with personalized, timely feedback on their performance, progress, and areas for improvement. These systems use machine learning algorithms to analyse student responses, identify patterns and trends, and generate actionable insights for both students and instructors. By offering targeted feedback and guidance, AI-powered courses support continuous learning and skill development (Brynjolfsson& Mitchell, 2017).

Remote Collaboration: AI technologies facilitate remote collaboration and peer-to-peer interaction among students, regardless of their physical location. Collaborative tools such as online forums, discussion boards, and virtual classrooms enable students to engage in meaningful discussions, share ideas, and collaborate on projects in a virtual environment. These collaborative experiences foster social learning, teamwork, and communication skills, enriching the overall learning experience.

Table 2. Various learning management systems for education

Name	Characteristics	Expertise
QUERIUM	⊗ Used for STEM education. ⊗ Instructional insight provided by the system to the scholars showing the areas for upscaling.	⊗ Perfecting performance of the students.
KIDSENSE	⊗ Interpretation of strong algorithms. ⊗ Enactment of vocabulary ⊗ Conversion of speech to text	⊗ Used for the initial stages of learning.
BLIPPAR	⊗ Incorporate intelligent technology and augmented reality. ⊗ Enhance learning within the classroom environment. ⊗ Visualize interdisciplinary resources from subjects such as geography, biology, and physics in a collaborative graphic interface.	⊗ Investigation into augmented reality application
QUIZLET	⊗ Enhance access to intelligent online study materials. ⊗ Offer personalized learning pathways. ⊗ Utilize machine learning algorithms to analyse data from millions of study sessions.	⊗ Assessment - Utilizing online adaptive learning tools
CENTURY TECH	⊗ Leverages cognitive neuroscience principles and data analytics techniques. ⊗ Tracks student progress, identifies areas of knowledge gaps, and offers personalized learning recommendations. ⊗ Reduces time spent on lesson preparation, grading, and managing homework assignments.	⊗ Cognitive learning - Automated processes utilizing analytics research.
KNEWTON	⊗ An adaptive educational technology ⊗ A program named ALTA aids in identifying knowledge gaps in scholars. ⊗ Provides relevant academic assignments.	⊗ Adaptive learning - Managing and monitoring students' performance.
COUSERA	⊗ For studying business analytics, graphic design, and Python ⊗ Cloud Engineering	⊗ Online learning - Self-directed learning hub.

CONCLUSION

Higher education has become increasingly accessible due to the integration of technology and artificial intelligence in teaching, learning, and administration. Students who have access to the internet and technology often prefer technology-integrated learning over traditional classroom learning. Smart classrooms equipped with advanced technology offer endless opportunities for teachers and provide valuable feedback for student development. As a result, smart universities, equipped with cutting-edge technologies and artificial intelligence applications, are transforming the traditional university model into centres of learning and academic excellence in the higher education sector. These smart campuses resemble the cities of the future, offering innovative learning environments and opportunities. This chapter provides a detailed understanding of the opportunities of smart education within smart universities, supported by artificial intelligence applications.

REFERENCES

Annaswamy, A. M., Hussain, A., Chakraborty, A., & Cvetkovic, M. (2016). Foundations of infrastructure Cps. *Proceedings of American Control Conference*. Boston, MA: IEEE.

Balakrishna, C. (2012) Enabling technologies for smart city services and applications. *6th International Conference on Next Generation Mobile Applications, Services And Technologies (NGMAST)*, Paris, France, IEEE. DOI: 10.1109/NGMAST.2012.51

Bingimlas, K. (2009). Barriers to the successful integration of ICT in teaching and learning environments: A review of the literature. *Eurasia Journal of Mathematics, Science and Technology Education*, 5(3), 235–245. DOI: 10.12973/ejmste/75275

Borawska-Kalbarczyk, K., Tołwińska, B., & Korzeniecka-Bondar, A. (2019). From Smart Teaching to Smart Learning in the Fast-Changing Digital World. L. Daniela (Ed.)*Didactics of Smart Pedagogy,* 23–40. Cham: Springer Nature.

Boulton, A. (2015). Applying data-driven learning to the web. In Leńko-Szymańska, A., & Boulton, A. (Eds.), *Multiple Affordances of Language Corpora for Data-driven Learning* (pp. 267–295). John Benjamins., DOI: 10.1075/scl.69.13bou

Brynjolfsson, E., & Mitchell, T. (2017). What Can Machine Learning Do?*Workforce Implications.Science*, 358(6370), 1530–1534. DOI: 10.1126/science.aap8062 PMID: 29269459

Cham. K. M., M€akel€a, T. (2019). Valuation of emerging learning solutions. PROCEEDINGS OF EDMEDIA 2014—WORLD CONFERENCE ON EDUCATIONAL MEDIA AND TECHNOLOGY(pp. 168–172). Tampere, Finland: Association for the Advancement of Computing in Education.

Copeland, M. (2016). What is the difference between artificial intelligence, machine learning, and deep learning? *Nvidia.* https://blogs.nvidia.com/blog/2016/07/29/whats -difference-artificial-intelligencemachinelearning-deep-learning-ai/

Davison, M. (n.d).: AI and the Classroom – Machine Learning in Education. *True Information Architect: Education*, https://www.trueinteraction.com/ai-and-the -classroom-machine-learning-in-education/

Dillon, T., Potdar, V., Singh, J., & Talevski, A. (2011, May). Cyber-physical systems: Providing Quality of Service (QoS) in a heterogeneous systems-of-systems environment. In 5th IEEE International Conference on Digital Ecosystems and Technologies (IEEE DEST 2011) (pp. 330-335). IEEE.

Diwan, P. (2017) Artificial intelligence: Changing the education paradigm. *Chatbotslife*, https://chatbotslife.com/artificial-intelligence-changing-the-educationparadigma2 6fac41dd 5.

Eric E.(2017) The Art of SEO: Mastering Search Engine Optimization.*O'Reilly Media, Inc. Online Document.*

Gaffney, M. (2010). Enhancing teachers' take-up of digital content: Factors and design principles in technology adoption. http://www.thelearningfederation.edu.au/verve/_resources/ Enhancing_Teacher_Takeup_of_Digital_Content_Report.PDF

Goksel, N., & Bozkurt, A. (2019). *Artificial Intelligence in Education: Current Insights and Future Perspectives. Handbook of Research on Learning in the Age of Transhumanism*. IGI Global.

Gros, B. (2016). The design of smart educational environments. *Smart Learning Environment*, 3(15), 15. Advance online publication. DOI: 10.1186/s40561-016-0039-x

Gros, B. (2016). *The Dialogue Between Emerging Pedagogies and Emerging Technologies,The Future of Ubiquitous Learning*. Springer.

Hagen, P. (2011). *The Changing Nature of Participation in Design: A practice-based study of social technologies in early design research*. University of Technology Sydney.

Hammer, M., & Champy, J. (1993). *Reengineering the Corporation: A Manifesto for Business Revolution*. Harper Business.

Han, Y., Chunyan, M., Cyril, L., & Timothy, J. W. (2017). Towards AI-powered personalization in MOOC learning. *NPJ Science of Learning*, 2(15), 15. Advance online publication. DOI: 10.1038/s41539-017-0016-3

Hirschberg, J., & Manning, C. D. (2015). Advances in natural language processing. *Science*, 349(6245), 261–266. DOI: 10.1126/science.aaa8685 PMID: 26185244

Hramiak, A., & Boulton, H. (2013). Escalating the use of Web 2.0 Technology in Secondary Schools in the United Kingdom: Barriers and Enablers beyond Teacher Training. *Electronic Journal of e-Learning*, 11(2), 91–100.

Hwang, G. J. (2014). Definition, framework, and research issues of smart learning environments - a context aware ubiquitous learning perspective. *Smart Learning Environments*, 1(1), 4. DOI: 10.1186/s40561-014-0004-5

Infrastructure, S. Getting More from Strategic Assets.(2016).*CSIC (Cambridge Centre for Smart Infrastructure and Construction), Cambridge, UK*.http://www -smartinfrastructure.eng. cam.ac.uk/files/the-smart-infrastructure-paper

James, J. (2019). *Artificial intelligence & future warfare: implications for international security.* Defense& Security Analysis., DOI: 10.1080/14751798.2019.1600800

Kaimara, P., & Deliyannis, I. (2019). Why should I play this game? The role of motivation in smart pedagogy. Didactics of Smart Pedagogy: Smart Pedagogy for Technology Enhanced Learning, 113-137.

Konnikova, M. (2014) Will MOOCs be flukes? *The New Yorker.* https:// www .newyorker.com/science/maria-konnikova/moocs-failure-solutions2020/06/01

Kumar, K. A., & Gupta, M. P. (2015). How to make a Smart Campus. *Smart Campus Programme in IIT Delhi. Technical Report IIT*, Delhi.

Kwok, L. F. (2015). A vision for the development of i-campus. *Smart Learning Environments*, 2(2).

Marzano, G., & Martinovs, A., andUsca S. (2019). Mechatronics Education: Needs and Challenges. Environment. Technology. Resources. *Proceedings of the 12th International Scientific and Practical Conference.* Volume II, 214-217.

Microsoft Education Blog. (2020) AI technology helps students who are deaf learn. *Online document.*https://blogs.microsoft.com/ai/ai-powered-captioning/

Moneim, R. A. (2020). Towards a smart University in the light of 21 st century skills. An-Najah University Journal for Research, B. *Humanities (Washington)*, 34(6).

Morimoto, R. (2010). Estimating the benefits of effectively and proactively maintaining infrastructure with the innovative smart infrastructure sensor system. *Socio-Economic Planning Sciences*, 44(4), 247–257. DOI: 10.1016/j.seps.2010.07.005

Oblinger, D. (2006). Bootstrapped learning proposer information pamphlet for broad agency announcement, 07-04.http://fs1.fbo.gov/EPSData/ODA/ Synopses/4965/ BAA0704/BLPIPfin al.pdf

Pelgrum, W. J., & Doornekamp, B. G. (2009). Indicators on ICT in primary and secondary education. https://ec.europa.eu/education/moreinformation/doc/ ictindicrep_en.pdf

Pishva, D., & Nishantha, G. G. D. (2008). Smart classrooms for distance education and their adoption to multiple classroom architecture. *Journal of Networks*, 3(5), 54–64. DOI: 10.4304/jnw.3.5.54-64

Potter, J. R. (2019). Artificial Intelligence and Swarming in Maritime Systems. *Marine Technology Society Journal*, 53(5), 64–67.

Radhakrishnan, T. K., Balasubramanian, S. (2010) Modelling and control of multivariable process using intelligent techniques. *Sensors & Transducers*, 121(10).

Riley, T. (2017). Artificial intelligence goes deep to beat humans at poker. *Science Magazine*. https://www.sciencemag.org/news/2017/03/artificial-intelligence-goes-deepbeat-humans-poker

Rudd, T., Morrison, J., Facer, K., & Gifford, C. (2006) Futurelab: What if...? Re-imagining learning spaces.*Telearn Archives. Online document.* https://telearn.archivesouvertes.fr/file/index/docid/190334/filename/rudd-2006

Schroer, A. (2018). Companies Using AI in Education to Enhance the Classroom. *Bullettin.Com. Artificial Intelligence.*https://builtin.com/artificialintelligence/ai-in-education

Shahzadi, I., Amin, S., & Chaudhary, K. M. (2013). Drivers of supply chain performance enhancing organizational output: An exploratory study for manufacturing sector. *Facilities Management*, 5(14), 53–64.

Siau, K. (2018). Education in the age of artificial intelligence: How will technology shape learning? *Global Analyst*, 7(3), 22.

Taleb, Z., & Hassanzadeh, F. (2015). Toward smart school: A comparison between smart school and traditional school for mathematics learning. *Procedia: Social and Behavioral Sciences*, 171, 90–95. DOI: 10.1016/j.sbspro.2015.01.093

Torres, S. J., Avariento, J. P., & Rambla, D. (2015). Enhancing integrated indoor/outdoor mobility in a smart campus. *International Journal of Geographical Information Science*, 29(11), 1–14.

Van Laar, E., van Deursen, A. J. M., van Dijk, J. A. G. M., & de Haan, J. (2017). The relation between 21st-century skills and digital skills: A systematic literature review. *Computers in Human Behavior*, 72, 577–588. DOI: 10.1016/j.chb.2017.03.010

Vander, A. (2018) The Shift to Digital Learning: 10 Benefits. Online document. https://www.gettingsmart.com/2015/11/the-shift-to-digital-learning-10-benefits/ last accessed 2020/05/30.

Wogu, I. A. P., Misra, S., Assibong, P. A., Apeh, H. A., Awogu-Maduagwu, E., Maskeliunas, R., & Damasevicius, R. (2018, February). Artificial Intelligence, MOOC's and the dilemma of teaching and learning in tertiary institutions: A critical appraisal. In *International Conference on Information Systems and Management Science (ISMS)*, University of Malta (pp. 22-23).

Wogu, I. A. P., Olu-Owolabi, F. E., Assibong, P. A., Agoha, B. C., Sholarin, M., Elegbeleye, A., & Apeh, H. A. (2017, October). Artificial intelligence, alienation and ontological problems of other minds: A critical investigation into the future of man and machines. In *2017 International Conference on Computing Networking and Informatics (ICCNI)* (pp. 1-10). IEEE.

Wogu, I. A. P., Olu-Owolabi, F. E., Atayero, A. A., Sholarin, M. A., Ugbogu, P. C., Ogbuehi, U. K., & Akoleowo, V. O. (2016). The changing face of education and the dilemma of Massive Open Online Courses (MOOCs) in Nigeria's tertiary institutions: Implications for development. In 3rd International Conference on African Development Issues. Retrieved from https://scholar. google. com/citations

Zhu, Z. T., Yu, M. H., & Riezebos, P. (2016). A research framework of smart education. Smart learning environments, 3, 1-17.

Chapter 14
Challenges of Artificial Intelligence (AI) in Language Learning

Farhat Jokhio
University of Sindh, Pakistan

Ghazala Shaukat
University of Sindh, Pakistan

Saima Shaikh
University of Sindh, Pakistan

ABSTRACT

The present research investigation is an effort to explain the importance of the mother tongue in human life, including academic achievement, intellectual development and enculturation. This research has also focused on the challenges and opportunities of artificial intelligence in language learning. The method of narrative review of the literature was used to review recent research on artificial intelligence in language learning. The findings of this review are consistent with various research done in the field of Language and artificial intelligence, which highlight the critical role of technologies of artificial intelligence in Language learning along with some challenges associated with the context and meaning of Language.

DOI: 10.4018/979-8-3373-0219-5.ch014

INTRODUCTION

A child's first comprehension of the world around him, the learning of concepts, and his perception of existence start with his mother tongue. Mother tongue plays a very influential role in an individual's personality development, and has a powerful impact on how we think, perceive, feel and express emotions. Mother tongue is of the most significant importance in human communication and has a powerful influence on every aspect of our lives. (Dogara, 2023; Nishanthi, 2020; Sirbo, 2015). It helps a child in his mental, moral and emotional development. (Normohammadi, 2008). The mother tongue can establish a direct relationship between heart and mind influencing every part of our lives (Kundal, 2014). Nwali (2014), in his research on the influence of the mother tongue, found that mother tongue as an important force behind academic achievement. He further recommended the use of the mother tongue in education, recognizing the immense influence of the mother tongue in a child's education. The role of the mother tongue in academic achievement has also been prioritized in similar research. Omebe (2002) has clearly emphasized that home is the first informal educational instruction to which the child is actively exposed and prepared to face formal education. According to him, the child learns many things from home before going to school in their mother tongue, including speech, and names of people, animals and objects which add to a child's learning later at school. Mother tongue influences the intellectual development of the child as well. (Normohammadi, 2008; Plessis, 2008). It is an essential tool for learning and preserving values, norms and overall culture; it is a carrier of culture, in fact. Mother tongue is the Language we use to think, feel and express emotions and, most significant source of learning another language. (Kundal, 2014). All these and many other types of research on the importance of the mother tongue have emphasized the role of the mother tongue in every aspect of human life.

Researchers in the field of artificial intelligence have also recognized the importance of Language and have devised many programs to understand languages and their use. Artificial intelligence is changing Language in data for the purpose of learning and teaching, specifically online education. Due to quick advancements in artificial intelligence in the field of Language, it has become essential to understand the role of artificial intelligence in Language so that native Language, a powerful source of human culture and a predictor of academic performance and cognitive development, can be preserved and communicated to the next generations successfully. Therefore, this research was devised to highlight the importance of the mother tongue in human life and further to review the role of AI technologies in language learning.

Significance and objectives

This research was devised to highlight the importance of the mother tongue and its impact on an individual's academic achievement, intellectual development and enculturation. Further, to understand the use of artificial intelligence programs and Challenges of such programs/technologies in language learning. For this purpose, the method of narrative review of the literature was employed. This research will help to understand the role of Language, specifically the mother tongue, in human life. It will explain the technologies of artificial intelligence which are in use in Language and learning .understanding the contribution of artificial intelligence in Language will help to preserve native languages in the future, where the use of artificial intelligence will occupy almost all areas of life.

LITERATURE REVIEW

Impact of mother tongue on academic achievement, intellectual or cognitive development and enculturation.

Mother tongue is the first Language that a child learns from birth. It is also called the native Language and home language. This language child learns and speaks at home, especially with their mother. This is the Language that a child hears from birth. Mother tongue is the most excellent source of perception of the world. Mother tongue is also a source of maintaining and transmitting culture; it is the most critical part of communication. The mother tongue is a source of enculturation and cultural awareness and the basis of a civilization that binds people together. Language is the sign of the cultural identity of ethnic groups; there, the development, continuation and life of culture are highly associated with learning native languages. Dogara (2023) states, "Language is a vital factor in a nation's development. It is the carrier of a country's intangible heritage, showing the nation's ethno cultural, mythological, and psychological experiences and ideas".

Mother tongue also plays an influential role in a child's cognitive development. Research has demonstrated that cognitive development, as well as intellectual development, is relatively faster in those children who are fluent in their mother tongue. It has also been noted that if a student is educated in his/her mother tongue, the level of success of his or her educational achievement is more excellent than someone taught in a medium other than their mother tongue. (Nishanti2020). Children who are taught in their mother tongue are more efficient in developing cognitive skills. Mother Language was found to be the solid supporting force behind intellectual/ cognitive development. (Normohammadi, 2008).

Mother tongue and academic achievement are positively correlated. As a medium of instruction, the mother tongue in education increases students' motivation and learning skills. Awopetu (2016) concluded that using a mother tongue in the classroom was influential in fostering children's learning abilities. Children perform better when they get an education in their mother tongue, which shows the importance of the mother tongue in academic achievement. In a study of the medium of instruction, Ali (2018) suggested the inclusion of indigenous languages as a medium of instruction along with mainstream languages in Sindh, Pakistan. Other researchers also propose the same suggestions (Shah& Shirai, 2016).Researches on cross-national differences in math achievement were found to be related with many secondary math abilities, which mean cultural and social factors play very crucial part in producing those differences. A number of possible predictive factors were examined in researches, including language as well, school systems, teaching styles and teacher-student relationship.Reserach by Stigler, Lee, and Stevenson (1986) has shown that cross-national differences among Chinese, Japanese, and American children in counting and memory exercises may be largely a function of differences in these languages related to counting and numbers. These and many other researchers have found the importance of a native or mother tongue as an important factor behind students' achievement in all subjects. (References 5 researches).

Artificial intelligence

Artificial Intelligence (AI) has occupied almost every aspect of human lives, the primary role of everything big and small; artificial intelligence is all around. With the technology of deep learning in medicine, AI has already reached an expert level in diagnosing diseases with the technology of deep learning in medicine and the synthesis of speech by reading the neural activity of the cerebral cortex. Artificial intelligence can create realistic photos and videos that are difficult to differentiate from real ones. Chat boats have been created to help the process of communication. "Definitions of artificial intelligence begin to shift based on the goals that are trying to be achieved with an AI system. Generally, people invest in AI development for one of these three objectives: build systems that think exactly like humans do (strong AI), get systems to work without figuring out how human reasoning works (weak AI), and Use human reasoning as a model but not necessarily the end goal" (as cited in Marr, 2018, para. 7). (Viktorivna et al., 2022).

Artificial intelligence and language learning

Artificial intelligence is deeply immersed in our lives. It has become the focus of the attention of experts from almost all fields of knowledge. For the past few years, many experts have expressed their concerns about the adverse effects of artificial intelligence. However, very little we know about the involvement of AI ‘in language. This research will help to sort out the advantages of AI in language learning and the challenges it has caused for the future of human Language. Working of AI

Artificial intelligence must overcome some challenges.

AI technologies must control three challenges to be successful in a non-vision world, Language, context and reasoning (Srinivasan, 2016). A review article in MIT, technology's AI's language problem, emphasizing language problems, identified those AI language technologies (IBM et al. Go) process language similarly as humans do. Most current implementations approach the text as data rather than as Language. Understanding of the context is another issue related to Language. Natural language processing of the text needs to be processed in the proper context. This right context is, in fact, the focus of technology on language structure, not only on words. To overcome this problem with Language, Natural language understanding is proposed in place of the mechanical approach of natural language processing (Srinivasan, 2016). Computational statistics mainly drives current methods for natural language processing (NLP). These methods convert the text into data without understanding the text and then learn from patterns in that particular data. Loss of meaning and context occurs due to this process. To overcome this problem of AI with Language, the Process of Natural language understanding must be employed to get the meaning of the written text and context. Artificial intelligence is also involved in understanding dead languages, preserving endangered languages and learning new languages (Text Inspector, 2023).

CONCLUSION

Importance of the mother tongue is of great value in the communication process, transference of cultural values and norms from one generation to the next, and in transferring knowledge. The role of the mother tongue in academic achievement, intellectual development and enculturation is undeniable in the light of research and direct observations. In order to preserve, learn and teach languages, predominantly native or endangered languages, artificial intelligence technologies for Language should be learned to achieve this objective.

Recommendations

Education institutions must embrace the modern methods /technologies of artificial intelligence to improve the teaching and learning of languages. Even though there may be some problems, risks and features to overcome or work on, artificial intelligence and Language should continue to develop together. AI specialists in Sindh, Pakistan, must focus on learning and adopting technologies of AI for Language to teach the Sindhi language and other native languages. This review has not used statistical methods to understand AI's language technologies; statistical methods are recommended for future research to get a more accurate picture of the problem.

REFERENCES

Ali, S. S. (2018). Mother Tongue or the Other Tongue? That is the Question! *International Research Journal of Arts and Humanities*, 46(46), 1–14.

Awopetu, A. V. (2016). Impact of mother tongue on Children's learning abilities in the early childhood classroom. *Procedia: Social and Behavioral Sciences*, 233, 58–63. DOI: 10.1016/j.sbspro.2016.10.131

Dogara, G. (2023).Mother tongue, A tool for cultural awareness. (Retrieved https://www.thisdaylive.com/index.php/2022/01/09/mother-tongue-a-tool-for-cultural-awakeness?amp

KUNDAL, D. D. B. (2014). Importance of Mother Language. *International Journal (Toronto, Ont.)*, 2(9), 4.

Lesia Viktorivna, K., Andrii Oleksandrovych, V., Iryna Oleksandrivna, K., & Nadia Oleksandrivna, K. (2022). *Artificial Intelligence in Language Learning: What Are We Afraid Of.* Arab World English Journal.

Normohammadi, R. (2008). Mother Tongue, a Necessary Step to Intellectual Development. *Journal of Pan-Pacific Association of Applied Linguistics*, 12(2), 25–36.

Nwali, O. S. (2014). Impact of mother tongue on the academic achievement of the child. *Knowledge Review*, 30(1), 5–12.

Omebe, S. E. (2002). *Counseling the parents for effective provision of learning environment for the Nigerian child. The learning environment of the Nigerian child. Journal of the Nigerian Society for Educational Psychologists*. NISEP.

Plessis, S. D. (2008). Talk to your child cleverly. They were retrieved on August 5, 2008.

Shirazi, K., & Shah, U. (2016). Education in mother tongue: Need of the time: A case study of a public sector college at Jamshoro. *Science International (Lahore)*, 28(3), 3197–3201.

Sirbu, A. (2015). The significance of Language as a tool of communication. Scientific Bulletin" Mircea cel Batran. *Naval Academy*, 18(2), 405.

Srinivasan, V. (2016). Context, Language, and Reasoning in ai: three key challenges.

Conclusion

As we reach the conclusion of *AI, Corporate Social Responsibility, and Marketing in Modern Organizations*, it is clear that the integration of Artificial Intelligence (AI), Corporate Social Responsibility (CSR), and marketing has the potential to fundamentally reshape the way modern organizations operate. This book has explored the multifaceted impact of AI across these domains, demonstrating how forward-thinking companies can leverage AI to create more responsible, ethical, and customer-focused business practices.

Throughout this book, we have seen how AI is far more than a technological tool for operational efficiency. It is a transformative force that can drive innovation, enhance decision-making, and open new pathways for responsible business conduct. In the context of CSR, AI has been shown to play a crucial role in helping companies meet their sustainability goals, improve supply chain transparency, and promote ethical business practices. The powerful analytical capabilities of AI allow organizations to monitor and reduce their environmental footprint, ensure fair labor practices, and build more resilient business models in the face of global challenges such as climate change and social inequality.

From a marketing perspective, AI offers businesses unprecedented insights into consumer behavior and preferences. Through predictive analytics, machine learning, and AI-driven personalization, companies are now able to engage with customers on a deeper, more meaningful level. By aligning marketing strategies with CSR initiatives, businesses can build stronger brand loyalty and trust, as consumers increasingly favor companies that demonstrate a commitment to social and environmental responsibility.

The intersection of AI, CSR, and marketing is not without its challenges. Ethical considerations, such as data privacy, algorithmic bias, and the unintended consequences of AI, are issues that organizations must confront as they adopt these technologies. However, as discussed throughout this book, these challenges also present opportunities for companies to lead the way in responsible AI use. By embracing transparency, fairness, and inclusivity, businesses can position themselves as pioneers in ethical AI adoption, setting standards for the industry and building trust with stakeholders.

As we look to the future, the role of AI in shaping modern organizations will only grow in significance. The integration of AI with CSR and marketing is not a passing trend but a fundamental shift in how businesses operate, engage with society, and respond to consumer expectations. Companies that invest in AI-driven CSR initiatives and ethical marketing strategies will be better positioned to succeed in an increasingly competitive and socially conscious marketplace.

The key takeaway from this book is that AI, when used thoughtfully and responsibly, has the power to drive positive change—not just for businesses, but for society as a whole. The fusion of AI with CSR and marketing presents an exciting opportunity to create a more sustainable, ethical, and customer-centric business landscape. As technology continues to evolve, so too must our approach to its adoption, ensuring that AI serves as a force for good in the modern world.

In closing, *AI, Corporate Social Responsibility, and Marketing in Modern Organizations* aims to inspire business leaders, marketers, and CSR professionals to think critically about the potential of AI in their organizations. By embracing AI as a tool for both innovation and responsibility, companies can create lasting value, not just for their shareholders, but for the communities and environments in which they operate. As we move forward, it is our collective responsibility to ensure that AI is used in ways that contribute to a better, more equitable future for all.

Muhammad Nawaz Tunio
University of Sufism and Modern Sciences, Bhitshah, Pakistan

Compilation of References

Abedin, B. (2021). Managing the tension between opposing effects of explainability of artificial intelligence: A contingency theory perspective. *Internet Research*, 32(2), 425–453. DOI: 10.1108/INTR-05-2020-0300

Adams, D., & Wright, B. (2023). Enhancing Customer Experience with AI: A Case Study Approach. *Journal of Customer Experience Management*, 14(1), 1–12. DOI: 10.1108/JCEM-05-2022-0135

Adula, M., Birbirsa, Z. A., & Kant, S. (2023). The effect of interpersonal, problem solving and technical training skills on performance of Ethiopia textile industry: Continuance, normative and affective commitment as mediators. *Cogent Business & Management*, 10(3), 2286672. Advance online publication. DOI: 10.1080/23311975.2023.2286672

Afridi, S. A., Afsar, B., Shahjehan, A., Khan, W., Rehman, Z. U., & Khan, M. A. (2023). Impact of corporate social responsibility attributions on employee's extra-role behaviors: Moderating role of ethical corporate identity and interpersonal trust. *Corporate Social Responsibility and Environmental Management*, 30(2), 991–1004. DOI: 10.1002/csr.2017

Afshan, G., Shahid, S., & Tunio, M. N. (2021). Learning experiences of women entrepreneurs amidst COVID-19. *International Journal of Gender and Entrepreneurship*, 13(2), 162–186. DOI: 10.1108/IJGE-09-2020-0153

Ahmed, R., & Štreimikienė, D. (2021). Environmental Issues and Strategic Corporate Social Responsibility for Organizational Competitiveness. Journal of Competitiveness. .DOI: 10.7441/joc.2021.02.01

Ahmed, M., & Khan, N. (2020). Challenges of AI Adoption in Small Businesses: A Review. *Journal of Small Business Management*, 58(1), 1–20. DOI: 10.1080/00472778.2019.1659663

Ajiga, D. I., Ndubuisi, N. L., Asuzu, O. F., Owolabi, O. R., Tubokirifuruar, T. S., & Adeleye, R. A. (2024). AI-driven predictive analytics in retail: A review of emerging trends and customer engagement strategies. *International Journal of Management & Entrepreneurship Research*, 6(2), 307–321. DOI: 10.51594/ijmer.v6i2.772

Akbar, F., Bon, A. T. B., Alshaikh, M. E., & Wadood, F. (2021). Mediating effects of inbound innovations openness on entrepreneurial mindset and firm outcome. *Review of International Geographical Education Online*, 11(5), 519–541.

Akın, N. (2024). Digital marketing strategies for digital entrepreneurs: Emerging trends and future research directions. In *New strategy models in digital entrepreneurship* (pp. 296-319).

Akram, U., Fülöp, M., Tiron-Tudor, A., Topor, D., & Căpu neanu, S. (2021). Impact of Digitalization on Customers' Well-Being in the Pandemic Period: Challenges and Opportunities for the Retail Industry. *International Journal of Environmental Research and Public Health*, 18(14), 7533. Advance online publication. DOI: 10.3390/ijerph18147533 PMID: 34299984

Al Alawi, A. M., Al Kindi, K., Al Shukaili, A., & Ahmed, E. R. (2023). Entrepreneurial practices, innovation, and job creation: The role of demographics and inventiveness as moderators. *International Journal of Innovation Science*. Advance online publication. DOI: 10.1108/IJIS-12-2022-0232

Alahi, M. E. E., Sukkuea, A., Tina, F. W., Nag, A., Kurdthongmee, W., Suwannarat, K., & Mukhopadhyay, S. C. (2023). Integration of IoT-enabled technologies and artificial intelligence (AI) for smart city scenario: Recent advancements and future trends. *Sensors (Basel)*, 23(11), 5206. DOI: 10.3390/s23115206 PMID: 37299934

Alameeri, M. S. (2023). Contextual effects of expertise adoption, subjective wellbeing, entrepreneurial behavioral microfoundations and social relations on entrepreneurial innovation: a investigation of SMEs in Kuwait.

Ali, J. (2023). *AI-driven software engineering. AEI, 3(1)*. None-None., DOI: 10.54254/2977-3903/3/2023030

Ali, S. S. (2018). Mother Tongue or the Other Tongue? That is the Question! *International Research Journal of Arts and Humanities*, 46(46), 1–14.

Alshareef, N., & Tunio, M. N. (2022). Role of leadership in adoption of blockchain technology in small and medium enterprises in Saudi Arabia. *Frontiers in Psychology*, 13, 911432. DOI: 10.3389/fpsyg.2022.911432 PMID: 35602740

Amershi, S., Weld, D., Vorvoreanu, M., Fourney, A., Nushi, B., Collisson, P., & Horvitz, E. (2019, May). Guidelines for human-AI interaction. In *Proceedings of the 2019 CHI conference on human factors in computing systems* (pp. 1-13). DOI: 10.1145/3290605.3300233

Anderson, C., & McCormick, J. (2021). AI and Small Business: Overcoming Barriers to Adoption. *Small Business Economics*, 57(1), 1–20. DOI: 10.1007/s11187-020-00371-4

Anderson, S., & Brown, T. (2023). The Future of AI in Small Business Operations. *Journal of Business Operations Research*, 48(1), 1–20. DOI: 10.1007/s41112-023-00304-9

Anguera-Torrell, O., Aznar-Alarcón, J., & Vives-Perez, J. (2020). COVID-19: Hotel industry response to the pandemic evolution and to the public sector economic measures. *Tourism Recreation Research*, 46(2), 148–157. DOI: 10.1080/02508281.2020.1826225

Anjorin, K. (2024). Harnessing artificial intelligence to develop strategic marketing goals. *International Journal of Management & Entrepreneurship Research*, 6(5), 1625–1650. DOI: 10.51594/ijmer.v6i5.1127

Annaswamy, A. M., Hussain, A., Chakraborty, A., & Cvetkovic, M. (2016). Foundations of infrastructure Cps. *Proceedings of American Control Conference*. Boston, MA: IEEE.

Arboretti, R., Ceccato, R., Pegoraro, L., & Salmaso, L. (2022). Design of experiments and machine learning for product innovation: A systematic literature review. *Quality and Reliability Engineering International*, 38(2), 1131–1156. DOI: 10.1002/qre.3025

Arshad, M. Z., Meirun, T., Javaid, M., Ali, M., Arshad, M. H., & Maneerat, C. (2020). The importance of learning mindset and entrepreneurial mindset on SMEs outcome. *International Journal of Disaster Recovery and Trade Continuity*, 11(1), 1220–1228.

Asefa, K., & Debela, K. L. "Effect of Transformational Leadership on Organizational Performance: The Mediating Role of Employee Commitment and Expert Systems (AI) Inclusion in Ethiopia," *2023 International Conference on Communication, Security and Artificial Intelligence (ICCSAI)*, Greater Noida, India, 2023, pp. 305-310, DOI: 10.1109/ICCSAI59793.2023.10421269

Ato Sarsah, S., Tian, H., Dogbe, C. S. K., Bamfo, B. A., & Pomegbe, W. W. K. (2020). Effect of entrepreneurial mindset on radical innovation outcome among manufacturing SMEs: The mediating role of absorptive capacity. *Journal of Strategy and Administration*, 13(4), 551–570.

Awopetu, A. V. (2016). Impact of mother tongue on Children's learning abilities in the early childhood classroom. *Procedia: Social and Behavioral Sciences*, 233, 58–63. DOI: 10.1016/j.sbspro.2016.10.131

Ayeni, O. (2024). Ai in education: A review of personalized learning and educational technology. *GSC Advanced Research and Reviews*, 18(2), 261–271. DOI: 10.30574/gscarr.2024.18.2.0062

Azhar, M., & Akhtar, M. J. (2020). Social media: A catalyst for entrepreneurship and marketing. *South Asian Journal of Marketing & Management Research*, 10(11), 62–70. DOI: 10.5958/2249-877X.2020.00087.9

Aziz, K., Dua, S., & Gupta, P. (2024). Revolutionizing influencer marketing: Harnessing the power of data analytics and artificial intelligence (AI). In *Advances in Data Analytics for Influencer Marketing: An Interdisciplinary Approach* (pp. 41–66). Springer Nature Switzerland. DOI: 10.1007/978-3-031-65727-6_4

Baah, C., Amponsah, K. T., Issau, K., Ofori, D., Acquah, I. S. K., & Agyeman, D. O. (2021). Examining the interconnections between sustainable logistics practices, environmental reputation and financial performance: A mediation approach. *Vision (Basel)*, 25(1), 47–64. DOI: 10.1177/0972262920988805

Babiak, K., & Trendafilova, S. (2011). CSR and environmental responsibility: Motives and pressures to adopt green management practices. *Corporate Social Responsibility and Environmental Management*, 18(1), 11–24. DOI: 10.1002/csr.229

Babiak, O. (2023). Threads and upgrades of AI technology in the new media era. *Грааль Науки*, (24), 441–448. DOI: 10.36074/grail-of-science.17.02.2023.080

Bahta, D., Yun, J., Islam, R., & Bikanyi, K. (2020). How does CSR enhance the financial performance of SMEs? The mediating role of firm reputation. *Ekonomska Istrazivanja*, 34(1), 1428–1451. DOI: 10.1080/1331677X.2020.1828130

Balakrishna, C. (2012) Enabling technologies for smart city services and applications. *6th International Conference on Next Generation Mobile Applications, Services And Technologies (NGMAST)*, Paris, France, IEEE. DOI: 10.1109/NGMAST.2012.51

Barutcu, S., Yaldir, A., & Hasiloglu, S. B. (2017). From mass to personalized mobile marketing strategies: The new dimensions through expert systems. *European Scientific Journal*, 13(10), 400–409. DOI: 10.19044/esj.2017.v13n10p400

Basco, R., & Rodríguez, M. (2009). Studying the Family Enterprise Holistically. *Family Business Review*, 22(1), 82–95. DOI: 10.1177/0894486508327824

Bassford, C. (2021, November 10). Why Now is the Perfect Time for Hotels to Adopt Contactless. Shiji Insights and Publications. https://insights.shijigroup.com/why-now-is-the-perfect-time-for-hotels-to-adopt-contactless/

Behringer, K., & Szegedi, K. (2016). The Role Of CSR In Achieving Sustainable Development – Theoretical Approach. *European Scientific Journal*, 12(22), 10–10. DOI: 10.19044/esj.2016.v12n22p10

Bello, S. M., & Muazu, M. H. (2023). The 21st century innovative marketing strategies for halal entrepreneurs in the various segments of the halal industry. In *Contemporary discourse of halal and Islamic entrepreneurship: Trends and future opportunities* (pp. 223–235). Springer Nature Singapore., DOI: 10.1007/978-981-99-6427-7_15

Bettiol, M., Di Maria, E., & Finotto, V. (2012). Marketing in SMEs: The role of entrepreneurial sensemaking. *The International Entrepreneurship and Management Journal*, 8(2), 223–248. DOI: 10.1007/s11365-011-0174-3

Bhuiyan, M. S. (2024). The role of AI-enhanced personalization in customer experiences. *Journal of Computer Science and Technology Studies*, 6(1), 162–169. DOI: 10.32996/jcsts.2024.6.1.17

Bibi, M. (2019). Execution of artificial intelligence approach in human resource management functions: Benefits and challenges in Pakistan. *Sarhad Journal of Management Sciences*, 5(1), 113–124. DOI: 10.31529/sjms.2018.5.1.8

Bingimlas, K. (2009). Barriers to the successful integration of ICT in teaching and learning environments: A review of the literature. *Eurasia Journal of Mathematics, Science and Technology Education*, 5(3), 235–245. DOI: 10.12973/ejmste/75275

Birhane, M., Amentie, C., Borji, B., & Kant, S. Are Ethiopian Coffee Farmers Proficient to Predict Capital Structure with Mediation of AI Based Knowledge Systems and Asset Liquidity? In AI in Agriculture for Sustainable and Economic Management (pp. 199-215). CRC Press.

Blanke, J. M. (2020). Protection for 'Inferences drawn': A comparison between the general data protection regulation and the california consumer privacy act. *Global Privacy Law Review, 1*(2).

Borawska-Kalbarczyk, K., Tołwińska, B., & Korzeniecka-Bondar, A. (2019). From Smart Teaching to Smart Learning in the Fast-Changing Digital World. L. Daniela (Ed.)*Didactics of Smart Pedagogy,* 23–40. Cham: Springer Nature.

Boston, (2017). Corporate Social Responsibility in the Hospitality Sector, Boston Hospitality Review | Boston Hospitality Review. (2017, January 27). © 2023 Boston University. https://www.bu.edu/bhr/2017/01/27/hospitalitycsr/

Boulton, A. (2015). Applying data-driven learning to the web. In Leńko-Szymańska, A., & Boulton, A. (Eds.), *Multiple Affordances of Language Corpora for Data-driven Learning* (pp. 267–295). John Benjamins., DOI: 10.1075/scl.69.13bou

Bozkurt, A. (2023). Generative AI, synthetic contents, open educational resources (OER), and open educational practices (OEP): A new front in the openness landscape. *Open Praxis*, 15(3), 178–184. DOI: 10.55982/openpraxis.15.3.579

Bresciani S, Rehman SU, Alam GM, Ashfaq K, Usman M (2022). Environmental MCS package, perceived environmental uncertainty and green performance: in green dynamic capabilities and investment in environmental management perspectives. Rev Int Bus Strat(ahead-of-print).

Brochado, A., Rita, P., & Margarido, A. (2016). High tech meets high touch in upscale hotels. *Journal of Hospitality and Tourism Technology*, 7(4), 347–365. DOI: 10.1108/JHTT-07-2016-0038

Brooks, J., & Brown, K. (2022). AI-Driven Customer Engagement: Trends and Innovations. *Journal of Business Trends*, 34(2), 1–20. DOI: 10.1007/s11187-021-00411-4

Brown, K., & Davis, L. (2022). Data Privacy and AI Ethics in Customer Engagement Strategies. *Journal of Business Ethics*, 173(2), 1–18. DOI: 10.1007/s10551-021-04735-5

Brown, T., & Green, D. (2023). The Future of AI in Small Business Marketing. *JMR, Journal of Marketing Research*, 60(1), 1–20. DOI: 10.1177/00222437221110004

Brynjolfsson, E., & Mitchell, T. (2017). What Can Machine Learning Do? *Workforce Implications.Science*, 358(6370), 1530–1534. DOI: 10.1126/science.aap8062 PMID: 29269459

Buhmann, A., & Fieseler, C. (2021). Towards a deliberative framework for responsible innovation in artificial intelligence. *Technology in Society*, 64, 101475. DOI: 10.1016/j.techsoc.2020.101475

Calvo, J. (2018). High-Tech Start-Ups in Japan: Cogent Labs, AI-OCR Solutions for Automated Business Process Outsourcing. *International Journal of Entrepreneurship and Innovation*, 10(4), 1–15. DOI: 10.2478/ijek-2018-0011

Campbell, C., Sands, S., Ferraro, C., Tsao, H. Y. J., & Mavrommatis, A. (2020). From data to action: How marketers can leverage AI. *Business Horizons*, 63(2), 227–243. DOI: 10.1016/j.bushor.2019.12.002

Carbonell, P., & Escudero, A. (2010). The effect of market orientation on innovation speed and new product performance. *Journal of Business and Industrial Marketing*, 25(7), 501–513. DOI: 10.1108/08858621011077736

Carole, K. S., Armand, T. P. T., & Kim, H. C. (2024, February). Enhanced experiences: Benefits of AI-powered recommendation systems. In *2024 26th International Conference on Advanced Communications Technology (ICACT)* (pp. 216-220). IEEE.

Carson, G., O'Connor, C., & Simmons, G. (2020). The crucial role of market intelligence in the development of small business marketing capabilities. *Journal of Small Business and Enterprise Development*, 27(5), 797–816. DOI: 10.1108/JSBED-12-2019-0394

Chalmers, D., MacKenzie, N. G., & Carter, S. (2020). Artificial Intelligence and Entrepreneurship: Implications for Venture Creation in the Fourth Industrial Revolution. *Entrepreneurship Theory and Practice*, 44(6), 1–22. DOI: 10.1177/1042258720934581

Cham. K. M., M€akel€a, T. (2019). Valuation of emerging learning solutions. PROCEEDINGS OF EDMEDIA 2014—WORLD CONFERENCE ON EDUCATIONAL MEDIA AND TECHNOLOGY(pp. 168–172). Tampere, Finland: Association for the Advancement of Computing in Education.

Chaturvedi, R., & Verma, S. (2023). Opportunities and challenges of AI-driven customer service. In *Artificial intelligence in customer service: The next frontier for personalized engagement* (pp. 33–71). IGI Global. DOI: 10.1007/978-3-031-33898-4_3

Chelliah, M. K., Aravindan, K. L., & Muthaiyah, S. (2022). Entrepreneurial mindset and innovations openness promote the outcome of services SMEs: The mediating role of cost leadership. *Administrative Sciences*, 13(1), 1. DOI: 10.3390/admsci13010001

Cheng, S. H. (2023). Impact of generative artificial intelligence on footwear design concept and ideation. *Engineering Proceedings*, 55(1), 32.

Chen, J., Liu, Z., Huang, X., Wu, C., Liu, Q., Jiang, G., Pu, Y., Lei, Y., Chen, X., Wang, X., Zheng, K., Lian, D., & Chen, E. (2024). When large language models meet personalization: Perspectives of challenges and opportunities. *World Wide Web (Bussum)*, 27(4), 42. DOI: 10.1007/s11280-024-01276-1

Chintalapati, S., & Pandey, S. (2021). Artificial intelligence in marketing: A systematic literature review. *International Journal of Market Research*, 64(1), 38–68. DOI: 10.1177/14707853211018428

Chowdhary, C. L., Reddy, G. T., & Parameshachari, B. D. (2022). *Computer vision and recognition systems: Research innovations and trends*. Apple Academic Press. DOI: 10.1201/9781003180593

Chowdhury, S., Dey, P., Joel-Edgar, S., Bhattacharya, S., Rodriguez-Espindola, O., Abadie, A., & Truong, L. (2023). Unlocking the value of artificial intelligence in human resource management through AI capability framework. *Human Resource Management Review*, 33(1), 100899. DOI: 10.1016/j.hrmr.2022.100899

Chukwuka, E. J., & Dibie, K. E. (2024). Strategic Role of Artificial Intelligence (AI) on Human Resource Management (HR) Employee Performance Evaluation Function. *International Journal of Entrepreneurship and Business Innovation*, 7(2), 269–282. DOI: 10.52589/IJEBI-HET5STYK

Clark, M., & Taylor, H. (2021). AI in E-commerce: Enhancing Customer Experience and Sales. *Journal of E-commerce Research*, 12(4), 1–18. DOI: 10.1007/s12345-021-01123-2

COM. (2011)681 - Renewed EU strategy 2011-14 for Corporate Social Responsibility - EU monitor. (n.d.). https://www.eumonitor.eu/9353000/1/j4nvkkpftveemt7_j9vvik7m1c3gyxp/vitwrzhm31gk#:~:text=Definition%3A%20the%20Commission%20puts%20forward,prerequisite%20for%20meeting%20that%20responsibility

Cooper, A., & Taylor, J. (2020). AI-Driven Strategies for Enhancing Customer Experience. *Journal of Marketing Management*, 36(5), 1–12. DOI: 10.1080/0267257X.2020.1748125

Copeland, M. (2016). What is the difference between artificial intelligence, machine learning, and deep learning? *Nvidia*. https://blogs.nvidia.com/blog/2016/07/29/whats-difference-artificial-intelligencemachinelearning-deep-learning-ai/

Country profile – inbound tourism | Tourism Dashboard. (UNWTO,2021). https://www.unwto.org/tourism-data/country-profile-inbound-tourism

Davenport, T. H. (2018). *The AI advantage: How to put the artificial intelligence revolution to work*. MIT Press. DOI: 10.7551/mitpress/11781.001.0001

Davenport, T., Guha, A., Grewal, D., & Bressgott, T. (2020). How artificial intelligence will change the future of marketing. *Journal of the Academy of Marketing Science*, 48(1), 24–42. DOI: 10.1007/s11747-019-00696-0

Davison, M. (n.d).: AI and the Classroom – Machine Learning in Education. *True Information Architect: Education*, https://www.trueinteraction.com/ai-and-the-classroom-machine-learning-in-education/

Del Prete, M. (2021). Emotional artificial intelligence: Detecting and managing customer emotions in automated customer service. *Journal of Service Research.* Advance online publication. DOI: 10.1177/10946705211015680

Dereso, C. W., Kant, S., Muthuraman, M., & Tufa, G. (2023). Effect of Point of Service on Health Department Student's Creativity in Comprehensive Universities of Ethiopia: Moderating Role of Public-Private Partnership and Mediating Role of Work Place Learning. In: Jain, S., Groppe, S., Mihindukulasooriya, N. (eds) Proceedings of the International Health Informatics Conference. Lecture Notes in Electrical Engineering, vol 990. Springer, Singapore. https://doi.org/DOI: 10.1007/978-981-19-9090-8_13

Desai, D. (2022). Hyper-personalization: an AI-enabled personalization for customer-centric marketing. In *Adoption and Implementation of AI in Customer Relationship Management* (pp. 40-53). IGI Global. DOI: 10.4018/978-1-7998-7959-6.ch003

Dey, S., & Shukla, D. (2020, March). Analytical study on use of AI techniques in tourism sector for smarter customer experience management. In *2020 International Conference on Computer Science, Engineering and Applications (ICCSEA)* (pp. 1-5). IEEE. DOI: 10.1109/ICCSEA49143.2020.9132925

Dillon, T., Potdar, V., Singh, J., & Talevski, A. (2011, May). Cyber-physical systems: Providing Quality of Service (QoS) in a heterogeneous systems-of-systems environment. In 5th IEEE International Conference on Digital Ecosystems and Technologies (IEEE DEST 2011) (pp. 330-335). IEEE.

Diwan, P. (2017) Artificial intelligence: Changing the education paradigm. *Chatbotslife*, https://chatbotslife.com/artificial-intelligence-changing-the-educationparadigma2 6fac41dd 5.

Dogara, G. (2023).Mother tongue, A tool for cultural awareness. (Retrieved https://www.thisdaylive.com/index.php/2022/01/09/mother-tongue-a-tool-for-cultural-awakeness?amp

Du, M., & Li, Y. (2023). *Tax avoidance, CSR performance and financial impacts: evidence from BRICS economies*. International Journal of Emerging Markets., DOI: 10.1108/IJOEM-05-2022-0747

Durga, P., Godavarthi, D., Kant, S., & Basa, S. S. (2024). Aspect-based drug review classification through a hybrid model with ant colony optimization using deep learning. *Discov Computing*, 27(1), 19. DOI: 10.1007/s10791-024-09441-w

Edwards, K., & Parker, M. (2022). The Role of AI in Optimizing Customer Service Operations. *Operations Management Research*, 15(2), 1–18. DOI: 10.1007/s12063-021-00205-4

Efendioğlu, İ. (2023). The change of digital marketing with artificial intelligence.. DOI: 10.33422/7th.iarmea.2023.07.101

Eman, N. E., Jamshed, K. A., Al-Ghazali, B. M., Jamshaid, S., Shamsi, A. I., & Kainat, N. E. (2023). Role and Impact of Social Media in Tourism for Women Entrepreneurs: A Study on Family Business Women Entrepreneurs. In Women's Empowerment Within the Tourism Industry (pp. 116-131). IGI Global. DOI: 10.4018/978-1-6684-8417-3.ch009

Eric E.(2017) The Art of SEO: Mastering Search Engine Optimization.*O'Reilly Media, Inc. Online Document.*

Eriksson, T., Bigi, A., & Bonera, M. (2020). Think with me, or think for me? on the future role of artificial intelligence in marketing strategy formulation. *The TQM Journal*, 32(4), 795–814. DOI: 10.1108/TQM-12-2019-0303

Essential Corporate Social Responsibility Statistics in. 2023 • ZipDo. (2023, June 13). ZipDo. https://zipdo.co/statistics/corporate-social-responsibility/

EUR-Lex - 52011DC0568 - EN - EUR-Lex. (n.d.). EUR-Lex - 52011DC0568 - EN - EUR-Lex. https://eur-lex.europa.eu/legal-content/EN/ALL/?uri=CELEX%3A52011DC0568

Evans, M., & Turner, R. (2022). AI in Small Business Operations: Efficiency and Productivity. *Journal of Business Operations*, 33(2), 1–18. DOI: 10.1016/j.jbo.2021.100441

Family Firm Facts - Family Owned Business Institute - Grand Valley State University. (FamilyFirm, 2023). https://www.gvsu.edu/fobi/family-firm-facts-5.htm#:~:-text=85%20percent%20of%20start%2Dups,(FFI%20Global%20Data%20Points)

Fandos-Roig, J. C., S'anchez-García, J., Tena-Monferrer, S., & Callarisa-Fiol, L. J. (2021). Does CSR help to retain customers in a service company? *Sustainability (Basel)*, 13(1), 1–21. DOI: 10.3390/su13010300

Fang, J. (2023). Research on the design of business models and transformation management of new entrepreneurial ventures driven by artificial intelligence. *BCP Business & Management*, 49, 36–41. DOI: 10.54691/bcpbm.v49i.5383

Feranita, F., Kotlar, J., & De Massis, A. (2017). Collaborative innovation in family firms: Past research, current debates and agenda for future research. *Journal of Family Business Strategy*, 8(3), 137–156. DOI: 10.1016/j.jfbs.2017.07.001

Fern'andez-Gago, R., Cabeza-García, L., & Godos-Díez, J. L. (2020). How significant is corporate social responsibility to business research? *Corporate Social Responsibility and Environmental Management*, 27(4), 1809–1817. DOI: 10.1002/csr.1927

Fes, N. (2021, December 13). TOP 10 OLDEST HOTELS IN EUROPE. https://www.tourism-review.com/oldest-hotels-in-europe-attract-visitors-with-history-and-charm-news12320

Fikadu, G., Kebede, K., & Kant, S. (2023). Entrepreneurship Mindset to Nurture the Halal Food Firm Future in Ethiopia. *Journal of Islamic Fiscal and Trade Research*, 3(1), 43–56.

Franklin, A. (2023). Implementing Corporate Social Responsibility Strategies to Enhance the Profitability of Firms (Doctoral dissertation, Walden University).

Gaffney, M. (2010). Enhancing teachers' take-up of digital content: Factors and design principles in technology adoption. http://www.thelearningfederation.edu.au/verve/_resources/ Enhancing_Teacher_Takeup_of_Digital_Content_Report.PDF

Gao, B., Wang, Y., Xie, H., Hu, Y., & Hu, Y. (2023). Artificial intelligence in advertising: Advancements, challenges, and ethical considerations in targeting, personalization, content creation, and ad optimization. *SAGE Open*, 13(4), 21582440231210759. Advance online publication. DOI: 10.1177/21582440231210759

Gao, Y., & Liu, H. (2023). Artificial intelligence-enabled personalization in interactive marketing: A customer journey perspective. *Journal of Research in Interactive Marketing*, 17(5), 663–680. DOI: 10.1108/JRIM-01-2022-0023

Gatti, L., Vishwanath, B., Seele, P., & Cottier, B. (2019). Are we moving beyond voluntary CSR? Exploring theoretical and managerial implications of mandatory CSR resulting from the new Indian companies act. *Journal of Business Ethics*, 160(4), 961–972. DOI: 10.1007/s10551-018-3783-8

Gaurav, K., & Mahato, J. (2023). Role of Artificial Intelligence in Creating Excellence in Entrepreneurship: A Literature Review. *International Journal of Computational Science*, 8(4), 1–14. DOI: 10.17010/ijcs/2023/v8/i4/173266

Gimpel, H., Graf-Seyfried, V., Laubacher, R., & Meindl, O. (2023). Towards artificial intelligence augmenting facilitation: AI affordances in macro-task crowdsourcing. *Group Decision and Negotiation*, 32(1), 75–124. DOI: 10.1007/s10726-022-09801-1 PMID: 36643885

Goksel, N., & Bozkurt, A. (2019). *Artificial Intelligence in Education: Current Insights and Future Perspectives. Handbook of Research on Learning in the Age of Transhumanism*. IGI Global.

Govindan, K. (2022). Theory Building Through Corporate Social Responsibility 4.0 for Achieving SDGs: A Practical Step Toward Integration of Digitalization With Practice- Based View and Social Good Theory. *IEEE Transactions on Engineering Management*.

Grimstad, S., Glavee-Geo, R., & Fjørtoft, B. (2020). SMEs motivations for CSR: An exploratory study. *European Business Review*, 32(4), 553–572. DOI: 10.1108/EBR-01-2019-0014

Gros, B. (2016). The design of smart educational environments. *Smart Learning Environment*, 3(15), 15. Advance online publication. DOI: 10.1186/s40561-016-0039-x

Gros, B. (2016). *The Dialogue Between Emerging Pedagogies and Emerging Technologies,The Future of Ubiquitous Learning*. Springer.

Guerola-Navarro, V., Gil-Gomez, H., Oltra-Badenes, R., & Soto-Acosta, P. (2024). Customer relationship management and its impact on entrepreneurial marketing: A literature review. *The International Entrepreneurship and Management Journal*, 20(2), 507–547. DOI: 10.1007/s11365-022-00800-x

Guo, Y., Li, Y., Liu, D., & Xu, S. X. (2024). Measuring service quality based on customer emotion: An explainable AI approach. *Decision Support Systems*, 176, 114051. DOI: 10.1016/j.dss.2023.114051

Gupta, R., & Sharma, A. (2020). AI-Driven Marketing Strategies for Small Businesses: A Case Study Approach. *JMR, Journal of Marketing Research*, 57(5), 1–12. DOI: 10.1177/0022243720927657

Gupta, S., Hanssens, D., Hardie, B., Kahn, W., Kumar, V., Lin, N., Ravishanker, N., & Sriram, S. (2006). Modeling customer lifetime value. *Journal of Service Research*, 9(2), 139–155. DOI: 10.1177/1094670506293810

Gürlek, M., & Kilic, I. (2021). A true friend becomes apparent on a rainy day: Corporate social responsibility practices of top hotels during the COVID-19 pandemic. *Current Issues in Tourism*, 24(7), 905–918. DOI: 10.1080/13683500.2021.1883557

Gusenbauer, M., Schweiger, N., Matzler, K., & Hautz, J. (2023). Innovation Through Tradition: The Role of Past Knowledge for Successful Innovations in Family and Non-family Firms. *Family Business Review*, 36(1), 17–36. Advance online publication. DOI: 10.1177/08944865221147955

Guyo, D. M., Kero, C. A., & Kant, S. (2025). Is Marketing Intermediaries' Mediation Required for Livestock and Products Marketing to Improve the Economic Status of Pastoralist Communities in Ethiopia? In AI in Agriculture for Sustainable and Economic Management (pp. 216-234). CRC Press.

Guyo, K., & Kero, C. A. "Mediation of Marketing Intermediaries and AI Adoption Between Livestock Products Marketing and Economic Status of Pastoralist in Ethiopia," *2023 International Conference on Communication, Security and Artificial Intelligence (ICCSAI)*, Greater Noida, India, 2023, pp. 311-316, https://doi.org/DOI: 10.1109/ICCSAI59793.2023.10421261

Hadi, N., & Udin, U. (2020). Testing the Effectiveness of CSR Dimensions for Small Business Entrepreneurs. *Journal of Open Innovation*. Advance online publication. DOI: 10.3390/joitmc7010006

Hagen, P. (2011). *The Changing Nature of Participation in Design: A practice-based study of social technologies in early design research*. University of Technology Sydney.

Hakeem, A., Raissi, N., & Matoussi, H. (2024). Rationality and dynamism on entrepreneurial mindset to the pace of internationalization: The moderating role of ecoapproachal munificence. *Journal of International Entrepreneurship*, •••, 1–35.

Hammer, M., & Champy, J. (1993). *Reengineering the Corporation: A Manifesto for Business Revolution*. Harper Business.

Han, T. (2023). On the copyright of content generated by artificial intelligence. *SHS Web of Conferences, 178*, 01019. https://doi.org/DOI: 10.1051/shsconf/202317801019

Han, Y., Chunyan, M., Cyril, L., & Timothy, J. W. (2017). Towards AI-powered personalization in MOOC learning. *NPJ Science of Learning*, 2(15), 15. Advance online publication. DOI: 10.1038/s41539-017-0016-3

Harrison, J., & Thompson, M. (2023). Enhancing Customer Loyalty through AI-Powered Personalization. *Journal of Consumer Marketing*, 40(1), 1–15. DOI: 10.1108/JCM-05-2022-5231

Hasan, R., Shams, S., & Rahman, M. (2021). Consumer trust and perceived risk for voice-controlled artificial intelligence: The case of Siri. *Journal of Business Research*, 131, 591–597. DOI: 10.1016/j.jbusres.2020.12.012

Hendrix, T. (2015). *Marketing for entrepreneurs: How to promote one's own craft.*

Hicham, N., Nassera, H., & Karim, S. (2023). Strategic framework for leveraging artificial intelligence in future marketing decision-making. *Journal of Intelligent Management Decision*, 2(3), 139–150. DOI: 10.56578/jimd020304

Hirschberg, J., & Manning, C. D. (2015). Advances in natural language processing. *Science*, 349(6245), 261–266. DOI: 10.1126/science.aaa8685 PMID: 26185244

Hollebeek, L. D., Sprott, D. E., & Brady, M. K. (2021). Rise of the machines? Customer engagement in automated service interactions. *Journal of Service Research*, 24(1), 3–8. DOI: 10.1177/1094670520975110

Hou, J., Yao, Y., Hameed, J., Kamran, H., Nawaz, M., Aqdas, R., ... & Patwary, A. (2021). The role of artificial and nonartificial intelligence in the new product success with moderating role of new product innovation: A case of manufacturing companies in China. *Complexity, 2021*(1). https://doi.org/DOI: 10.1155/2021/8891298

Hramiak, A., & Boulton, H. (2013). Escalating the use of Web 2.0 Technology in Secondary Schools in the United Kingdom: Barriers and Enablers beyond Teacher Training. *Electronic Journal of e-Learning*, 11(2), 91–100.

Hu, Y. (2023). Literature in the age of artificial intelligence. 1781-1787. https://doi.org/DOI: 10.2991/978-2-38476-092-3_228

Huang, M. H., & Rust, R. T. (2018). Artificial intelligence in service. *Journal of Service Research*, 21(2), 155–172. DOI: 10.1177/1094670517752459

Huang, M. H., & Rust, R. T. (2021). Engaged to a robot? The role of AI in service. *Journal of Service Research*, 24(1), 30–41. DOI: 10.1177/1094670520902266

Hu, J. (2024). Dynamic content generation in large language models with real-time constraints. https://doi.org/DOI: 10.31219/osf.io/xje3w

Hwang, G. J. (2014). Definition, framework, and research issues of smart learning environments - a context aware ubiquitous learning perspective. *Smart Learning Environments*, 1(1), 4. DOI: 10.1186/s40561-014-0004-5

Idonije, P. I., Dangana, E. A., Ameh, A. A., & Okafor, G. O. (2022). Entrepreneurial Mindset and Sustainable Job Creation: A Investigation of Small and Medium Firms in South-South, Nigeria. Journal of Trade Administration. *Innovation and Inventiveness*, 1(1), 254–277.

Idowu, S. O., Capaldi, N., Zu, L., & Gupta, A. D. (Eds.). (2013). *Encyclopedia of corporate social responsibility* (Vol. 21). Springer. DOI: 10.1007/978-3-642-28036-8

Igudia, E., Uba, C. D., & Wale-Oshinowo, B. (2020). Understanding Small Trade Entrepreneurial Activity in the Nigerian Bottom of The Pyramid (BoP) and Informal Economy.

Infrastructure, S. Getting More from Strategic Assets.(2016).*CSIC (Cambridge Centre for Smart Infrastructure and Construction), Cambridge, UK.*http://www-smartinfrastructure.eng. cam.ac.uk/files/the-smart-infrastructure-paper

Ismail, H. N., Mohd Puzi, M. A., Banki, M. B., & Yusoff, N. (2019). Inherent factors of family business and transgenerational influencing tourism business in Malaysian islands. *Journal of Tourism and Cultural Change*, 17(5), 624–641. DOI: 10.1080/14766825.2018.1549058

Jabo, B., & Kant, S. "Impact of Technical CRM on Ethiopia Bank Human-Computer Interface and Competitive Advantage as Mediators of Performance," 2024 IEEE International Conference on Computing, Power and Communication Technologies (IC2PCT), Greater Noida, India, 2024, pp. 679-682, https://doi.org/DOI: 10.1109/IC2PCT60090.2024.10486237

Jackson, G., & Apostolakou, A. (2010). Corporate Social Responsibility in Western Europe: An Institutional Mirror or Substitute? *Journal of Business Ethics*, 94(3), 371–394. DOI: 10.1007/s10551-009-0269-8

Jacobides, M. G., Brusoni, S., & Candelon, F. (2021). The evolutionary dynamics of the artificial intelligence ecosystem. *Strategy Science*, 6(4), 412–435. DOI: 10.1287/stsc.2021.0148

James, J. (2019). *Artificial intelligence & future warfare: implications for international security.* Defense& Security Analysis., DOI: 10.1080/14751798.2019.1600800

Jamshaid, S., Malik, N. I., Haider, A. A., Jamshed, K., & Jamshad, S. (2020, December). Overthinking hurts: rumination, worry and mental health of international students in China during Covid-19 pandemic. In *International Joint Conference on Arts and Humanities (IJCAH 2020)* (pp. 17-24). Atlantis Press. DOI: 10.2991/assehr.k.201201.004

Jamshed, K. A., Afzal, M. I., Al-Ghazali, B. M., Jamshaid, S., Eman, N. E., & Shamsi, A. I. (2023b). Tourism as an Empowerment Tool in Sustainable Development: Evidence From the Hospitality Industry of China. In Women's Empowerment Within the Tourism Industry (pp. 132-146). IGI Global.

Jamshed, K. A., Shah, S. H. A., & Al-Ghazali, B. M. (2023a). Family Tourism Businesses and Post Pandemic: An Overview of the Hospitality Industry of Europe. Women's Empowerment Within the Tourism Industry, 102-115.

Jamshed, K. A., Shah, S. H. A., & Al-Ghazali, B. M. (2023e). Family Tourism Businesses and Post Pandemic: An Overview of the Hospitality Industry of Europe. Women's Empowerment Within the Tourism Industry, 102-115.

Jamshed, K. A., Shah, S. H. A., & Jamshaid, S. (2023c). Social Innovation and Environment: An Overview of the Tourism and Hospitality Industry of Europe. Frugal Innovation and Social Transitions in the Digital Era, 144-156.

Jamshed, K., Shah, S. H. A., Rahman, E. Z., & Din, Z. U. (2023d, February 15). Green Transformational Leadership Impact on Pro Environmental Behavior with Mediating Mechanism of Moral. . . ResearchGate. https://doi.org/DOI: 10.37896/jxu17.2/017

Jiang, W., & Wong, J. (2016). Key activity areas of corporate social responsibility (CSR) in the construction industry: A study of China. *Journal of Cleaner Production*, 113, 850–860. DOI: 10.1016/j.jclepro.2015.10.093

Jia, P., & Stan, C. (2021). Artificial Intelligence Factory, Data Risk, and VCs' Mediation: The Case of ByteDance, an AI-Powered Startup. *Journal of Risk and Financial Management*, 14(5), 1–18. DOI: 10.3390/jrfm14050203

Jiddi, F. E. (2023). Does corporate social responsibility result in better hotel guest attitudinal and behavioral loyalty? *Heliyon*, 9(8), e18669. DOI: 10.1016/j.heliyon.2023.e18669 PMID: 37560643

Jocic, M. R., Morris, M. H., & Kuratko, D. F. (2023). Familiness and innovation outcomes in domestic firms: The mediating role of entrepreneurial mindset. *Journal of Small Trade Administration*, 61(4), 1345–1377.

Just, J. (2024). Natural language processing for innovation search–Reviewing an emerging non-human innovation intermediary. *Technovation*, 129, 102883. DOI: 10.1016/j.technovation.2023.102883

Kaimara, P., & Deliyannis, I. (2019). Why should I play this game? The role of motivation in smart pedagogy. Didactics of Smart Pedagogy: Smart Pedagogy for Technology Enhanced Learning, 113-137.

Kai, P., & Generoso, M. J. I. A. I. I. (2024). Emerging technologies adoption and market positioning of ai products in china. *International Journal of Research Studies in Management*, 12(2). Advance online publication. DOI: 10.5861/ijrsm.2024.1023

Kaliyamoorthy, R., & Theeban, K. P. (2013). Entrepreneurial marketing strategies in business enhancement of private higher education institutions (PHEI) in Malaysia. *International Journal on Global Business Management & Research*, 2(1), 16.

Kamkankaew, P., Thanitbenjasith, P., Sribenjachot, S., Sanpatanon, N., Phattarowas, V., & Thanin, P. (2024). How artificial intelligence is helping businesses grow and thrive: The transformative role of artificial intelligence in thai b2c digital marketing. *IJSASR*, 4(1), 137–164. DOI: 10.60027/ijsasr.2024.3651

Kanitz, R., Gonzalez, K., Briker, R., & Straatmann, T. (2023). Augmenting organizational change and strategy activities: Leveraging generative artificial intelligence. *The Journal of Applied Behavioral Science*, 59(3), 345–363. DOI: 10.1177/00218863231168974

Kannan, D., Shankar, K. M., & Gholipour, P. (2022a). Paving the way for a green transition through mitigation of green manufacturing challenges: A systematic literature review. *Journal of Cleaner Production*, 368, 132578. DOI: 10.1016/j.jclepro.2022.132578

Kant, S., & Adula, M. (2024). Human-Machine Interaction in the Metaverse in the Context of Ethiopia. In Impact and Potential of Machine Learning in the Metaverse (pp. 196-212). IGI Global. DOI: DOI: 10.4018/979-8-3693-5762-0.ch008

Kant, S., & Adula, M. (2024). AI Learning and Work Attitude Mediation Between Reward and Organizational Support in Ethiopia. In Gomathi Sankar, J., & David, A. (Eds.), *Generative AI for Transformational Management* (pp. 109–136). IGI Global., DOI: 10.4018/979-8-3693-5578-7.ch005

Karamthulla, M. J., Muthusubramanian, M., Tadimarri, A., & Tillu, R. (2024). Navigating the future: AI-driven project management in the digital era. *International Journal for Multidisciplinary Research*, 6(2), 1–11. DOI: 10.36948/ijfmr.2024.v06i02.15295

Katper, N. K., Tunio, M. N., Hussain, N., Junejo, A., & Gilal, F. G. (2020). COVID-19 crises: Global economic shocks vs Pakistan economic shocks. *Advances in Science. Technology and Engineering Systems Journal*, 5(4), 645–654. DOI: 10.25046/aj050481

KATRAGADDA, V. (2023). Automating Customer Support: A Study on The Efficacy of Machine Learning-Driven Chatbots and Virtual Assistants. *IRE Journals, 7*(1), 600-601.

Katsikea, E., Theodosiou, M., & Makri, K. (2019). The interplay between market intelligence activities and sales strategy as drivers of performance in foreign markets. *European Journal of Marketing*, 53(10), 2080–2108. DOI: 10.1108/EJM-06-2017-0402

Kaur, H. (2019). Search engine optimization and its latest trends: A review. *Think India Journal*, 22(17), 2052–2062.

Kaushik, P., Miglani, S., Shandilya, I., Singh, A., Saini, D., & Singh, A. (2023). HR Functions Productivity Boost by using AI. *International Journal on Recent and Innovation Trends in Computing and Communication*, 11(8), 701–713. DOI: 10.17762/ijritcc.v11i8s.7672

Kedi, W. E., Ejimuda, C., Idemudia, C., & Ijomah, T. I. (2024). AI software for personalized marketing automation in SMEs: Enhancing customer experience and sales. *World Journal of Advanced Research and Reviews*, 23(1), 1981–1990. DOI: 10.30574/wjarr.2024.23.1.2159

Khadka, S., Rai, B., & Khadka, A. K. (2023). AI-driven customization in financial services: Implications for social innovation in Nepal. *NCC Journal*, 8(1), 1–11. DOI: 10.3126/nccj.v8i1.63128

Khan, S., & Iqbal, M. (2020, June). AI-powered customer service: Does it optimize customer experience? In *2020 8th International Conference on Reliability, Infocom Technologies and Optimization (Trends and Future Directions)* (ICRITO) (pp. 590-594). IEEE. DOI: 10.1109/ICRITO48877.2020.9197876

Khan, S., & Iqbal, M. (2020, June). AI-Powered Customer Service: Does it optimize customer experience? In *2020 8th International Conference on Reliability, Infocom Technologies and Optimization (Trends and Future Directions)(ICRITO)* (pp. 590-594). IEEE.

Kim, H., & Lee, S. (2022). AI and Digital Transformation in Small Businesses. *Digital Transformation Journal*, 8(2), 1–20. DOI: 10.1016/j.dtj.2021.100567

Koi-Akrofi, J. (2023). *CSR Paradigms, Consumer Behaviour, and Business Performance: A Literature-Based Analysis*. TEXILA INTERNATIONAL JOURNAL OF MANAGEMENT., DOI: 10.21522/TIJMG.2015.09.01.Art003

Konina, O. (2024). Improving business innovation management through artificial intelligence. *J. Tr.Chal. Art. Intell.*, 1(1), 21–32. DOI: 10.61552/JAI.2024.01.003

Koning, R., Hasan, S., & Chatterji, A. (2022). Experimentation and start-up performance: Evidence from A/B testing. *Management Science*, 68(9), 6434–6453. DOI: 10.1287/mnsc.2021.4209

Konnikova, M. (2014) Will MOOCs be flukes? *The New Yorker*. https:// www.newyorker.com/science/maria-konnikova/moocs-failure-solutions2020/06/01

Kortetm¨aki, T., Heikkinen, A., & Jokinen, A. (2022). Particularizing nonhuman nature in stakeholder theory: The recognition approach. *Journal of Business Ethics*, •••, 1–15. DOI: 10.1007/S10551-022-05174-2/TABLES/2

Kothari,C. R.(2004). Research methodology: Methods and techniques. New Age International

Koumentakis, S. (2021, November 21). Family businesses and economy - KOUMENTAKIS AND ASSOCIATES. KOUMENTAKIS & ASSOCIATES Law Firm. https://koumentakislaw.gr/en/articles/family-businesses-and-the-economy/

Kumar, K. A., & Gupta, M. P. (2015). How to make a Smart Campus. *Smart Campus Programme in IIT Delhi. Technical Report IIT*, Delhi.

Kumar, T. A. (2024). Personalized entrepreneurial training programs using data analytics to match founders with the right skill development.

Kumar, S., & Rana, R. (2020). The Role of Artificial Intelligence in Transforming Customer Service Experience in Small Businesses. *Journal of Business Research*, 110, 1–10. DOI: 10.1016/j.jbusres.2020.01.011

Kumar, T. (2023). Integration of intelligent AI & SEO: A review of various factors. [IJNMS]. *International Journal of New Media Studies*, 10(1).

KUNDAL, D. D. B. (2014). Importance of Mother Language. *International Journal (Toronto, Ont.)*, 2(9), 4.

Kuzior, A., Sira, M., & Brożek, P. (2023). Use of artificial intelligence in terms of open innovation process and management. *Sustainability (Basel)*, 15(9), 7205. DOI: 10.3390/su15097205

Kwok, L. F. (2015). A vision for the development of i-campus. *Smart Learning Environments*, 2(2).

Lantos, G. P. (2014). Marketing for entrepreneurs. *Journal of Product and Brand Management*, 23(2), 140–143. DOI: 10.1108/JPBM-05-2013-0311

Larsson, S., & Heintz, F. (2020). Transparency in artificial intelligence. *Internet Policy Review*, 9(2). Advance online publication. DOI: 10.14763/2020.2.1469

Latha, R. (2024). Is artificial intelligence really influencing the marketing strategies and consumer behaviour?. Salud Ciencia Y Tecnología - Serie De Conferencias, 3, 896. DOI: 10.56294/sctconf2024896

Lee, J., & Jeong, H. (2022). A study on implications of AI education policy using keyword analysis. *Journal of The Korean Association of Information Education*, 26(5), 397–406. DOI: 10.14352/jkaie.2022.26.5.397

Lee, J., Suh, T., Roy, D., & Baucus, M. (2019). Emerging Technology and Business Model Innovation: The Case of Artificial Intelligence. *Journal of Open Innovation*, 5(3), 1–14. DOI: 10.3390/joitmc5030044

Lehrer, C., Wieneke, A., Vom Brocke, J., Jung, R., & Seidel, S. (2018). How big data analytics enables service innovation: Materiality, affordance, and the individualization of service. *Journal of Management Information Systems*, 35(2), 424–460. DOI: 10.1080/07421222.2018.1451953

Lesia Viktorivna, K., Andrii Oleksandrovych, V., Iryna Oleksandrivna, K., & Nadia Oleksandrivna, K. (2022). *Artificial Intelligence in Language Learning: What Are We Afraid Of.* Arab World English Journal.

Lewis, C., & Roberts, A. (2020). AI-Powered Customer Insights for Business Growth. *Journal of Business Insights*, 45(4), 1–15. DOI: 10.1007/s41112-020-00264-7

Lindquist, D. H., & Dautaj, Y. (2021). AI in international arbitration: Need for the human touch. *J. Disp. Resol.*, 39.

Liu, Q. (2022). Analysis of collaborative driving effect of artificial intelligence on knowledge innovation management. *Scientific Programming*, 2022, 1–8. DOI: 10.1155/2022/8223724

Liu, Q., & Liang, F. (2022). Artificial intelligence opportunities and challenges for enterprise management: A review and research hotspot. *Journal of Management Science and Engineering*, 20(5), 1–15. DOI: 10.1117/12.2659278

Liu, Y. (2023). Implications of generative artificial intelligence for the development of the media industry. *AEI*, 1(1), 29–36. DOI: 10.54254//1/2023006

Liu, Y., Chen, Y., Ren, Y., & Jin, B. (2021). Impact mechanism of corporate social responsibility on sustainable technological innovation performance from the perspective of corporate social capital. *Journal of Cleaner Production*, 308, 127345. Advance online publication. DOI: 10.1016/j.jclepro.2021.127345

Ljepava, N. (2022). Ai-enabled marketing solutions in marketing decision making: ai application in different stages of marketing process. Tem Journal, 1308-1315. https://doi.org/DOI: 10.18421/tem113-40

Lourens, M., Raman, R., Vanitha, P., Singh, R., Manoharan, G., & Tiwari, M. (2022). Agile Technology and Artificial Intelligent Systems in Business Development. *International Conference on Computer, Communication, and Computational Sciences*, 1-10. DOI: DOI: 10.1109/IC3I56241.2022.10073410

Lumpkin, G. T., & Brigham, K. H. (2011). Long–term orientation and intertemporal choice in family firms. *Entrepreneurship Theory and Practice*, 35(6), 1149–1169. DOI: 10.1111/j.1540-6520.2011.00495.x

Lyon, T. P., & Maxwell, J. W. (2010). Does Green Corporate Social Responsibility Benefit Society? In Issues of the Day (pp. 90-91). Routledge.

Ma, C., Yu, C., & Latif, Y. (2023). CSR and Sustainable Growth in China's Technology Firms between 2010 and 2021. *Sustainability (Basel)*, 15(3), 2101. Advance online publication. DOI: 10.3390/su15032101

Makhloufi, L., Laghouag, A. A., Ali Sahli, A., & Belaid, F. (2021). Effect of entrepreneurial mindset on innovation capability: The mediating role of absorptive capability and organizational learning capabilities. *Sustainability (Basel)*, 13(10), 5399. DOI: 10.3390/su13105399

Mandal, P. (2018). Marketing information and marketing intelligence: Roles in generating customer insights. *International Journal of Business Forecasting and Marketing Intelligence*, 4(3), 311. DOI: 10.1504/IJBFMI.2018.092786

Mandinach, E. B. (2012). A perfect time for data use: Using data-driven decision making to inform practice. *Educational Psychologist*, 47(2), 71–85. DOI: 10.1080/00461520.2012.667064

Mansour, M., Aman, N., Al-Ghazali, B. M., & Shah, S. H. A. (2022). Perceived corporate social responsibility, ethical leadership, and moral reflectiveness impact on pro-environmental behavior among employees of small and medium enterprises: A double-mediation model. *Frontiers in Psychology*, 13, 967859. DOI: 10.3389/fpsyg.2022.967859 PMID: 36507031

Mao, Y. (2023). Current state and future development of artificial intelligence in marketing. *Applied and Computational Engineering*, 6(1), 536–541. DOI: 10.54254/2755-2721/6/20230884

Marcelja, G. (2023). AI-powered communication. In *Молодые исследователи: новые векторы диалога* (pp. 87-93).

Marion, T. J., Moghaddam, M., Ciuccarelli, P., & Wang, L. (2023). AI for user-centered new product development: From large-scale need elicitation to generative design. In *The PDMA Handbook on Innovation and New Product Development.*

Martínez-López, F. J., & Casillas, J. (2013). Artificial intelligence-based systems applied in industrial marketing: An historical overview, current and future insights. *Industrial Marketing Management*, 42(4), 489–495. DOI: 10.1016/j.indmarman.2013.03.001

Martin, P., & Clark, H. (2022). The Impact of AI on Service Delivery in Small Businesses. *Service Management Research*, 34(3), 1–15. DOI: 10.1108/SMR-08-2021-0027

Marzano, G., & Martinovs, A., andUsca S. (2019). Mechatronics Education: Needs and Challenges. Environment. Technology. Resources. *Proceedings of the 12th International Scientific and Practical Conference*. Volume II, 214-217.

Massa, L., & Tucci, C. L. (2013). Business model innovation. The Oxford handbook of innovation management, 20(18), 420-441.

Mathafena, R. B., & Msimango-Galawe, J. (2023). Entrepreneurial mindset, customer mindset and opportunity exploitation in driving trade outcome: Moderating effect of interfunctional coordination. *Journal of Entrepreneurship in Emerging Economies*, 15(3), 538–565. DOI: 10.1108/JEEE-03-2021-0114

Mehrotra, A. (2019, April). Artificial intelligence in financial services: Need to blend automation with human touch. In *2019 International Conference on Automation, Computational and Technology Management (ICACTM)* (pp. 342-347). IEEE. DOI: 10.1109/ICACTM.2019.8776741

Meles, A., Salerno, D., Sampagnaro, G., Verdoliva, V., & Zhang, J. (2023). The influence of green innovation on default risk: Evidence from Europe. *International Review of Economics & Finance*, 84, 692–710. DOI: 10.1016/j.iref.2022.11.036

Memon, A. B., Meyer, K., & Tunio, M. N. (2022). Toward collaborative networking among innovation laboratories: A conceptual framework. *International Journal of Innovation Science*, 14(2), 282–301. DOI: 10.1108/IJIS-04-2021-0069

Mendes, A. C., Ferreira, F. A., Kannan, D., Ferreira, N. C., & Correia, R. J. (2022). A BWM approach to determinants of sustainable entrepreneurship in small and medium- sized enterprises. *Journal of Cleaner Production*, 371, 133300. DOI: 10.1016/j.jclepro.2022.133300

Mesir, M. (2019). The role of artificial intelligence in decision making in small businesses. *Indian Journal of Science and Technology*, 12(18), 1–6. DOI: 10.17485/ijst/2019/v12i18/144586

Meyer, C., Cohen, D., & Nair, S. (2020). From automats to algorithms: The automation of services using artificial intelligence. *Journal of Service Management*, 31(2), 145–161. DOI: 10.1108/JOSM-05-2019-0161

Michael, O. (2023). Natural language processing relevance to online business. *Swb*, 01(03), 37–42. DOI: 10.61925/SWB.2023.1305

Microsoft Education Blog. (2020) AI technology helps students who are deaf learn. *Online document.*https://blogs.microsoft.com/ai/ai-powered-captioning/

Miller, D., & Le Breton-Miller, I. (2021). Brief reflections on family firm research and some suggested paths forward. *Journal of Family Business Strategy*, 12(1), 100410. DOI: 10.1016/j.jfbs.2020.100410

Mirzani, Y. (2024). Artificial intelligence and innovation management: Transformative forces shaping organizational creativity. *Epra International Journal of Multidisciplinary Research (IJMR)*, 511-518. https://doi.org/DOI: 10.36713/epra16272

MNE Guidelines - OECD. (2023). MNE Guidelines - Organisation for Economic Co-operation and Development. https://mneguidelines.oecd.org/mneguidelines/

Mohamed, E., Osman, M. E., & Mohamed, B. A. (2024). The impact of artificial intelligence on social media content. *Journal of Social Sciences (New York, N. Y.)*, 20(1), 12–16. DOI: 10.3844/jssp.2024.12.16

Momanyi, J. S. (2023). Entrepreneurial Mindset, Trade Incubation, Trade Strategies and Outcome of Start-ups in Nairobi City County, Kenya (Doctoral dissertation, University of Nairobi).

Moneim, R. A. (2020). Towards a smart University in the light of 21 st century skills. An-Najah University Journal for Research, B. *Humanities (Washington)*, 34(6).

Morimoto, M. (2017). Personalization, perceived intrusiveness, irritation, and avoidance in digital advertising. In *Digital Advertising* (pp. 110–123). Routledge. DOI: 10.4324/9781315623252-7

Morimoto, R. (2010). Estimating the benefits of effectively and proactively maintaining infrastructure with the innovative smart infrastructure sensor system. *Socio-Economic Planning Sciences*, 44(4), 247–257. DOI: 10.1016/j.seps.2010.07.005

Motiwalla, L., Deokar, A. V., Sarnikar, S., & Dimoka, A. (2019). Leveraging data analytics for behavioral research. *Information Systems Frontiers*, 21(4), 735–742. DOI: 10.1007/s10796-019-09928-8

Moura, S., Reis, J. L., & Rodrigues, L. S. (2021). The Artificial Intelligence in the Personalisation of the Customer Journey–a literature review.

Musyaffi, A., Sari, D., & Respati, D. (2021). Understanding of Digital Payment Usage During COVID-19 Pandemic: A Study of UTAUT Extension Model in Indonesia. Journal of Asian Finance. *Economics and Business*, 8, 475–482. DOI: 10.13106/jafeb.2021.vol8.no6.0475

Nafizah, U., Roper, S., & Mole, K. (2023). Estimating the innovation benefits of first-mover and second-mover strategies when micro-businesses adopt artificial intelligence and machine learning. *Small Business Economics*, 62(1), 411–434. DOI: 10.1007/s11187-023-00779-x

Nascimento, A. M., & Meirelles, F. D. S. (2022). Factors Influencing the Adoption Intention of Artificial Intelligence in Small Businesses. In *Proceedings of* ISLA 2022, https://aisel.aisnet.org/isla2022/20

Nascimento, A. M., de Melo, V. V., Queiroz, A. C. M., Brashear-Alejandro, T., & de Souza Meirelles, F. (2021). Artificial intelligence applied to small businesses: The use of automatic feature engineering and machine learning for more accurate planning. *Revista de Contabilidade e Organizações*, 15, 1–15.

Nasution, S., Andini, G., Prawira, Y., & Azzahra, D. (2019). *Marketing strategy analysis of nano tea product based on mangosteen peel (gracinia mangostana) to promote functional foods industry*. Indonesian Journal of Business and Entrepreneurship., DOI: 10.17358/ijbe.5.3.263

Naumov, N. (2019). The impact of robots, artificial intelligence, and service automation on service quality and service experience in hospitality. In *Robots, artificial intelligence, and service automation in travel, tourism and hospitality* (pp. 123–133). Emerald Publishing Limited., DOI: 10.1108/978-1-78756-687-320191007

Nelson, P., & White, J. (2021). Implementing AI in Small Business: Best Practices and Strategies. *Journal of Innovation Management*, 9(3), 1–14. DOI: 10.1108/JIM-04-2020-0072

Németh, R., & Koltai, J. (2023). Natural language processing. *Intersections*, 9(1), 5–22. DOI: 10.17356/ieejsp.v9i1.871 PMID: 36568020

Nicolescu, L., & Tudorache, M. T. (2022). Human-computer interaction in customer service: The experience with AI chatbots—a systematic literature review. *Electronics (Basel)*, 11(10), 1579. DOI: 10.3390/electronics11101579

Niu, L. (2024). New applications of online education content analysis based on natural language processing technology. https://doi.org/DOI: 10.4108/eai.17-11-2023.2342790

Noranee, S. and Othman, A. (2023). Understanding consumer sentiments: exploring the role of artificial intelligence in marketing. Jmm17 Jurnal Ilmu Ekonomi Dan Manajemen, 10(1), 15-23. DOI: 10.30996/jmm17.v10i1.8690

Normohammadi, R. (2008). Mother Tongue, a Necessary Step to Intellectual Development. *Journal of Pan-Pacific Association of Applied Linguistics*, 12(2), 25–36.

Nsom, N. K. (2021). Evaluating the Measures of Enhancing Trade Growth in Sub-Saharan Africa: The Case of Cameroon.

Ntapiapis, N. (2023). Artificial intelligence in digital marketing: Descriptive analysis of companies' artificial intelligence strategies with random sampling. *Etkileşim*, 6(12), 368–387. DOI: 10.32739/etkilesim.2023.6.12.226

Nwali, O. S. (2014). Impact of mother tongue on the academic achievement of the child. *Knowledge Review*, 30(1), 5–12.

Nyoach, T. D., Lemi, K., Debela, T., & Kant, S. (2024). Does Organizational Commitment Mediate the Relationship between Employee Relationship Management and Bank Performance? The Case of Banks in Ethiopia. *International Journal of Organizational Leadership*, 13(2), 355–376. DOI: 10.33844/ijol.2024.60419

Oblinger, D. (2006). Bootstrapped learning proposer information pamphlet for broad agency announcement, 07-04.http://fs1.fbo.gov/EPSData/ODA/ Synopses/4965/ BAA0704/BLPIPfin al.pdf

Ogundipe, D. (2024). Ai and product management: A theoretical overview from idea to market. *International Journal of Management & Entrepreneurship Research*, 6(3), 950–969. DOI: 10.51594/ijmer.v6i3.965

Omebe, S. E. (2002). *Counseling the parents for effective provision of learning environment for the Nigerian child. The learning environment of the Nigerian child. Journal of the Nigerian Society for Educational Psychologists*. NISEP.

Osiyevskyy, O., Umantsiv, Y., & Kavun, O. (2024). Strategy for striking the omnichannel balance in Retail 4.0. *Strategy and Leadership*. Advance online publication. DOI: 10.1108/SL-12-2023-0120

Ouyang, Y., Wang, L., Yang, A., Shah, M., Belanger, D., Gao, T., . . . Zhang, Y. (2021). The next decade of telecommunications artificial intelligence. *arXiv preprint arXiv:2101.09163*.

Pandey, S. (2020). Exploring the role of Artificial Intelligence (AI) in transforming HR functions: An Empirical Study in the Indian Context. *International Journal of Scientific Research and Engineering Development*, 3(5), 719–732.

Pandey, S., Gupta, S., & Chhajed, S. (2021). *ROI of AI: Effectiveness and Measurement. International Journal Of Engineering Research & Technology* (Vol. 10). Ijert.

Panigrahi, A., Pati, A., Sahu, B., Das, M. N., Nayak, D. S. K., Sahoo, G., & Kant, S. (2023). En-MinWhale: An ensemble approach based on MRMR and Whale optimization for Cancer diagnosis. *IEEE Access : Practical Innovations, Open Solutions*, 11, 113526–113542. DOI: 10.1109/ACCESS.2023.3318261

Papagiannis, N. (2020). *Effective SEO and content marketing: The ultimate guide for maximizing free web traffic*. John Wiley & Sons. DOI: 10.1002/9781119628682

Park, G. (2019). The changing wind of data privacy law: A comparative study of the European Union's General Data Protection Regulation and the 2018 California Consumer Privacy Act. *UC Irvine L. Rev.*, 10, 1455.

Park, J., Oh, C., & Kim, H. Y. (2024). AI vs. human-generated content and accounts on Instagram: User preferences, evaluations, and ethical considerations. *Technology in Society*, 79, 102705. DOI: 10.1016/j.techsoc.2024.102705

Patel, N., & Kumar, S. (2021). Leveraging AI for Customer Segmentation and Targeting. *Journal of Targeting. Measurement and Analysis for Marketing*, 29(3), 1–15. DOI: 10.1057/s41270-020-00112-3

Patel, S., & Desai, R. (2020). AI and Customer Analytics: Enhancing Business Performance. *Business Analytics Journal*, 14(4), 1–14. DOI: 10.1002/baj.2324

Pelgrum, W. J., & Doornekamp, B. G. (2009). Indicators on ICT in primary and secondary education. https://ec.europa.eu/education/moreinformation/doc/ictindicrep_en.pdf

Pellas, N. (2023). The influence of sociodemographic factors on students' attitudes toward AI-generated video content creation. *Smart Learning Environments*, 10(1), 57. Advance online publication. DOI: 10.1186/s40561-023-00276-4

Perrini, F. (2006). Corporate social responsibility: doing the most good for your company and your cause.

Ping, N. L. (2019, December). Constructs for artificial intelligence customer service in e-commerce. In *2019 6th International Conference on Research and Innovation in Information Systems (ICRIIS)* (pp. 1-6). IEEE. DOI: 10.1109/ICRIIS48246.2019.9073486

Pishva, D., & Nishantha, G. G. D. (2008). Smart classrooms for distance education and their adoption to multiple classroom architecture. *Journal of Networks*, 3(5), 54–64. DOI: 10.4304/jnw.3.5.54-64

Plessis, S. D. (2008). Talk to your child cleverly. They were retrieved on August 5, 2008.

Poli, T. A. (2024). Mediating Role of Entrepreneurship Capability in Sustainable Outcome and Women Entrepreneurship: An Evidence from a Developing Country. *Journal of Ecohumanism*, 3(3), 2006–2019. DOI: 10.62754/joe.v3i3.3553

Popescu, C. C. (2018). Improvements in business operations and customer experience through data science and Artificial Intelligence. In *Proceedings of the International Conference on Business Excellence* (Vol. 12, No. 1, pp. 804-815). DOI: 10.2478/picbe-2018-0072

Potter, J. R. (2019). Artificial Intelligence and Swarming in Maritime Systems. *Marine Technology Society Journal*, 53(5), 64–67.

Prentice, C., & Nguyen, M. (2020). Engaging and retaining customers with AI and employee service. *Journal of Retailing and Consumer Services*, 56, 102186. DOI: 10.1016/j.jretconser.2020.102186

Radhakrishnan, T. K., Balasubramanian, S. (2010) Modelling and control of multivariable process using intelligent techniques. *Sensors & Transducers*, 121(10).

Raji, M. A., Olodo, H. B., Oke, T. T., Addy, W. A., Ofodile, O. C., & Oyewole, A. T. (2024). E-commerce and consumer behavior: A review of AI-powered personalization and market trends. *GSC Advanced Research and Reviews, 18*(3), 066-077.

Ramachandran, K. K., Suma, S., Banerjee, D., Mathew, B., Cheepurupalli, N. R., & Mohan, C. R. (2024). The effectiveness of influencer marketing in the age of AI. *Journal of Informatics Education and Research*, 4(2).

Rawool, V., Foroudi, P., & Palazzo, M. (2024). AI-powered voice assistants: Developing a framework for building consumer trust and fostering brand loyalty. *Electronic Commerce Research*, •••, 1–33. DOI: 10.1007/s10660-024-09850-5

Raza, A., Tursoy, T., Seraj, M., Shaikh, E., & Ali, M. (2024). Impact of financial behavior and experience on financial literacy: A study of universities in Pakistan. *Innovation Economics Frontiers*, 27(1), 32–42. DOI: 10.36923/economa.v27i1.240

Reddy, S. R. B. (2022). Enhancing customer experience through AI-powered marketing automation: Strategies and best practices for Industry 4.0. *Journal of Artificial Intelligence Research*, 2(1), 36–46.

Responsibility, W. I. C. S. 4 Types | HBS Online. (2021, April 8). Business Insights Blog. https://online.hbs.edu/blog/post/types-of-corporate-social-responsibility

Riley, T. (2017). Artificial intelligence goes deep to beat humans at poker. *Science Magazine*. https://www.sciencemag.org/news/2017/03/artificial-intelligence-goes-deepbeat-humans-poker

Roberts, A., & Miller, J. (2023). AI and Customer Feedback Analysis: Improving Service Quality. *Journal of Service Quality Management*, 20(1), 1–15. DOI: 10.1177/10946705221110003

Roberts, L., & Harris, J. (2021). Ethical Considerations in AI-Driven Customer Engagement. *Journal of Business Ethics*, 170(4), 1–14. DOI: 10.1007/s10551-020-04603-1

Roberts, M., & Jones, E. (2021). Overcoming Technological Barriers in AI Adoption for Small Businesses. *Technological Forecasting and Social Change*, 165, 1–15. DOI: 10.1016/j.techfore.2021.120543

Robertsson, H. (2023, January 16). How the largest family enterprises are outstripping global economic growth. www.ey.com. https://www.ey.com/en_gl/family-enterprise/family-business-index

Roediger, H. L.III. (2006). Reviewing Book Chapters. In Sternberg, R. J. (Ed.), *Reviewing scientific works in psychology* (pp. 89–100). American Psychological Association., DOI: 10.1037/11288-006

Romano, A. (2022, May 25). The World's Oldest Hotel Has Been in the Same Family for 52 Generations. Travel + Leisure. https://www.travelandleisure.com/hotels-resorts/japanese-hotel-oldest-in-the-world

Rosário, A. (2021). Research-based guidelines for marketing information systems. *International Journal of Business Strategy and Automation*, 2(1), 1–16. DOI: 10.4018/IJBSA.20210101.oa1

Roundy, P. T. (2022). Artificial intelligence and entrepreneurial ecosystems: Understanding the implications of algorithmic decision-making for startup communities. *Journal of Engineering, Entrepreneurship, and Technology*, 10(3), 1–19. DOI: 10.1108/JEET-07-2022-0011

Rozaq, M., Hastjarjo, S., & Slamet, Y. (2021). How novice entrepreneurs learn about digital marketing communication strategies? *Jurnal ASPIKOM*, 6(2), 345–359. DOI: 10.24329/aspikom.v6i2.936

Rudd, T., Morrison, J., Facer, K., & Gifford, C. (2006) Futurelab: What if...? Re-imagining learning spaces.*Telearn Archives. Online document*. https://telearn.archivesouvertes.fr/file/index/docid/190334/filename/rudd-2006

S.V., N. (. (2023). Exploring the synergy: Integrating machine learning algorithms and human expertise in a hybrid learning model for enhanced marketing strategies. *The Review of Contemporary Scientific and Academic Studies*, 3(12). Advance online publication. DOI: 10.55454/rcsas.3.12.2023.003

Sadhu, A. K. R., Parfenov, M., Saripov, D., Muravev, M., & Sadhu, A. K. R. (2024). Enhancing customer service automation and user satisfaction: An exploration of AI-powered chatbot implementation within customer relationship management systems. *Journal of Computational Intelligence and Robotics*, 4(1), 103–123.

Sahoo, S., & Raghu, Y. (2023). Digital marketing strategies used by novice entrepreneurs in promoting their business—A study in Bangalore. *SJCC Management Research Review*, 103-119.

Salem, I., Elbaz, A., Elkhwesky, Z., & Ghazi, K. (2021). The COVID-19 pandemic: The mitigating role of government and hotel support of hotel employees in Egypt. *Tourism Management*, 85, 104305–104305. DOI: 10.1016/j.tourman.2021.104305 PMID: 36567706

Sanyaolu, E., & Atsaboghena, R. (2022). Role of Artificial Intelligence in Human Resource Management: Overview of its benefits and challenges. *ResearchGate*, (December), 1–8.

Saunders, M., Lewis, P., & Thornhill, A. (2007). Research methods. *Business Students 4th edition Pearson Education Limited, England, 6*(3), 1-268

Saunders, M. N. K., Lewis, P., Thornhill, A., & Bristow, A. (2015). *Understanding research philosophies and approaches: Research methods for business students.* Pearson.

Savitri, E., Dp, E., & Syahza, A. (2021). Can innovation mediate the effect of adaptability, entrepreneurial mindset on trade outcome? *Advanced Science Letters*, 11(8), 2301–2312.

Schiavone, F., Pietronudo, M., Sabetta, A., & Bernhard, F. (2022). Designing AI implications in the venture creation process. *International Journal of Entrepreneurial Behaviour & Research*, 28(7), 1–25. DOI: 10.1108/IJEBR-06-2021-0483

Schroer, A. (2018). Companies Using AI in Education to Enhance the Classroom. *Bullettin.Com. Artificial Intelligence.*https://builtin.com/artificialintelligence/ai-in-education

Sekaran, U., & Bougie, R. (2016). *Research methods for business: A skill building approach.* John Wiley & Sons.

Senyapar, H. (2024). Artificial intelligence in marketing communication: A comprehensive exploration of the integration and impact of AI. *Technium Social Sciences Journal*, 55, 64–81. DOI: 10.47577/tssj.v55i1.10651

Shafique, I., Kalyar, M. N., & Mehwish, N. (2021). Organizational ambidexterity, green entrepreneurial orientation, and environmental performance in SMEs context: Examining the moderating role of perceived CSR. *Corporate Social Responsibility and Environmental Management*, 28(1), 446–456. DOI: 10.1002/csr.2060

Shah, S. H. A., Jamshed, K. A., Saleem, S., Bashir, M., & Kiani, O. I. (2022a). Sustainable Development in the Hospitality Industry of Europe: Role of Green HRM Practices. In Sustainable Development of Human Resources in a Globalization Period (pp. 49-67). IGI Global.

Shah, S. H. A., Jamshed, K., Saleem, S., Al-Ghazali, B. M., & Kiani, O. I. (2023b). Rebuilding Tourism in Asia for Future (Post-COVID-19). In Resilient and Sustainable Destinations After Disaster (pp. 109-119). Emerald Publishing Limited.

Shah, K., Arjoon, S., & Rambocas, M. (2016). Aligning Corporate Social Responsibility with Green Economy Development Pathways in Developing Countries. *Sustainable Development (Bradford)*, 24(4), 237–253. DOI: 10.1002/sd.1625

Shah, S. H. A., Al-Ghazali, B. M., Bhatti, S., Aman, N., Fahlevi, M., Aljuaid, M., & Hasan, F. (2023a). The Impact of Perceived CSR on Employees' Pro-Environmental Behaviors: The Mediating Effects of Environmental Consciousness and Environmental Commitment. *Sustainability (Basel)*, 15(5), 4350. DOI: 10.3390/su15054350

Shah, S. H. A., Sultana, A., Gul, A., Sajjad, S., Aziz, S., Basit, A., & Qadir, A. (2020b). Transformational leadership influence on innovation directly and indirectly through affective commitment in hotel industry of Malaysia. *International Review of Management and Marketing*, 10(6), 22–28. DOI: 10.32479/irmm.10761

Shahzadi, I., Amin, S., & Chaudhary, K. M. (2013). Drivers of supply chain performance enhancing organizational output: An exploratory study for manufacturing sector. *Facilities Management*, 5(14), 53–64.

Shahzad, M., Qu, Y., Javed, S., Zafar, A., & Rehman, S. (2020). Relation of environment sustainability to CSR and green innovation: A case of Pakistani manufacturing industry. *Journal of Cleaner Production*, 253, 119938. DOI: 10.1016/j.jclepro.2019.119938

Shaikh, E., Khoso, I., & Chandio, F. (2019). Effects of Corporate Social Responsibility on Organizational Performance: A Conceptual and Literature Review. Grassroots (17260396), 53(1).

Shaikh, E., Tunio, M. N., Khoso, W. M., Brahmi, M., & Rasool, S. (2022). The COVID-19 pandemic overlaps entrepreneurial activities and triggered new challenges: A review study. In *Managing human resources in SMEs and start-ups: International challenges and solutions* (pp. 155-182). DOI: 10.1142/9789811239212_0008

Shaikh, E., Watto, W. A., Brahmi, M., Tunio, M. N., & Lighari, S. N. (2023). Customer satisfaction and customer loyalty: An empirical case study on the impact of benefits generated through smartphone applications. *International Journal of Public Sector*.

Shaikh, E., Brahmi, M., Thang, P. C., Watto, W. A., Trang, T. T. N., & Loan, N. T. (2022). Should i stay or should i go? explaining the turnover intentions with corporate social responsibility (CSR), organizational identification and organizational commitment. *Sustainability (Basel)*, 14(10), 6030. DOI: 10.3390/su14106030

Shaikh, E., Tunio, M. N., & Qureshi, F. (2021). Finance and women's entrepreneurship in DETEs: A literature review. In *Entrepreneurial Finance* (pp. 191–209). Innovation and Development.

Sharma, P., Massis, A., & Gagné, M. (2014). Family business: A fertile ground for research on time, teams and positive organizational study. *European Journal of Work and Organizational Psychology*, 23(5), 674–679. DOI: 10.1080/1359432X.2014.900046

She, J., Jiang, J., Ye, L., Hu, L., Bai, C., & Song, Y. (2020, February 20). 2019 novel coronavirus of pneumonia in Wuhan, China: Emerging attack and management strategies. *Clinical and Translational Medicine*, 9(1), 19. DOI: 10.1186/s40169-020-00271-z PMID: 32078069

Shirazi, K., & Shah, U. (2016). Education in mother tongue: Need of the time: A case study of a public sector college at Jamshoro. *Science International (Lahore)*, 28(3), 3197–3201.

Siau, K. (2018). Education in the age of artificial intelligence: How will technology shape learning? *Global Analyst*, 7(3), 22.

Sigué, S. P., & Biboum, A. D. (2020). Entrepreneurial marketing and social networking in small and medium service enterprises: A case study into business dealings in Cameroon. *Journal of African Business*, 21(3), 338–354. DOI: 10.1080/15228916.2019.1625022

Simmou, W., Govindan, K., Sameer, I., Hussainey, K., & Simmou, S. (2023). Doing good to be green and live clean!-Linking corporate social responsibility strategy, green innovation, and environmental performance: Evidence from Maldivian and Moroccan small and medium-sized enterprises. *Journal of Cleaner Production*, 384, 135265. DOI: 10.1016/j.jclepro.2022.135265

Singh, P., & Rana, A. (2022). Implementing AI in Small Business Marketing Strategies. *Marketing Intelligence & Planning*, 40(2), 1–12. DOI: 10.1108/MIP-04-2021-0103

Singh, R., & Kumar, V. (2021). AI and Customer Relationship Management: Enhancing Customer Engagement. *Journal of Business and Industrial Marketing*, 36(3), 1–15. DOI: 10.1108/JBIM-06-2020-0273

Sirbu, A. (2015). The significance of Language as a tool of communication. Scientific Bulletin" Mircea cel Batran. *Naval Academy*, 18(2), 405.

Sjödin, D., Parida, V., Palmié, M., & Wincent, J. (2021). How AI capabilities enable business model innovation: Scaling AI through co-evolutionary processes and feedback loops. *Journal of Business Research*, 134, 574–587. DOI: 10.1016/j.jbusres.2021.05.009

Smyrnios, K., Tanewski, G., & Romano, C. (1998). Development of a Measure of the Characteristics of Family Business. *Family Business Review*, 11(1), 49–60. DOI: 10.1111/j.1741-6248.1998.00049.x

Solutions, F. B. (2013). Family Business Solutions. Your Guide to a Family Constitution.

Sönmez, S., Apostolopoulos, Y., Lemke, M., & Hsieh, Y. (2020). Understanding the effects of COVID-19 on the health and safety of immigrant hospitality workers in the United States. *Tourism Management Perspectives*, 35, 100717–100717. DOI: 10.1016/j.tmp.2020.100717 PMID: 32834958

Sood, A., Sharma, R., & Bhardwaj, A. (2021). Artificial intelligence research in agriculture: A review. *Online Information Review*, 46(6), 1054–1075. DOI: 10.1108/OIR-10-2020-0448

Srinivasan, V. (2016). Context, Language, and Reasoning in ai: three key challenges.

Stoilova, E. (2021). AI chatbots as a customer service and support tool. *ROBONOMICS: The Journal of the Automated Economy*, 2, 21–21.

Stokes, D. (2000). Putting entrepreneurship into marketing: The processes of entrepreneurial marketing. *Journal of Research in Marketing and Entrepreneurship*, 2(1), 1–16. DOI: 10.1108/14715200080001536

Straker, K., Wrigley, C., & Rosemann, M. (2015). Typologies and touchpoints: Designing multi-channel digital strategies. *Journal of Research in Interactive Marketing*, 9(2), 110–128. DOI: 10.1108/JRIM-06-2014-0039

Suganthi, L. (2020). Investigating the relationship between corporate social responsibility and market, cost and environmental performance for sustainable business. *South African Journal of Business Management*, 51(1), 1–13. DOI: 10.4102/sajbm.v51i1.1630

Suhartanto, D., Syarief, M., Nugraha, A., Suhaeni, T., Masthura, A., & Amin, H. (2021). Millennial loyalty towards artificial intelligence-enabled mobile banking: Evidence from Indonesian Islamic banks. *Journal of Islamic Marketing*, 13(9), 1958–1972. DOI: 10.1108/JIMA-12-2020-0380

Sundarambal, B., Karthikeyini, C., Bommi, R. M., Subramanian, S., & Lokesh, M. (2023, December). AI-based content management system. In *2023 International Conference on Data Science, Agents & Artificial Intelligence (ICDSAAI)* (pp. 1-8). IEEE.

Sycara, K., & Lewis, M. (2004). Integrating intelligent agents into human teams.

Taleb, Z., & Hassanzadeh, F. (2015). Toward smart school: A comparison between smart school and traditional school for mathematics learning. *Procedia: Social and Behavioral Sciences*, 171, 90–95. DOI: 10.1016/j.sbspro.2015.01.093

Taylor, S., & Smith, P. (2020). AI and Customer Loyalty: Enhancing Relationships. *Customer Relationship Management Journal*, 12(2), 1–15. DOI: 10.1007/s12345-020-01107-3

Tekic, Z., & Füller, J. (2023). Managing innovation in the era of AI. *Technology in Society*, 73, 102254. DOI: 10.1016/j.techsoc.2023.102254

Teng, Y., Wu, K., & Xu, D. (2021). The Association Between Fear of Coronavirus Disease 2019, Mental Health, and Turnover Intention Among Quarantine Hotel Employees in China. *Frontiers in Public Health*, 9, 668774. Advance online publication. DOI: 10.3389/fpubh.2021.668774 PMID: 34136457

Thirupathi, L., Sunkara, S. H., Boodala, I. R., & Vempati, V. S. (2024). Personalization and customization strategies with AI in service marketing. In *Integrating AI-driven technologies into service marketing* (pp. 499–524). IGI Global. DOI: 10.4018/979-8-3693-7122-0.ch024

Tjano, R. N., & Janse van Rensburg, L. J. (2020). The association of self-efficacy and entrepreneurial intentions on the commitment of the next generation in domestic-owned agritrade. *Acta Commercii*, 20(1), 1–12.

Torres, S. J., Avariento, J. P., & Rambla, D. (2015). Enhancing integrated indoor/outdoor mobility in a smart campus. *International Journal of Geographical Information Science*, 29(11), 1–14.

Townsend, D. (2023). Leveraging Generative AI Tools Like ChatGPT for Start-ups and Small Business Growth. *Entrepreneurial Exchange*, 7(2), 1–12. DOI: 10.32617/902-641b18d332731

Tran, M. T. (2024). Unlocking the AI-powered customer experience: Personalized service, enhanced engagement, and data-driven strategies for e-commerce applications. In *Enhancing and Predicting Digital Consumer Behavior with AI* (pp. 375–382). IGI Global. DOI: 10.4018/979-8-3693-4453-8.ch019

True Gen'. Generation Z and its implications for companies. (2018, November 12). McKinsey & Company. https://www.mckinsey.com/industries/consumer-packaged-goods/our-insights/true-gen-generation-z-and-its-implications-for-companies

Tulcanaza-Prieto, A., Cortez-Ordoñez, A., & Lee, C. (2023). Influence of customer perception factors on AI-enabled customer experience in the Ecuadorian banking environment. *Sustainability (Basel)*, 15(16), 12441. DOI: 10.3390/su151612441

Tunio, M. N., Yusrini, L., & Shoukat, G. (2021). Corporate social responsibility (CSR) in hotels in Austria, Pakistan, and Indonesia: Small and medium enterprise spillover of COVID-19. In *Handbook of research on entrepreneurship, innovation, sustainability, and ICTs in the post-COVID-19 era* (pp. 263-280). IGI Global.

Tunio, M. N., Yusrini, L., & Shoukat, G. (2021). Corporate social responsibility (CSR) in hotels in Austria, Pakistan, and Indonesia: Small and medium enterprise spillover of COVID-19. In *Handbook of Research on Entrepreneurship, Innovation, Sustainability, and ICTs in the Post-COVID-19 Era* (pp. 263-280). IGI Global.

Tunio, M. N. (2020). Role of ICT in promoting entrepreneurial ecosystems in Pakistan. [JBE]. *Journal of Business Ecosystems*, 1(2), 1–21. DOI: 10.4018/JBE.2020070101

Tunio, M. N., Chaudhry, I. S., Mughal, F., & Shaikh, E. (2022). Marketing mode and survival of the entrepreneurial activities of nascent entrepreneurs. In *Big data analytics* (pp. 1–18). Auerbach Publications. DOI: 10.1201/9781003307761-1

Tunio, M. N., Chaudhry, I. S., Shaikh, S., Jariko, M. A., & Brahmi, M. (2021). Determinants of the sustainable entrepreneurial engagement of youth in developing country—An empirical evidence from Pakistan. *Sustainability (Basel)*, 13(14), 7764. DOI: 10.3390/su13147764

Tunio, M. N., Jariko, M. A., Børsen, T., Shaikh, S., Mushtaque, T., & Brahmi, M. (2021). How entrepreneurship sustains barriers in the entrepreneurial process—A lesson from a developing nation. *Sustainability (Basel)*, 13(20), 11419. DOI: 10.3390/su132011419

Tunio, M. N., Shaikh, E., Katper, N. K., & Brahmi, M. (2023). Nascent entrepreneurs and challenges in the digital market in developing countries. *International Journal of Public Sector Performance Management*, 12(1-2), 140–153. DOI: 10.1504/IJPSPM.2023.132244

Uba, C. D., Igudia, E., & Wale-Oshinowo, B. (2022). Understanding small trade entrepreneurial activity in the Nigerian bottom of the pyramid and informal economy. *International Journal of Entrepreneurship and Small Business*, 46(3), 353–375. DOI: 10.1504/IJESB.2022.124461

Usman, F. O., Eyo-Udo, N. L., Etukudoh, E. A., Odonkor, B., Ibeh, C. V., & Adegbola, A. (2024). A critical review of AI-driven strategies for entrepreneurial success. *International Journal of Management & Entrepreneurship Research*, 6(1), 200–215. DOI: 10.51594/ijmer.v6i1.748

Usmani, U. A., Happonen, A., & Watada, J. (2023, June). Human-centered artificial intelligence: Designing for user empowerment and ethical considerations. In *2023 5th international congress on human-computer interaction, optimization and robotic applications (HORA)* (pp. 1-7). IEEE.

Us, Y., Pimonenko, T., & Lyulyov, O. (2023). Corporate Social Responsibility and Renewable Energy Development for the Green Brand within SDGs: A Meta-Analytic Review. *Energies*, 16(5), 2335. DOI: 10.3390/en16052335

Van Laar, E., van Deursen, A. J. M., van Dijk, J. A. G. M., & de Haan, J. (2017). The relation between 21st-century skills and digital skills: A systematic literature review. *Computers in Human Behavior*, 72, 577–588. DOI: 10.1016/j.chb.2017.03.010

Vander, A. (2018) The Shift to Digital Learning: 10 Benefits. Online document. https://www.gettingsmart.com/2015/11/the-shift-to-digital-learning-10-benefits/ last accessed 2020/05/30.

Vaska, S., Massaro, M., Bagarotto, E., & Mas, F. (2021). The Digital Transformation of Business Model Innovation: A Structured Literature Review. *Frontiers in Psychology*, 11, 539363. Advance online publication. DOI: 10.3389/fpsyg.2020.539363 PMID: 33584396

Vats, I., Kirilenko, O., & Novak, V. (2024). Benefits of using artificial intelligence in core HR processes. *Monthly Informational and Analytical Journal*, 3(-), 8–12. Advance online publication. DOI: 10.37634/efp.2024.3.1

Veloso, C., Magalhães, D., Sousa, B., Walter, C., & Valeri, M. (2021). Encouraging consumer loyalty: the role of family business in hospitality. Journal of Family Business Management. .DOI: 10.1108/JFBM-10-2021-0134

Venkateswaran, N. (2023). AI-driven personalization in customer relationship management: Challenges and opportunities. *Journal of Theoretical and Applied Information Technology*, 101(18), 7392–7399.

Venkateswaran, P. S., Dominic, M. L., Agarwal, S., Oberai, H., Anand, I., & Rajest, S. S. (2024). The role of artificial intelligence (AI) in enhancing marketing and customer loyalty. In *Data-Driven Intelligent Business Sustainability* (pp. 32–47). IGI Global.

Verganti, R., Vendraminelli, L., & Iansiti, M. (2020). Innovation and design in the age of artificial intelligence. *Journal of Product Innovation Management*, 37(3), 212–227. DOI: 10.1111/jpim.12523

Vinithkumar, S., & Sanjeev, S. (2019). Artificial Intelligence in Human Resource Management. *International Journal of Research and Analytical Reviews*, 6(1), 20–24.

Wang, Y. (2023). Synthetic realities in the digital age: Navigating the opportunities and challenges of AI-generated content. *Authorea Preprints*.

Wang, Y. Y., Yu, D., Ju, Y. C., & Acero, A. (2008). An introduction to voice search. *IEEE Signal Processing Magazine*, 25(3), 28–38. DOI: 10.1109/MSP.2008.918411

Weng, W. (2021). Effect of internet of things on marketing intelligence and business strategy: An organizational capability perspective. *International Journal of Electronic Commerce Studies*, 12(2), 209. DOI: 10.7903/ijecs.1906

What is Corporate Social Responsability (CSR)? HEC Paris. (2019). https://www.hec.edu/en/faculty-research/centers/society-organizations-institute/think/so-institute-executive-factsheets/what-corporate-social-responsability-csr

Who we are. (2023). Deloitte. https://www.deloitte.com/global/en/about.html

Williams, S., & Murphy, D. (2023). Learning from Each Other: UK Global Businesses, SMEs, CSR and the Sustainable Development Goals (SDGs). *Sustainability (Basel)*, 15(5), 4151. Advance online publication. DOI: 10.3390/su15054151

Wilson, K., & Harris, M. (2021). AI and Customer Relationship Management: Enhancing Engagement and Loyalty. *Journal of Business and Industrial Marketing*, 36(3), 1–18. DOI: 10.1108/JBIM-05-2020-0221

Wilson, R., & Brown, S. (2021). AI in Retail: Transforming Customer Engagement and Experience. *Retail and Distribution Management*, 49(6), 1–20. DOI: 10.1108/IJRDM-04-2021-0163

Wirba, A. V. (2023). Corporate Social Responsibility (CSR): The Role of Government in promoting CSR. *Journal of the Knowledge Economy*, 15(2), 1–27. DOI: 10.1007/s13132-023-01185-0

Wogu, I. A. P., Olu-Owolabi, F. E., Atayero, A. A., Sholarin, M. A., Ugbogu, P. C., Ogbuehi, U. K., & Akoleowo, V. O. (2016). The changing face of education and the dilemma of Massive Open Online Courses (MOOCs) in Nigeria's tertiary institutions: Implications for development. In 3rd International Conference on African Development Issues. Retrieved from https://scholar. google. com/citations

Wogu, I. A. P., Misra, S., Assibong, P. A., Apeh, H. A., Awogu-Maduagwu, E., Maskeliunas, R., & Damasevicius, R. (2018, February). Artificial Intelligence, MOOC's and the dilemma of teaching and learning in tertiary institutions: A critical appraisal. In *International Conference on Information Systems and Management Science (ISMS)*, University of Malta (pp. 22-23).

Wogu, I. A. P., Olu-Owolabi, F. E., Assibong, P. A., Agoha, B. C., Sholarin, M., Elegbeleye, A., & Apeh, H. A. (2017, October). Artificial intelligence, alienation and ontological problems of other minds: A critical investigation into the future of man and machines. In *2017 International Conference on Computing Networking and Informatics (ICCNI)* (pp. 1-10). IEEE.

Wu, C. J., Raghavendra, R., Gupta, U., Acun, B., Ardalani, N., Maeng, K., & Hazelwood, K. (2022). Sustainable AI: Environmental implications, challenges and opportunities. *Proceedings of Machine Learning and Systems*, 4, 795–813.

Wu, L., Shao, Z., Yang, C., Ding, T., & Zhang, W. (2020). The Impact of CSR and Financial Distress on Financial Performance—Evidence from Chinese Listed Companies of the Manufacturing Industry. *Sustainability (Basel)*, 12(17), 6799. Advance online publication. DOI: 10.3390/su12176799

Wu, Y. (2022). Machine learning approaches for retail bank marketing practice. *BCP Business & Management*, 23, 931–937. DOI: 10.54691/bcpbm.v23i.1475

Wynn, M., & Jones, P. (2022). IT Strategy in the Hotel Industry in the Digital Era. *Sustainability (Basel)*, 14(17), 10705. Advance online publication. DOI: 10.3390/su141710705

Xue, Y., Jiang, C., Guo, Y., Liu, J., Wu, H., & Hao, Y. (2022). Corporate Social Responsibility and High-quality Development: Do Green Innovation, Environmental Investment and Corporate Governance Matter? *Emerging Markets Finance & Trade*, 58(11), 3191–3214. DOI: 10.1080/1540496X.2022.2034616

Xu, Y., Shieh, C. H., van Esch, P., & Ling, I. L. (2020). AI customer service: Task complexity, problem-solving ability, and usage intention. *Australasian Marketing Journal*, 28(4), 189–199. DOI: 10.1016/j.ausmj.2020.03.005

Yams, N., Richardson, V., Shubina, G., Albrecht, S., & Gillblad, D. (2020). Integrated AI and innovation management: The beginning of a beautiful friendship. *Technology Innovation Management Review*, 10(11), 5–18. DOI: 10.22215/timreview/1399

Yan, J. (2023). Prediction of consumer behavior based on machine learning algorithm.. https://doi.org/DOI: 10.4108/eai.26-5-2023.2334304

Yang, M. (2018). International entrepreneurial marketing strategies of MNCs: Bricolage as practiced by marketing managers. *International Business Review*, 27(5), 1045–1056. DOI: 10.1016/j.ibusrev.2018.03.004

Yarlagadda, R. T. (2017). *AI automation and its future in the United States. International Journal of Creative Research Thoughts*. IJCRT., DOI: 10.32628/IJCRT

Yau, K., Saad, N., & Chong, Y. (2021). Artificial intelligence marketing (aim) for enhancing customer relationships. *Applied Sciences (Basel, Switzerland)*, 11(18), 8562. DOI: 10.3390/app11188562

Yawalkar, M. V. V. (2019). A study of artificial intelligence and its role in human resource management. [IJRAR]. *International Journal of Research and Analytical Reviews*, 6(1), 20–24.

Yim, S., Bae, Y. H., Lim, H., & Kwon, J. (2019). The role of marketing capability in linking CSR to corporate financial performance. *European Journal of Marketing*, 53(7), 1333–1354. DOI: 10.1108/EJM-08-2017-0526

Yu, J., Lee, K., & Hyun, S. (2021). Understanding the influence of the perceived risk of the coronavirus disease (COVID-19) on the post-traumatic stress disorder and revisit intention of hotel guests. *Journal of Hospitality and Tourism Management*, 46, 327–335. DOI: 10.1016/j.jhtm.2021.01.010

Yuniarthe, Y. (2017, September). Application of artificial intelligence (AI) in search engine optimization (SEO). In *2017 International Conference on Soft Computing, Intelligent System and Information Technology (ICSIIT)* (pp. 96-101). IEEE. DOI: 10.1109/ICSIIT.2017.15

Zanfardini, M., Aguirre, P., & Tamagni, L. (2016). The evolution of CSR's research in tourism context: A review from 1992 to 2012. *Anatolia*, 27(1), 38–46. DOI: 10.1080/13032917.2015.1083207

Zarantonello, L., & Schmitt, B. H. (2023). Experiential AR/VR: A consumer and service framework and research agenda. *Journal of Service Management*, 34(1), 34–55. DOI: 10.1108/JOSM-12-2021-0479

Zhang, L., & Wei, W. (2021). Influencer marketing: A comparison of traditional celebrity, social media influencer, and AI influencer. *Boston Hospitality Review*, 1-11.

Zhang, L., & Su, W. (2023). Corporate social responsibility, internal control, and firm financial performance. *Frontiers in Psychology*, 13, 977996. Advance online publication. DOI: 10.3389/fpsyg.2022.977996 PMID: 36660285

Zhang, Y., & Li, P. (2023). Predictive Analytics in Small Business Decision-Making. *Journal of Decision Systems*, 32(1), 1–20. DOI: 10.1080/12460125.2022.2150345

Zhu, Z. T., Yu, M. H., & Riezebos, P. (2016). A research framework of smart education. Smart learning environments, 3, 1-17.

Zohuri, B. (2023). Charting the future the synergy of generative AI, quantum computing, and the transformative impact on economy, society, jobs market, and the emergence of artificial super intelligence. *Current Trends in Engineering Science*, 3(7), 1–4. DOI: 10.54026/CTES/1050

Zou, Z., Liu, Y., Ahmad, N., Sial, M., Badulescu, A., Zia-ud-Din, M., & Badulescu, D. (2021). What Prompts Small and Medium Enterprises to Implement CSR? A Qualitative Insight from an Emerging Economy. *Sustainability (Basel)*, 13(2), 952. Advance online publication. DOI: 10.3390/su13020952

About the Contributors

Muhammad Nawaz Tunio Dr. Tunio's dedication to academic excellence is further evidenced by his teaching and administrative roles at various universities, where he has mentored students, organized international conferences, and contributed to developing curricula in Business Administration and Management.

***

Rohit Sabnis is a Research Associate at College of Healthcare Management and Economics, Gulf Medical University, UAE. He is MBA from Kurukshetra University Kurukshetra (A state government public university), India. He has published research papers in international journals and participated in various international conferences, workshops, and seminars. He worked as a management trainee and intern in the Thumbay Hospital, United Arab Emirates (UAE); Decathlon, Zirakpur, India; and Bajaj Allianz General Insurance, India. He completed various MOOCs from Copenhagen Business School, University of New Mexico, University of California, Irvine, University of London, and many other. His areas of interest are Entrepreneurship, consumer behavior, marketing strategies and strategic management. He is inspired with thought leadership and a regular contributor to educational magazines, debates, and cultural activities. He can be reached at rohit27.sr@gmail.com

Metasebia Adula is an Assistant Professor at the College of Business and Economics, Department of Management, Bule Hora University, Ethiopia.

Ali Akaak is an academic and professional in business and tourism management. He has a doctorate's degree in Management Studies (Tourism Management and Development) from the University of Exeter Business School in the United Kingdom. He has over 15+ years of experience in academic and administrative positions in public and private universities. Dr. Akaak is the head of the human resource management section at the University of Technology and Applied Sciences-Salalah. He has published and presented papers at conferences about strategic planning, destination management, tourism development, labor unions, and social entrepreneurs. Also, Dr. Akaak has been a member of several societies, including the Environment Society of Oman (ESO), Omani Society of Human Resources (OSHRM), World Tourism Association for Cultural and Heritage (WTACH), Tour Guiding Committee at the General Directorate of Heritage and Tourism-Dhofar, Green Destination Organization, New Generation Group (NGG) at the Anglo-Omani Society.

Atanu Bhattacharya, Associate Professor & Head of the Department, School of International Hospitality & Tourism Management ITM Vocational University, Vadodara. Atanu Bhattacharya began his career in 2010 with Radisson Hotels, rising to the position of Lobby Manager before transitioning to academia in 2014. He has since been affiliated with esteemed institutions across India, including Golden Regency Institute, AIMS College of Hotel Management, Regal College of Hotel Management & Tourism, Om Sterling Global University, and Medhavi Skills University. Mr. Bhattacharya has authored 13 international research papers and holds publishing authority for 6 Indian patents under Intellectual Property Rights. His extensive industry and academic experience make him a distinguished figure in hospitality and tourism education.

Indraneel Bose is currently working as Associate professor at Swami Vivekanand Subharti University Meerut UP in Hotel Management Department.

Ajay Chandel is working as an Associate Professor at Mittal School of Business, Lovely Professional University, Punjab. He has 14 years of teaching and research experience. He has published papers in SCOPUS, WOS, and UGC listed Journals in areas like Social Media Marketing, E-Commerce, and Consumer Behaviour. He has published cases on SMEs and Social Entrepreneurship in The Case Centre, UK. He also reviews The Case Journal, Emerald Group Publishing, and International Journal of Business and Globalisation, Inderscience. He has authored and developed MOOCs on Tourism and Hospitality Marketing under Epg-Pathshala- A gateway to all postgraduate courses (a UGC-MHRD project under its National Mission on Education Through ICT (NME-ICT).

Shivani Dhand is an Associate Professor (14+ years of experience),a Certified SHRM (Society for Human Resource Management)faculty in the department of Mittal School of Business of Lovely Professional University.She is NLP(Neuro Linguistics Programming) Practioner She is also a member of the Indian Society for Training and Development (ISTD) and the Indian Society of Labour Economics. She is also a core committee member and Mentor of an NGO(Shalini Fellowship) Shivani Dhand has worked in an IT company as an HR. She has published 15 research papers in various journals which include Scopus-indexed, UGC care and peer-reviewed journals. She is a certified POSH trainer. She has worked with CPSC (Columbo Plan Staff College) Manila Philippines, and trained the faculty and Principals of various Institutions in Bhutan (2015). In 2016, She worked on one of the projects," Austria as an Innovation leader in EU in Austria and was awarded as best presentation and Excellent paper. Her research is situated in the field of Startups, HR Practices Human Resource Management, Entrepreneurship, and social entrepreneurship with a special focus on academic entrepreneurship.

Garima Jain is currently working as Assistant professor at Swami Vivekanand Subharti University Meerut UP in Hotel Management Department.

Farhat Jokhio, Ph.D., is an Assistant Professor with 20 years of teaching experience, specializing in research methods and positive psychology. Her research focuses on parenting, drug addiction, and juvenile crime in Sindh. She is currently a research supervisor for M.Phil. students, guiding their work in applied psychology.

Shashi Kant is an Assistant Professor at the College of Business and Economics, Department of Management, Bule Hora University, Ethiopia.

Preet Kanwal completed her Post-Doctoral Fellowship at the ESG, University of Quebec in Montreal, Canada, furthering research expertise in her field. During her Post Doctoral Fellowship, she worked on exploring demographic sensitivity and its impact on discrimination in HEIs while considering insights from Canada and India. Dr. Kanwal is an academician and researcher with over 20 years of experience in Human Resource Management. She holds a PhD in Human Resource Management from I.K. Gujral Punjab Technical University, Punjab, India, where she conducted an empirical study on the quality of work life in the textile industry of Punjab, India. She also has international experience teaching MBA students from Victoria University (Online), Australia, and Sunway University (Online), Malaysia. Dr. Kanwal's research interests revolve around the quality of work-life, work-life balance, industrial relations, labour laws, social security and labour welfare, organizational stress, and behaviour, particularly in the context of the textile industry. She has presented her research at numerous national and international conferences and published her work in Scopus-indexed and UGC-listed Journals. Additionally, she has authored several book chapters on related topics, underscoring her commitment to advancing knowledge in her field. Her contributions extend beyond teaching and research; she has been actively involved in organizing and leading training sessions, workshops, and conferences, both as a participant and as a session chair. Currently she is working on a funded project titled, "Empowering Women Artisans for Vision Viksit Bharat@2047: Financial Inclusion, Market Access, and Skill Development in Selected States of India".

Thi Minh Ngoc Luu is currently the Head of the Department of Economics and Management at the International School, Vietnam National University, Hanoi. She has over 17 years of experience in teaching and researching human resource management, management control, corporate governance, individual and organizational behavior, leadership, and sustainable development.

Shashank Mittal has done his FPM in Organizational behavior and Human Resource from Indian Institute of Management Raipur. He holds B. Tech from I.E.T. Lucknow. His post FPM work experience includes almost five years of industry and academics exposures in multiple roles. Prior to joining FPM, he has over two years of industrial experience and three years of teaching experience in various organizations. He has published multiple papers in ABDC ranked and SSCI indexed journals of international repute such as Journal of Knowledge Management, Journal of Behavioral and Experimental Finance, International Journal of Conflict Management, Journal of Management and Organization and Current Psychology. His current research interest includes Social identity, Knowledge exchanges, Status, Proactive helping, Employer branding, Organizational justice, and Humanitarian relief management. He enjoys badminton and cycling during leisure time.

Tafese Niguse is a PhD Scholar at the College of Business and Economics, Department of Marketing Management, Bule Hora University, Ethiopia.

Sachin Kumar Pandey is an Assistant Professor at the Quantum School of Hospitality and Tourism, Quantum University, Roorkee. He has one year of academic experience at Jaipur National University, Jaipur, and five years of industry experience with leading hotels such as Radisson Blu, Le Meridien, and JW Marriott. His background combines practical industry knowledge with academic insight, enriching the learning experience for his students.

Alok Prasad is a seasoned academic and industry professional with over 26 years of teaching experience at prestigious institutions such as Amity University (Noida), IP University (Delhi), and UPTU (Lucknow). He currently leads the Quantum School of Hospitality and Tourism at Quantum University, Roorkee.In addition to his academic career, Dr. Prasad has 6 years of industry experience with the Jaypee Group and Oberoi Group, where he held various management roles. His expertise lies in hospitality management, curriculum development, and professional training.

Sachin Kumar Raut As an innovative educator and strategist with a PhD in strategic decision-making, I bring a unique blend of academic rigour and industry insight to business education. My teaching philosophy revolves around interactive learning, tailoring methods like gamification and advanced technology to diverse student needs, and fostering an inclusive and dynamic learning environment. I focus on integrating real-world examples with theoretical concepts, preparing students for the evolving global business landscape. Beyond the classroom, I actively engage in industry collaborations and research, contributing to esteemed journals and taking on key roles in course development and accreditation processes. My approach is not just about teaching; it's a reciprocal journey of continuous learning and growth. I am dedicated to inspiring students to become lifelong learners and responsible global citizens equipped to tackle tomorrow's challenges.

Syed Bilawal Ali Shah, born on Jan 1, 1992, is a distinguished petroleum geologist. He holds a Ph.D. in Petroleum Geology from the University of Malaya, Malaysia. With a strong academic foundation, including a Bachelor's degree in Earth Sciences, he has excelled in areas like petroleum geophysics, geological mapping, and basin modeling. Dr. Bilawal's career began as an Internee Geologist at OGDCL in Pakistan, where he gained valuable exploration experience. He furthered his research skills as a Research Assistant at the University of Malaya. Notably, Dr. Bilawal has authored numerous research publications, focusing on hydrocarbon potential, reservoir characterization, and source rock analysis. His work has earned international recognition. He is also a visionary leader, founding CALWASS to support academic excellence. His multilingual proficiency, including English, French, Urdu, Hindi, Pashto, and Malay, demonstrates his global outlook. Dr. Syed Bilawal Ali Shah's contributions to petroleum geology and academia continue to shape the industry, making him a respected figure in the field.

Vikas Sharma is an alumnus of IHM Gwalior. He has 7 years of experience, including teaching and industry experience in luxury brands like ITC grand Bharat Gurugram, The Leela Ambience Hotel and Residences Gurugram and Le Meridian Gurugram. Currently he is associated with Swami Vivekanand Subharti University, Bhikaji Cama Subharti college of Hotel Management as Assistant Professor. Also He is currently pursuing PhD in Hotel Management from Swami Vivekanand Subharti University and has completed Masters in Travel and Tourism Management. He has 7 patents published and also published 8 research papers in various national and international journals. He has attended 15 FDPs and workshops. He has also presented research papers in many national and international conferences.

Ghazala Shoukat is an Associate Professor in the Department of Sociology at the University of Sindh, with 20 years of teaching experience. She earned her Ph.D. in Sociology with research focused on the social assessment of female education and its impact on poverty alleviation in Sindh, Pakistan. Currently, she is a postdoctoral scholar at the National Institute of Historical and Cultural Research (NIHCR) at Quaid-e-Azam University, Islamabad, where her research explores Empowering Women's Leadership for Political Representation in Sindh: A Multi-Dimensional Analysis. Dr. Shoukat's work contributes to understanding the intersection of education, poverty, and gender representation in Pakistan, aiming to enhance women's roles in leadership and political spheres.

Sandeep Kumar Singh is a faculty in the area of Information Systems and Analytics at Jindal Global Business School, O.P. Jindal Global University, Sonipat. Prior to joining Jindal Global Business School, he worked as an Assistant Professor at JKLU Jaipur for two years. He has earned his Ph.D. in computational physics from Antwerpen University, Belgium. His PhD work focused on mathematical modeling and simulation of two-dimensional materials. Post to his PhD, he worked as a research scientist in Sweden for four years in energy storage systems, bioelectronics. He also did MTech in industrial mathematics and scientific computing from IIT Madras, Chennai. His current research interests are to apply complex mathematical modeling in the business and financial world.

Ankit Srivastava is currently working as Assistant professor at Swami Vivekanand Subharti University Meerut UP in Hotel Management Department.

Mohit Yadav is an Associate Professor in the area of Human Resource Management at Jindal Global Business School (JGBS). He has a rich blend of work experience from both Academics as well as Industry. Prof. Mohit holds a Ph.D. from Department of Management Studies, Indian Institute of Technology Roorkee (IIT Roorkee) and has completed Master of Human Resource and Organizational Development (MHROD) from prestigious Delhi School of Economics, University of Delhi. He also holds a B.Com (Hons.) degree from University of Delhi and UGC-JRF scholarship. He has published various research papers and book chapters with reputed publishers like Springer, Sage, Emerald, Elsevier, Inderscience etc. and presented research papers in national and International conferences both in India and abroad. He has many best paper awards on his credit too. He is reviewer of various international journals like Computers in Human Behavior, Policing etc. His areas of interest are Organizational Behavior, HRM, Recruitment and Selection, Organizational Citizenship Behavior, Quality of work life and role.

Index

A

B

C

D

E

F

G

H

I

L

M

N

P

S

U

V

www.ingramcontent.com/pod-product-compliance
Lightning Source LLC
LaVergne TN
LVHW080601300926
849162LV00005B/1017
9798337302195